Jainism in North India

I : Pārśvanātha, the twenty-third *Tīrthaṅkara* of the Jainas.
From a Palm-leaf manuscript of the *Kalpa-Sūtra* of the thirteenth century.

Jainism in North India
800 BC – AD 526

BY

Chimanlal J. Shah, MA

With a Foreword by the

Rev. H. Heras, S.J.

Director, Indian Historical Research Institute

St Xavier's College, Mumbai

D.K. Printworld (P) Ltd.

New Delhi

Cataloging in Publication Data — DK
[Courtesy: D.K. Agencies (P) Ltd. <docinfo@dkagencies.com>]

Shah, Chimanlal J.
Jainism in north India, 800 BC – AD 526 / by Chimanlal J. Shah : with a foreword by H. Heras.
xxvi, 296 p., 25 cm.
Reissued with fresh typeset. Originally published: Bombay: Longmans, Green & Co., 1932.
Includes bibliographical references (p.)
Includes Index.
ISBN 812460309X

1. Jainism — India — History I. Title.

DDC 294.409 54 21

ISBN 81-246-0309-X
First published in 1932
Reissued in this format 2007

Published and printed by:
D.K. Printworld (P) Ltd.
Regd. office : *'Sri Kunj'*, F-52, Bali Nagar
New Delhi - 110 015
Phones : (011) 2545-3975; 2546-6019; *Fax* : (011) 2546-5926
E-mail: dkprintworld@vsnl.net
Web: www.dkprintworld.com

To
My Father

ACKNOWLEDGMENT

THE author takes this opportunity of thanking the trustees of Sheth Anandji Kalyanji for their kind help, which has rendered possible the publication of this work.

Preface

Mr C. J. SHAH is one of the pioneer students of the Indian Historical Research Institute, and his work will undoubtedly be of great credit to his *Alma Mater*. Being himself a Jaina, he took up the early history of Jainism as the subject of his research, and the result of his studies is embodied in the present book.

Jainism is the most overlooked among all the great religions of India. The present work will disclose whatever is historical and legendary in the early history of this religion, the doctrines of its founder, the divisions among his disciples, the spreading of the new faith and the continuous struggle with its sister-faith, Buddhism, which it has survived in the country that witnessed the birth of both of them.

Two limits will be found in this history of Jainism by Mr Shah — one geographical, the other chronological. Jainism was soon spread all over south India, and it formed there a new community with different *guru*s, different practices and even a different ritual. In short, the history of Jainism in south India is totally different from the history of Jainism in north India, and forms by itself a different historical unit. That is the reason why Mr Shah has limited his work geographically to *Āryāvarta*.

The other limit of Mr Shah's work is chronological. His history stops at AD 526, when the list of canonical works of Jainism was finally drawn up in the Vallabhī Council. This event was a landmark in the history of Jainism. Prior to it Jainism was in a state of primitive simplicity that was totally lost after the codification of its religious books. After this date Jainism appears crystallized, and loses its genuineness and sincerity. Mr Shah has selected for his work the early period, which is much more interesting and of much greater cultural value.

As regards the method followed in this work, nothing will, it is expected, be objected against it even by the most scrupulous historians. Certainly there is never a human work totally flawless. This, and the fact that it is the first work of Mr Shah, will sufficiently commend the following pages to the benevolence of readers and critics. I ought however to mention that he has not been satisfied by seeing what other authors have said or propounded

— since that is not research but mere compilation. He has studied the sources themselves, has criticized opinions, has discussed controversial points, has compared sources with sources and has thus finally elucidated one of the most obscure periods in the history of India, with the criticism and impartiality proper to a historian.

The work of Mr Shah is No. 6 in the series of "Studies in Indian History of the Indian Historical Research Institute." It is to be expected that its appearance will communicate new encouragement to his successors, the present research workers of the Institute. Many an obscure point still exists in India's past which demands the sincere work of rising historians of India for the benefit of posterity. The work of the historian is the investigation of truth. And truth will always reveal itself if we look for it with constancy, with sincerity and with an unprejudiced mind. Then truth itself will be the crown of our efforts.

H. HERAS, S.J.

BOMBAY,
15th January 1931.

Contents

I. JAINISM BEFORE MAHĀVĪRA

II. MAHĀVĪRA AND HIS TIMES

I

II

III

IV

III. JAINISM IN ROYAL FAMILIES 800 – 200 BC

I

V. MATHURĀ INSCRIPTIONS

VI. STATE OF JAINISM DURING THE GUPTA PERIOD

VII. JAINA LITERATURE OF THE NORTH

VIII. JAINA ART IN THE NORTH

List of Abbreviations

A.H.R.S.	Andhra Historical Research Society.
A.R.	Asiatic Researches.
A.S.I.	Archaeological Survey of India. (Annual Reports.)
A.S.R.	*Reports of the Archaeological Survey of India*. (Cunningham)
A.S.W.I.	Archaeological Survey of Western India.
B.D.G.P.	*Bengal District Gazetteers, Patna.*
B.D.G.P.	*Bengal District Gazetteers, Puri.*
B.O.D.G.P.	*Bihar and Orissa District Gazetteers, Patna.*
B.O.R.I.L.	Bandarkar Oriental Research Institute Library.
C.H.I.	*Cambridge History of India.*
C.I.I.	*Corpus Inscriptionum Indicarum.*
E.B.	*Encyclopaedia Britannica.*
E.C.	*Epigraphia Carnatica.*
E.I.	*Epigraphia Indica.*
E.R.E.	*Encyclopaedia of Religion and Ethics.*
H.M.I.	*History of Mediaeval India.*
H.O.S.	Harvard Oriental Series.
I.A.	*Indian Antiquary.*
I.H.Q.	*Indian Historical Quarterly.*
J.A.O.S.	*Journal of the American Oriental Society.*
J.A.S.B.	*Journal of the Asiatic Society of Bengal.*

J.B.B.R.A.S.	*Journal of the Bombay Branch of the Royal Asiatic Society.*
J.B.O.R.S.	*Journal of the Bihar and Orissa Research Society.*
J.D.L.	*Journal of the Department of letters. (Calcutta.)*
J.G.	*Jaina Gazette.*
J.P.A.S.B.	*Journal and Proceedings of the Asiatic Society of Bengal.*
J.R.A.S.	*Journal of the Royal Asiatic Society.*
J.S.S.	*Jaina Sāhitya Saṁśodhaka.*
M.A.R.	*Mysore Archaeological Report.*
M.E.	*Marathi Encyclopaedia.*
Q.J.M.S.	*Quarterly Journal of the Mythical Society.*
S.B.B.	Sacred Books of the Buddhists.
S.B.E.	Sacred Books of the East.
S.B.J.	Sacred Books of the Jainas.
Z.D.M.G.	Zeitschrift der Deutschen Morgenländischen Gesellschaft.

List of Illustrations

Maps

Introduction

I

Of all Indological studies Jainism[1] has been particularly unfortunate in that the little that is done for it stands in vivid contrast with the vast undone. Even Buddhism, a veritable sister of Jainism in point of contemporaneous glory as well as rivalry, has not, as is borne out by many an evidence, lacked its due from the scholar-world. This indifference towards Jainism becomes all the more unmerited when we look at the other side of the shield; for Buddhism has practically disappeared from India, whereas the Jaina community not merely exists but wields a considerable influence over the political and economical destinies of this vast country.[2] Although as Mrs Stevenson has observed : "It is no longer in any sense a court religion, nevertheless the influence that it wields in India today is enormous. Its great wealth and its position as the religion *par excellence* of moneylenders and bankers makes it, especially in native states, the power behind the throne; and if anyone doubts its influence, he need only count up the number of edicts prohibiting the slaying of animals on Jaina sacred days that have recently been issued by the rulers of the independent states."[3] The Jainas "form, in fact, a very large and, from their wealth and influence, a most important division of the population of India."[4]

Hertel is certainly right when he says that "Amongst European scholars there are comparatively few persons who realize the full importance of Jainism, and the mighty influence which it was, and is, exercising on Indian civilization, especially on Indian religion and morals, arts and sciences,

1. The word Jainism is derived from जैन, the adjectival form from जिन, a way common to the names of many other religions as well as systems of philosophy — e.g. Mahommedanism from Mahommedan, Christianity from Christian, Zoroastrianism from Zoroastrian, and so forth (but not Buddhism, Manuism or Benthamism), or again, Dvaitism or Advaitism from द्वैत or अद्वैत, Fatalism from fatal, and so on.
2. Cf. Jaini, *Outlines of Jainism*, p. 73.
3. Stevenson (Mrs), *The Heart of Jainism*, p. 19.
4. *Works of Wilson*, I., p. 347.

literature and languages."[1] Neither is there any particular enthusiasm forthcoming in this direction from Indian scholars except for a few eminent men like Jaini, Jayaswal, Ghosal and others of their ilk. But the partiality of scholars towards Buddhism is not without sound reasons, for there is no denying that Buddhism had at one time been so extensive that it was not at all exaggerating to call it the religion of the Asiatic continent. But while it is true that Jainism was certainly restricted to a smaller area, there is evidence enough, as brought out by Mr N.C. Mehta, that Jaina paintings found a place even on the walls of the cave-temples of Chinese Turkestan.[2]

But this partiality towards Buddhism has unfortunately given rise to some fantastic and even untoward conclusions by, notably, some European scholars, who it must be conceded were at the time of their research virtually deprived of all benefit from any authentic comparative study of Jainism which is so imperative in view of the fact that the past history of these two sister-faiths runs well-nigh parallel. Fortunately for us many such fanciful conclusions have of recent years been corrected by scholars both in the East and the West. We shall notice below only a few of these fads. "Buddhism in proper," says W.S. Lilly, "survives in the land of its birth in the form of Jainism. What is certain is that Jainism came into notice when Buddhism had disappeared from India."[3] Says Mr Wilson : "From all credible testimony, therefore, it is impossible to avoid the inference that the Jainas are a sect of comparatively recent institution, who first came into power and patronage about the eighth and ninth century: they probably existed before that date as a division of the Bauddhas, and owed their elevation to the suppression of that form of faith to which they contributed."[4]

Writers like Colebrooke have erred on the other extreme in believing Gautama Buddha to have been the pupil of Mahāvīra, on the ground that one of the latter's pupils (Indrabhūti) bears the name of Gotamasvāmī or Gotama.[5] Echoes Edward Thomas : "A schism took place after Mahāvīra. Indrabhūti was raised to the rank of a deified saint, under the synonymous designation of Buddha (for Jina and Buddha bear the same meaning

1. Hertel, *On the Literature of the Śvetāmbaras of Gujarat*, p. 1.
2. Mehta, *Studies in Indian Painting*, p. 2. According to Hemacandra, and other Jaina traditions also, Jainism was not limited to India of today. — Hemacandra, *Pariśiṣṭaparvan* (ed. Jacobi), pp. 69, 282. Cf. *M.E.*, XIV., p. 319.
3. Lilly, *India and its Problems*, p. 144.
4. Wilson, op. cit., p. 334.
5. Jacobi, *Kalpa-Sūtra*, p. 1.

according to both Buddhists and Jainas)."[1] But the fact is that Jina means "the Conqueror" and Buddha "the Knower."

In his paper read at a meeting of the Royal Asiatic Society Mr Colebrooke has said : "It is certainly probable, as remarked by Dr. Hamilton and Major Delamaine, that the Gautama of the Jainas and the Buddhas is the same personage; and this leads to the further surmise that both these sects are branches of one stock. According to the Jainas, one of Mahāvīra's eleven disciples left spiritual successors; that is, the entire succession of Jaina priests is derived from one individual, Sudharma Svāmī. Two only out of eleven survived Mahāvīra — viz. Indrabhūti and Sudharma : the first, identified with Gautama Svāmī, has no spiritual successor in the Jaina sect. The proper inference seems to be that the followers of this surviving disciple are not of the sect of Jina, rather that there have been none. Gautama's followers constitute the sect of Buddha, with tenets in many respects analogous to those of the Jainas, or followers of Sudharma, but with a mythology or fabulous history of deified saints quite different."[2]

Such hurried conclusions and identifications on both sides on grounds of chance similarity of certain names or dogmas are not only not history but not logic either. In the words of Dr. Jacobi such an identification "can only be maintained on the principles of Fluellen's logic : 'there is a river in Macedon: and there is also, moreover, a river at Monmouth. It is called Wye at Monmouth; but it is out of my prains what is the name of the other river. But 'tis all one: 'tis alike as my fingers is to my fingers. and there is salmons in both.'"[3]

Even a distinguished scholar like Dr. Hopkins connected Mahāvīra exclusively with "idolatry, demonology and man-worship." "Of all the great religious sects of India," says the same scholar in connection with Jainism, "that of Nātaputta is perhaps the least interesting, and has apparently the least excuse for being."[4] Neither are the final remarks of the learned Orientalist in any sense toned down. "A religion in which the chief points insisted upon are," he concludes, "that one should deny God, worship man and nourish vermin has indeed no right to exist, nor has it had as a

---

1. Thomas (E.), *Jainism or the Early Faith of Aśoka,* p. 6.
2. Colebrooke, *Miscellaneous Essays,* II., pp. 315, 316.
3. Jacobi, *I.A.,* IX., p. 162.
4. Hopkins, *Religions of India,* p. 296.

system much influence on the history of thought."[1] These conclusions of Hopkins are so much out of the way that we hope to get very near the truth by a merciless process of negating these ill-founded and ill-adduced findings of his. For yet, like other things that have according to him "no right to exist," Jainism "has existed for over two millennia, and has produced excellent types of men — both monks and householders — and has offered real guidance and solace to many a seeking and believing votary."[2]

And Dr. Hopking is not the only one of his kind, but he must be distinguished from the rest in that he was neither loth nor perverse in being corrected and purged of these ill-founded conclusions of his. For in the course of a letter to Śrī Vijaya Indra Sūri he remarks : "I found at once that the practical religion of the Jainas was one worthy of all commendation, and I have since regretted that I stigmatised the Jaina religion as insisting on denying God, worshipping man and nourishing vermin as its chief tenets without giving regard to the wonderful effect this religion has on the character and morality of the people. But as is often the case, a close acquaintance with a religion brings out its good side and creates a much more favourable impression of it as a whole than can be obtained by an objective literary acquaintance."[3]

Small wonder, therefore, that, as a result of such immature studies, Jainism was for a long time looked upon as an offshoot of Buddhism, which fact naturally failed to rouse the curiosity of research students in this branch of Oriental study. It went on like this for some time, but thanks to scholars like Jacobi and Bühler it is no longer denied that Jainism had an independent genesis. As a matter of fact, Jainism has now recovered much of the ground lost, owing to the strenuous efforts of these two eminent scholars. The former's introduction to his edition of the *Kalpa-Sūtra of Bhadrabāhu* and his learned article on *Mahāvīra and his Predecessors*,[4] published in 1879 and in 1880 respectively, and the latter's essay, *Uber die Indische Secte der Jaina* (*The Indian Sect of the Jainas*), read in 1877 were, in fact, the first rational, scientific and comprehensive accounts of the Jaina religion. The fame of these eminent scholars, and the great ability and philosophical acumen with which they treated the subject, attracted the attention of learned Europe to this great

1. Hopkins, *Religions of India*, p. 297.
2. Belvalkar, *Brahma-Sūtras*, pp. 120, 121.
3. Cf. Shah, *J.G.*, XXIII, p. 105.
4. *I.A.*, IX, pp. 158 ff.

religion, and the inquiry which Jacobi and Bühler started has continued to the present day, and has been fruitful of great results. Happily there has been a positive change in the outlook towards Jainism, and it has been restored to its due place among the religions of the world, in view of the glorious part it played in the past and its contribution to the progress of world culture and civilization, which is not inferior to the contribution of any other *religion on the globe.*

In this very connection Smith has to say that "it may well be doubtful if Buddhism can be correctly described as having been the prevailing religion of India as a whole at any time." He therefore condemns the phrase "Buddhist period" used by many writers as "false and misleading"; for, he says, "neither a Buddhist nor a Jaina period ever existed," in the sense that "neither heresy ever superseded Brahmanical Hinduism."[1] Nevertheless there is no denying that both these faiths have left a permanent impress upon the pages of Indian history, and their contribution to Indian thought, life and culture has been inestimable. Our object, therefore, in the present thesis, is to chalk out the extent of Jainism in general — and not of a particular sect of it, such as Śvetāmbara, Digambara or Sthānakavāsī — in north India, and to trace the history of its *vicissitudes* as they obtained in that part of India.

II

We shall not attempt to relate here, neither shall we venture to sketch in outline, the mighty developments of the dogmas, the institutions and the destinies of this great religion. We shall hardly be able to thrash out the questions arising in connection with the sources of Jaina history, the immensely variegated traditions, the dual form in which Jaina sacred literature has been handed down in resonance either with the Śvetāmbara or Digambara convention. Ours will therefore be an attempt to follow the fortunes of a people, stout and sturdy, great and glorious, both in making a history for themselves and for their religion, and to estimate, in howsoever tentative and fragmentary a fashion, the intrinsic worth of their contribution, particularly to the rich and fruitful cultural stream of north India.

There are special reasons that bring out the long-felt need of a book of this nature, besides that the theme has met with scant attention from scholars, considering the literary output, during the last century and a quarter, in various other departments of Oriental studies. In the first place, the history of north India can never be complete unless it is as well written in the light of Jainism, in view of the immense changes in the laity as well as

1. Smith, *Oxford History of India*, p. 55.

royalty wrought by this religion. Secondly, any survey of Indian philosophies cannot but be imperfect without comprising the Jaina philosophy; this applies all the more aptly to the region lying to the north of the Vindhyas — the land where Jainism was born. Thirdly, if a well-connected and exact account of Indian rituals, customs, traditions, institutions, art and architecture is the theme of the researcher, then the chequered career of Jainism in the north — interspersed as it is by numerous foreign invasions when no institution however sacred, no religion however potent, was absolutely safe — must naturally secure a pre-eminent place in such a thesis. Says Johannes Hertel in this connection: "Characteristic of Indian narrative art are the narratives of the Jainas. They describe the life and manners of the Indian population in all its different classes, and in full accordance with reality. Hence Jaina narrative literature is, amongst the huge mass of Indian literature, the most precious source not only of folklore in the most comprehensive sense of the word, but also in the history of Indian civilization."[1] Finally, no study has so potent an influence in forming a nation's mind and civilization as a critical and careful survey of its past history, and it is through such study alone that an unreasoning and superstitious worship of the past is replaced by a legitimate and manly admiration.

Regarding the literary contribution of the Jainas it would take a fairly big volume to give a history of all that the Jainas have contributed to the treasures of Indian literature. Jainas have contributed their full share to the religious, ethical, poetical and scientific literature of ancient India. Taking a comprehensive review of the contribution of the Jainas to Indian culture Mr. Barth observes : "They have taken a much more active part in the literary and scientific life of India. Astronomy, grammar, and romantic literature owe a great deal to their zeal."[2]

In the realm of art, the elaborately carved friezes in the cave-temples and dwellings on the Udayagiri and Khaṇḍagiri Hills, the richly decorated *āyāgapaṭṭas* and *toraṇas* of the Mathurā find, the beautiful free-standing pillars

1. Hertel, op. cit., p. 8.
2. Barth, *The Religions of India*, p. 144.

on the mountain masses of Girnār and Śatruñjaya, the admirable architecture in the Jaina temples at Mount Abu, and elsewhere, are sufficient to evoke the interest of any student of Indian history. Likewise it is impossible, in the region of religion, to appreciate the real force that was behind the great Śaṅkarācārya or the great Dayānanda without following the reactions of centuries of Jaina and Buddhist influence.

These movements in literature, art and religion could not have succeeded but under the wings of royal patronage. Hence our study must necessarily start with tracing the fortunes of Jainism at royal courts, as in its course it "becomes the state religion of certain kingdoms, in the sense that it was adopted and encouraged by certain kings, who carried with them many of their subjects."[1]

But the task is certainly a thorny one. There is no single work which is a complete survey of Jainism in north India; yet it is no mere blank, neither any medley of historical and legendary names, religious parables, and epic and Āgamic myths, heaped up pell-mell. For then in vain have the thousands of ancient Jaina *sādhus* and scholars toiled to preserve those elaborate compositions handed down from generation to generation by a feat of memory which is considered a miracle in modern days; and in vain, too, most eminent Indian and foreign scholars and antiquarians have worked during the last hundred and fifty years, if it be still impossible to put together the results of their learned researches in the shape of a connected history such as is intelligible to the general reader and useful to the student.

Although many portions of Jaina history are still obscure, and although many questions of details are still a bone of contention, to construct a general history of the Jaina epochs is happily no longer a desperate undertaking. Desperate or not, we must frankly disclaim any pretensions to discoveries of our own, as well as to extend in any way the limits of Oriental scholarship and research.

In conclusion a word must be added with regard to the denotation of the term "north India." In a limited sense the expression "south India" is applied only to the districts lying south of the Kṛṣṇā and the Tuṅgabhadrā rivers, the portion north of these rivers usually being called the Deccan. But south and north India, south and north respectively of the Narbadā and the Mahānadī,

---

1. Smith, op. cit., p. 55.

form a unit by themselves, and it is in this sense that the term is here used. "It is to the south of the Tapti river that the Deccan plateau proper begins. The Narbada river is the real parting of Hindustan from the Deccan (Peninsular India)."[1] And it is in this territory that nearly half the Jainas, out of the total population of about twelve lakh, reside today. And these Jainas, six lakh or so in number, are historically and socially, and also religiously, a definite unit by themselves, even as they are by traditions, customs and habits distinctly northern. As among the Buddhists so among the Jainas, this division between north and south, though geographical in its origin, "has extended in the end to the doctrines taught, the question of the canon of scripture, and the entire body of the traditions and usages."[2]

1. Srinivasachari and Aiyangar, *History of India,* pt. I., p. 3.
2. Barth, op. cit., p. 145.

CHAPTER I

Jainism before Mahāvīra

"THE history of ancient India," says a modern historian, "is a history of thirty centuries of human culture and progress. It divides itself into several distinct periods, each of which, for a length of several centuries, will compare with the entire history of many a modern people."[1] In these "thirty centuries of human culture and progress" the Jaina contribution is a solid synthesis of many-sided developments in art, architecture, religion, morals and sciences; but the most important achievement of the Jaina thought is its ideal of *Ahiṁsā* — non-violence — towards which, as the Jainas believe, the present world is slowly, though imperceptibly, moving. It was regarded as the goal of all the highest practical and theoretical activities, and it indicated the point of unity amidst all the diversities which the complex growth of culture inhabited by different peoples produced.

The name Jainism indicates the predominantly ethical character of the system. As the Buddhists are the followers of Buddha, the Enlightened, the Jainas are the followers of *Jina*, the Victor, a title applied to all the *tīrthaṅkara*s of the Jainas.[2]

The generic names of a *jina* express the ideas entertained by his votaries about his achievement. He is *Jagataprabhu*, Lord of the world; *Sarvajña*, Omniscient; *Trikālavit*, Knower of the three times (past, present and future); *Kṣīṇakarmā*, Destroyer of corporeal action; *Adhīśvara*, Supreme Lord; *Devādhideva*, God of gods, and similar epithets of obvious purport; whilst others are of a more specific character, as *tīrthakara* or *tīrthaṅkara*, *kevalī*, *arhat* and *jina*. The first implies one who has crossed over (*tīryate anena*) — that is, the ocean; *kevalī* is the possessor of *kevala*, or spiritual nature, free from its

1. Dutt, op. cit., p. 1.
2. It is also applicable to all those men and women who have conquered their lower nature, and who have by means of a thorough victory over all attachments and antipathies realized the highest. Cf. Radhakrishnan, *Indian Philosophy*, I, p. 286.

investing sources of error; *arhat* is one entitled to the homage of gods and men; and *jina* is the victor of all human passions and infirmities.[1]

The religion propounded by such a *jina* is called Jainism, and it is known by some such designations as *Jaina-darśana, Jaina-śāsana, Syādvāda-dṛṣṭi, Jaina-dharma*, etc. His followers are called Jainas, generally known as *śravakas*.[2]

It is really difficult, nay impossible, to fix a particular date for the origin of Jainism. Nevertheless, modern research has brought us at least to that stage wherein we can boldly proclaim all those worn-out theories about Jainism being a later offshoot of Buddhism or Brāhmanism as gross ignorance or, to repeat, as erroneous misstatements. On the other hand we have progressed a step further, and it would be now considered an historical fallacy to say that Jainism originated with Mahāvīra without putting forth any new grounds for justifying this statement. This is because it is now a recognized fact that Pārśva, the twenty-third *tīrthaṅkara* of the Jainas, is an historical person, and Mahāvīra, like any other *jina*, enjoyed no better position than that of a reformer in the galaxy of the *tīrthaṅkara*s of the Jainas.[3]

The question whether religion is as old as the human race, or whether it is the growth of a later stage, is as little open to solution by historical research as that of its origin and essence; it can be answered only by psychology and is a purely philosophical inquiry. No tribe or nation has yet been met with destitute of belief in some higher beings, which indication is most essential to what is known as religion in the abstract.

Coming to religion in concrete — that is, to a particular belief or faith — we find that there also arises the same question whether it is as old as

---

1. Hemacandra, *Abhidhānacintāmaṇi*, chap. I, vv. 24-25.
2. अस्य च जैनदर्शनस्य प्रकाशयिता परमात्मा रागद्वेषाद्यान्तररिपुजेतृत्वादन्वर्थकजिननामधेयः। जिनोऽर्हन् स्याद्वादी तीर्थंकर इति चानर्थान्तरम्। अत एव तत्प्रकाशितं दर्शनमपि जैनदर्शनमर्हत्प्रवचनं जैनशासनं स्याद्वाददृष्टिरनेकान्तवाद इत्याद्यभिधानैर्व्यपदिश्यते . — Vijayadharmasūri, *Bhandarkar Commemoration Volume*, p. 139.
3. For a better understanding of the later part of the chapter we shall give below a list of the 24 *tīrthaṅkara*s of this age : 1. Ṛṣabha, 2. Ajita, 3. Sambhava, 4. Abhinandana, 5. Sumati, 6. Padmaprabha, 7. Supārśva, 8. Candraprabha, 9. Puṣpadanta or Suvidhi, 10. Śītala, 11. Śreyāṁsa, 12. Vāsupūjya, 13. Vimala, 14. Ananta, 15. Dharma, 16. Śānti, 17. Kunthu, 18. Ara, 19. Malli, 20. Munisuvrata, 21. Nimi, 22. Nemi or Ariṣṭanemi, 23. Pārśva (Pārśvanātha), 24. Vardhamāna, also named Vīra, Mahāvīra, etc. Everyone of them has a discriminative symbol or *lāñchaṇa* for himself, and this is always found on Jaina idols representing them — e.g. the symbol of Pārśva is a hooded snake, and that of Vardhamāna is a lion. Cf. एतस्यामवसर्पिण्यामृषभोऽजितसंभवौ . . . , etc. — Hemacandra, op. cit., vv. 26, 27, 28.

the human race, or whether it is a growth of a later stage in human life. Here we are confronted with a more or less universal claim, which is put forth by every religion, and which, to put it frankly, shortly comes to this: ours is the eternal and universal religion and others are heretics. To strengthen and justify this claim of eternity we find almost everywhere a lot of legendary literature which indulges in religious parables and canonical myths. Whether this is human weakness, or whether there is one religion which can justify its claim to eternity and universality, is no business of ours to say. That is beyond the lines that we have marked out for our purpose here. We shall limit ourselves to what Jainism has to say on this crucial question.

To the Jainas, Jainism has been revealed again and again in everyone of these endless succeeding periods of the world by innumerable *tīrthaṅkaras*.[1] Of the present age the first *tīrthaṅkara* was Ṛṣabha and the last two were Pārśva and Mahāvīra. The lives of these *tīrthaṅkaras* are found fully worked out both in the Jaina canonical literature and in individual *caritras* (life-sketches) written by various Jaina *gurus*.[2] Of these Ṛṣabha is said to be 500 poles in stature, and he is believed to have lived for 8,400,000 *pūrva* years, while both Pārśva and Mahāvīra lived for 100 and 72 years respectively.[3] If we just compare the lives of these *tīrthaṅkaras* we find that there is a distinct decrement from Ṛṣabha. The one before Pārśva — namely, Nemi — attained the age of 1000 years.[4] This return to reason in the stature and years of the last two *tīrthaṅkaras* induced some scholars to draw a probable inference that the last two alone are to be considered as historical personages.[5]

Talking of Pārśva, Lassen says: "The opinion that this Jina was a real person is specially supported by the circumstance that the duration of his life

1. Hemacandra has enumerated in his *Abhidhānacintāmaṇi* the 24 *jinas* who have appeared in the past *utsarpiṇī* period and 24 others of the future age. उत्सर्पिण्याम्, etc. and भाविन्यां तु, etc. — vv. 50-56. He concludes : एवं सर्वावसर्पिण्युत्सर्पिणीषु जिनोत्तमा : . . . — v. 56.
2. Among the *sūtras* see Bhadrabāhu's *Kalpa-Sūtra,* or Sudharma's *Āvaśyaka,* etc.; to mention a few individual *caritras* we have पार्श्वनाथचरित्रम् by Hemavijayagaṇi ; शान्तिनाथमहाकाव्यम् by Śrī Munibhadrasūri ; मल्लिनाथचरित्रम् by Vinayacandrasūri and also by Haribhadra; महावीरस्वामिचरित्रम् by Nemicandra, and so on.
3. *Kalpa-Sūtra, sūt.* 227, 168, 147. According to the Jainas one *pūrva* is equal to 70,560,000,000,000 years. Cf. *Saṁgrahaṇī-Sūtra,* v. 262.
4. *Kalpa-Sūtra, sūt.* 182.
5. Stevenson (Rev.), *Kalpa-Sūtra,* Int., p. xii.

does not at all transgress the limits of probability as is the case with his predecessors.[1]

No doubt history cannot draw inferences on such grounds, but the period of Indian history with which we are concerned is greatly wanting in data on which we can base our authoritative conclusions. "It is almost impossible," observes Dutt, "to fix any precise date in the history of India before Alexander the Great visited the land."[2] It is really inexplicable why everything has been recorded since the advent of Lord Mahāvīra, the product of the great Indian synthesis, and also why authentic records are missing previous to this. With all this, it is not a hopeless task to fix an historical date for Pārśva, the twenty-third *tīrthaṅkara* of the Jainas. The contemporary literature of the time of Mahāvīra and Buddha throws a great deal of light on this important question of Jaina history, and, as we shall see, the evidence put forward by the Jaina *sūtras* is also not less worthy of note.

Taking Pārśva, the object of our search here, we find that there is no authoritative data in the form of an inscription or a monument which is directly connected with him, but there are inscriptions and monuments from which an indirect inference can safely be drawn.

Reviewing the Jaina inscriptions from Mathurā we find that there is a reference to Ṛṣabha in a dedication to him by lay votaries.[3] Moreover, we find here that most of the inscriptions are dedicated to more than one *arhat*.[4] "All of them, whether bearing kings' names or not, clearly belong to the Indo-Scythic period, or — if the era of Kanishka and his successors is identified with *Śaka*-era — to the first and second century AD."[5] If Mahāvīra was the founder, it can with all impunity be said that there is certainly no great gulf of time that divides him from the people of whose dedication to Mahāvīra we have spoken above, since they come only some six centuries after him, which fact would place them at once in possession of much intimate knowledge as to the foundation of the religion. But, over and above this, the dedication is to more than one *arhat*, and particularly to Ṛṣabha, which fact makes it

---

1. Lassen, *I.A.*, II, p. 261.
2. Dutt, op. cit., p. 11.
3. प्रीयताम्भगवानृषभश्रीः (May the divine Ṛṣabha be pleased). — *E.I.*, I, p. 386 ; Ins. No. VIII.
4. नमो अरहंत्ततानं (Adoration to the *arhats*). — Ibid., p. 383 ; Ins. No. III.
5. Ibid., p. 371.

clear as regards both the authenticity of a very ancient beginning of the religion, and the probable succession of numerous *tīrthaṅkaras* in the meanwhile.

Furthermore, we have a monumental proof in one of the greatest *tīrthas*[1] of the Jainas, the hill of Samet-Śikhar[2] in Bengal, which is known also as Pārasnāth Hill. It is situated in the Hazaribag district. Both in the *Kalpa-Sūtra*, recorded and proved to have been composed by Bhadrabahu, and hence which can be traced as far back as *c.* 300 BC,[3] and also in other Jaina literature we find that on the eve of his *nirvāṇa* Pārśva came down to this hill and went to *mokṣa* from here.[4]

Coming to contemporary literature we find many reliable statements and coincidences that leave no doubt as to the historicity of Pārśva's life. For our purpose here we need not examine the veracity of all these references, but we shall merely enumerate just a few which are most striking and highly convincing.

According to the Jaina scriptures Jaina *sādhus* and nuns were known as *nigaṇṭhas* and *nigaṇṭhins* — Sanskrit *nirgranthas* — etymologically meaning "without any ties."[5] This is also apparently corroborated by the Buddhist canon;[6] Varāhamihira[7] and Hemacandra[8] call them *nirgranthas*, whilst other writers substitute synonyms, such as *vivasana*,[9] *muktāmbara*, etc. The name *nirgrantha* for the Jaina religious men occurs also in the edicts of Aśoka under the form of *nigaṇṭha*.[10] The *piṭakas* of the Buddhas often mention the *nigaṇṭhas*

1. *Tīrtha,* according to Jaina terminology, means a place of pilgrimage.
2. "Samet-Śichara, called in Major Rannel's map Pārsonaut, is situated among the hills between Bihar and Bengal ; its holiness is great in the eyes of the Jainas, and it is said to be visited by pilgrims from the remotest provinces of India." — Colebrooke, op. cit., II, p. 213. There is a celebrated temple of Pārśva in that place.
3. Charpentier, *Uttarādhyayana-Sūtra,* Int., pp. 13, 14.
4. See *Kalpa-Sūtra, sūt.* 168 ; निर्वाणामासन्नं संमेताद्रौ ययौ प्रभुः — Hemacandra, *Triṣaṣṭi-Śalākā, Parva* IX, v. 316, p. 219.
5. See *Uttarādhyayana,* Lecture or *Adhyayana* XII, 16 ; XVI, 2 ; *Ācārāṅga,* pt. II., *Adhyayana* III, 2, and *Kalpa-Sūtra, sūt.* 130, etc.
6. See *Dīgha Nikāya,* I., p. 57 ; *Buddhism in Translations* (Har. Or. Series), III, pp. 224, 342-43, 469, 484, etc. ; *Mahā Parinibbāṇa Sutta,* chap. v., 267, etc. Cf. Rhys Davids, S.B.E., III, p. 166.
7. शाक्योपाध्यायार्हतनिर्ग्रन्थनिमित्त . . . etc. — Varāhamihira, *Bṛhat-Saṁhitā, Adhyayana* LI, v. 21 : "In Varāhamihira's (sixth century) *Bṛhat-Saṁhitā,* LX. 19 (ed. Kern), *Nagna,* "Naked," is the official designation of a Jaina *Yati.*" — Barth, op. cit., p. 145.
8. निर्ग्रन्थो भिक्षुः . . . etc. — Hemacandra, *Abhidhānacintāmaṇi,* v. 76.
9. विवसनसमय . . . etc. — Pansikar, *Brahmasūtra-Bhāṣya,* p. 252 (2nd edn.).
10. Bühler, *E.I.,* II, p. 272.

as opponents of Buddha and his followers. Wherever they are mentioned in the Buddhist canon it is mostly to refute their belief, and thus to assert the superiority of the faith of Lord Buddha.[1] These facts prove two things: that the Jaina monks were called *nigaṇṭhas*, and that, as far as the Buddhist writings reach, the Jainas and Buddhists were great rivals.[2]

Coming to Mahāvīra, we find that his father, Siddhārtha, was of Kāśyapa *gotra*, belonging to the clan of the *jñātr̥*-kṣatriyas.[3] This is the reason why Mahāvīra was known as Jñātr̥putra in his own days.[4] Now, in Pāli, *nāta* is equivalent of *jñāti*, and hence Jñātr̥putra means Nātaputta, which more resembles Nāyaputta, "a *Biruda* of Mahāvīra used in the *Kalpa-Sūtra* and the *Uttarādhyayana-Sūtra*."[5] Thus the titles Nigaṇṭhanātha, Nigaṇṭha-Nātaputta, and also merely Nātaputta refer to none else but Mahāvīra. "The discovery of the real name of the founder of the Jainas," says Dr Bühler, "belongs to Professor Jacobi and myself. The form *Jñātr̥putra* occurs in the Jaina and northern Buddhist books; in Pāli it is *Nātaputta*, and in Jaina Prākr̥t *Nāyaputta*. *Jñāta* or *Jñāti* appears to have been the name of the Rajput clan from which the *Nirgrantha* was descended."[6]

Again coming back to the Buddhist canon, we find in an old book of the Sinhalese canon, the *Sāmagāma-Sutta*, a reference to Nigaṇṭha-Nātaputta's death in Pāvā.[7] Furthermore, a reference to the doctrine of the *nigaṇṭhas*, as given in Buddhist canonical literature, confirms the identity of the *nigaṇṭhas* with the Jainas. "The *Nigaṇṭha-Nātaputta* knows and sees all things, claims perfect knowledge and faith, teaches annihilation by austerities of the old *karmas* and prevention by activity of new *karma*. When *karma* ceases all ceases."[8] There are indeed many such references to Mahāvīra and his theory in the old

---

1. See *Aṅguttara Nikāya*, III, 74 ; *Mahāvagga*, VI, 31, etc.
2. "Among the religious sects of non-Buddhistic persuasion are the *Nirgranthas* or Jainas, the adversaries whom Ashvaghosha detests with greater virulence than brāhmaṇas." — Nariman, *Sanskrit Buddhism*, p. 199 (2nd edn.) ; see also Mitra, *The Sanskrit Buddhist Literature in Nepal*, p. 11.
3. नायकुलचंदे, Cf. *Kalpa-Sūtra*, *sūt*. 110 ; see also ibid., *sūt*. 20, etc. ; *Ācārāṅga-Sūtra*, pt. III., *Adhyayana* XV, 4.
4. Ibid., pt. I., VII, 12, and VIII, 9.
5. Jacobi, *Kalpa-Sūtra*, Int., p. 6.
6. Bühler, *I.A.*, VII, p. 143, n. 5. See also: "We owe to Professor Jacobi the suggestion, which is undoubtedly correct, that the teacher, who is thus styled in the sacred books of the Buddhists, is identical with Mahāvīra," etc. — *C.H.I.*, I, p. 160.
7. Z.D.M.G., XXXIV, p. 749. Cf. Bühler, *The Indian Sect of the Jainas*, p. 34.
8. *Aṅguttara Nikāya*, III., 74. Cf. S.B.E., XLV, p. xv.

II : *Nirvāṇa* of Pārśvanātha on Mt. Sammeta.
From a Palm-leaf manuscript of the *Kalpa-Sūtra* of the thirteenth century.
(Copyright: Āgamodaya Samiti)

books of the Buddhas, but we shall limit ourselves to one which is very helpful in tracing this history as far back as Pārśvanātha.

There is a reference to Nātaputta's system in the *Sāmaññaphala-Sutta*, which is as follows: *Cātuyāma Saṁvara Saṁvuto*, which has been interpreted by Jacobi as referring to the Jaina term *cāturyāma*. "It is applied," says the learned scholar, "to the doctrine of Mahāvīra's predecessor, Pārśva, to distinguish it from the reformed creed of Mahāvīra, which is called *Pāñcyāma Dharma*."[1]

To understand this interpretation of Dr Jacobi we must know beforehand that the original religion of Pārśva had laid down four great vows for the guidance of his followers, and they are as follows: *ahiṁsā*, non-killing; *sunṛta*, truthful speech; *asteya*, not stealing; and *aparigraha*, renouncing of all illusory objects. Mahāvīra being a reformer also saw that in the society in which he was moving, *brahmacarya* — chastity — must be made a separate vow, quite distinct from the *aparigraha* vow of Pārśvanātha.[2]

Referring to this reformation in the Jaina church by Mahāvīra, Jacobi observes: "The argumentation in the text presupposes a decay of the morals of the monastic order to have occurred between Pārśva and Mahāvīra, and this is possible only on the assumption of sufficient interval of time having elapsed between the last two Tīrthaṅkaras, and this perfectly agrees with the common tradition that Mahāvīra came 250 years after Pārśva."[3]

Thus from the Buddhist *grantha*s themselves we get sound proofs which help us to ascertain the historical character of Pārśva's life. Besides this there is one thing which sounds very strange when we consider all these references about Nātaputta and his philosophy that are available in the Buddhist canon. With all these refutations and references about them in the canonical works of the rival faith the Jainas could ignore their adversaries. It follows from this that the *nirgrantha*s were considered by the Buddhas an important sect, while the *nirgrantha*s in their turn did not think it worthwhile to take any notice of the sister faith. These strange coincidences of both the Buddhist and the Jaina literature go a long way to prove the existence of Jainism much before the advent of Buddha and Mahāvīra.

1. Jacobi, *I.A.*, IX, p. 160.
2. व्रतानि . . . पञ्चव्रतानि . . . etc. — See *Kalpa-Sūtra, Subodhikā-Ṭīkā*, p. 3.
3. Jacobi, S.B.E. XLV, pp. 122-23.

"The *Nirgranthas,*" observes Dr Jacobi, "are frequently mentioned by the Buddhists, even in the oldest part of the *Piṭakas.* But I have not yet met with a distinct mention of the Buddhas in any of the old Jaina *Sūtras*, though they contain lengthy legends about Jamāli, Gośāla and other heterodox teachers. As this is just the reverse position to that which both sects mutually occupy in all aftertimes, and as it is inconsistent with our assumption of a contemporaneous origin of both creeds, we are driven to the conclusion that the *nirgranthas* were not a newly founded sect of Buddha's time. This seems to have been the opinion of the *Piṭakas* too; for we find no indication of the contrary in them."[1]

So much about references in Buddhist canons: now we shall see what the Hindu scriptures and legends have to say about Jainism. Though they seem to be somewhat later than Mahāvīra and his times, they go a step further than the Buddhist canon. And, strangely enough, they more or less support the belief of the Jainas that Ṛṣabha was the first Jina of this age.

From *Viṣṇu Purāṇa* we learn that the brāhmaṇas too have a Ṛṣabha whose life more or less coincides with that of the Jaina one.[2] In the *Bhāgavata Purāṇa* also a detailed account of the life of one Ṛṣabha is given, and from that it is evident that it is none other than the first Jaina *tīrthaṅkara* himself. A note on *Bhāgavata-Purāṇa* in Wilson's *Viṣṇu Purāṇa* has it: "That work enters much more into detail on the subject of Ṛṣabha's devotion, and particularises circumstances not found in any other *Purāṇa.* The most interesting of these are the scenes of Ṛṣabha's wanderings, which are said to be Koṅka, Vankāṭa, Kuṭaka, and Southern Karnāṭaka, or the western part of the peninsula; and the adoption of the Jaina belief by the people of those countries."[3]

Of the remaining *tīrthaṅkaras*, Sumati, the fifth *tīrthaṅkara,* is evidently identical with Bharata's son Sumati, of whom it is said in the *Bhāgavata* that he "will be irreligiously worshipped by some infidels as a divinity." Besides this, "Arishṭanemi, the twenty-second Tīrthaṅkara, is connected with Kṛshṇa's

1. Jacobi, *I.A.*, IX, p. 161.
2. Nābhi had by his queen Maru the magnanimous Ṛṣabha, and he had a hundred sons, the eldest of whom was Bharata. Having ruled with equity and wisdom, and celebrated many sacrificial rites, he resigned the sovereignty of the earth to the heroic Bharata, etc. — Cf. Wilson, *Viṣṇu Purāṇa,* p. 163.
3. Ibid., p. 164 n.

myth through Rājīmatī, daughter of Ugrasena."[1] From all these references from the *Viṣṇu* and *Bhāgavata* Purāṇas Jacobi concluded ". . . there may be something historical in the tradition which makes Ṛshabha the first Tīrthaṅkara."[2] However, it is not to be forgotten that according to some scholars these Purāṇas belong to a later date, and hence much weight cannot be put on their authority,[3] in spite of scholars like Smith, who would not like to disparage the authority of the Purāṇic lists.[4]

Leaving the *tīrthaṅkara*s aside we find there is a reference to Jaina philosophy in one of the oldest *sūtra*s of the Hindus. In the *Brahma-Sūtras*, which are believed by Telang[5] and others to be as old as the fourth century BC, we find a refutation of Jaina Syādvāda and of the Jaina theory about the soul.[6] There are also many more references about Jainism in the *Mahābhārata*, the *Manu-Smṛti*, the *Śivasahasra*, the *Taittirīya Āraṇyaka*, the *Yajurveda-Saṁhitā* and other Hindu scriptures, but we shall not deal with them here.[7]

Finally, we shall refer to what some of the most ancient and most sacred of the Jaina *sūtra*s and some of the most eminent scholars of our day have to say on the historicity of Pārśva and his predecessors. Before we directly refer to any part of Jaina literature we shall see what can be gathered about this particular point from the salient features of the period itself. "As a general account of the facts," says Jarl Charpentier, "the statement that the main part of the canon originated with Mahāvīra and his immediate successors may probably be trusted."[8] But the Jainas go a step further than this. According to them the *pūrva*s were the oldest sacred books, dating as far back as the first *tīrthaṅkara*, Ṛṣabha. There is also another more reliable tradition upon which Professor Jacobi rightly lays stress as containing some truth, and it is this that

1. Jacobi, op. cit., p. 163. See also "Neminātha, an uncle to Kṛshṇa and the twenty-second Tīrthaṅkara of the Jainas," etc. — Cf. Mazumdar, op. cit., p. 551.
2. Jacobi, op. and loc. cit.
3. Cf. Wilson, op. cit., I, pp. 328-29.
4. "Modern European writers have been inclined to disparage unduly the authority of the *Purāṇic* lists, but closer study finds in them much genuine and valuable historical tradition." — Cf. Smith, *Early History of India*, p. 12 (4th edn.).
5. S.B.E. VIII, p. 32. "*Nyāya-Darśana* and *Brahma-Sūtra* (*Vedānta*) were composed between AD 200 and 450" — Jacobi. Cf. *J.A.O.S.*, XXXI, p. 29.
6. Cf. Pansikar, op. cit., p. 252.
7. Hiralal, H., *Ancient History of the Jaina Religion*, pt. II, pp. 85-89.
8. Charpentier, op. cit., p. 12.

the *pūrvas* were taught by Mahāvīra himself, and that the *aṅgas* were then composed by his *gaṇadharas*.[1]

From this it becomes clear that Mahāvīra and his *gaṇadharas* who succeeded him were the authors of the Jaina Āgamic literature. When we say that Mahāvīra was the author we do not mean that he actually wrote them, but that whatever is recorded there was taught by him. "For authorship in India depended chiefly on the matter, the words being rather irrelevant, provided the sense be the same."[2] Furthermore, from certain peculiarities of the Jaina literature itself we can also mark that along with the religion it can be traced as far back as Vardhamāna and some time even before him. But we shall not touch any of these characteristic features here, since we are going to deal with them in our chapter on "Jaina Literature."

Now when in such canonical literature of the Jainas we find more or less unanimous and reliable reference to Pārśva there is no reason to doubt their authenticity. Take for instance the *Kalpa-Sūtra* of the days of Bhadrabāhu. It has referred to all the *tīrthaṅkaras* of the Jainas. Its references to Pārśva and Mahāvīra *dharma* have, however, been dealt with. The most important passage is the one in the *Bhagavatī* wherein is described a dispute between Kālāsavesiyaputta, a follower of Pārśva, and some disciple of Mahāvīra. It ends with the former's begging permission to stay with him "after having changed the law of the four vows for the law of the five vows enjoining compulsory confession."[3] In Śīlāṅka's commentary on the *Ācārāṅga* the same distinction is made between the *cāturyāma* of Pārśva's followers and the *pāñcayāma* of Vardhamāna's *tīrtha*.[4]

The same thing is repeated also in the *Uttarādhyayana*. To quote Dasgupta: "The story in the *Uttarādhyayana* that a disciple of Pārśva met a disciple of Mahāvīra and brought about the union of the old Jainism and that propounded by Mahāvīra seems to suggest that this Pārśva was probably an historical person."[5]

Coming to modern scholars we find that there is a general unanimity about the historical character of Pārśva's life. Just to mention a few among

1. Jacobi, S.B.E., XXII, Int., p. 45.
2. Jacobi, *Kalpa-Sūtra*, p. 15.
3. तए णं से कालासवेसियपुत्त अणगारे थेरे भगवंतो वंदइ नमंसइ २ (त्ता) एवं वदासी — इच्छामि णं भंते। तुब्भं . . . — Cf. *Bhagavatī-Sūtra, Śataka* I, *sūt.* 76. Cf. also Weber, *Fragment der Bhagavatī*, p. 185.
4. स एव चतुर्यामभेदाच्चतुर्धा, etc. — Cf. *Ācārāṅga-Sūtra, Śrutaskandha* II, vv. 12-13. p. 320.
5. Dasgupta, *History of Indian Philosophy* I, p. 169. Cf. also तओ केसिं बुवन्तं तु गोयमो इणमठ्ठावी . . . — *Uttarādhyayana-Sūtra, Adhyayana* XXIII, v. 25.

the older generation of Sanskrit scholars in the West, we find that Colebrooke,[1] Stevenson[2] and Edward Thomas[3] strongly believed that Jainism was older than both Nāttaputta and Sākyaputta. "I take Pārśvanātha," says Colebrooke, "to have been the founder of the sect of the Jainas, which was confirmed and thoroughly established by Mahāvīra and his disciple Sudharma; by whom, and by his followers, both Mahāvīra and his predecessor, Pārśvanātha, have been venerated as deified saints (*Jinas*), and are so worshipped by the Jainas of this day."[4]

On the other side some German scholars, like Bühler[5] and Jacobi,[6] refuted the arguments put forward by H.H. Wilson,[7] Lassen[8] and others. "These particulars," says Jacobi, "about the religion of the Jainas previous to the reform of Mahāvīra are so matter-of-fact like, that it is impossible to deny that they may have been handed down by a trustworthy tradition. Hence we must infer that the *Nirgranthas* already existed previous to Mahāvīra — a result which we shall render more evident in the sequel by collateral proofs."[9]

Coming to our own day we have three of the greatest writers on Indian philosophy — Drs Belvalkar,[10] Dasgupta[11] and Radhakrishnan[12] — and historians and scholars like Charpentier,[13] Guérinot,[14] Mazumdar,[15] Frazer,[16] Elliot,[17] Poussin[18] and others, who hold the same opinion. "Jainism has suffered," observes Belvalkar, "in estimation as an ethical and metaphysical system by being deemed as more or less contemporaneous in origin with the other more evolved philosophical systems like the Sāṁkhya, Vedānta and Buddhism. The fact is that Mahāvīra inherited the ontology of his system from a remoter ancestry, and he probably did little more than transmit it unchanged to succeeding generations."[19]

In his learned preface to the *Uttarādhyayana* Dr Charpentier observes: "We ought also to remember both that the Jaina religion is certainly older than Mahāvīra, his reputed predecessor, Pārśva, having almost certainly

1. Colebrooke, op. cit., II, p. 317.
2. Stevenson (Rev.), *op.* and *loc. cit.*
3. Thomas (Edward), op. cit., p. 6.
4. Colebrooke. *op.* and *loc. cit.*
5. Bühler, *The Indian Sect of the Jainas*, p. 32.
6. Jacobi, S.B.E., XLV, p. xxi.
7. Wilson, op. cit., I, p. 334.
8. Lassen, *I.A.*, II, p. 197.
9. Jacobi. *I.A.*, IX, p. 160.
10. Belvalkar, *The Brahma-Sūtras*, p. 106.
11. Dasgupta, op. cit., p. 173.
12. Radhakrishnan, op. cit., p. 281.
13. Charpentier, *C.H.I.*, I, p. 153.
14. Guérinot, *Bibliographie Jaina*, Int., p. xi.
15. Mazumdar, op. cit., pp. 262 ff.
16. Frazer, *Literary History of India*, p. 128.
17. Elliot, *Hinduism and Buddhism*, I, p. 110.
18. Poussin, *The Way to Nirvāṇa*, p. 67.
19. Belvalkar, op. cit., p. 107.

existed as the real person, and that consequently the main point of the original doctrine may have been codified long before Mahāvīra."[1] Lastly, Dr Guérinot says: "There can no longer be any doubt that Pārśvanātha was an historical personage. According to the Jaina tradition he must have lived a hundred years, and died 250 years before Mahāvīra. His period of activity therefore corresponds to the 8th century BC. The parents of Mahāvīra were followers of the religion of Pārśva."[2]

From all these overwhelming proofs about the existence of a *tīrthaṅkara* or *tīrthaṅkara*s before Mahāvīra we can, without any fear of historical fallacy, affirm that modern research goes rightly as far back as the days of Pārśvanātha. About the other *tīrthaṅkara*s we shall not endorse the opinion of Mazumdar, who, even at the risk of entirely disregarding the Jaina tradition, lays down that Ṛṣabha Deva, the first *tīrthaṅkara* of the Jainas, "was a king of the Vairāja dynasty in Bithoor (29th century BC)."[3] We shall merely conclude in the words of Dr Jacobi that "we must close our researches here content to have obtained a few glimpses into the prehistorical development of Jainism. The last point which we can perceive is Pārśva; beyond him all is lost in the mist of fable and fiction."[4]

1. Charpentier, *Uttarādhyayana,* Int., p. 21.
2. Guérinot, *op.* and *loc. cit.*
3. Mazumdar, *op.* and *loc. cit.*
4. Jacobi, op. cit., p. 163.

III : Pārśvanātha, the twenty-third *Tīrthaṅkara* of the Jainas (Gujarat).

CHAPTER II

Mahāvīra and his Times

I

WE have already dealt with Pārśva, the predecessor of Mahāvīra, in the previous chapter. There is very little in connection with him that we can glean out from any other source but the Jaina *sūtras*. From the Buddhist canonical literature we inferred that there was some such thing as the *cāturyāma-dharma* of Pārśva. All that we know about him is only through Jaina canonical literature, which has also been the basis for all those historians and scholars who have written about him.

We need not put down here all that the Jainas have to say about Pārśva, because it is impossible to deal with that part of Jaina history which forms the period between the last two *tīrthaṅkaras*, mainly for two reasons — viz. that, in the first place, what we know about them is chiefly through mere tradition, and that, in the second place, there is so much that is contradictory even there. It would be enough to say that Pārśva was born of a king named Aśvasena, who was a ruling magnate at Benares, and that his mother's name was Vāmā.[1] Furthermore, according to the Jaina belief there were 16,000 monks, 38,000 nuns, 164,000 laymen and 327,000 laywomen who formed his whole following.[2] Pārśva is said to have lived for one hundred years, for seventy years of which he was engrossed in seeking *nirvāṇa*.[3]

Coming to Mahāvīra we find that, according to Jaina tradition, he came about two hundred and fifty years after his predecessor.[4] The period of Indian history when Mahāvīra lived is called the rationalistic age. Its duration differs

1. *Kalpa-Sūtra, sūt*. 150 ; see also अवातरद्वामास्वामिन्या उदरे . . . etc. — Hemacandra, *Triṣaṣṭi-Śalākā, Parva* IX. v. 23, p. 196 ; Charpentier, *C.H.I.*, I., p. 154.
2. *Kalpa-Sūtra, sūt*. 161-164.
3. Ibid., *sūt*. 168 ; see also सप्ततिर्व्रतपालने । इत्यायुर्वत्सरशतं . . . etc. — Hemacandra, op. cit., v. 318, p. 219 ; Mazumdar, op. cit., p. 551.
4. श्रीपार्श्वनिर्वाणात् पञ्चाशदधिकवर्षशतद्वयेन श्रीवीरनिर्वाणं. — *Kalpa-Sūtra, Subodhikā-Ṭīkā*, p. 132. "As he is said to have died 250 years before the death of Mahāvīra, he may probably have lived in the 8th century BC" — *C.H.I.*, I., p. 153.

with different authors, but generally the limit can be put as between 1000-200 BC.[1] The age of epic India had passed away. The Kurus, the Pāñcālas, the Kośalas, and the Videhas of the Gangetic Valley no more existed. It was in this period that the Āryans issued out of the Gangetic Valley and founded Hindu kingdoms even in the southernmost parts of India; suffusing their new settlements with their glorious civilization.

And this is precisely a period which is marked by a great flourish of religion in India. "Her ancient religion, which the Hindu Āryans had practised and proclaimed for fourteen centuries, had degenerated into forms."[2] India was now to witness the commencement of a great revolution. Whether for the better or for the worse, she had to face a great upheaval in the Hindu fold. "Religion in its true sense had been replaced by forms. Excellent social and moral rules were disfigured by the unhealthy distinctions of caste, by exclusive privileges for brāhmaṇas and by cruel laws for śūdras. Such exclusive caste privileges did not help to improve the brāhmaṇas themselves. As a community they became grasping and covetous, ignorant and pretentious, until *brāhmaṇa-sūtrakāra*s themselves had to censure the abuse in the strongest terms."[3]

The institution of priesthood among the Hindus is certainly a later growth; for although the word brāhmaṇa is used in the *Ṛgveda*[4] (which Veda goes back to the earliest times of Āryan culture in India), it only meant "singers of sacred songs."[5] And it was now that they came to designate a class of religious functionaries. As time went on the office seems to have become hereditary, and by and by the brāhmaṇas came to be regarded with higher and higher honour.[6] With it their pretensions also rose higher and higher, but they could not yet form an exclusive caste. This was the situation before the Āryans had advanced beyond the Seven Rivers, at the mouth of the Indus, where they

---

1. Cf. Dutt, op. cit. (Contents); Mazumdar, op. cit. (Contents).
2. Dutt, op. cit., p. 340.
3. Ibid., p. 341; see also "(Brahmans) who neither study nor teach the *Veda* nor keep sacred fires become equal to *Śūdras.*" — *Vāsishṭha*, III., 1. Cf. Bühler, S.B.E., XIV., p. 16.
4. Griffith, *The Hymns of the Rigveda*, II., pp. 96, 97, etc. (2nd edn.).
5. Cf. Tiele, *Outlines of the History of Religion*, p. 115.
6. "In course of time the priest's connection with the sovereign appears to have assumed permanency, and probably become hereditary." — Cf. Law, N.N., *Ancient Indian Polity*, p. 44.

had originally settled after their separation from the Iranians.[1] But with a diffusion of the Hindu-Āryans over the region south-east of the Seven Rivers, and their settlement on the Ganges and the Jumna, the Vedic religion gave birth to brāhmanism, or the hierarchy of brāhmaṇas.[2]

With brāhmanism came the rigidity of caste system, which "was still a pliable institution in the Epic period, but the rules of caste were made more rigid and inflexible in the Rationalistic period, and it was impossible for the members of a lower caste to enter within the pale of priesthood."[3] This state of things resulted in brāhmaṇas being entirely relieved of manual labour, and being fed on the resources of the industrial classes without doing anything worthwhile to compensate the other classes.[4] They had become idlers to such an extent that they were not prepared to acquire that learning which alone could justify their exemption from labour. Vasiṣṭha felt the abuse and the injustice keenly, and protested against idlers being supported and fed, in terms which could be indicted only when Hinduism was still the religion of a living nation.[5]

The abuses begotten of the privileges of the caste system combined with the circumstance that writing was unknown, or at any rate was not generally employed for literary purposes, contributed to give increasing influence to the brāhmaṇas.[6] Subject at first to the princes and nobles, and dependent on them, they began by insinuating themselves into their favour, and representing that the protection and liberty of brāhmaṇas were part of the duties of the princes and nobles. Gradually they set themselves up as the exclusive guardians and interpreters of "revelation" (*Śruti*) and "tradition" (*Smṛti*), in virtue of their being masters of instruction.[7] By far the greater

1. "It is not so easy to trace the relations between *Brahmarshideśa* and the earlier Āryan settlements in the land of the Seven Rivers." — *C.H.I.*, I., p. 51.
2. Cf. Tiele, op. cit., pp. 112, 117. "The language of the *Rigveda*, the oldest form of Vedic Sanskrit, belongs to the country of the Seven Rivers. The language of the *Brāhmaṇas* and of the later Vedic literature in the country of the Upper Jumna and Ganges (*Brahmarshideśa*) is transitional." — *C.H.I.*, I., p. 57.
3. Dutt, op. cit., p. 264. Cf. Crooke, *E.R.E.*, II., p. 493.
4. Cf. McCrindle, *Ancient India*, p. 209.
5. "The King shall punish that village where Brahmans, unobservant of their sacred duties and ignorant of the Vedas, subsist by begging ; for it feeds robbers." — *Vāsishṭha*, III, 4. Cf. Bühler, S.B.E., XIV., p. 17.
6. Cf. Tiele, op. cit., p. 121.
7. "To this class the knowledge of divination among the Indians is exclusively restricted, and none but the Sophists is allowed to practise that art." — McCrindle, op. and loc. cit.

number of works on religion were composed with a view to the sacrificial service.[1] They constitute the four Vedas, each Veda having different *Brāhmaṇas*. These *Brāhmaṇas* are generally "marked by narrow formalism, childish mysticism and superstitious talks about all kinds of trifles, such as may be expected where a pedantic and powerful priesthood is invested with unlimited spiritual authority."[2]

The *yajña* ceremony was so organized and arranged that by and by it became more and more elaborate and involved, and this required a constant increase in the number of ministrants, all of whom were of necessity brāhmaṇas. Sometimes they went to such an extent that the reverence for the *devas* (gods) also perceptibly diminished as they placed themselves on their level.[3] Behind the doctrine of the sacrificial service the popular understanding was that "a suitable combination of rites, rituals and articles of sacrifice had the magical power of producing the desired effect — a shower of rain, the birth of a son, the routing of a huge army, etc. The sacrifices were enjoined generally not so much for any moral elevation as for the achievement of objects of practical welfare."[4]

Thus the social ideal of brāhmaṇas was the unlimited power that hierarchy conferred and the strict separation of castes. Various useful callings were in this rigid society branded as sinful, and men were prevented from withdrawing even from shameful occupations to which birth condemned them. Highest claims were made by the brāhmaṇas, and they were also the recipients of the most extravagant privileges. This went on to such an extent that even the unlimited authority of the king was considered to be at their service.[5] The very religious bent of the ancient Indians was such that the royal priest [6] was an important personage from the very earliest times of

1. The sacrificial ceremonial at the consecration of a king (*rājasūya*), the very common horse-sacrifice (*aśvamedha*), the proper human-sacrifice (*puruṣamedha*), and the general sacrifice (*sarvamedha*) were the most important. At these four sacrifices human victims were really offered in ancient times, but as the manners grew more gentle this practice began to decline ; though not with universal approval, finally it fell into disuse.
2. Tiele, op. cit., p. 123.
3. They held "the supreme place of divinity and honour." — Cf. McCrindle, op. and loc. cit.
4. Dasgupta, op. cit., I., p. 208. Cf. also Law, N. N., op. cit., p. 39.
5. "They were divinely appointed to be the guides of the nation and the councillors of the king, but they could not be kings themselves." — Law, N.N., op. cit., p. 45.
6. Also called *purohit*, etymologically meaning "placed in front, appointed."

which we have any record. Woman was considered a non-entity in the social organization, and the śūdra was despised out and out.[1]

Naturally such a state of society was not destined to hold a long time. And it did end with the appearance of Mahāvīra on one side, and Buddha Śākyaputta on the other. "It is said of the French Revolution," says Dutt, "that it was mainly brought about by two causes: the oppression of the kings and the intellectual reaction set in by the philosophers of the 18th century. The Buddhist revolution in India is still more distinctly the result of similar causes. The oppression of brāhmanism made the people sigh for a revolution, and the work of the philosophers opened the path to such a revolution."[2]

Dr Hopkins goes a little further and lays stress on the psychology of the people with whom these developments first originated. "To a great extent," says the learned scholar, "both Jainism and Buddhism owed their success to the politics of the day. The kings of the East were impatient of the Western Church; they were pleased to throw it over. . . . The West was more conservative than the East. It was the home of the rites it favoured. The East was but a foster-father."[3]

But we are not out to invent any anti-brāhmaṇa prejudice for the explanation of this great Indian revolution. It was "an expression of the general ferment of thought which prevailed at the beginning of the epic period."[4] We need not understand it as a mere "result of kṣatriya protest against the caste exclusiveness of brāhmaṇas,"[5] because "the ground had been well prepared for the growth of a new belief and new doctrines outside the orthodox bull-work of brāhmanism."[6] Furthermore, the hypothesis of development from which the history of a religion sets out is based on the principle that all changes and transformations in religions, whether they appear from a subjective point of view to indicate decay or progress, are the results of natural growth, and find in it their best explanation.

Coming to our own period we find that this attitude is corroborated by

---

1. Cf. Tiele, op. cit., pp. 129-30. Manu, in spite of his oft-quoted line : यत्र नार्यस्तु पूज्यन्ते रमन्ते तत्र देवताः prohibited woman even the performance of sacramental rites — a prohibition which he places on woman and the śūdra alike. — Cf. chaps. V, 155 ; IX., 18 ; and IV., 80.
2. Dutt, op. cit., p. 225.
3. Hopkins, op. cit., p. 282.
4. Radhakrishnan, op. cit., I., p. 293.
5. Srinivasachari and Iyangar, op. cit., p. 48.
6. Frazer, op. cit., p. 117.

gradual changes in the history of Indian thought and Indian outlook on life. "Tendencies to question the authority of the Vedas," says Kunte, "were shown long before Buddha Gautama succeeded in organising opposition to the Vedic polity, social and religious."[1] The same is the opinion of other scholars also. "Buddhism and Jainism," says Jacobi, "must be regarded as religious developments out of brāhmanism, not by sudden reformation, but prepared by a religious movement going on for a long time."[2] There is nothing unreasonable if we say that the echo of what was to come on some future date was already audible in the Upaniṣads, which had anticipated the new system in all its directions. "The pioneers of this new system," says Dr Dasgupta, "probably drew their suggestions from the sacrificial creed and from the Upaniṣads, and built their systems independently by their own rational thinking."[3] Mr Dutt traces this change in the mind of the people as far back as the eleventh century BC — that is, five centuries before the time of which we are now speaking. According to him, "earnest and thoughtful Hindus had ventured to go beyond the wearisome rituals of the *Brāhmaṇa* literature, and had inquired into the mysteries of the soul and its creator."[4]

This was the state of things in the Hindu-fold, and hence, naturally, the Jaina-fold also could not escape its evil effects.[5] We have already seen that Mahāvīra had to make certain distinctions in the four great vows put forward by his predecessor, and this initiative on his part ultimately resulted in the five great vows propounded by him. The state of society was such that people would try to take advantage, if any loopholes were available, for a free and easy life; which brings into broad relief Mahāvīra's making clear in all its aspects the *dharma* of Pārśva.[6]

II

It was amidst this changing flux of thought that Mahāvīra moved, and wove out for himself the solution of the riddle of the cosmos, which placed man's fate, for weal or woe, here and hereafter, in man's own hands, and tought him to look not beyond himself for hope or aid. The nation was prepared

1. Kunte, op. cit., pp. 407, 408.
2. Jacobi, S.B.E., XXII., Int., p. 32.
3. Dasgupta, op. cit., I., p. 210.
4. Dutt, op. cit., p. 340.
5. ". . . in the 250 years that elapsed between his death and the coming of Mahāvīra abuses became so rife . . ." — Stevenson (Mrs), op. cit., p. 49.
6. See *Kalpa-Sūtra, Subodhikā-Ṭīkā*, p. 3 ; Jacobi, S.B.E., XLV., pp. 122, 123.

when he began to preach, for his spiritualism was understood and appreciated, and gradually even the brāhmaṇas recognized him as a great teacher.[1] "Intellectual brāhmaṇas also joined the ranks of Jainas as of Buddhists from time to time owing to conviction as well as for honour, and contributed to the maintenance of the reputation of the Jainas for learning."[2]

Jainism spread slowly among the poor and the lowly, for it was then a strong protest against caste privileges. It was a religion of equality of man. Mahāvīra's righteous soul rebelled against the unrighteous distinction between man and man, and his benevolent heart hankered for a means to help the humble, the oppressed and the lowly. The beauty of a holy life, of a sinless, benevolent career, flashed before his mind's eye as the perfection of human destiny, as the heaven on earth; and, with the earnest conviction of a prophet and a reformer, he proclaimed this as the essence of religion. His world-embracing sympathy led him to proclaim this method of self-culture and holy living to suffering humanity, and he invited the poor and lowly to end their suffering by cultivating brotherly love and universal peace. The brāhmaṇa and the śūdra, the high and the low, were the same in his eyes. All could equally effect their salvation by a holy life, and he invited all to embrace his catholic religion of love.[3] It spread slowly — as Christianity spread in Europe in early days — until Śreṇika, Kūṇika, Candragupta, Samprati, Kharavela and others embraced Jainism during the first few glorious centuries of Hindu rule in India.

Like brāhmanism, Jainism also is based on the so-called dogmas of the transmigration of the soul, and seeks for deliverance from the endless succession of rebirths.[4] But it pronounces the brāhmanic penance and abstinences inadequate to accomplish this, and aims at attaining, not union with the universal spirit,[5] but *nirvāṇa* — that is, absolute release from all

1. प्रभुः अपापापुर्यां . . . जगाम, तत्र . . . बहवो ब्राह्मणाः मिलिताः . . . चतुश्चत्वारिंशच्छतानि द्विजाः प्रव्रजिताः. —*Kalpa-Sūtra, Subodhikā-Ṭīkā*, pp. 112, 118.
2. Vaidya (C. V.), *H.M.I.*, III., p. 406.
3. सर्व्वसत्वानं हितसुखायास्तु (May it be for the welfare and happiness of all creatures). — Bühler, *E.I.*, II., pp. 203, 204 ; Ins. No. XVIII.
4. "He for whom there is no bondage whatever in this world . . . etc., has quitted the path of birth." — Jacobi, S.B.E., XXII., p. 213.
5. "There were two principal world theories in ancient India. One, which was systematised as the Vedānta, teaches in its extreme form that the soul and the universal spirit are identical and the external world an illusion." — Elliot, op. cit., I., p. 106.

bodily forms and activities.[1] Without denying the existence of the *devas* (gods), at any rate at first, it places each *jina* above them and recognizes them as subordinate to a perfect saint.[2] It differed from brāhmanism, as primitive Christianity differed from the Jewish hierarchy, by rejecting outward works or theological knowledge as a mark of holiness,[3] and seeking it in gentleness, in purity of heart and life, in mercy, and self-denying love for a neighbour. Above all, it is distinguished by its relation to castes. Mahāvīra comes neither to oppose them nor to level everything. On the other hand, he adopts a doctrine that men are born in lower or higher castes, determined by their sins or good works in a former existence; but it teaches at the same time that by a life of purity and love, by becoming a spiritual man, everyone may attain at once the highest salvation. Caste makes no difference to him; he looks for the man even in the *cāṇḍāla;*[4] the miseries of existence beset all alike, and his law is a law of grace for all. Therefore the most salutary change that Mahāvīra brought about was his effort to show how circumstantial indeed caste system was, and how easy it was for a spiritual man to break the fetters of caste system.

This is Jainism in general. It is quite popular in its character, and its instrument is preaching rather than instruction. Coming to Mahāvīra we find that he too, like Buddha, was born of a kṣatriya aristocratic family. In fact, all along, it has been the Jaina belief that a Jina must always come from a kṣatriya or some such noble family.[5] Now it so happened that because of certain actions on his part in his former lives.[6] Mahāvīra had first to take

---

1. आत्यन्तिको वियोगस्तु देहादेर्मोक्ष उच्यते.— Haribhadra, *Ṣaḍdarśana Samuccaya,* v. 52.
2. देवाधिदेवं सर्वज्ञं श्रीवीरं प्रणिदध्महे . . . — Hemacandra, *Pariśiṣṭaparvan,* Canto I, v. 2 ; . . . जिनेन्द्रो . . . सुरासुरेन्द्रसंपूज्यः . . . — Haribhadra, op. cit., vv. 45, 46.
3. "One does not become a Śramaṇa by the tonsure, nor a Brahman by the sacred syllable *'OM,'* nor a *Muni* by living in the woods, nor a *Tāpasa* by wearing (clothes) Kuśa-grass and bark." — Jacobi, S.B.E., XLV., p. 140.
4. सोवागकुलसंभूओ . . . हरिएस बलो . . . etc. — *Uttarādhyayana,* Lecture XII, 1. "Harikeśa-Bala was born in a family of *Svapākas* (*kāṇḍālas*) ; he became a monk and a sage," etc. — Jacobi, op. cit., p. 50.
5. "It never has happened, nor does it happen, nor will it happen, that Arhats, . . . be born of poor families, . . . beggars' families, or Brāhmanical families. For indeed Arhats . . . are born in high families, . . . in families belonging to the race of *Ikshvāku,* or in other such-like families of pure descent on both sides." — Jacobi, S.B.E., XXII., p. 225.
6. According to the Jaina belief whatever we are in our present life is a net result of all our *karmas* committed during our previous births. All *karmas* are generally considered to be imperishable, indescribable, and indestructible unless they take →

the form of an embryo in the womb of a brāhmaṇa lady named Devānandā, the wife of the brāhmaṇa Ṛṣabhadatta,[1] and, as usual with the lives of all such big prophets, there is a popular legend about Mahāvīra also that when the god Śakra (Indra), "the chief of kings and gods,"[2] came to know about this, it was arranged by him to transfer the embryo from Devānandā's womb to that of kṣatriyāṇī Triśalā, the wife of the kṣatriya king Siddhārtha of the Kāśyapa-*gotra*, belonging to the clan of the jñātṛ-kṣatriyas.[3] Although at the instance of a miracle, Mahāvīra ultimately belongs to kṣatriya origin.

Curiously enough this legend has been worked out in sculptures also. Some specimens of Jaina sculptures from Mathurā bear testimony to it with an exactness which is really surprising, which fact shows that this legend can be traced historically to the very beginning of the Christian era, and therefore it can safely be said that it must have had some connection either with the life of Mahāvīra or that it must have been connected with one or the other social characteristics of those days.

We know from *Kalpa-Sūtra* that the god Indra had sent Hariṇegameṣī to carry out this command of his.[4] This Hariṇegameṣī is generally interpreted as "Negamesī of Hari"— i.e., "Negamesī, the servant of Indra."[5] Dr Bühler observes: "A Jaina sculpture representing Naigamesa, a small tīrthaṅkara and a female with a small infant, can only be taken to refer to the most famous legend, in which the deity plays a part — viz. the exchange of the embryos of Devānandā and Triśalā."[6]

On the very face of it this legend of Mahāvīra seems strange enough, but it must be admitted that tales stranger and more legendary in nature also have been told by other religions about their own prophets. What strikes us

---

→ effect. Now Mahāvīra had committed the *karman* relating to name and *gotra* in one out of twenty-seven visible lives which he had to pass before he was destined to be born on this earth as the last Jaina prophet. It was because of this *karman* that he had first to take his birth in the family of a brāhmaṇa. तच्च जीचैर्गोत्रं भगवता स्थूलसप्तविंशतिभवापेक्षया तृतीय पैवे बद्धं — *Kalpa-Sūtra, Subodhikā-Ṭīkā*, p. 26. Cf. also Jacobi, op. cit., pp. 190, 191.

1. ततश्च्युत्वा तेन मरीचिभवबद्धेन नीचैर्गोत्रकर्मणा . . . ऋषभदत्तस्य ब्राह्मणस्य देवानन्दायाः ब्राह्मणयाः कुक्षो उत्पन्नः. — *Kalpa-Sūtra, Subodhikā-Ṭīkā*, p. 29.
2. Cf. S.B.E., XXII., p. 225.
3. After eighty-two days the embryo was removed. समणे भगवं महावीरे . . . बासीइ . . . ब्भित्ताए साहरिए . . . — *Kalpa-Sūtra, Subodhikā-Ṭīkā*, pp. 35, 36.
4. Jacobi, op. cit., pp. 223 ff.
5. Bühler, op. cit., p. 316.
6. Ibid., p. 317. Cf. also *Mathura Sculptures*, Plate II ; *A.S.R.*, XX., Plate IV, 2-5.

most is not the nature of the tradition, but the spirit behind it. Does it mean, from this attitude on the part of the Jainas, that their monastical order was originally intended only for the kṣatriyas? It seems not; because, tracing from the days of Mahāvīra down to our own times, we find that some of the greatest and most prominent figures of the Jaina fold were brāhmaṇas as well. From Indrabhūti[1] down, right to the last *gaṇadhara* of Mahāvīra, all were brāhmaṇas. Then in later history we have prominent *gurus* and scholars like Siddhasena and Haribhadra who also were originally brāhmaṇas.[2]

It may be that just at the beginning of the rationalistic period, when brāhmaṇas were more or less at the height of their glory, and when other castes were getting more and more conscious of their previous subordination to brāhmaṇas, this belief on the part of the Jainas got a certain definite form. The Buddhists also seem to have entertained a similar feeling, emphasizing the prominence of the kṣatriya touch in their church. In one of his sermons at Benares, Buddha speaks of his religion as that "for the sake of which noble youths fully give up the world and go forth into the houseless state."[3]

With all this it must be borne in mind that the Jainas did not mind the brāhmaṇas becoming Jaina *gurus* and enjoying the highest posts in the Jaina church, but they made this distinction, that a born brāhmaṇa may become a *kevalī* and attain *mokṣa*, but he cannot become a *tīrthaṅkara*. This may be just to wipe off the common belief of the people of those days that brāhmaṇas alone were entitled to be at the top in all spiritual matters. We know from authentic sources that during the early days there was nothing like the brāhmaṇas enjoying monopoly about religious and other ceremonial affairs. "Numerous instances have also been cited to show that men of low birth actually entered the priestly caste by their knowledge and virtues; that priestly caste did not acquire a monopoly of religious learning; that they often came as humble

---

1. "There is a legend about Indrabhūti which shows how much he was attached to his teacher. At the time of Mahāvīra's death he was absent. On his return, hearing of his beloved teacher's sudden decease, he was overcome with grief. He became aware that the last remaining bond which tied him to the *Saṁsāra* was the feeling of love he still entertained for his teacher. Therefore he cut asunder that bond, and thus *Chinnapiyabaṁdhane* he reached the stage of *Kevalin.* He died a month after Māhāvīra's *Nirvāna.*" — Jacobi, *Kalpa-Sūtra,* Int., p. 1.
2. "Siddhaseṇa Divākara, the son of a Brahman minister. . . . Haribhadra was originally a learned Brahman. . . . " — Stevenson (Mrs), op. cit., pp. 76, 80.
3. Rhys Davids and Oldenberg, S.B.E., XIII., p. 93.

IV : Ornamental Slab representing the transfer of Māhavīra's embryo by Naigameṣa.
(Copyright: Archaeological Survey of India)

pupils to Kṣatriya kings to acquire religious learning."[1] "They did not," observes Tiele, "yet form an exclusive caste, for kings and kings' sons are also designated as sacred singers, and perform priestly functions, though, like many of the nobles also, they generally had their house-priests (*purohits*)."[2]

Anyhow, as we have already remarked, in later history, by insinuations and pretensions, brāhmaṇas came to be recognized as spiritual guardians and benefactors of society,[3] though "at any rate the older hymns contained occasional references to a brāhmaṇa or a brāhmaṇa's son, in later hymns these are more numerous."[4] This might surely have moved the kṣatriyas and other castes to pull down the brāhmaṇas from the heights of their self-acquired superiority and to deprive them of some of their many privileges.

Dr Jacobi, in interpreting this particular incident of Mahāvīra's life, seems to have drawn some far-fetched conclusions. He begins with the hypothesis that Siddhārtha, the father of Mahāvīra, had two wives — one the kṣatriyāṇī, Triśalā, and the other the brāhmaṇī, Devadattā. Furthermore, he believes that Mahāvīra was really born of Devadattā, but afterwards he was proclaimed to have been born of Triśalā just with a view to get him the importance and greatness accruing from the aristocratic connection on his mother's side, and to entitle him to the patronage of his relations.[5] We see no use in drawing imaginary inferences from such incidents as these that are connected with a prophet's life, but we might get something from the atmosphere of the time in interpreting such a dogmatic assertion of the Jaina canonical books as that a brāhmaṇa can be everything but a *tīrthaṅkara.*

Thus Mahāvīra is believed to have been born of Triśalā, near the town of Vaiśālī,[6] nearly twenty-seven miles north of Patna. His father, Siddhārtha, seems

1. Dutt, op. cit., p. 264.
2. Tiele, op. cit., p. 116. "Previous to the origin of caste, and even in the period when the functions were not yet stereotyped, the king could sacrifice for himself and his subjects unaided." — Law, N.N., op. cit., p. 41.
3. "They had frequently, however, to encounter grave resistance from the princes ; generally, however, they contrived, either by assumption and arrogance or by cunning, to attain their end." — Tiele, op. cit., p. 121.
4. Ibid., p. 115.
5. Cf. Jacobi, S.B.E., XXII., Int., p. xxxi.
6. This Vaiśālī is identified with the modern Besarh in the Hājīpur subdivision of Muzaffarpur.

to have been a chieftain of Kuṇḍagrāma village,[1] and his mother, Princess Triśalā, was the sister of the chieftain of Vaiśālī, the capital of Videha, and was related also to Bimbisāra, king of Magadha.[2] In Nandivardhana and Sudarśanā he had his eldest brother and sister respectively. Mahāvīra was married to one Yaśodā, who belonged to the Kauṇḍinya *gotra*, and he had by her a daughter named Anojjā, also called Priyadarśanā.[3] She was married to his nephew *rājaputra* Jamāli, "a future disciple of his father-in-law and the propagator of the first schism in the Jaina church."[4] Mahāvīra lived a householder's life till he was thirty years old, but just after the decease of his parents he left his home with the permission of his elder brother and entered the spiritual career,[5] "which in India, just as the Church in the Western country, seems to have offered a field for ambitious younger sons."[6]

According to the Jaina belief Māhavīra's parents were worshippers of Pārśva and followers of the *śramaṇas*.[7] "Mahavira's doctrines are spoken of in the *Sūtras* not as his doctrines but *decreta*, or old-established truths — *Pannattas*. All this would be next to impossible if he had been like Buddha, the original founder of his religion; but it is just what one would expect to be the record of a reformer's life and preaching."[8] He is said to have been praised and hymned by both gods and men in the following sweet words: "Obtain the pre-eminent highest rank (i.e. final liberation) on that straight road which the Jinas have taught."[9]

1. "Just outside Vaiśālī lay the suburb Kuṇḍagrāma — probably surviving in the modern village of Basukund — and here lived a wealthy nobleman, Siddhārtha, head of a certain warrior-clan called the Jñātṛkas." — *C.H.I.*, I., p. 157.
2. Cf. Frazer, op. cit., pp. 128-31. According to the Jaina *sūtra*s Triśalā was called Videhadattā and Priyakāriṇī, and that is why Mahāvīra was called "Videhadatta's son." Cf. Jacobi, op. cit., pp. 193 194, 256.
3. राजा समरवीरोऽथ यशोदां कन्यकां निजाम्। प्रदातुं वर्धमानाय . . . भर्तुर्यशोदायामजायत। . . . दुहिता प्रियदर्शना॥ — Hemacandra, *Triṣaṣṭi-Śalākā, Parva* X, vv. 125, 154, p. 16.
4. Charpentier, *C.H.I.*, I., p. 158. राजपुत्रो . . .। जमालिः . . . प्रियदर्शनाम्॥ — Hemacandra, op. cit., v. 155, p. 17.
5. समणे भगवं महावीरे . . . तीसं वासाइं कट्टु . . . विदेहंसि मुंडे भवित्ता, etc. — *Kalpa-Sūtra, Subodhikā-Ṭīkā*, pp. 89, 96.
6. Radhakrishnan, op. cit., p. 287.
7. महावीरस्म अम्मापियरो पासावच्चिज्जा . . . etc. — *Ācārāṅga*, pt. II., *sūt.* 178, p. 422. Cf. Jacobi, op. cit., p. 194. "His parents had, according to a tradition which seems trustworthy, been followers of Pārśva, the previous Tīrthaṅkara; as has already been pointed out, the doctrine of Mahāvīra was scarcely anything else than a modified or renovated form of Pārśva's creed." — Charpentier, op. cit., p. 160.
8. Jacobi, *I.A.*, IX., p. 161.
9. Jacobi, S.B.E., XXII., p. 258. "He had proclaimed the highest law of the Jinas." — Ibid., XLV., p. 288.

Having left the house, Mahāvīra went through the usual career of an ascetic. He wandered for more than twelve years, resting only during the rainy-season.[1] For about the first thirteen months "the venerable ascetic Mahāvīra wore clothes."[2] After that time he walked about naked, casting aside every kind of garment. By uninterrupted meditation, unbroken chastity and the most scrupulous observation of the rules concerning eating and drinking he fully subdued his senses. He was out to neglect his body for twelve years, and with equanimity he was prepared to bear, undergo and suffer all calamities arising from any sources.[3] Thus it is but natural that in a state of forgetfulness as this, Mahāvīra was not conscious whether or not he was dressed. There was nothing like any deliberate move on his part that he should go about naked. The robe that he was putting on during his wanderings was taken away from him in halves by some brāhmaṇa friend of his father named Soma.[4] What came in the prophet's life in a more or less unconscious state of his mind was not meant to be literally adopted by his followers. There is no such rigidity visible in the canonical literature of the Jainas. In the *Uttarādhyayana-Sūtra* the following words are put in the mouth of Sudharman: "My clothes being torn, I shall (soon) go naked," or "I shall get a new suit"; such thoughts should not be entertained by a monk.

"At one time he will have no clothes, at another he will have some; knowing this to be a salutary rule, a wise (monk) should not complain about it."[5] In short, it comes to this, that a monk should be indifferent to all such superficialities. With all this, the general rule adopted for the discipline of the whole class was that monks should try to get on with one cloth, and if essential they may keep two.[6]

---

1. "When the rainy-season has come and it is raining, many living beings are originated and many seeds just spring up . . . . Knowing this (state of things) one should not wander from village to village, but remain during the rainy-season in one place." — Jacobi, S.B.E., XXII., p. 136.
2. समणे भगवं महावीरे संवच्छरं साहियं मासं चीवरधारी हुत्था तेणं परं अचेलए पाणिपडिग्गहिए. — *Kalpa-Sūtra, Subodhikā-Ṭīkā, sūt*. 117, p. 98. Cf. S.B.E., XXII., pp. 259, 260.
3. Cf. ibid., p. 200.
4. ततः पितुर्मित्रेण ब्राह्मणेन गृहीतं. — *Kalpa-Sūtra, Subodhikā-Ṭīkā*, p. 98. Cf. Hemacandra, op. cit., v. 2, p. 19.
5. Jacobi, S.B.E., XLV., p. 11.
6. Jacobi, S.B.E., XXII., p. 157. "The Jaina rules about dress are not so simple ; for they allow a Jaina monk to go naked or to wear one, two or three garments, but a young strong monk should as a rule wear but one robe. Mahāvīra went about naked, and so did the *jinakalpikas*, or those who tried to imitate him as much as possible. But they also were allowed to cover their nakedness." — Ibid., Int., p. xxvi.

Twelve years thus spent in self-penance and meditation were not fruitless. "During the thirteenth year Mahāvīra . . . , not far from an old temple . . . , under a *śāla-tree*, being engaged in deep meditation, reached the highest knowledge and intuition, called *kevala*, which is infinite, supreme, unobstructed, unimpeded, complete, and full."[1]

During these twelve years of preparatory self-mortification Vardhamāna had gone through numerous places, most of which are very difficult to identify today. Roaming about in countries inhabited by savage tribes, rarely having a shelter in which to rest for a night, and visiting even wild tribes of the country called Lāḍha, he had to endure the most painful and dangerous treatment from the barbarous inhabitants.[2] Thereafter he was recognized as omniscient, as a *kevalin* comprehending all subjects, and as an *arhat* for whom there is no secret in this world to learn.[3] By this time he was already forty-two, and the remaining thirty years of his life he passed in teaching his religious system, organizing his order of ascetics, and wandering about preaching his doctrines and making converts. He apparently visited all the great towns of north and south Bihar, dwelling principally in the kingdoms of Magadha and Aṅga. Most of the rainy-seasons were spent round about his native town, Vaiśālī;[4] at Rājagṛha, the old capital of Magadha; at Campā,[5] the capital of ancient Aṅga; at Mithilā, the kingdom of Videha, and at Śrāvastī.[6]

"His wanderings seem to have covered a wide area, and on occasions he visited Rājagṛha, the capital of Magadha, and other towns, where the

1. Ibid., p. 263. Cf. Ibid., p. 201.
2. Cf. Charpentier, op. cit., p. 158 ; Radhakrishnan, op. cit., p. 287. "Mahāvīra wandered for more than twelve years in Lāḍha, in Vajjabhūmi and Subhabhūmi, the Rāḍha of today in Bengal." — Dey, *The Geographical Dictionary of Ancient and Mediaeval India,* p. 108. According to Dr Bühler the Rārh of today in Bengal. Cf. Bühler, *Indian Sect of the Jainas,* p. 26.
3. Cf. Jacobi, op. cit., pp. 263, 264.
4. "Under the name of Kuṇḍa-gāma the city of Vaiśālī is mentioned as the birthplace of Mahāvīra, the Jaina Tīrthaṅkara, who was also called Vesali, or the man of Vaiśālī." — Day, op. cit., p. 107.
5. Campā is a very sacred place to the Jainas, inasmuch as it was the resort of Mahāvīra for three rainy seasons during his wanderings. It is known also as the birthplace and the place of death of Vāsupūjya, the twelfth *tīrthaṅkara* of the Jainas. Cf. ibid., p. 44.
6. "Śrāvastī, also called Sahet-Mahet, is the Candrapura or Candrikāpurī of the Jainas. It is known as the birthplace of the third *tīrthaṅkara* Sambhavanātha and the eighth Tīrthaṅkara Candraprabha of the Jainas." — Ibid., p. 190. "In that period in that age the venerable ascetic Mahāvīra stayed the first rainy season in Asthikagrāma, three rainy seasons in Campā and Prishṭi-Campā, twelve in Vaiśālī and Vanijagrāma, fourteen in Rājagṛha and the suburb of Nālandā . . . , one in Śrāvastī, one in the town of Pāpā in King Hastipāla's office of the writers." — Jacobi, op. cit., p. 264.

V : During the thirteenth year, under a Śāla tree, Mahāvīra reached the highest knowledge and intuition called *Kevala*.
From a Palm-leaf manuscript of the *Kalpa-Sūtra* of the thirteenth century.

utmost honour was shown to him."[1] Furthermore, looking to the schisms in the Jaina church in his own day, the number of Mahāvīra's followers, as believed by the Jainas, does in no way discredit him. He had an excellent community of 14,000 *śramaṇas*, 36,000 nuns, 159,000 male lay-votaries, 318,000 female lay-votaries, and something like 5400 others who either knew the fourteen *pūrvas* or were *kevalins*, and so on.[2]

Thus having become a *kevalin* at the age of forty-two at Jṛmbhikagrāma,[3] situated on the River Ṛjupālikā, near the Pārasnāth hills, and having wandered for about thirty years as a reformer in the Jaina church, Lord Mahāvīra died at the age of seventy-two[4] in the house of King Hastipāla's scribe in Pāvāpurī,[5] near Rājagṛha, a place still visited by thousands of Jaina pilgrims. According to the traditional Jaina chronology this event is believed to have taken place in the year 527 BC, differing by sixteen years from the *nirvāṇa* of Buddha according to the chronology of Ceylon, or 543 BC.[6] This date of Mahāvīra is based on three verses repeated in many commentaries and chronological works.[7] "These verses, which are quoted in a large number of commentaries and chronological works, but the origin of which is by no means clear, give the adjustment between the eras of Vira and Vikrama, and form the basis of the earlier Jaina chronology."[8] Merutuṅga's[9] *Vicāiraśreṇī* is based on them, and

1. Charpentier, op. and loc. cit. "The extent of his sphere of influence almost corresponds with that of the kingdom of Śrāvastī or Kosala, Videha, Magadha, and Aṅga — the modern Oudh, and the provinces of Tirhut and Bihar in western Bengal." — Bühler, op. cit., p. 27.
2. Jacobi, op. cit., pp. 267-68.
3. Also called Jṛbhakagrāma or Jṛmbhilā. — Stevenson (Mrs), op. cit., p. 38.
4. "Mahāvīra lived thirty years as a householder, more than twelve years in a state inferior to perfection, something less than thirty years as a *Kevalin*, forty-two years as a monk — seventy-two years on the whole." — Jacobi, op. cit., p. 269.
5. Pāpā-Pāvāpurī, about seven miles to the south-east of Bihar (town) and two miles to the north of Giriyek. According to Stevenson's *Kalpa-Sūtra*, Mahāvīra died here while he was spending the Paryuṣaṇa (Pajjuṣaṇa) at the palace of Hastipāla, king of Pāpā. There are four beautiful Jaina temples in an enclosure which marks the site of his death. Annual (*Dīpāvalī*) Dīvālī was started to commemorate Mahāvīra's death. Cf. Dey, op. cit., p. 148.
6. Cf. Jacobi, *Kalpa-Sūtra*, Int., p. 8.
7. "None of the sources in which these announcements appear is older than the twelfth century AD. The latest is found in Hemacandra, who died in the year AD 1172." — Bühler, op. cit., p. 23.
8. Bühler, *I.A.*, II., p. 363.
9. "Merutuṅga, a famous Jaina author, composed in V.S. 1361= AD 1304 his work the *Prabhandhaciṅtāmaṇi* and about two years later his *Vicāraśreṇi*. . . ." — Charpentier, *I.A.*, XLIII., p. 119.

they specify 470 years as the interval between Vikramāditya and the *nirvāṇa* of Mahāvīra.

The translation of the three verses is as follows[1] :

1. Pālaka, the Lord of Avantī, was anointed during that night in which the *arhat* and *tīrthaṅkara* Mahāvīra entered *nirvāṇa.*
2. Sixty are (the years) of King Pālaka, but one hundred and fifty-five are (the years) of the Nandas; one hundred and eight those of the Mauryas, and thirty those of Pusamitra (Puṣyamitra).
3. Sixty (years) ruled Balamitra and Bhānumitra, forty Nabhovāhana; thirteen years likewise lasted the rule of Gardabhilla, and four are the years of Śaka.[2]

Thus, according to Merutuṅga, 470 years elapsed between the *nirvāṇa* and Vikramāditya's era, which corresponds to the year 527 before the Christian era.[3] In coming to this period of 470 years according to Merutuṅga, we get 255 years as the interval between the beginning of the era of Vikrama and the reign of the Mauryas. This comes to 312 BC as the date of Candragupta's *abhiṣeka,* according to the Jaina tradition.[4] Now, subtracting 255 from 470 we get 215 years as the period between Candragupta and the *nirvāṇa*. This period of 215 years is not subscribed to by all, for Hemacandra, in his *Pariśiṣṭaparvan*, writes: "And thus 155 years after the liberation of Mahāvīra Candragupta became king."[5] Adding 155 to 312 BC we get the *nirvāṇa* of Mahāvīra in 467 BC. Merutuṅga no doubt refers to this statement of Hemacandra, but about it he says nothing more than that it is in contradiction with other works.[6]

The date of Mahāvīra as worked out by Jacobi[7] and Charpentier[8] is based on the data supplied by these two Jaina *gurus*. Both the learned scholars

---

1. "That they were not composed by Merutuṅga himself or any of his contemporaries is certain, because at that time the Jaina authors had long ago ceased to write in Prākṛt." — Charpentier, op. cit., p. 120.
2. जं रयणिं कालगओ . . . सगस्स चऊ. . . . — *Vicāraśreṇi*, p. 1. MS., B.O.R.I.L., No. 378 of 1871-1872.
3. Fifty-seven years elapsed between the commencement of the *Saṁvat* and the Christian eras.
4. "The Jaina authorities give the year of his accession as 313 (312) BC, a date at which the canon of the Jaina scriptures was fixed." — Cf. *C.H.I.*, I., p. 698.
5. एवं च श्रीमहावीर . . . चंद्रगुप्तोऽभवन्नृपः. — Jacobi, *Pariśiṣṭaparvan,* Canto VIII, v. 339.
6. तच्चिन्त्यम् यत एवं ६० वर्षाणि त्रुट्यन्ति। अन्यग्रंथैः सह विरोधः. — *Vicāraśreṇī,* op. cit., p. 1.
7. Jacobi, *Kalpa-Sūtra,* Int., pp. 6-10.
8. Charpentier, op. cit., pp. 118-23, 125-33, 167-78.

have worked out their conclusions with so much minuteness and historical accuracy that we need not repeat here the grounds put forward by them for justifying their opinions. They rightly agree in accepting the chronological fact put forward by Hemacandra, and come to the inevitable conclusion that the date of this epoch must be somewhere about 467 BC.[1]

"I have tried to show," says Charpentier, "that the chronological list on which the Jainas found this assumption of a period of 470 years between the death of Mahāvīra and the commencement of the Vikrama era is almost entirely valueless. The line of rulers composed in order to fill up the time is wholly unhistorical and can by no means be trusted. . . ."[2] Leaving aside the wholly hypothetical basis of the Jaina tradition, the other grounds put forward by the eminent scholars are the contemporary existence of both Mahāvīra and Buddha, and the more trustworthy historical facts put forward by Hemacandra.

That the two prophets were different persons, contemporaries and founders of rival communities of monks, is now an established fact. "But, if we believed the Jaina tradition to be right, when it asserts the death of Mahāvīra to have taken place 470 years before Vikrama, or 527 BC, we might doubt whether this is possible. For the death of Buddha, the date of which was first, and in my opinion rightly, fixed by General Cunningham and Professor Max Müller, occurred in 477 BC; and as all sources are unanimous in telling us that he was then 80 years old, he must have been born in 557 BC. From this it is clear that if Mahāvīra died in 527 BC, Buddha at that stage was only 30 years of age, and as he did not attain Buddhahood and gained no followers before his 36th year — i.e. about 521 BC — it is quite impossible that he should never have met Mahāvīra. Moreover, both are stated to have lived during the reign of Ajātaśatru, who became king eight years before the death

---

1. No doubt there are other scholars who hold the contrary opinion, but their discussions having been rendered obsolete by Jacobi and Charpentier we shall not dwell upon them any further. Just to mention a few amongst them: Burgess, *I.A.*, II., p. 140 ; Rice (Lewis), *I.A.*, III., p. 157 ; Thomas (Edward), *I.A.*, VIII., p. 30 ; Pathak, *I.A.*, XII., p. 21 ; Hoernle, *I.A.*, XX., p. 360 ; Guérinot, *Bibliographie Jaina*, Int., p. VII, and so on.
2. Charpentier, op. cit., p. 125. "Not only is the number of years (155) allotted in the *Gāthās* to the reign of the Nandas unduly great, but also the introduction of Pālaka, Lord of Avantī, in the chronology of the Magadha kings looks very suspicious." — Jacobi, op. cit., p. 8.

of Buddha, and reigned 32 years; this makes it even more impossible to believe in the dates mentioned above."[1]

Coming to Hemacandra's statement in his *Pariśiṣṭaparvan*, Dr Charpentier says: "We may assume with Jacobi that he (Hemacandra) took as correct the tradition of 255 years elapsing between the accession of Candragupta and the Vikrama era. This would then make the time between the death of Mahāvīra and the accession of Vikrama till 255 + 155 = 410 years, and involve the conclusion that Mahāvīra died in 467 BC, which in my opinion is the date best fitted for all circumstances connected with it, and may be deemed the right one."[2]

Over and above these there are also other considerations, which in one way or the other help us to come to this date of Mahāvīra's death. We need no more discuss them here, but just to enumerate: the traditional date of Bhadrabāhu's death and his connection with Candragupta;[3] the date of the third schism in the Jaina church and its relation with the Maurya king, Balabhadra;[4] the connection between the date put in the *Kalpa-Sūtra* of Bhadrabāhu as finally settled by Devardhigaṇin and the date of the great council held at Vallabhī in the year of Dhruvasena's succession,[5] and finally the date of Suhastin, the disciple of Sthūlabhadra and his connection with Samprati,[6] grandson and successor of Aśoka.[7]

---

1. Charpentier, op. cit., pp. 131-32. "To return to our discussions of the date of the *Nirvāṇa*, it is obvious that the year 467 BC, which we inferred from Hemacandra's record, cannot be far wrong, because it agrees so well with the adjusted date of Buddha's *Nirvāṇa*, 477 BC, a synchronism which by our previous research has been established as necessary." — Jacobi, op. cit., p. 9.
2. Charpentier, op. cit., p. 175.
3. This date of Bhadrabāhu's death is 170 A.V., which is equal to 357 BC according to the traditional date, and 297 according to the date of Jacobi and Charpentier, and considering Bhadrabāhu's connection with Candragupta the year 357 BC is to be totally excluded.
4. This schism originated in 214 A.V., and according to Merutuṅga the Maurya rule dates from 215 A.V.; and hence Hemacandra's calculations, according to which the Maurya dynasty begins 155 years after the *nirvāṇa*, seem more reasonable.
5. That date is either 980 or 993 A.V., which, taking 467 BC as the date of Mahāvīra's *nirvāṇa*, is equal to AD 526, which exactly corresponds to the year of Dhruvasena's succession to the throne of Vallabhī.
6. This date is 245 A.V. according to Merutuṅga, and this more or less agrees with the chronology of Hemacandra, according to which Candragupta began his rule in 155 A.V., because, as Aśoka died ninety-four years after Candragupta, the date of Samprati comes to 249 A.V.
7. Cf. Charpentier, op. cit., pp. 175-76 ; Jacobi, op. cit., pp. 9-10.

With such historical data before us one thing is clear, that the conclusion which we have arrived at is quite in harmony with the various facts connected with and depending upon the date under consideration. Still, however, 467 BC cannot be taken as the real year of Mahāvīra's death, though it cannot be far wrong, because there is no ground to assume that Hemacandra took as correct the tradition that two hundred and fifty-five years elapsed between the accession of Candragupta and the Vikrama era, and thereby came to the conclusion that according to the Jaina tradition Candragupta began his dynasty in 312 BC. No doubt a precise date for the accession of Candragupta seems, with our present evidence impossible;[1] but still, without dwelling further upon a matter of so much uncertainty, an earlier date seems more reasonable and more in keeping with the contemporary historical atmosphere and with certain events of Candragupta's own life. Scholars like Dr Thomas (F.W.),[2] Smith[3] and others agree in putting Candragupta's succession from 325–321 BC, or thereabout.[4] Taking this as our basis, we get *c.* 480–467 BC as the date of Mahāvīra's *nirvāṇa*, and this *fits* in with the adjusted date of Buddha's *nirvāṇa*, 477 BC, "which has been proved correct within very narrow limits."[5] This is because it is obvious that the *nirvāṇa* of both these teachers can be separated by a few years only.[6] Moreover, the acceptance of some such period for the *nirvāṇa* of Vardhamāna in no way contradicts any of the considerations that we have already put forth.

However, before we pass on to the reformed Jaina church of Mahāvīra, we shall have to say a few words on the *misunderstanding* of the revolution that had been brought about in the chronology of this period by the so-called correct evidence as put forward by Mr Jayaswal, Mr Banerji and others.[7] As we shall see in our chapter entitled "Jainism in Kaliṅga Deśa," until very recently it was believed, by these scholars, with Vincent Smith[8] and others,

1. "Our defective knowledge of the chronology is in striking contrast to the trustworthy information which we possess concerning the country and its administration." — Thomas (F.W.), *C.H.I.*, I., p. 473.
2. Ibid., pp. 471-72.
3. Smith, *Early History of India*, p. 206 (4th edn.).
4. "The date of Candragupta's accession has been fixed by Professor Kern between 321 and 322; accordingly the date of the *Nirvāṇa* is somewhere between 477 and 475 BC; and this date is probably correct within a few years, as it nearly agrees with the adjusted date of Buddha's *Nirvāṇa* in 477 BC" — Jacobi, *Pariśiṣṭaparvan*, Int., p. 6.
5. Jacobi, op. and loc. cit.
6. Cf. Dasgupta, op. cit., I., p. 173.
7. Jayaswal, *J.B.O.R.S.*, III., pp. 425-72, and IV., pp. 364 ff. ; Banerji (R.D.), *J.B.O.R.S.*, III., pp. 486 ff.
8. Smith, *J.R.A.S.*, 1918, pp. 543-47.

that the inscription of Khāravela was dated in the year 165 of the Maurya era, *Rāja-Muriya Kāle*, equivalent to 170 BC. The significance of the date of the record was emphasized by a reference in another passage to some Nandarāja having excavated a canal in Kaliṅga three hundred years earlier — that is to say, 470 BC.[1] This Nandarāja being identified with Nandivardhana, the ninth Śaiśunāga king, whose date was previously taken as about 418 BC, Smith went to the extent of revolutionizing the whole Śaiśunāga chronology, and put *c.* 554 BC for the previous 491 BC of Ajātaśatru, and *c.* 582 BC for *c.* 519 BC of Bimbisāra.[2] From this change in the chronology of the contemporary dynasty of both Buddha and Mahāvīra, and from a reference in the body of the inscription about an image of *jina* being taken away by a Nanda king, both Smith[3] and Jayaswal[4] came to the conclusion that the Khāravela record supports the old traditional dates for the death of Mahāvīra, 527 BC, and the death of Buddha, 543 BC.

As we shall see later on, all these inferences based on the Khāravela inscription are of no account considering the latest reading suggested by Mr Jayaswal. According to it there is nothing like any reference to the Maurya era; but this factor is of very little importance, because we come practically to the same date of the inscription, taking into consideration the reference made to the great Indo-Greek king, Demetrios. The most significant change that has been brought about is that the canal referred to was excavated in the year 103 of the Nanda era and not three hundred years earlier.[5] Thus the sole basis on which Mr Smith hurriedly took the step of pushing back the whole Śaiśunāga chronology by something like fifty years now falls to the ground. "I have been so impressed," said the great historian, "by the new evidence,

1. Smith, *J.R.A.S.*, 1918, p. 546.
2. "In the third edition of my *Early History of India* (1914) I placed the accession of Nandivardhana doubtfully about 418 BC. He must now go back to *c.* 470 BC, or possibly to an earlier date. That finding involves putting back Ajātaśatru or Kuṇika (No. 5 Śaiśunāga) to at least *c.* 554 BC, and his father Bimbisāra or Śreṇika (No. 4) to at least *c.* 582 BC," — Smith, op. cit., pp. 546-47. In his first edition (1904) Smith has put 401 BC for Nandivardhana, p. 33 ; see ibid., p. 41 ; ibid., p. 51 (4th edn. 1924).
3. "According to Pāli tradition Mahāvīra predeceased Buddha. But other reasons support the date 467 BC, as advocated by Charpentier, and this fits in with the traditional date of Bhadrabāhu, who was the contemporary of Candragupta Maurya. The year 527 (528-7) BC, the most commonly quoted date for the death of Mahāvīra, is merely one of several dates, but it is supported by the Khāravela inscription." — Ibid., p. 49. Cf. ibid., p. 50.
4. Jayaswal, *J.B.O.R.S.*, XIII., p. 246.
5. Ibid., p. 221 ff.

that in my forthcoming book, *The Oxford History of India*, now being printed, I have inserted earlier periods for the Śaiśunāgas and Nandas,"[1] but now the very person (Jayaswal) who was rightly relied upon to this extent by Mr Smith, and who deserves greater credit for keeping up to his conviction, has more or less completely altered his first reading of the inscription after working at it for a pretty long time.

Coming to Jayaswal, he says: "It also proves that to have Jina images about or rather before 450 BC means that the date of Mahāvīra's *nirvāṇa* must be what we get from the various Jaina chronological data read with the Purāṇic and Pāli material, which all harmonise in fixing it to be 545 BC . . ."[2] This sounds rather strange. There is no reason why this King Nanda referred to here should be identified particularly with Nandivardhana, the Śaiśunāga whose era has been identified by Jayaswal with the Nanda era referred to above on the basis of Alberuni and other historical grounds.[3]

This King Nanda, as we shall see in our next chapter, is, according to Dr Charpentier, better identified with one of the Nine Nandas, the first of whom "seems not to be very unfavourably judged by Hemacandra."[4] If this identification is accepted, the historical period of having Jaina images would be somewhere in the very beginning of the fourth century BC. Even granting that this King Nanda is to be identified with Nandivardhana, whose date, according to Jayaswal, comes to about 457 BC, there is no historical fallacy committed or any Jaina tradition disregarded if we say that there must have been Jaina images about or rather before 450 BC. There is no reason why, just because of this, the *nirvāṇa* of Mahāvīra cannot be somewhere about 467 BC, and should go so far back as 545 BC, because, according to so many traditions, whether right or wrong, image-worship is no new development in the Jaina church.[5]

But the fixing of 545 BC as the date of Mahāvīra's *nirvāṇa* is nothing else but disregarding some of the real historical facts and coincidences of the

1. Smith, *J.R.A.S.*, 1918, p. 547.
2. Jayaswal, op. cit., p. 246. This date of Jayaswal is based also on the chronological facts that he has worked out after consulting the Pāli, Purāṇic and Burmese traditions. Cf. *J.B.O.R.S.*, I., p. 114.
3. Jayaswal, *J.B.O.R.S.*, XIII., pp. 240-41.
4. Charpentier, op. cit., pp. 171-72.
5. तए णं सा दोवई रायवरकन्ना . . . जेणेव जिणघरे . . . जिणपडिमाणं . . . पणामं करेइ . . . *Jñātā, sūt.* 119, p. 210.

Jaina annals. It is true no doubt that this period of Indian history is chequered with numerous traditions, Jaina, Buddhist or Hindu, and sometimes because of some or the other interest or object in view they are so arranged by later writers that it has become an impossible task to find out the real truth behind the whole show. Now, according to the Jaina tradition, the whole interval between Ajātaśatru and Candragupta has been filled up by Udāyin and the Nine Nandas,[1] while writers like Merutuṅga tell us that the Nanda rule lasted for one hundred and fifty-five years. On the other hand Hemacandra has allotted only ninety-five years for the Nandas, by which he rightly means the Nine Nandas. However, the chronological period of 480–467 BC that we have put down for Mahāvīra's *nirvāṇa* is — as is often inevitable in our efforts to reconstruct the mosaic of ancient Indian history from the few pieces which have as yet been found — an attempt to do little more than define the limits of possible hypothesis in this instance. For greater certainty we must be content to wait until the progress of archaeological research has furnished us with more adequate materials.

III

Coming to the reformed Jaina church of Mahavira or Jainism as such we find that it is not possible to talk at length about that either. All that can be done within a limited scope like this is to mark its salient features and its beliefs about the ordinary problems, inquiries and difficulties of a man's spiritual life. Reflection is the moving spirit of philosophy. Early philosophical reflection engages itself with searching for the origin of the world, and it attempts to formulate the law of causation. In this respect Jainism is atheistic, if by atheism we understand the belief that there is no eternal supreme God, Creator and Lord of all things. "The atheism of the Jainas means denial of a divine creative spirit."[2] The Jainas flatly deny such a supreme God, but they believe in the eternity of existence, universality of life, immutability of the law of *karma*, and supreme intelligence as the means to self-liberation.

1. Cf. Rapson, *C.H.I.*, I., p. 313.
2. Hopkins, op. cit., pp. 285-86. "Their only real gods are their chiefs or teachers, whose idols are worshipped in the temples." — Ibid.

To the Jainas there is no need to assume any first cause of the universe.[1] They deny the existence of an intelligent first cause[2] and repudiate the theory of the creation of the world out of nothing or out of a series of accidents. To the Jaina thinker the systematic working of the law of nature cannot be a product of luck or accident. He cannot conceive how a non-creative God suddenly becomes creative. "If God created the universe," asks Ācārya Jinasena, "where was he before creating? If he was not in space, where did he localize the universe? How could a formless or immaterial substance like God create the world of matter? If the material is to be taken as existing, why not take the world itself as unbegun? If the creator was uncreated, why not suppose the world to be itself self-existing?" Then he continues: "Is God self-sufficient? If he is, he need not have created the world. If he is not, like an ordinary potter, he would be incapable of the task, since, by hypothesis, only a perfect being could produce it. If God created the world as a mere play of his will, it would be making God childish. If God is benevolent and if he has created the world out of his grace, he would not have brought into existence misery as well as felicity."[3]

If it is argued that everything that exists must have a maker, then that maker himself would stand in need of another maker, and we would be landed in a cycle, the way from which to escape is to assume the reality of a self-subsisting maker who is the author of everything else. Here again is raised the problem that if it is possible for one being to be self-subsistent and eternal, is it not possible for more things and beings to be uncreated and substantive? Then the Jaina mind puts forth the hypothesis of a number of substances, and the world is explained on the theory of the necessity of all substances to manifest themselves. "The whole universe of being, of mental and material factors has existed from all eternity, undergoing an infinite number of revolutions produced by the powers of nature without the

---

1. कर्तास्ति कश्चिद् जगतः स चैकः
स सर्वगः स स्ववशः स नित्यः।
इमाः कुहेवाकविडम्बनाः स्यु-
स्तेषां न येषामनुशासकस्त्वम् ॥६ ॥
Hemacandra, *Syādvādamañjarī* (ed. Motilal Ladhaji), v. 6, p. 24 ; see ibid., p. 14 ff.
2. Radhakrishnan, op. cit., I., p. 289. Cf. also Vijayadharmasūri, *Bhandarkar Commemorative Volume*, pp. 150-51.
3. Latthe, *Introduction to Jainism*, pp. 85-87 ; Jinasena, *Ādi Purāṇa*, chap. III. Cf. Bhandarkar, *Report on Sanskrit MSS, 1883-1884*, p. 118.

intervention of any external deity. The diversities of the world are traced to the five co-operating conditions of time (*kāla*), nature (*svabhāva*), necessity (*niyati*), activity (*karma*), and desire to be and act (*udyama*)."[1]

With all this such a belief on the part of the Jainas did not make them materialistic in the sense of one of the inchoate philosophical systems called "materialism," or in the sense of Cārvāka, whose motto was to make merry while life lasted, since he thought that the body turned to ashes turns not to life again. In his manual on Jainism Mr Warren has nicely put the difference between the Jaina and these philosophical systems of thought. "An alternative to the doctrine of a kind of almighty creator governing the universe," says the learned scholar, "is the theory of soulless materialist atheism which affirms that life and consciousness are the outcome of the massing and activity of material atoms, to be dissipated at death; but for those who find neither of these theories satisfactory there is the theory roughly outlined in this book, a theory which neither denies the existence of the soul nor starts with the presumption of a creator, but makes each individual the master of his own destiny, holds out immortality for every living being, and insists upon the very highest rectitude of life, up to final perfection, as a necessary means to permanent happiness now and hereafter."[2]

Here arises the question, if there is no such being distinct from the world called God, what are the characteristics of the authority which is implicitly believed by the Jainas? Unless the characteristics are known it may come to believing the words of an arbitrary and tyrannical law-giver. Furthermore, however the authority may be true, teaching presupposes true knowledge. Going to the very root of religion we find that the definition of religion as the relation between man and superhuman powers in which he believes is by no means philosophical, nor does it in any sense apply to Jainism. On the other hand it leaves unanswered the question of the essence of religion. "Man's desire for an explanation of the existence of misery, for its relief to extinction, and for a consequent increase of happiness, is the ground of religion."[3] The powers mentioned above are designedly not described as supersensual as visible deities would thus be excluded, and moreover, they are superhuman,

---

1. Radhakrishnan, op. cit., p. 330.
2. Warren, *Jainism*, p. 2. "Man! Thou art thine own friend ; why wishest thou for a friend beyond thyself?" — Jacobi, S.B.E., XXII., p. 33.
3. Warren, op. cit., p. 1.

never in reality but in the estimation of the worshippers.[1] Nevertheless this is a weakness which is more or less universal, and hence, naturally, the Jainas are not expected to be free from it. Leaving this aside, we have already seen that Jainism is, as it were, a pure and perfect light thrown over the world by one who has subdued all his senses and passions, and who has thereby become free from all *karmas*.[2]

The *śāstras* that form the fundamental basis of Jainism are based on the teaching of such spiritual leaders as Pārśva and Mahāvīra, who once lived on earth in flesh and blood. Their teaching was first imparted to *gaṇadharas*,[3] who were the chief disciples of *jina*, the omnipotent seer of the universal and infinite light, while they in their turn handed it over to a line of *gurus* who come down to our own days.[4] Thus it is with these *jinas* that lies the source of all that we are going to say about Jainism in the following pages.

The sources for this are no doubt of a comparatively later date, and it is not difficult to distinguish between what was original and what was transformed. For, as Charpentier has rightly observed, "the inflexible conservatism of the small Jaina community in holding fast to its original insitutions and doctrine" has been its strongest safeguard;[5] and it is this conservatism that, in spite of periods of severe afflictions, has enabled the Jainas to preserve their canons to a large extent untainted. There are indications in bas-reliefs of the first and the second century AD of their authenticity, going back to a much earlier period, and its oldest elements "may very well go back to the time of the first disciple of Mahāvīra, or at any rate to the council of Pāṭalīputra, which was held, according to tradition,

---

1. Cf. Tiele, op. cit., p. 2.
2. जिनेन्द्रो . . . रागद्वेषविवर्जितः . . . कृत्स्नकर्मक्षयं कृत्वा संप्राप्तः परमं पदम् . . . — Haribhadra, *Ṣaḍdarśana Samuccaya*, vv. 45, 46. "It is the opinion of Jainism that only that knowledge is true which is purged of the infatuating elements of anger, hatred, or other passions ; that only he who is all-knowing is able to map out the path of rectitude which shall lead to final beatitude in life everlasting ; and that omniscience is impossible in any in whom the infatuating elements are found to exist." — Warren, op. cit., p. 3.
3. Beginning from Indrabhūti and ending with Prabhava, Mahāvīra had altogether eleven *gaṇadharas*.
4. प्रक्रान्तशास्त्रस्य वीरजिनवरेन्द्रापेक्षयाऽर्थतः आत्मागमत्वं तच्छिष्यं तु पञ्चमगणधरं सुधर्मं . . . तच्छिष्यं च जंबू . . . परम्परागमतां प्रतिपिपादयिषुः सूत्रकारः . . . आह . . . — *Jñātā, Ṭīkā*, p. 1.
5. Charpentier, *C.H.I.*, I., p. 169.

under the Maurya king, Candragupta, at the end of the fourth century BC."[1] The transformations happened principally in matters of detail, and the unconscious modifications which all religions and institutions tend to undergo in matters of practice rather than in the principles underlying them.

Coming again to the definition of religion we find that the chief functions of religion are the work of relieving misery, explaining its existence, and of increasing the real happiness of life. We shall now briefly see what has been the working of the Jaina thought and how far it has succeeded in considering these difficulties and requirements of man's spiritual life. According to Jainism, then, everything that there is, was, or ever will be, has been classified as either animate (*jīva*) or inanimate (*ajīva*); and has been defined as that in which there is Origination, Destruction and Permanence. It is with this *tripadī* that Mahāvīra welcomes his great converts from the brāhmaṇa fold and his *gaṇadhara*s when they joined the Jaina church, and, having received which, they composed the twelve *aṇga*s.[2]

This division of the universe, according to the Jaina metaphysics, into two everlasting, uncreated, coexisting but independent categories — the living (*jīva*) — also used to connote life, vitality, soul or *consciousness*[3] — and the non-living (*ajīva*) — is, according to the Jainas, a perfect division and as such unassailable. The *ajīva* is further divided into *dharma, adharma, ākāśa, pudgala,*[4] and to these some also add *kāla*.[5] The *jīva*, or the soul, except in its final stage of liberation (*nirvāṇa*), is always in combination with *ajīva*, and thereby brings into existence a kind of energy which is known as *karma*, and which cannot conduce to freedom, perfection or peace. These *karma*s, or deeds of the soul,

---

1. Macdonell, *India's Past*, p. 71 ; Jacobi, op. cit., Int., pp. xl-xlii ; Ghosal, *Dravya-saṁgraha*, S.B.J., I., pp. 3-4.
2. एकादशानां त्रिपदीग्रहणपूर्वकं एकादशाङ्ग . . . etc. — *Kalpa-Sūtra, Subodhikā-Ṭīkā*, pp. 112-18. इन्द्र-भूतिः . . . त्रिपदीं प्राप्य द्वादशांगों रचितवान् . . . etc. — Ibid., p. 115. जाते संघे चतुर्धैवं . . . इन्द्रभूतिप्रभृतीनां त्रिपदीं व्याहरत् प्रभुः — Hemacandra, *Triṣaṣṭi-Śalākā, Parva* X, v. 165, p. 70.
3. Stevenson (Mrs), op. cit., p. 94.
4. Things enjoyable by the senses, the five senses themselves, the mind, the *karma*s, and all other material objects are called *pudgala*s, or matters. All material things are ultimately produced by the combination of atoms. The smallest individual particle of matter is called an atom (*aṇu*). In their atomic theory "we place the Jainas first, because they seem to have worked out their system from the most primitive notions about matter." — Jacobi, *E.R.E.*, II., p. 199.
5. भेदाश्च धर्माधर्माकाशपुद्गलाः . . . — Haribhadra, op. cit., p. 50. Yogendrācārya in his *Paramātma Prakāśa* includes *Kāla*, v. 142.

VI : The eleven Gaṇadharas of Lord Mahāvīra.
From a Palm-leaf manuscript of the *Kalpa-Sūtra* of the thirteenth century.

in conjunction with matter (*pudgala*) are either good or bad, and it is on account of them that the soul has to suffer all the experiences of this world process, including births and rebirths.[1] So here lies the source of all our miseries, and hence to explain these two forms — *jīva* and *ajīva* — and their mutual connections on a broad basis, Jaina *śāstrakāra*s have put forward nine categories (*nava tattva*s), which are as follows :

Jīva, ajīva, puṇya, pāpa, āśrava, saṁvara, bandha, nirjarā and *mokṣa*.[2] All these substances have been very minutely worked out by Jaina metaphysics, but we need not go into all these details.[3]

Those forms that have consciousness belong to the first category — viz. *jīva* — and those that have not this quality are *ajīva*s.[4] As just remarked, in our worldly existence both *jīva*, or the soul, and *ajīva*, or the non-soul, go together, and thus the soul in combination with our body becomes the doer of all actions whether good or bad. The soul in its pure state is possessed of Infinite Perception or Faith (*ananta-darśana*), Infinite Knowledge (*ananta-jñāna*), Infinite Bliss (*ananta-sukha*), and Infinite Power (*ananta-vīrya*).[5] It is all-perfect, enjoying as it does these four infinities, which the soul has a right to enjoy when it is in its true eternal character.[6]

Ordinarily however, with the exception of a few released souls (*mukta-jīva*s), all the other *jīva*s (*saṁsārin*s) have their purity and power covered with a thin veil of *karma* matter which has been accumulating in them from

---

1. "Matter is without consciousness; soul is conscious. Matter has no choice but to be moulded by the soul. The connection of soul and matter is material, and it is affected by the soul's activity. The bondage is called Karma, since it is the Karma or deed of the soul. It is material, forming a subtle bond of extremely refined Kārmic matter which keeps the soul from flying up to its natural abode of full knowledge and everlasting peace." — Jaini, op. cit., p. 26 कर्त्ता शुभाशुभं कर्म भोक्ता कर्मफलस्य च . . . — Haribhadra, op. cit., v. 48.
2. जीवाजीवौ तथा पुण्यं पापमाश्रवसंवरौ।
बन्धश्च निर्जरामोक्षौ नव तत्त्वानि तन्मते॥
— Haribhadra, op. cit., v. 47. Cf. also Kundakundācārya, *Pañcāstikāyasāra*, v. 108.
3. Cf. Stevenson (Mrs), op. cit., pp. 299-311.
4. चैतन्यलक्षणो जीवो, यश्चैतद्वैपरीत्यवान्। अजीवः स . . . — Haribhadra, op. cit., v. 49.
5. "The Jainas distinguish between *Darśana* and *Jñāna*. *Darśana* is the knowledge of things without their details — e.g. I see a cloth. *Jñāna* means the knowledge of details — e.g. I not only see the cloth but know to whom it belongs, of what quality it is, where it was prepared, etc. In all cognition we have first *Darśana* and then *Jñāna*. The pure souls possess infinite general perception of all things as well as infinite knowledge of all things in all their details." — Dasgupta, op. cit., I., p. 129.
6. Jaini, op. cit., p. 1.

beginningless time. The natural qualities of the soul are thus more or less obscured, and consequently various conditions of weal (*puṇya*) and woe (*pāpa*) are experienced. This is how we get the next two categories — viz. *puṇya* and *pāpa*.

In *puṇya* we include those matters that are connected with the soul and are the result of good and virtuous actions. Those that are contradictory to these are called *pāpas*.[1] *Puṇya* is the meritorious kind of *karma*, while *pāpa* is the sinful kind of it. When the soul is thus striving under such auspicious (*śubha*) and inauspicious (*aśubha*) *karmas* it is helped by the activity of the mind, speech and body, which fact either helps the inflow of such kārmic matter and thereby the soul gets bound to them, or acts as a bar to it. It is here that we get *āśrava*, *saṁvara* and *bandha*.

The activity of the mind, speech and body which makes the inflow of kārmic matter into the soul possible is technically called *āśrava*, while the same sort of activity which acts as a bar to such an inflow is called *saṁvara*. The actual investing of the soul by this matter is called *bandha*.[2] Thus according to the Jaina *mata* it is we who are responsible for our own condition. "In whatever degree we are ignorant, in pain, unhappy, unkind, cruel or weak, it is because, since birth and even previously in the infinite past, we are and have been acquiring and incorporating into ourselves (*āśrava*, *bandha*) — by the attraction and assimilation of subtle, unseen, though real physical matter (*pudgala*) — energies (*karma*) which clog the natural wisdom, knowledge, blissfulness, love, compassion and strength of the soul, and which excite us to unnatural action."[3]

---

1. पुण्यं सत्कर्मपुद्गलाः। — Haribhadra, op. cit., v. 49. पापं तद्विपरीतं तु . . . — Ibid., V. 50.
2. . . . मिथ्यात्वाद्यास्तु हेतवः।
   यस्तैर्बन्धः स विज्ञेय आश्रवो जिनशासने॥
   संवरस्तन्निरोधस्तु बन्धो जीवस्य कर्मणः।
   अन्योन्यानुगमात्कर्मसम्बन्धो यो द्वयोरपि॥ — Ibid., vv. 50-51.
3. Warren, op. cit., p. 5. "The natural perfections of the pure soul are sullied by the different kinds of Karma matter. Those who obscure right knowledge of details (*Jñāna*) are called *Jñānāvaraṇīya* ; those which obscure right perception (*Darśana*), as in sleep, are called *Darśanāvaraṇīya* ; those which obscure the bliss-nature of the soul and thus produce pleasure and pain are *Vedanīya*, and those which obscure the right attitude of the soul towards faith and right conduct, *Mohanīya*." — Dasgupta, op. cit., I., pp. 190-91. In addition to these four kinds of *Karma* there are other four kinds of *Karma*, which are called *āyuṣ-karma*, *nāma-karma*, *gotra-karma* and *antarāya-karma*. They determine respectively the duration of life, the character of our individuality, the family or the nationality, and the inborn energy which hinders or obstructs the progress or success of the soul.

With all these handicaps in the form of *karmas* none need be disappointed about his own spiritual growth. Though the *karmas* of man are determining him in various ways, yet there is in him infinite capacity or power for right action (*ananta-vīrya*), so that *karma* can never subdue this freedom and capacity though this may be suppressed from time to time by the influence of *karma*. The Jaina *śāstras* say that by means of a strict religious life and austerities all these *karmas* can be destroyed, and the soul can ultimately achieve its natural state in *mokṣa*. That is why Dr Bühler says: "The accusation that *Nātaputta* embraced fatalism must therefore be regarded as an invention and an outcome of sect hatred, as well as of the wish to throw discredit on their opponents."[1]

Thus the purging of the *karmas*, or rather their destruction, is called *nirjarā*, and the utter annihilation of all *karmas* or the complete freedom of the soul from kārmic matter is called *mokṣa*.[2] Thus *nirjarā* is possible by a change in the soul, or by reaping the effects of *karmas*, or by penances before their time of fruition. When all the *karmas* are destroyed *mokṣa*, or liberation, is effected.[3]

From the above characteristics of these different categories one thing is clear — that they are in one way or the other connected with the soul until it obtains the final release from corporeal sufferance by deification through a perfect disengagement from both good and evil. It is due to this that *jīva*, deluded by the kārmic forces, experiences ignorance, misery and wretchedness in this world. Such a revolving of *jīva* in this phenomenal world is called *saṁsāra*, and to get free from this *saṁsāra*, which is the result of the delusion of the soul, is to achieve *mokṣa*, or final emancipation. It is nothing extraneous to be obtained by *jīva*, but it is merely its getting off from the clutches of kārmic fetters and achieving its own natural state.[4]

---

1. Bühler, op. cit., p. 32. Cf. Jacobi, *I.A.*, IX., pp. 159-60.
2. बद्धस्य कर्मणः शाटो यस्तु सा निर्जरा मता। आत्यन्तिको वियोगस्तु देहादेर्मोक्ष उच्यते॥ — Haribhadra, op. cit., v. 52.
3. विपाकात्तपसा वा कर्मपरिशाटो कर्मात्मसंयोगध्वंसः निर्जरा ; कृत्स्नकर्मक्षयलक्षणः मोक्षः . . . — Umāsvātivācaka, *Tattvārthādhigama-Sūtra* (ed. Motilal Ladhaji), p. 7, n.
4. आत्मनः स्वभावसमवस्थानम् . — Ibid. . . . स्वभावजं सौख्यम् . — Hemacandra, *Yoga-śāstra, Prakāśa* or chap. XI., v. 61, p. 1, MS., *B.O.R.I.L.*, No. 1315, of 1886-1892.

In short, *mokṣa* is a state in which the soul is quite free from all kārmic forces. *Karmas* are like clouds to it, and when it gets absolved from them the perfectly pure spirit shines with all its lustre, like the open sun, and this is its *mokṣa*. In this process there is nothing like any one thing taking the place of the other, but merely the obstructive agent is done away with. So when a bird gets free from its cage, what is meant is not putting anything else in its place in the cage, but only removing the cage, which acted as an obstruction to the freedom of the bird. Similarly when the soul achieves *mokṣa* it merely experiences what potentially is its own craving and nothing new, by the utter destruction of all forces — all *puṇya* and *pāpa karmas*. Thus when *mokṣa* is achieved the pure and free *ātmā* gets to its own natural state, liberated from the material body and its veils — that is to say, the absolved soul shines with all its refulgence, bliss, knowledge and power.

Having thus understood the source of all conditions of weal and woe the question that arises now is how to attain *mokṣa*. Jainism seems to show a way out of the misery of life by proposing austerity, inward and outward, as the means. The way to *nirvāṇa* is naturally revealed by *jina*. It lies through the *ratnatraya*, or "the Three Jewels" of *samyag-darsana* (right belief), *samyag- jñāna* (right knowledge) and *samyak-cāritra* (right conduct).[1] Under a form at first sight perceptibly different we at once recognize here the *tri-ratna* of the Buddhists — viz. Buddha, the Law and the *saṁgha*.[2]

The "Three Gems," which according to the Jainas result in the spirit's attainment of deliverance, form the fundamental basis of Jaina *yoga*, which, says Hemacandra, is the cause of *mokṣa* (salvation).[3] The first of these tells us that faith in *jina* or in the *tattvas* propounded by him is right belief.[4] Its negative aspect is again scepticism of a kind which hampers all serious thought.

---

1. सम्यग् दर्शनज्ञानचारित्राणि मोक्षमार्गः — Umāsvātivācaka, op. cit., chap. I., *sūt*. 1. Cf. Haribhadra, op. cit., v. 53.
2. Barth, op. cit., p. 147. "It is interesting to compare these Three Jewels with the Buddhist *Tri-Ratna* : Buddha, the Law and the Order ; and with the Mohammedan Triad : Happiness (*Khera*), Mercy (*Mera*), Prayer (*Bandagī*) ; and again with the Pārsi Trio : Holy Mind, Holy Speech and Holy Deeds." — Stevenson (Mrs), op. cit., p. 247.
3. चतुर्वर्गे अग्रणीर्मोक्षो योगस्तस्य च कारणम्॥ ज्ञानश्रद्धानचारित्ररूपं रत्नत्रयं च सः — Hemacandra, op. cit., chap. I., v. 15, p. 1.
4. तत्त्वार्थश्रद्धानं सम्यग्दर्शनम् . — Umāsvātivācaka, op. cit., chap. I., *sūt*. 2. The *tattvas* referred to here are the *nava-tattvas* mentioned above. Haribhadra, op. cit., p. 53.

All that *samyag-darśana* wants to achieve is that "instead of being blighted by cold logic and cunning sophistry, or eaten away by the corrosion of scepticism, it may grow into the tree of knowledge and fructify into the world-blessing fruit of righteous conduct."[1] Thus the most important of the Three Jewels is *samyag-darśana,* because it saves us from the soul-emptying, puzzling void of scepticism. On the other hand, right knowledge enables us to examine in detail all that the mind has inculcated through convictions. In short it gives a right and clear insight into the same *tattva*s. Right know-ledge is in fact knowledge of the Jaina creed or of the doctrines as laid down by *jina.*[2] Briefly, the intellect helped by faith finally helps to lead to right conduct, which is the goal.

There may be right *jñāna* and *darśana,* but if they are not accompanied by *cāritra* all is useless. Right conduct consists in the strict observance of all the precepts laid down by *jina,* through which *nirvāṇa* is attained. The goal being *mokṣa,* naturally right conduct must be such as to keep the body down and lift the soul. Succinctly, it means giving up all sinful activities of the mind, speech and body.[3]

In practical life this practice of right conduct is divided into two broad divisions: *sādhu-cāritra,* or the conduct of a *sādhu,* and *gṛhastha-cāritra,* or the conduct of a layman; but we shall not enter into all these details here. For our purpose, suffice it to say that naturally the rules for ascetics are stricter than those for laymen, and provide, as it were, a shorter, though harder, route to *nirvāṇa,* which is the goal of the layman as well, but one which he reaches by a longer and slower process.

On the whole the rigour of Jaina discipline anticipates a great amount of strength of will and character before it can be easily taken up by anybody. Beginning with the five great vows of non-killing (*ahiṁsā*), truth (*satya*),

---

1. Jaini, op. cit., p. 54.
2. . . . तत्त्वानां . . . ।
   . . . अवबोधस्तमत्राहुः सम्यग्ज्ञानं . . . ॥
   — Hemacandra, op. cit., chap. I., v. 16, p. 1. The Jainas acknowledge five kinds of *jñāna,* and mark with great precision the five degrees of knowledge that lead to Omniscience : (1) *mati-jñāna* (sense-knowledge), (2) *śruta-jñāna* (testimony), (3) *avadhi-jñāna* (knowledge of the remote), (4) *mana-paryāya-jñāna* (thought-reading), (5) *kevala-jñāna* (Omniscience).
3. सर्वसावद्ययोगानां त्यागश्चारित्रमुच्यते. — Ibid., chap. I., v. 18, p. 2.

non-stealing (*asteya*), chastity (*brahmacarya*) and non-attachment (*aparigraha*),[1] and the three-fold restraint of the mind, speech and body Jaina discipline goes to the final stage of a man's spiritual career when he desires neither life nor death and when he may take up the vow of *anaśana*, which in a stricter sense means "fasting which precedes and ends with death."[2]

The whole Jaina discipline has been so minutely and exhaustively worked out that it would make a study by itself.[3] We shall merely state here in brief all that we have already said about the Jaina view of life and salvation and then pass on to some other salient features of Jainism. To sum up in the words of Kundakundācārya:

"The soul which is the agent of its own karma, and the enjoyer of the fruits thereof, as conditioned by its own karma, gets blinded by the veil of ignorance and roams about in the world of *saṁsāra*, which is limited for the faithful and unlimited for the unfaithful.

Suppressing or annihilating the veil of ignorance which clouds the faculty of perception and will, well equipped with the Three Jewels, the undaunted pilgrim that has conquered the suffering and pain due to environment, beckoned by the ideal of self-knowledge wades through the paths and reaches the Divine city of Perfection."[4]

Thus when once the soul, overpowered with the four *kaṣāyas* (passions) — anger, vanity, intrigue and greed — and the senses, and perforce kept away from its natural state by good and bad energies called *karmas*, gets free from all such obstructive and foreign forces, it is said to enjoy all the attributes of God.[5] "By the absence of karma, omniscient and embracing the whole world in its view, it attains undisturbable, supersensual and infinite bliss."[6]

---

1. अहिंसा सत्यमस्तेयब्रह्मचर्यापरिग्रहाः । . . . विमुक्तये ॥. — Hemacandra, op. cit., chap. I., v. 19, p. 2.
2. . . . मरणकाला य अणसणा. — *Uttarādhyayana-Sūtra,* chap. XXX., v. 9.
3. "The value of Jaina philosophy lies not only in the fact that it, unlike Hinduism, has co-related ethical teaching with its metaphysical system but also in the amazing knowledge of human nature which its ethics display." — Stevenson (Mrs), op. cit., p. 123.
4. Kundakundācārya, *Pañcāstikāyasāra,* S.B.J., III., 75-76.
5. "In a word, believers in the creation theory make God a man, bring him down to the level of need and imperfection; whereas Jainism raises man to Godhood and inspires him to reach as near Godhood as possible by steady faith, right perfection, right knowledge, and above all, a spotless life." — Jaini, op. cit., p. 5.
6. Kundakundācārya, op. cit., v. 151 (trans. Jaini, op. cit., p. 77).

Really speaking such a soul puts forward the ideal of God in the Jaina church,[1] and once it has reached these heights it has never to fall. Says Umāsvāti:

दग्धे बीजे यथाऽत्यन्तं प्रादुर्भवति नाङ्कुरः।
कर्मबीजे तथा दग्धे न रोहति भवाङ्कुरः॥

"Just as when a seed is totally burnt, no sprout comes forth, so also when the seed in the form of karma is burnt, there is no more worldly existence."[2]

Thus, "though there is no such being distinct from the world called God, yet certain of the elements of the world when properly developed obtain deification. God is only the highest, noblest and fullest manifestation of the powers which lie latent in the soul of man."[3]

It may not be out of place to remark that among such omniscient souls some are called *tīrthaṅkara*s because of the presence of the *karma* called *nāma-karma*,[4] and whose one distinctive mark is their own natural awakening without anybody preaching to them, and who in their embodied condition preached and propounded the truth. The others are mere *kevalins*, or *sāmānya-siddha*s, who are disembodied, steady and bliss-unending.[5] The *tīrthaṅkara*s with their unique godliness propound divinity and with their extraordinary supernatural beauty, power, glory and lustre leave an everlasting impression over the world.

Really speaking, *tīrthaṅkara* is a peculiar term of Jainism. It is very often used to denote one who forms the *caturvidhasaṁgha* (the fourfold order) of monks, nuns and male and female lay-followers, but, rightly speaking, a *tīrthaṅkara* is he who sheds spiritual rays which bathe the ocean of this phenomenal world in a pure light, and it is through this that one is enabled to reach the heights of spiritual well-being. These *tīrthaṅkara*s, by endowing fresh vigour, and giving new light and revival to *dharma*, bless the world and leave it ahead of all previous ages.[6] It is natural that none else than the one

---

1. कर्मक्षयस्य करणेन भवतीश्वरो न पुनर्नित्यमुक्तः कश्चिदेकः सनातन ईश्वरः।. — Vijayadharmasūri, op. cit., p. 150.
2. Umāsvātivācaka, op. cit., chap. X., *sūt.* 8, p. 201. अकर्मकीभूतः परमात्मा न पुनः कर्मवानर्हति भवितुम् मुक्तिं प्राप्य न पुनरधोऽवतारः . . . — Vijayadharmasūri, op. and loc cit.
3. Radhakrishnan, op. cit., I., p. 331.
4. Just as the *karma* called *gotra-karma* came in the way of Mahāvīra's being born to a kṣatriyāṇī so we get here *Nāma-Karma.* तीर्थंकरनामसंज्ञं न यस्य कर्मास्ति . . . — Hemacandra, op. cit., chap. XI., v. 48, p. 30.
5. Cf: Jaini, op. cit., p. 2.
6. "When a new Tīrthaṅkara rises, the followers of the preceding ones follow him, as the followers of Pārśva followed Mahāvīra." — Stevenson (Mrs), op. cit., p. 241.

who has rightly subdued all the good or bad forces that surround the soul can attain heights, and as a mark of their great victory all *tīrthaṅkaras* are called *jinas*, or victors. "The soul which has perfect perception, perfect knowledge, infinite bliss and infinite power,"says Yogendrācārya, "is a perfect saint, and being self-manifested, is known as *Jina-Deva* (or the divine conqueror)."[1] All these omniscient souls, after their span of life on this earth is over, reach final emancipation or *mokṣa*.[2] Thus *nirvāṇa* or the final liberation of the Jainas is a state of being, without qualities and relation, and remote from all chances of rebirth. Like the Buddhists, it is not an escape into *nirvāṇa* or nothingness.[3] It is an escape from the body though not from existence. "It is not the fact of existence which is the evil in the eyes of the Jainas; it is life which is bad."[4] The body being separated from the soul, the animate being gains freedom from the trammels of the successive series of existences, and thus *nirvāṇa* is not the annihilation of the soul but its entry into a state of blessedness which has no end. "(The liberated) is not long or small . . . ; not black nor blue . . . ; not bitter nor pungent . . . ; is without body, without resurrection, without contact (of matter), is not feminine nor masculine nor neuter; he perceives, he knows, but there is no analogy (whereby to know the nature of the liberated soul); its essence is without form; there is no condition of the unconditioned."[5]

Coming to some of the prominent features of Jainism, the first thing that would strike us most is the ideal of *ahiṁsā* as propounded by it. Kundakundācārya states that "*Jīva* is conscious, formless, characterised by *upayoga*, attached to karma, the lord, the agent, the enjoyer (of the fruits of karma), the pervader of bodies (large or small); that which goes upward to

1. Cf. Jaini, op. cit., p. 78.
2. As a matter of detail we may observe that the Digambara sect of the Jainas agrees with the Buddhists in maintaining that no woman has the capacity of attaining *nirvāṇa.* To the Digambaras, before she can ever reach *mokṣa* she has to undergo rebirth as a man, while to the Śvetāmbaras the path of *mokṣa* is open to all, whether man or woman. अस्ति स्त्रीनिर्वाणं पुंवत् (Like man there is *Nirvāṇa* for woman), says Śākaṭāyanācārya in his "स्त्रीमुक्ति-केवलिभुक्तिप्रकरणयुग्मम्." — Cf. *J.S.S.*, II., Nos. 3-4, Appendix 2, v. 2.
3. "Buddhists . . . seem . . . to use their common word *Nirvāṇa* as connoting extinction not only of desire, with which the Jainas would agree, but also of the soul itself, which they would indignantly deny." — Stevenson (Mrs), op. cit., p. 172.
4. Barth, op. cit., p. 147.
5. Jacobi, S.B.E., XXII., p. 52.

the end of *loka*, being free from the *impurity* of karma."[1] Life to the Jainas is universally the same, and it is governed by the same immutable law of cause and effect. Not only is man endowed with *jīva*, but also all creatures, including plants, animals, birds, insects; and even atomic and invisible beings, like the smallest particles of the elements of the earth, the fire, the water and the wind are endowed with the soul (*jīva*). This hylozoistic theory, as Jacobi calls it, is an important characteristic of the Jainas, and "pervades their whole philosophic system and code of morals."[2] It is quite different from the animistic belief in the existence of spirits in stones, trees and running brooks.[3] The latter had to be propitiated with bloody sacrifices, destroying other forms of precious life, but according to the Jainas life in all its forms is sacred, and as it moves towards the same goal it is not to be disturbed or disintegrated by any kind of violence. This is the rationale or psychology underlying perhaps by far the most dominating characteristic of Jainism — viz. the principle of *ahiṁsā*.[4]

Ahiṁsā, as defined by Hemacandra, is as follows :

न यत्प्रमादयोगेन जीवितव्यपरोपणम्।
त्रसानां स्थावराणां च तदहिंसाव्रतं मतम्॥

"Not to destroy life, either five-, four-, three-, or two-sensed or immovable (*i.e.* one-sensed), even though carelessness is considered as keeping the vow of non-killing."[5]

The implications of this doctrine are perhaps nowhere better illustrated than in a story contained in Hemacandra's *Yogaśāstra*. It is related therein that in the days of King Śreṇika there was a butcher named Kālasaukarika who was known for his cruelty. He had a son named Sulasa, who was a great devotee of Lord Mahāvīra, and hence on grounds of religion he was on good terms with Abhayakumāra, the son of the King Śreṇika, This butcher's mentality was so wild and fierce that it had become more or less impossible to win him over to the *ahiṁsā* of the Jainas. Śreṇika being a staunch

1. Kundakundācārya, S.B.J., III., 27 ; Cf. *Dravyasaṁgraha*, S.B.J., I., pp. 6-7.
2. Jacobi, op. cit., Int., p. xxxiii.
3. The animistic belief that nearly everything is possessed of a soul proves that Jainism is older than Mahāvīra and Buddha. This must have appeared at a very early time, when higher forms of religious beliefs and cults had not yet, more generally, taken hold of the Indian mind. Cf. Jacobi, op. cit., XLV., Int., p. xxxiii.
4. Cf. Smith, *Oxford History of India*, p. 53.
5. Hemacandra, op. cit., chap. I., v. 20, p. 2. (For trans, see Stevenson (Mrs), op. cit., p. 234.)

follower of Mahāvīra was very much worried at this, and so being actuated with a high sense of duty he told the butcher :

. . . सूनां विमुञ्च यत्।
दास्येऽहमर्थमर्थस्य लोभात्त्वमसि सौनिकः॥

"If you leave your profession, I shall bestow wealth on you, for it is through greed of wealth that you are a butcher."

This request on the part of the king had no effect on Kālasaukarika. With all light-mindedness he replied:

सूनायां ननु को दोषो यया जीवन्ति मानवाः।
तां न जातुं त्यजामीति . . .॥

"What harm is there in butchery by which human beings subsist ? I am not going to leave it."

Thus when the king saw that there was no way open to him he put him into a dark well, where he was left hanging the whole night; but even there the butcher's mentality led him to draw figures of animals on the wall of the well and destroy them then and there. After this he caught some dangerous disease and went to hell.

Just after the death of his father Sulasa's relatives gathered around him and tried to persuade him to continue the family profession, but he told them: "As life is dear to me so also is the case with other animals, and having seen such fruits who would be prepared to live by killing?" All this had little or no effect on Sulasa's relatives, and they even showed their readiness to share the fruits of his life. Then Sulasa, pretending to kill a buffalo, gave a stroke with his father's axe on his leg and fell senseless on the ground. After a short time he regained consciousness and addressed his relatives :

. . . बन्धवो यूयं विभज्य मम वेदनाम्। ". . . Relatives! You (now) share my pain," but they could do nothing more than merely console him. Then he again told them, as if reminding them of their original promise:

. . . व्यथामियतीमपि। न मे ग्रहीतुमीशिध्वे तत्कथं नरकव्यथाम्॥ "If you cannot take this much misery how can you the miseries of hell?" Thus Sulasa won over his relatives to his way of thinking, and having taken the twelve vows of the Jainas went to heaven.[1]

---

1. Hemacandra, *Yogaśāstra* (with his own commentary), chap. II., v. 30, pp. 91-95. Very often heaven is taken to mean *mokṣa*, but it is not so. To the Jainas *mokṣa* is that stage from which the soul has never to return. According to Jainism there is a limit to life in heaven, but when the soul reaches *mokṣa* it enjoys bliss for ever.

The moral of this story is obvious. It illustrates the extreme insistence of the Jaiṅas on the principle of *ahiṁsā*, no less than the theory of *karma*. "Viler than unbelievers," says the *Yogaśāstra*, quoting the law of Manu to the effect that animals may be slain for sacrifice, "are those cruel ones who make the law that teaches killing."[1]

In their practical life also the respect of the Jainas for everything that has life is surprising, looking to the hurry and worry of this workaday world of ours. Whatever criticism we desire to offer about Jainism as it is in practice, there is no denying the fact that the great ideal of *ahiṁsā* of the Jainas was actuated by feelings of love and friendship towards all beings, and hence for our purpose suffice it to make a mere statement of facts, and a few remarks based on them. To a *sādhu* the rule of wounding nothing means that he must carry three articles with him — a straining-cloth for his drinking-water, a broom, and a veil before his mouth lest he might unconsciously swallow or crush any invisible animalcule. "This duty also necessitates the ascetic to pluck in the most painful manner his hair, which, according to the original custom, he must do away with at his consecration — a peculiar custom of the Jainas, which is not found among the other penitents of India."[2]

Even so, for fear of outraging the vow of *ahiṁsā*, a layman also observes so many precautions in daily life; but something which is rather striking is not to eat and, if possible, not to drink after sunset, that he might not swallow insects through mistake; and hence says Hemacandra: "Who would take food at night when human beings because of their eyesight being obstructed by deep darkness cannot see the insects falling in the eatable?"[3] Looking to all these practices if is clear that "no Hindu sect has carried *ahiṁsā* farther — *i.e.* respect for and abstinence from everything that has life."[4]

In spite of all this rigidity of practical details, there is nothing to warrant the conclusion that Jainism, literally obeyed, cannot hold the world together, but would lead nations to subjection, inaction and beggary. "It is only prejudice and garbled accounts of Jainism that have led to its being misunderstood. "Do your duty. Do it as humanly as you can." This, in brief, is the primary

1. Cf. Hopkins, op. cit., p. 288.
2. Bühler, op. cit., p. 15.
3. Hemacandra, op. cit., MS., chap. III., v. 49, p. 8.
4. Barth, op. cit., p. 145.

precept of Jainism. Not-killing cannot interfere with one's duties."[1] The Jaina *ahiṁsā* is not the *ahiṁsā* of a weakling but that of a brave soul which is or wants to be above all the evil forces of this world. Hemacandra rightly based it on the maxim: "Look upon other beings as you would look upon yourself."[2] An instance from the *Uttarādhyayana-Sūtra* amply illustrates the Jaina attitude towards the poorest, the lowliest and the lost.

Harikeśa was a *śvapāka* or *cāṇḍāla*. He became a great sage, possessed of the highest virtues, with his senses wholly subdued. Once when on his begging tours he approached the enclosure of a brāhmanical sacrifice, and observed:

"O brāhmaṇas, why do you tend the fire, and seek external purity by water? The clever ones say that external purity, which you seek for, is not the right thing."

"You (use) kuśa-grass, sacrificial poles, straw and wood, you touch water in the evening and in the morning; thereby you injure living beings, and in your ignorance you commit sins again and again.

"The law is my pond, celibacy my bathing-place, which is not turbid, and throughout clear for the soul; penance is my fireplace; right exertion is my sacrificial ladle; the body the dried cowdung; karma is my fuel; self-control, right exertion and tranquillity are the oblations, praised by the sages, which I offer."

Small wonder then that the *Uttarādhyayana* proclaims: "The value of penance has become visible, birth appears of no value! Look at the holy Harikeśa, the son of a *svapāka*, whose power is so great."[3]

This illustration also serves to indicate some of the moral virtues sought to be inculcated by the early Jainas. Really speaking, the characteristic feature of this religion is its claim to universality, and at its back is that great and glorious ideal of *ahiṁsā*, which puts before its saviours not the ideal of a hermit striving to secure his own redemption, but the ideal of a monk, enrolled in a brotherhood, and striving to save others. "It . . . declares its object to be to lead all men to salvation and to open its arms — not only to the noble

1. Jaini, op. cit., p. 72.
2. आत्मवत् सर्वभूतेषु . . . — Hemacandra, op. cit., chap. II., v. 20, p. 3.
3. Jacobi, S.B.E., XLV., pp. 50-56.

Āryan, but also to the low born śūdra, and even to the alien, deeply despised in India, the *mlecha*."[1]

Besides this cosmopolitan spirit of freely admitting any class of lay adherents into its fold, and thus to communion,[2] the feeling with which a Jaina is to look towards other faiths is itself creditable. It shows to what extent Jainism was careful not to injure the feelings of others. Even Mrs Stevenson has to say: "One of the unique glories of Jainism is that it, unlike most Indian-born religions, believes in the possibility of aliens reaching its goal."[3] This catholic attitude of respect for others is a characteristic of some of the brightest luminaries of the Jaina church. Haribhadra begins his section on the Jainas in the *Ṣaḍdarśana Samuccaya* with the words:

पक्षपातो न मे वीरे न द्वेषः कपिलादिषु।
युक्तिमद्वचनं यस्य तस्य कार्यः परिग्रहः॥

"Neither have I any partiality towards Vīra, nor do I hate Kapila and others. Whose word is proper his conclusion should be accepted."[4]

In addition to this greatly democratic constitution of the Jainas the ideal of *ahiṁsā* has also nourished and given due prominence to the discipline of confession within the Jaina church. *Hiṁsā* or injury to a certain extent is inevitable in human life, and hence a daily confession and a day-to-day consciousness of sins or wrongs committed during the course of the day is a necessity for the ultimate goal to be achieved. This may not be called the unique feature of Jainism, but in the Jaina church the prominence given to it is no doubt unique. *Sāmāyika* and *pratikramaṇa,* the two disciplines which have directly resulted from it, play a very important part in the lives of both

---

1. Bühler, op. cit., p. 3. "The Jaina community is only divided into *Yatis* and *Śrāvakas*, and if in any part of India, the Jainas practically recognise the distinctions of caste, it is just the same with the Christians and Mahomedans of Southern India, and even with the Bauddhas of Ceylon. This has nothing to do with the religion, it is only the adoption of social distinctions, which are rooted too deeply in the mind of the Indian nation to be abolished by the word of a religious reformer." — Jacobi, *Kalpa-Sūtra,* Int., p. 4.
2. "Hieun Tsiang's notes on the appearance of Nirgrantha or Digambara in Kiapishi (Beal, *Si-Yu-ki,* I., p. 55) point apparently to the fact that they had, in the north-west at least, spread their missionary activity beyond the borders of India." — Bühler, op. cit., p. 4.
3. Stevenson (Mrs), op. cit., p. 243.
4. Haribhadra, op. cit., p. 39; see also
   भवबीजांकुरजनना रागाद्याः क्षयमुपागता यस्य।
   ब्रह्मा वा विष्णुर्वा, हरो जिनो वा नमस्तस्मै॥
   — Hemacandra, *Mahādevastotra*, v. 44.

the clergy and the laity. The *Āvaśyaka-Sūtra* of Sudharma goes to the extent of saying: "That is real knowledge which begins with *sāmāyika* and ends with *Bindusāra* (the fourteenth *Pūrva*). The result of this is right conduct and the result of *cāritra* is *nirvāṇa*."[1]

The vow of *sāmāyika*, by observing which one gets equanimity of the soul, lays it down that at least forty-eight minutes in a day must be given to meditation.[2] The most essential portion of which — *karemi bhante*, etc. may be translated thus:

"O Lord! I do *sāmāyika*. I renounce all sinful activities. Till I live, with mind, speech and body, neither will I do nor will I make others do them. For that (sin) O Lord! I revert from them; I condemn them in the presence of my spirit and preceptor, and I vow to keep my soul free from such actions."[3]

These were the very words uttered by Lord Mahāvīra just after he was consecrated as a *sādhu*.[4] One of the definitions offered of *sāmāyika* in the *Āvaśyaka-Sūtra* commented upon by Haribhadra is roughly as follows:

"He has rightly undergone the vow of *sāmāyika* who has attained the attitude of equality, which makes him look at all kinds of living beings as he looks towards himself.[5] No kind of asceticism (*tapas*) can be of any good so long as attachment and antipathy (*rāga* and *dveṣa*) do not leave the soul. It is only when a man learns to look upon all living beings with equality (*samatva*) that he can effect such a conquest over *rāga* and *dveṣa*."[6]

Coming to *paḍikamaṇum*, or Sanskrit *pratikramaṇa*, we find herein a frank confession of sins and a sincere desire for their forgiveness. It is repentance for faults that already attach to the soul. "When engaging in *pratikramaṇa* — i.e. confession — Jainas think of the sins that they may have committed against any being possessing any *indriya* and ask forgiveness. At this time they also think of any germs which they may have created by sinning against the laws

1. सामाइयमाईयं . . . ।
   . . . निव्वाणं ॥. — *Āvaśyaka-Sūtra*, v. 93, p. 69.
2. Cf. Stevenson (Mrs), op. cit., p. 215.
3. करेमि भंते! . . . वोसिरामि. — *Āvaśyaka-Sūtra*, p. 454.
4. कृतपञ्चमौष्टिकलोचो भगवान् . . . "करेमि सामाइअं . . . " उच्चरति. — *Kalpa-Sūtra, Subodhikā-Ṭīkā*, p. 96. Cf. *Āvaśyaka-Sūtra*, p. 281.
5. यः 'समः' मध्यस्थः, आत्मानमिव परं . . ., 'सर्वभूतेषु' . . ., तस्य सामायिकं भवति. — *Āvaśyaka-Sūtra*, p. 329.
6. Cf. Dasgupta, op. cit., I., p. 201.

of sanitation . . . etc."[1] This is the natural outcome of a teaching that encourages civic and philanthropic virtues born out of the principle of *ahiṁsā*, which in its active form means helping humanity in its struggle for emancipation. Moreover the social organization of the Jainas is so designed as to carry out in practice the ideals briefly indicated above.

We shall now pass on to a characteristic feature of Jaina philosophy which has been considered as the distinct contribution of the Jainas to Indian logic. It is common with all religions to insist upon and provide for perfect knowledge. Every religion tries to teach man to go beyond the phenomenon. Jainism does the same, but with this difference, that it does not recognize the real from a restricted point of view.

For this attainment of perfect knowledge Jainism has a philosophy of its own, and this is known as the doctrine of *syādvāda* or *anekāntavāda* of the Jainas. "The doctrine of *nayas* or standpoints is a peculiar feature of the Jaina logic."[2] We have already seen that the Jaina metaphysics starts with a dualistic division of the universe into *jīva* and *ajīva*, and that in them lies the *tripadī*[3] of *utpāda*, *vyaya* and *dhruva*, respectively meaning Origination, Destruction and Permanence. Here origination means no new creation, because to the Jaina mind the whole universe of being has existed from all eternity. This *guṇa* of origination (*utpāda*) is just to show that in a permanent universe — permanent meaning having no origin — there is always origination of its modes of manifestations.[4] Thus everything that is *sat*, or the conception of being to the Jaina mind, is neither the absolutely unchangeable, nor the momentary changing qualities or existences, but involves them both. "Being then, as is testified by experience, is that which involves a permanent unit, which is incessantly every moment losing some qualities and gaining new ones."[5] This is, in short, the theory of indefiniteness (*anekāntavāda*),[6] or "what

1. Stevenson (Mrs), op. cit., p. 101.
2. Radhakrishnan, op. cit., I., p. 298.
3. वस्तुतत्त्वं चोत्पादव्ययध्रौव्यात्मकम् . . . — Hemacandra, *Syādvādamañjarī*, p. 168. Cf. ibid., vv. 21-22.
   येनोत्पादव्ययध्रौव्ययुक्तं यत्सत्तदिष्यते ।
   अनन्तधर्मकं वस्तु तेनोक्तं मानगोचरः ॥
   — Haribhadra, op. cit., v. 57.
4. Cf. Warren, op. cit., pp. 22-23.
5. Dasgupta, op. cit., I., p. 175.
6. तत्त्वं . . . जीवाजीवलक्षणम्, अनन्तधर्मात्मकमेव . . . —Hemacandra, op. cit., p. 170.

we may call the relative pluralism of the Jainas as against the extreme absolutism of the Upaniṣads and pluralism of the Buddhists."[1] It is on this that the *syādvāda* dialectics of the Jainas are based. "On these premises it is obvious that concerning a given *padārtha*, we can make, from a divergent point of view, different, apparently contradictory, statements."[2]

The innumerable qualities of a thing cannot be predicated in one statement, but they are all implied by any statement which predicates one of the qualities of a thing. Everything has to be considered in four different aspects: the matter (*dravya*), space (*kṣetra*), time (*kāla*), and nature (*bhāva*). This is why "the doctrine of *syādvāda* holds that since the most contrary characteristics of infinite variety may be associated with a thing, affirmation, made from whatever standpoint (*naya*), cannot be regarded as absolute."[3] Thus to observe a thing in its various aspects from different points of view is what is meant by *syādvāda*. "It is the method of knowing or speaking of a thing synthetically."[4]

Very often *syādvāda* has been described as the doctrine of scepticism,[5] but it is more correct to call it the science of "the assertion of alternative possibilities."[6] "The *syādvāda* doctrine," says A.B. Dhruva, "is not a doctrine of doubt. It enables a man to look at things with a wide and liberal view. It teaches us how and in what manner to look at things of this universe."[7] It neither affirms nor denies the existence of a thing,[8] but only states that a thing is or is not, or is what is described to be from one out of several points of view with which reality might be comprehended. "The dynamic character of reality consists only with relative or conditional predication. It does not

---

1. Dasgupta, op. cit., I., p. 175 ; नैकानि मानानि . . . अनेकमान इति. — *Viśeṣāvaśyaka-bhāṣyam*, v. 2186, p. 895.
2. Belvalkar, op. cit., p. 112.
3. Dasgupta, op. cit., p. 179.
4. Warren, op. cit., p. 20.
5. Cf. Hultzsch, *E.I.*, VII., p. 113. "In contrast to the Nihilistic Buddhist, the Jaina assumes a doubtful attitude, so that he is termed the 'may-be philosopher,' *Syādvādin*, in opposition to the Buddhist, the philosopher of 'the void.' " — Hopkins, op. cit., p. 291.
6. Cf. Fleet, *I.A.*, VII., p. 107. "The view is called *Syādvāda*, since it holds all knowledge to be only probable. Every position gives us only a perhaps, a maybe, or a *syāt*. We cannot confirm or deny anything absolutely of any object. There is nothing certain on account of the endless complexity of things." — Radhakrishnan, op. cit., I., p. 302.
7. Kannoomal, *Saptabhaṅgi-Naya*, Int., p. 8.
8. उपाधिभदापहितं विरुद्ध
   नार्थेष्वसत्त्वं सदवाच्यते च।
   — Hemacandra, op. cit., v. 24, p. 194

deny the possibility of predication. Every proposition is true, but only under certain conditions — i.e. hypothetically. There is nothing certain on account of the endless complexity of things. It is the use in seven different ways of judgment which affirm and negate, severally and jointly, without self-contradiction, thus discriminating the several qualities."[1] Answering the seven questions from the seven points of view is called *saptabhaṅgī-naya*, or pluralistic arguments. This philosophical doctrine is very abstruse and recondite. It is highly technical, and we cannot do better than produce the following exposition of it:

"The great contention of the Advaitins was that there is only one really existing entity, the *Ātman*, the-One-only without-a-second (*ekamevādvitīyam*), and that this is permanent (*nitya*), all else being non-existent (*a-sat*), a mere illusion. Hence it was called the *ātma-vāda, eka-vāda* or *nitya-vāda*. Their stock argument was that just as there are no such entities as cup, jar, etc. — these being only *clay* under various names and shapes — so all the phenomena of the universe are only various manifestations of the sole entity, *Ātman*. The Buddhists on the other hand said that man had no real knowledge of any such permanent entity; it was pure speculation, man's knowledge being confined to changing phenomena — growth, decay and death. Their doctrine was therefore called *anitya-vāda*. Clay as a substance may be permanent, but as a jar it is impermanent — may come into existence and perish. In other words, being is not simple, as Advaitins assert, but complex; and any statement about it is only part of the truth. The various possibilities were classed under seven heads (*Sapta-bhaṅgi*), each beginning with the word *syāt*, which is combined with one or more of these terms: *asti* ('is'), *nāsti* ('is not'), and *avaktavya* ("cannot be expressed"). Thus you can affirm existence of a thing from one point of view (*syāt-asti*), deny it from another (*syāt-nāsti*), and affirm both existence and non-existence with reference to it at different times (*syāt-asti-nāsti*). If you should think of affirming both existence and non-existence at the same time from the same point of view, you must say that the thing cannot be spoken of (*syāt-avaktavyaḥ*). Similarly, under certain circumstances, the affirmation of existence is not possible (*syāt-asti-avaktavyaḥ);* and also both (*syāt-asti-nāsti-avaktavyaḥ*). What is meant by these seven modes is that a thing should not be considered as existing everywhere at all times, in all ways, and

1. Radhakrishnan, op. cit., I., p. 302 ; स्याद्वादो हि सापेक्षस्तथैकस्मिन . . . सदसत्त्वनित्यानित्यत्वाद्यनेकधर्माभ्युपगमः ।. — Vijayadharmasūri, op. cit., p. 151.

in the form of everything. It may exist in one place and not in another, and at one time and not at another."[1]

"The solution of Jainism is thus a reconciliation of the two extremes of Vedāntism and Buddhism on grounds of common-sense experience."[2] Both Jacobi and Belvalkar take it as in opposition to the agnosticism of Sañjaya Belātthiputta: "Whereas Sañjaya had said, "I cannot say if it is, and I cannot say if it is not," Mahāvīra declared, "I can say that the thing in a sense is, and I can say that the thing in a sense is not.""[3]

In short, *syādvāda* is a unique feature of the Jaina philosophy. No better example of the clarity, subtlety and profundity of the Jaina intellect could be given than this. Mahāvīra might be safely credited with the invention of this part of the Jaina dialectics.[4] The earliest mention of this in the Jaina canonical literature according to Dasgupta "probably occurs in Bhadrabāhu's (433-357 BC) commentary of *Sūtrakṛtāṅga-Niryukti*."[5] This statement on the part of the learned scholar is based on the authority of the late Dr Satis Chandra Vidyabhushana,[6] who has used the following verse of the *Niryukti* as the basis of his inference:

असियसयं किरियाणं
अक्किरियाणं च होइचुलसोती।
अन्नाणिय सत्तट्ठी
वेणइयाणं च बत्तीसा॥

"180 of the *kriyāvāda*, 84 of the *akriyāvāda*, 67 of the *ajñānavāda* and 32 are of *vaināyikavāda*."[7]

It seems from this that the late doctor was under a wrong impression that the above verse of the *Niryukti* contained a reference to *Saptabhaṅgī-Naya*. As a matter of fact we get here an enumeration of the three hundred and sixty-three divisions of the four heretical creeds believed by the Jainas.[8]

---

1. Cf. Bhandarkar, *Report on Sanskrit MSS*, 1883-84, pp. 95-96 ; Rice (E.P.), *Kanarese Literature*, pp. 23-24.
2. Dasgupta, op. cit., I., p. 175.
3. Belvalkar, op. cit., p. 114. Cf. Jacobi, S.B.E., XLV., p. xxvii ; Belvalkar and Ranade, op. cit., pp. 433 n., 454 ff.
4. Cf. Belvalkar, op. cit., p. 114.
5. Dasgupta, op. cit., I., p. 181, n. 1.
6. Vidyabhushana, *History of the Mediaeval School of Indian Logic*, p. 8 ; *History of Indian Logic*, p. 167.
7. *Sūtrakṛtāṅga* (Āgamodaya Samiti), v. 119, p. 209.
8. Cf. Jacobi, op. cit., Int., p. xxvi ; ibid., pp. 315 ff.

Really speaking, in our opinion the earliest mention of the seven *nayas* and of the *syādvāda* philosophy of the Jainas lies in the *Sthānāṅga*, the *Bhagavatī* and the other canonical books of the Jainas.[1] Finally, to quote Lala Kannoomal: "The philosophers teaching this doctrine have written voluminous works to explain and expound its truth, to explain its subtleties. If this method of thinking is adopted in looking at the various religious tenets and philosophical creeds prevailing in India, which appear to be mutually conflicting, occasioning considerable differences of opinions, a perceptible change towards the reconciliation might occur."[2]

If *ahiṁsā* may be generalized as the fundamental ethical virtue of Jainism,[3] *syādvāda* may be described as the central and unique feature of Jaina metaphysics, and the explicit denial of the possibility of a perfect being from all eternity with the message of "Man! thou art thine own friend," as the centre round which circles the Jaina ritual. All this combined with the ideal of *ahiṁsā* teaches:

He prayeth well, who loveth well
Both man and bird and beast,
He prayeth best who loveth best
All things both great and small ;

(COLERIDGE)

and that is why a Jaina always says :

खामेमि सव्वजीवे, सव्वे जीवा खमंतु मे।
मेत्ती मे सव्वभूएसु, वेरं मज्झं न केणइ॥

"I forgive all souls; let all souls forgive me. I am on friendly terms with all; I have no enmity with anybody."[4]

Now to misunderstand or to misinterpret any of these features is to deliberately judge in a wrong way what is properly called Jainism. Let us be candid then, and concede that Mahāvīra's ideals were lofty and holy, and that his message of equality of mankind and of all living beings proclaimed to the caste-stricken and *yajña*-ridden people of India was large-hearted and benevolent.

---

1. *Sthānāṅga* (Āgamodaya Samiti), p. 390, *sūt*. 552 ; *Bhagavatī* (Āgamodaya Samiti), *sūt*. 469, p. 592. For further references see Sukhlal and Becherdas, *Sammatitarka* of Siddhasena, III., p. 441, n. 10.
2. Kannoomal, op. cit., Int., p. 7.
3. Dasgupta, op. cit., p. 200.
4. *Āvaśyaka-Sūtra*, p. 763.

IV

With these few words about the reformed church of Mahāvīra we shall now very briefly deal with some of the most important schisms in the Jaina church. And we shall in conclusion place a few considerations before the reader as to how the Jaina community could manage to survive all these insurrections in the *saṁgha* of Lord Mahāvīra.

As usual with the life of all prophets and reformers, unfortunately the church of Mahāvīra had also to face in its own days and afterwards a group of heterodox teachers, including those that are known to the Jainas as the seven *ṇiṇhagas* — Sanskrit *ninhavas*[1] — meaning those who propound something else than what the *jina* has meant. The seven *ninhavas* are Jamāli, Tīsagutta, Āsāḍha, Aśvamitra, Gaṅga, Chalue, and Goṣṭāmāhila.[2] Of these the most prominent and also the most dangerous rival of Mahāvīra was Gośāla Maṅkhaliputta — who is evidently identical with Maṅkhali Gośālo mentioned in the Pāli *sūtras* as one of the "six heretical teachers" and opponents of Lord Buddha.[3] Little is known about him and about the sect of the Ājīvikas of which he was the founder. We are practically in the dark "regarding the doctrines and practices of that ascetic community, which would seem to have, at one time, rivalled in numbers and importance the two still existing great communities of the Buddhists and Jainas."[4] After Gośāla we may just mention Jamāli, the son-in-law of Mahāvīra, Tīsagutta, a holy man in the community, and others.[5]

Gośāla first met Mahāvīra at Rājagṛha, and there he at once became his disciple. He was called Gośāla because he was born in a cowshed.[6] His father was a mendicant friar, and all these circumstances combined to show the

1. बहुरय . . . । सत्तेए णिण्हगा . . . वद्धमाणस्स. — *Āvaśyaka-Sūtra*, v. 778, p. 311 ; अथ सप्तनिग्हस्वरूपं . . . लिख्यते. — Merutuṅga, *Vicāraśreṇi*, *J.S.S.*, II., Nos. 3-4, Appendix, pp. 11-12.
2. *Bhagavatī-Sūtra* (Āgamodaya Samiti), II., pp. 410-30.
3. Jacobi, *Kalpa-Sūtra*, Int., p. 1.
4. Hoernle, *Uvāsaga-Dasāo*, II., Int., p. XII. Cf. Bühler, *I.A.*, XX., p. 362.
5. "In the fourteenth year of Mahāvīra's office as a prophet his nephew and son-in-law, Jamāli, headed an opposition against him, and similarly, two years afterwards, a holy man in the community, named Tīsagutta, made an attack. Both these merely concerned trifles. . . . Jamāli, however, persisted in his heretical opinions till his death." — Charpentier, *C.H.I.*, I., p. 163.
6. *Kalpa-Sūtra, Subodhikā-Ṭīkā*, p. 102. "Gośāla, son of a professional mendicant, Maṅkhali, and his wife Bhaddā. He saw the light of day in the cowshed of the wealthy Brahmana Gobahula at Sāvatthī." Sastri (Banerji), *J.B.O.R.S.*, XII., p. 55.

humble origin of the founder of the community of religious mendicants called the Ājīvikas.[1] "In the seventh *Aṅga* . . . a man, Saddalaputta, is said to have been received by Gośāla into the Ājīvika community, and the *Bhagavatī-Sūtra,* the fifth *Aṅga,* gives us an account of the life of Gośāla as the acknowledged head of the community. Though the Buddhist scriptures . . . also frequently mention Gośāla Maṅkhaliputta as one of the leaders of the six religious mendicant communities whom Buddha singles out for special animadversion, they never explicitly connect him with the Ājīvikas, or state that he was their leader. But that on this point the Buddhist tradition did not really differ from the Jaina is shown by the fact that both attribute to him the holding of the religio-philosophical doctrine of the negation of the free-will and moral responsibility."[2]

We have already seen that the period under consideration — when the religious life of ancient India was undergoing such radical change — is the rationalistic age of our history. It is the formative period which produced great individual philosophers like Gośāla Maṅkhaliputta, Sañjaya Belāttaputta, and others. Really speaking, India was then passing through a period of such religious enthusiasm that ". . . we must emphasize the fact that philosophy in this period not only ceased to be a purely academic or ritualistic affair divorced from life and conduct; . . . it developed strong and eccentric personalities and introduced all manner of strange practices and penances. . . . It must be put to the credit of these "heretic" free-thinkers that they brought philosophy into the open and compelled it to concern itself with the daily life and conduct of the people. Thus of the sect of the Ājīvikas to which Maṅkhali Gośāla belonged we read — "They discard all clothing; they dispense with all decent habits; they lick their food out of their hands. . . . They will not eat fish or flesh nor drink liquor or gruel. Some of them beg at one house and accept but one handful of food, others at two or seven. Some take food only once a day, others once in two days, others once in seven days, others once in every half-month." And this was by no means an

1. The name "Ājīvikas," it appears, was originally meant to stigmatize Gośāla and his followers as "professionals," though no doubt in later times, when it became the distinctive name of a mendicant order, it has no longer that offensive meaning. — Hoernle, *E.R.E.*, I., p. 259.

2. Ibid.

isolated or exceptional case. It would seem as if a sort of premium was set upon boldness and originality of conception and independence and eccentricity of practice."[1]

Thus it is clear that in Gośāla Mahāvīra had one who was not only not an asset or a source of strength to his *saṁgha*, but had one who acted as a great obstruction to the progress of the Jaina church in the early days of its reformation, and this comparatively strengthened the position of the Buddhists, and gave a severe blow to the rising influence of Mahāvīra.[2] So the consequences of this meeting of Mahāvīra and Gośāla were certainly disastrous for both the teacher and the disciple. "The two men were so different in character and temper that after six years, owing to the insincerity and trickery of Gośāla, the companionship was dissolved."[3]

Having separated from his master, Gośāla made his headquarters in the house of a potter-woman at Śrāvastī, and seems to have gained considerable influence there.[4] Soon after his separation from Mahāvīra he proclaimed that he had attained to the highest stage of saintship, that of a *jina*. "This claim was put forth two years before Mahāvīra himself had reached his perfect enlightenment."[5] But according to the Jaina tradition it is only in the fourteenth year of his career as a prophet that Mahāvīra happened to visit Śrāvastī, and there for the first time he seems to have seen Gośāla in the last days of his life. It is also recorded that the dual and unsteady nature of Gośāla asserted itself, and later on he seems to have repented[6] his undesirable conduct against his master.[7]

1. Belvalkar and Ranade, *History of Indian Philosophy*, II., pp. 460-61.
2. "The bone of contention was a theory of reanimation which Gośāla formulated from his observation of periodical reanimation of plant-life, and generalized it to such an extent as to apply it indiscriminately to all forms of life." — Barua, *J.D.L.*, II., p. 8. Cf. also Sastri (Banerji), op. cit., p. 56.
3. Hoernle, op. cit., p. 259. "Gośāla, having learnt from him the possession of the *Tejaleśyā*, or power of ejecting flame, and having learnt from certain of the disciples of Pārśvanātha what is technically called the *Mahānimitta* of the eight *Aṅgas*, intending probably their scriptural doctrines, set up for himself as a Jina and quitted his master." — Wilson, op. cit., I., pp. 295-96.
4. स्वामिनः पार्श्वात्स्फटितः श्रावस्त्यां तेजोनिसर्गमातापयति. . . . — *Āvaśyaka-Sūtra*, p. 214.
5. Charpentier, *C.H.I.*, I., p. 159.
6. "Some Jainas believe that, because he so sincerely repented before his death, he went not to hell, but to one of the *Devalokas* — i.e. heavens. . . ." — Stevenson (Mrs), op. cit., p. 60.
7. Cf. ibid. "His last act was to acknowledge to his disciple the truth of Mahāvīra's statement respecting himself and to instruct them to bury him with every mark of dishonour and publicly to proclaim his shame." — Hoernle, op. cit., p. 260.

With all this there is one point which need not be overlooked. The relatiohship between Mahāvīra and Gośāla, or, in other words, the relative position of Maṅkhaliputta in the great wave of religious enthusiasm in India, needs some definite explanation. Dr Barua seems to be under some delusion when he says: "Suffice it to say, that the evidences from either the Jaina or the Buddhist sources of information, do not bear out the Jaina pious belief that Gośāla was one of the two false disciples of Mahāvīra, and tend rather to prove the contrary. I mean that if the historian be called upon to pronounce a definite opinion on this disputed question he cannot but say that indebtedness, if any, was more on the side of the teacher than on that one who is branded by the Jaina as a false disciple."[1]

The delusion under which the learned scholar is labouring is that Mahāvīra first belonged to the religious order of Pārśvanātha, and that after one year, when he became undressed, he joined the Ājīvikas.[2] This is a hypothesis which not only disregards the authentic Jaina sources and traditions, but it shows an utter ignorance as to why the very followers of Gośāla were called Ājīvikas. As seen above, the distinction between the *dharma* of Pārśva and the *dharma* of Mahāvīra was a deliberate move on the part of the latter, and that the term Ājīvika was a term of contempt which was used by the Jainas and others to show the real nature of the Ājīvika sect.[3] Thus it is impossible that Mahāvīra should have joined the order of the Ājīvikas; neither was there a sect like this existing before Gośāla openly revolted against his teacher, since Gośāla himself was the originator of it.

It is an open fact that what little we know about Gośāla and his followers is based on either the Buddhist or the Jaina annals. "Their statement must, of course, be accepted with some caution; but their general trustworthiness is guaranteed by their agreement in all essential facts. This agreement possesses all the more value as the statements come from two independent sources of information."[4] A few isolated fragments which we can thus gather are, really speaking, not material which can entitle us to say that "indebtedness, if any, was more on the side of the teacher than on that one who is branded

1. Barua, op. cit., pp. 17-18.
2. Cf. ibid.
3. "It is clear that in the mouth of the Buddhists, 'Ājīvika' was the term of reproach applicable to a *Maskarin* or *Eka-daṇḍin* of the baser sort." — Hoernle, op. cit., p. 260.
4. Ibid., p. 261.

by the Jainas as a false-disciple." This becomes especially so when we know that the very traditions with the help of which we come to such a sweeping conclusion say something contrary to it.

The first point that the reputed doctor would like the critic to consider before judging one way or the other is "that the priority of Gośāla regarding *Jinahood* before Mahāvīra can be established beyond doubt by the history of Maṅkhaliputta in the *Bhagavatī*, confirmed in some important respects by the history of Mahāvīra in the *Kalpa-Sūtra.*"[1]

We wish this point had not been put for the consideration of the critic. It seems as if the writer wants to raise a deliberate misunderstanding about the whole episode. Nowhere in the *sūtras*, nor anywhere else in the whole of Jaina literature, is Gośāla said to have attained *jinahood.* What is said, as just remarked, is that Gośāla became a self-styled *jina* or *tīrthaṅkara.*[2] "Buddha charged him with incontinency."[3] So also did Mahāvīra. He is equally emphatic about it. In a dialogue in the *Sūtrakṛtāṅga* between Ārdraka, a disciple of Mahāvīra, and Gośāla the latter is reported to have said: "According to our law an ascetic . . . commits no sin . . . has intercourse with women."[4] He charges his followers with being "the slaves of women," and says that "they do not lead a life of chastity."[5] How could such a person who had become so notorious with his antinomian doctrines be expected and be said to have attained *jinahood*? This sounds particularly strange when, furthermore, the fact of his becoming a *jina* is based on the authority of the Jaina canon itself.

At another place the writer refers to the six previous births of Gośāla, with their particular periods as laid down in the *Bhagavatī-Sūtra,* and concludes: "The *Bhagavatī* account of the past reanimations of Gośāla, quaint and fanciful though it is, enables the historian to carry back the history of the Ājīvikas for 117 years counted backwards from Gośāla. . . ."[6] It seems that the popular tradition of the twenty-seven previous births of Mahāvīra has

1. Barua, op. cit., p. 18.
2. अजिणे जिणप्पलावी . . . अकेवली केवलिप्पलावी . . . विहरइ. — *Bhagavatī-Sūtra* (Āgamodaya Samiti), XV., p. 659. Cf. *Āvaśyaka-Sūtra*, p. 214 ; Charpentier, op. cit., p. 159.
3. Cf. Hoernle, op. cit., p. 261.
4. Jacobi, S.B.E., XLV., p. 411.
5. Ibid., pp. 245-70. Vijaya Rājendra Sūri, *Abhidhānarājendra*, II., p. 103.
6. Barua, op. cit., p. 7.

been set aside here. One does not know what entitles the writer to come to something like "the pre-Makkhali history of the Ājīvikas."[1]

In this fashion Dr Barua has put forward a few more points for the consideration of the critics, but everywhere, as he has himself said, his has been "a tremendous effort of imagination."[2] To go through, step by step, all the reasonings that he has put forward for maintaining his hypothesis based on his "intellectual sympathy"[3] towards the Ājīvikas would practically mean writing a small thesis on Gośāla. We need only say this much, that the learned doctor has mostly tried to disprove the Jaina and the Buddhist traditions with their own help. Moreover these are the traditions "which," observes Dr Jacobi, "in the absence of documents deserve most careful attention."[4]

With all this it may be granted that "Gośāla's philosophy was not entirely a new growth in the country."[5] It is certain that in the close environment of several conflicting theories and mutually contradictory dogmas what little Mahāvīra could achieve for the Jaina church was no doubt interconnected in the organic development of Indian thought.[6] Moreover, as observed by Dr Jacobi, it can also be said within its own limitations that "the greatest influence on the development of Mahāvīra's doctrine must . . . be ascribed to Gośāla, the son of Maṅkhali."[7] This is because both the theoretical and practical life of Gośāla probably had an abiding effect on the mind of Mahāvīra. To repeat: Gośāla was theoretically a fatalist. He believed that "there is no such thing as exertion or labour or power or vigour or manly strength, but all things are unalterably fixed."[8] While in his practical life he was "living in incontinency" (*abrahmacarya-vāsa*).[9] Thus naturally "the sin and shame of his life emphasized the need for stringent rules for the order, and the doctrine of absolute fatalism was to result in non-moral conduct. Jainism

1. Barua, op. cit., p. 7.
2. Ibid., p. 22.
3. Ibid.
4. Jacobi, op. cit., Int., p. xxxiii.
5. Barua, op. cit., p. 27.
6. "While Sañjaya's dialectics was mainly negative, Gośāla, by his *Terasiya*, or three-membered dialectics of 'it may be,' 'it may not be,' 'it may both be and not be,' had already paved the way for Mahāvīra's seven-membered *Syādvāda*." — Belvalkar and Ranade, op. cit., pp. 456-57. Cf. Hoernle, op. cit., p. 262.
7. Jacobi, op. cit., Int., p. xxix.
8. Hoernle, *Uvāsaga-Dasāo*, I., pp. 97, 115-16. Cf. ibid., II., pp. 109-10, 132.
9. *Majjhima-Nikāya*, I., 514 ff. Cf. Hoernle, *E.R.E.*, I., p. 261.

avoids this determinism . . . by teaching that, though karma decides all, we ourselves can affect our past Karma by our present life."[1]

Thus if at all Gośāla had an influence on the formulation of the reformed Jaina doctrine, and on the career of Mahāvīra, it is only thus far and no further. In addition to this we may add once again that just because of these unhappy schisms in the Jaina church "Mahāvīra's chances of founding an all-India religious movement were seriously jeopardised."[2]

This much about Gośāla himself. We have already seen that in the fourteenth year of Mahāvīra's life as a prophet Gośāla died. This event naturally coincides with the fact that he died 16 years prior to Mahāvīra, deducting 14 years from 30 of Mahāvīra as a prophet. Thus based on the date of Mahāvīra's *nirvāṇa*, which we have taken as approximately between 480-467 BC, Gośāla's death must be placed somewhere between 496-483 BC. As laid down in the *Bhagavatī-Sūtra*, this date of Gośāla is supported also by the fact that his death was coincident with the great war between King Kūṇiya (Ajātaśatru) and King Ceḍaga of Vaiśālī for the possession of an extraordinary elephant.[3] This elephant was given by Kūṇiya's father, King Bimbisāra, to his younger son Vehalla by his wife Cellaṇā, a daughter of King Ceḍaga. Having usurped the throne, Ajātaśatru tried to get the elephant from his younger brother, but the latter ran away with it to his grandfather in Vaiśālī. "Kūṇiya having failed peacefully to obtain the extradition of the fugitive commenced war with Ceḍaga."[4] Thus the war, which must have taken place somewhere about the time when Kūṇiya took upon himself the regal power, can be placed *c.* 496 BC.[5]

---

1. Stevenson (Mrs). op. cit., p. 60. "It was probably owing to Gośāla's conduct that Mahāvīra added a vow of chastity to the four vows of Pārśvanātha's order. . . ." — Ibid., p. 59. Cf. also ibid., p. 185 ; Hoernle, op. cit., p. 264.
2. Sastri (Banerji), op. cit., p. 56. "From the 6th to the 3rd century BC Buddhism under a common leader spread all over India and beyond. Divided counsel crippled Jainism at the start. But the Jainas have the satisfaction of knowing that the once-powerful Ājīvikas survive only as a memory." — Ibid., p. 58.
3. Hoernle, *Uvāsaga-Dasāo*, Appendix I, p. 7. एगहत्थिणावि णं पभू कूणिए राया पराजिणित्तए. — *Bhagavatī* (Āgamodaya Samiti), p. 316, *sūt*. 300. Cf. Hemacandra, *Triṣaṣṭi-Śalākā*, *Parva* X, vv. 205-06.
4. Hoernle, op. and loc. cit. Cf. also Tawney, *Kathākośa*, pp. 178-79. . . . न दद्यास्तदा युद्धसज्जो भवैमीति. — *Āvaśyaka-Sūtra*, p. 684.
5. Dr Hoernle, taking 484 BC as the date of Mahāvīra's death, puts *c.* 500 BC as the date (approximate) of Gośāla and of the war between Ajātaśatru and his grandfather. Cf. Hoernle, *E.R.E.*, I., p. 261.

Approaching the Ājīvika sect of the Jainas from an historical point of view we find that the sect did not die with its leader. Looking to the relation of the Ājīvikas with the Buddhists we see that the latter have "no cause for special resentment against either an Ājīvika or a Jaina. Buddhist rulers like Aśoka and Daśaratha bestow cave-dwellings on the Ājīvikas at Barābar and Nāgārjunī Hills in the same spirit as they build *Stūpas* for the Buddhists or order alms to the brāhmaṇas, elsewhere. The later resentment of the Buddhists centred round not the Jaina or the Ājīvika but the brāhmaṇas."[1]

The earliest mention of the Ājīvikas occurs in a brief record of the thirteenth year of Aśoka — that is to say, in 257 BC[2] — incised on the walls of two rock-hewn caves on Barābar Hill, near Gayā. It runs as follows: "King Piyadasi, in the 13th year of his reign, bestowed this cave on the Ājīvikas."[3]

The next mention occurs in the celebrated Pillar Edicts of Aśoka, where, referring to the functions of his censors of the Law of Piety, the emperor has included the Ājīvikas as one of those who will be looked after by them.[4] "Again, in the twentieth "regnal year," 250 BC, the sovereign presented a third costly rock-dwelling to the Ājīvikas."[5] A further early mention occurs in a brief record, incised on the walls of three rock-hewn caves on Nāgārjunī Hill in the first year of the reign of Aśoka's successor Daśaratha — i.e. in *c.* 230 BC. It runs as follows: "This cave was bestowed by His Majesty Daśaratha, immediately after his accession, on the venerable Ājīvikas, to be a dwelling-place for them, as long as sun and moon endure."[6]

---

1. Sastri (Banerji), op. cit., p. 55.
2. Taking Aśoka's coronation as about 270-269 BC, Cf. Smith, *Aśoka*, p. 73 (3rd edn.) ; Mookerji (Radhakumud), *Aśoka*, p. 37.
3. Hoernle, op. cit., p. 266. Cf. *I.A.*, XX., pp. 361 ff. ; Smith, *Aśoka*, p. 144 (1st edn.). Aśoka seems to have inherited his partiality towards the Ājīvikas from his parents, "if we may believe in the legends. The *Mahāvaṁsaṭīkā* (p. 126), as has been already noticed, refers to the family-preceptor of his mother, Queen Dharmā, being an Ājīvika of the name of Janasāna (*deviyā kulūpago Janasāno nāma eko Ājīvika*), whom King Bindusāra summoned to interpret the meaning of the Queen's dream before the birth of Aśoka; while in the *Divyāvadāna* (chap. XXVI), Bindusāra himself summons the Ājīvika ascetic Piṅgalavatsa for the examination of all his sons to find out who was the best to be his successor on the throne." — Mookerji (Radhakumud), op. cit., pp. 64-65. ". . . The Ājīvika saint, Piṅgalavatsa, summoned by the King, judged Aśoka as the fittest of his sons for the throne." — Ibid., p. 3.
4. Smith, op. cit., p. 155 ; *E.I.*, II., pp. 270, 272, 274.
5. Smith, op. cit., p. 54 (3rd edn.).
6. Hoernle, op. cit., p. 266. Cf. *I.A.*, XX., pp. 361 ff. ; Smith, op. cit., p. 145 (1st edn.).

Thus "of the seven caves, two in the Barābar Hill and three in the Nāgārjunī Hill mention the grant of those caves to the "Ājīvikas" (*Ājīvikehi*). In three cases the word *Ājīvikehi* had been deliberately chiselled off, every other letter entirely untouched."[1] It is really difficult to say who could have done this, but we know for certain that after King Daśaratha the Barābar Hills passed into the hands of the Jaina king, Khāravela. He was at Gorathagiri in the eighth year of his reign — i.e. just after the Aśoka-Daśaratha time. On epigraphic grounds also this can be ascertained by the remarkable façade of the Lomaśa Ṛṣi Cave.[2] As a pious Jaina, Khāravela might have "attempted to wipe off old scores by obliterating the hated name of the impostor Gośāla's Ājīvika followers."[3]

Writing on this Jaina-Ājīvika hostility in the domain of archaeology Mr Mookerji observes: "The last two Aśokan inscriptions in the Barābar caves, as shown here, and the three Nāgārjunī inscriptions of Daśaratha mention in common the grant of these caves to the Ājīvikas, but in three of these inscriptions there is detected an attempt to chisel away the word *ājīvikehi*, as if the name of this sect was not tolerated by somebody who was at such pains to wipe it off. Now, who was this somebody? Hultzsch conjectures it might have been the Maṅkhari Anantavarman, who assigned one of the Barābar caves to Kṛṣṇa, and two of the Nāgārjunī caves to Śiva and Pārvatī, and whose orthodox Hindu leaning did not favour the Ājīvikas. Dr Banerji Sastri puts forward a more convincing conjecture. He fastens the mischief on Khāravela, a Jaina, with the traditional hostility of his community to the Ājīvikas, a mischief that was thus committed much earlier than the times of Maṅkhari, when the Aśokan *Brāhmī-Lipi* was well-nigh forgotten."[4]

1. Sastri (Banerji), op. cit., p. 59.
2. Ibid., p. 60. Cf. also "A comparison of the two sites leaves hardly a doubt that the Goradhagiri façade and inscription are intimately connected with the Udayagiri (Khāravela) inscriptions and façades, both done by a Jaina who signed his creed in the mutilation of the letters 'Ājīvikehi.' " — Ibid., p. 61.
3. Ibid., p. 60. "He (Khāravela) naturally turned out the Ājīvikas, chiselled off their names and put in his Kaliṅgan troops in the Barābar Caves. The unfinished Lomaśa Ṛṣi he must have found quite handy. In any case Khāravela seems to have employed post-Mauryan craftsmen to polish up the walls." — Sastri (Banerji), *J.B.O.R.S.*, XII., p. 310.
4. Mookerji (Radhakumud), op. cit., p. 206. "Hultzsch's view is untenable: (1) He assumes without assigning any reason that Anantavarman in the 6th-7th century AD was familiar with Aśoka-Brāhmī of the 3rd century BC . . ." — Sastri (Banerji), op. cit., p. 57. The second reason put forward by the learned scholar is that Anantavarman, himself being a Hindu, had no special grievance against an Ājīvika, who was popularly

→

VII : Lomaśa Ṛṣī Cave, Barābar Hill.

Thus as a sect the Ājīvikas practically disappeared from India by the end of the second century BC,[1] though we find some such reference to it in the literature of the later period, as in Varāhamihira, Śīlāṅka's commentary on *Sūtrakr̥tāṅga*, Halāyudha's *Abhidhāna-Ratnamālā*, and in the inscriptional record on the walls of the Perumal temple at Poygaie, near Virinchipuram.[2] All these references are not directly connected with the Ājīvikas, nor are they in any way pure Ājīvika references. In many a place the term Ājīvika is used for the Digambara sect of the Jainas.[3]

With these few words about the first important schism in the Jaina church we shall pass on to the second epoch-making division — namely, the Śvetāmbara and the Digambara sects of the Jainas. Really speaking it is very difficult to say as to where lies the first origin of this division in the Jaina community. What both the Digambara and the Śvetāmbara traditions have to say on this and other points referring to each other is at times childish and very often quite unhistorical. Anyhow this much is certain, that this schism has done a lot of harm to the general progress and prosperity of the Jaina community. Both Jaina literature and Jaina history have suffered greatly from contradictory and retaliating traditions put forward by the two divisions. They look at each other as heretics, and sometimes worse than that.[4] In their zeal to keep up the prestige of belonging to the original church of Lord Mahāvīra none of them talks about its own origin, but both make a few sarcastic and sometimes disgraceful remarks about the origin and certain other beliefs of the rival sect.

Taking the Digambara traditions we find that the Digambaras themselves do not agree in their exposition of this division in the Jaina church. Ācārya

→ regarded as a follower of Viṣṇu or Kr̥ṣṇa. — Ibid. This is based on the authority of Kern (*I.A.*, XX., p. 361 ff.), but there is nothing in Jaina canonical or other literature to support this. Anyhow it may safely be said that it can hardly be a Hindu or a Buddhist who could have done this. "The only alternative left is a Jaina." Historically also "the Jaina-Ājīvika enmity makes it almost a certainty." — Sastri (Banerji), op. cit., p. 60. For Hultzsch's statement see *C.I.I.*, I., Int., p. xxviii (new edn., 1925).

1. Sastri (Banerji), op. cit., p. 53.
2. Hoernle, op. cit., pp. 266-67.
3. "There can be no doubt, therefore, that since the 6th century AD, when Varāhamihira used the term, the name has signified the Digambara sect of the Jainas." — Ibid., p. 266.
4. इय उप्पत्ती कहिया, सेवडयाणं च मग्गभट्टाणं।, etc. — Devasenasūri, *Bhāvasaṁgraha* (Soni's edn.), v. 160. p. 39. Cf. Premi, *Darśanasāra*, p. 57. मिच्छादंसणमिणमो . . . etc. — *Āvaśyaka-Sūtra*, p. 324.

Devasena says in his *Darśanasāra*: "The Śvetāmbara *Saṁgha* had its beginning in Vallabhīpura in Sourāṣṭra 136 years after the death of Vikrama."[1] This origin of the Śvetāmbaras according to the learned Ācārya was due "to the wicked and loose-charactered Jinacandra, the disciple of Ācārya Śānti, who was (in turn) the disciple of the venerable Bhadrabāhu."[2]

It is not clear which of the Bhadrabāhus is meant here. If this is the Bhadrabāhu of the days of Candragupta the period assigned to the schism would fall to the ground. But according to the Digambara tradition of the great famine in the days of Candragupta, the emigration of Bhadrabāhu and his votaries from the north, and the consequent separation of the Digambaras and the Śvetāmbaras, no other Bhadrabāhu is meant here.

Devasenasūri has said the same thing in *Bhāvasaṁgraha*, but in addition to it he talks of the famine which has been connected with the life of Bhadrabāhu. Here also Jinacandra is painted in the same colours. He is said to have murdered his *guru*, Ācārya Śānti, for rebuking him as being on the wrong path.[3] The curious thing is that he also puts the same date for the great schism.[4]

In both these Digambata traditions there is distinctly something wrong about the Bhadrabāhu mentioned here. There is something half said, or some other Bhadrabāhu is meant, or the traditions are put without any regard for the chronological facts of history. To whitewash these two statements Bhaṭṭāraka Ratnanandi introduced in his life of Bhadrabāhu the following facts: that in Bhadrabāhu's time the schism began under the name of *ardhaphalaka* (half-clothed); that Sthūlabhadra, who tried to oppose the propounder of such a change, was murdered by them; and that the final separation came after a long time because of Candralekhā, the daughter of the king of Ujjayinī and the wife of the king of Vallabhīpura.[5]

In contradiction to this there is another tradition which says that

1. छत्तीसे वरिससए . . . सोरट्ठे . . . उप्पण्णो सेवडो संघो।. — Premi, *Darśanasāra*, v. 11, p. 7.
2. Ibid., vv. 12-15.
3. सीसे सीसेण दीहदंडेण। थविरो घाएण मुओ . . . etc. — Devasenasūri, op. cit., v. 153, p. 38. Cf. Premi, op. cit., p. 56.
4. छत्तीसे वरिससए . . . सोरट्ठे उप्पण्णो सेवडसंघो . . . etc. — Devasenasūri, op. cit., v. 137, p. 35. Cf. Premi, op. cit., p. 55.
5. Premi, op. cit., p. 60. According to the Digambaras, "under Bhadrabāhu, the eighth age after Mahāvīra, the last Tīrthaṅkara, there rose the sect of *Ardhaphālakas* with later principles, from which developed the present sect of Śvetāmbaras (AD 80)." — Dasgupta, op. cit., I., p. 170.

Sthūlabhadra himself was opposed to the Digambara insistence on nakedness, and that after him his disciple Mahāgiri "revived "the ideal practice of nakedness." He was a real ascetic and recognised that under Sthūlabhadra's sway many abuses had crept into the order."[1] In this mission of his Mahāgiri was opposed by Suhastin, who was one of the leaders of the Jaina community under Mahāgiri.[2] According to the Śvetāmbaras the origin of the great schism lies under the following circumstances: In the town of Rathavīra there lived a man named Śivabhūti or Sahasramalla. Once his mother got angry with him and hence he left his house and became a Jaina *sādhu*. It so happened that after his consecration as a monk the ruling prince gave him a valuable blanket, and he felt enamoured of it. Seeing this his *guru* drew his attention to it, and thenceforth he became all naked and started the Digambara sect of the Jainas. His sister Uttarā also tried to follow in the footsteps of her brother, but Śivabhūti, thinking it to be inadvisable for women to remain naked, told her that a woman cannot get final liberation.[3]

The date put down by the Śvetāmbaras for this schism is 609 years after Mahāvīra,[4] and this comes to 139 years after the death of Vikrama, taking the traditional duration of 470 years as the period between Vikrama and the *nirvāṇa* of Mahāvīra. At least in their dates both the Digambara and the Śvetāmbara traditions fully agree. The former puts 136 years and the later 139, after Vikrama, as the period for this great division in the Jaina church. In spite of this agreement about the date they do not agree as to the circumstances under which arose this great division. Both Jinacandra and Śivabhūti look more like fictitious than like true historical persons, because the annals of both the rival faiths disclaim the fact of any such person belonging to their division. This is why Nathuram Premi, the learned Digambara scholar, says:

1. Stevenson (Mrs), op. cit., p. 73.
2. Ibid., p. 74. "I think that the divisions became marked from the time of Ārya-Mahāgiri and Ārya-Suhastin." — Jhaveri, *Nirvāṇa-Kalikā*, Int., p. 7.
3. This is given in the प्रवचनपरीक्षा of Upādhyāya Dharmasāgara. Cf. Hiralal (H.), op. cit., pt. II., p. 15. बोडियसिवभूइउत्तराहि इमं। . . . रहवीरपुरे समुप्पण्णं. — *Āvaśyaka-Sūtra*, p. 324.
4. छव्वससयाइं नवुत्तराइं तइया सिद्धिं गयस्स वीरस्स।
तो बोडियाण दिट्ठी रहवीरपुरे समुप्पण्णा॥
— Ibid., p. 323. "The origin of the Digambaras is attributed to Śivabhūti (AD 83), by the Śvetāmbaras as due to a schism in the old Śvetāmbara church. . . ." — Dasgupta, op. cit., I., p. 170.

"Can we not infer from this that nobody knew the origin of either of the two divisions? Something must be said, and so afterwards they have put down anything that came into their heads."[1] Though rather harsh, this remark is supported by the fact that both the sects agree in the line of *gurus* put down from the time of Mahāvīra only as far as Jambūsvāmī, who, according to the traditional date of Mahāvīra's *nirvāṇa,* died in 403 BC.[2] After Jambū both the parties have a list of succession of their teachers which is quite different, but they agree in their account of Bhadrabāhu of the days of Candragupta.[3] Really speaking, one cannot arrive at any definite conclusion from all these mutually conflicting traditions, and hence it is almost impossible to fix an exact date for this great schism in the Jaina community.

Along with these difficulties there are two things which should be particularly noticed. The first point is that the two divisions were based on the question whether the Jaina clergy should remain naked or should go about with some sort of garment to cover them. The second thing is the general unanimity about the period of the schism between the two divisions.

The very names of the two divisions connote what is meant by them. The Digambaras, or those who are clothed in air, maintained that absolute nudity is a necessary condition of saintship; the other division, or the Śvetāmbaras, those who are dressed in white, admit that Mahāvīra went about naked, but hold that the use of clothes does not impede the highest sanctity.[4] If this is the criterion, well, both need not quarrel as to which belongs to the original Jaina church, because, as laid down by their own traditions, the original Jaina church has no beginning and no end. Taking it historically and literally, we can say that the Śvetāmbaras are more akin to Pārśvanātha than to Mahāvīra, and Digambaras are nearer the latter, because Mahāvīra passed many years of his life as a prophet in a naked stage, while both Pārśva and his followers preferred to remain dressed.[5] Furthermore, if the authenticity of the

1. Premi, op. cit., p. 30.
2. Cf. Stevenson (Mrs), op. cit., p. 69.
3. Cf. Premi, op. and loc. cit.
4. "Nudity as a part of asceticism was practised by several sects in the time of Mahāvīra, but it was also reprobated by others (including all Buddhists) who felt it to be barbarous and unedifying." — Elliot, op. cit., p. 112.
5. Cf. Jacobi, S.B.E., XLV., pp. 119-29. "The probability is that there had always been two parties in the community: the older and weaker section, who wore clothes and dated from Pārśvanātha's time, and who were called Sthavira-Kalpa (the spiritual ancestors of the Śvetāmbara) ; and the Jina-Kalpa, or Puritans, who kept the extreme letter of the law as Mahāvīra had done, and who are the forerunners of the Digambara." — Stevenson (Mrs), op. cit., p. 79.

Śvetāmbara canonical literature is granted, we can go a step further and say that though the Digambaras followed the extreme letter of the law as Mahāvīra had done, the Śvetāmbaras in no way disregarded the law. This is because, as we have already remarked, that what Mahāvīra experienced in his state of forgetfulness he did not expect his followers to practise literally irrespective of what spiritual height they had reached.

With all this the point at issue is not as to which one of these two belonged to the original church, because it is difficult to define what really is or can be the original church of the Jaina community. This is not for a student of history to say. What he is concerned with is to mark out approximately the period whence this schism in the Jaina church had its distinct existence.

A detailed review of the facts before us is out of the question. What need be said is this, that the germ underlying this division had its origin in the days of Mahāvīra, when came Maṅkhaliputta, who made a cult out of it. After his death no doubt the Ājīvika force was greatly weakened, but there were some among the *nigaṇṭhas* themselves who sympathized with the Ājīvikas "on the points of nakedness, non-possession of a bowl, imperfect regard for life, distinctive mark of a staff and probably other matters."[1] This sympathy on their part might have manifested itself especially in the time of Bhadrabāhu, when, according to the Digambaras, the schism had its first beginning,[2] but there is no distinct separation as yet. We may now pass on to the Sthūlabhadra and Mahāgiri traditions, and then come down to the end of the first century AD when, according to both the Digambara and the Śvetāmbara traditions, the actual separation takes place.[3] Though the traditional legends put forward by the two divisions are in many respects highly coloured and extremely childish, one thing is clear, that at that particular period in Jaina history some conspicuous or unusual event or incident must have taken place which forms the basis of all these literary traditions. Nevertheless we cannot say that here

1. Hoernle, op. cit., p. 267 ff.
2. "It thus appears that the Jaina division into Digambara and Śvetāmbara may be traced back to the very beginning of Jainism, it being entirely due to the antagonism of the two associated leaders, Mahāvīra and Gośāla, who are the representatives of the two hostile sects." — Hoernle, op. cit., p. 268.
3. Mr Jhaveri, in his Introduction to his edition of *Nirvāṇa-Kalikā*, writes : "From the colophon of the work it appears that even in the first century of Vikrama the divisions of the Digambaras and the Śvetāmbaras were in existence. The colophon of the *Stutis* of Siddhasena Divākara confirms the existence of such division in ancient times." — Int., p. 7.

lies the actual separation of the two divisions, because in the Mathurā sculptures we have evidence that points out that the two divisions had till then many things in common which afterwards formulated some of the items on which the two parties could not agree.

To make matters more clear we might say that the chief points on which thc two parties particularly do not agree are the following: the insistence of the exchange of the embryo of Mahāvīra, to which the Digambaras do not subscribe; the beliefs that woman is not entitled to *mokṣa* and that *kevalins* do not take food, which are not acceptable to the Śvetāmbaras; and, finally, the Digambara belief in the complete disappearance of the ancient sacred literature of the Jainas.[1] Leaving aside some differenccs in rituals and other minor matters these are some of the prominent features on which the two divisions do not agree.

Now, taking the Mathurā sculptures, we find that the particular sculpture referring to the exchange of embryo of Lord Mahāvīra, which we have already mentioned, has represented in it *tīrthaṅkara* Mahāvīra in a naked state. The small ascetic at Nemesa's left knee, called in the inscription "divine . . . ," is no doubt meant for Mahāvīra, who is introduced by the artists with the attributes of a monk,[2] in order to show the subject to which the conversation refers, and he is represented so small because in reality he is not yet born and has not yet reached the position of an *arhat*.[3] Thus this one specimen of Mathurā sculpture has combined in itself the Digambara belief of nakedness and the Śvetāmbara tradition of the exchange of embryos. This shows that so far back as the first century of the Christian era an actual separation between the parties had not yet taken place.

Nevertheless it must be reiterated that the Jaina iconography in its initial stage is greatly marked with the undressed state of the Jaina *tīrthaṅkaras*, and this goes as far back as the second century BC, if not further. Mon Mohan Chakravarti, talking of the Jaina monuments on the Udayagiri and the

---

1. तेण कियं मयमेयं इत्थीणं अत्थि तब्भवे मोक्खो।
केवलणाणीण पुणो अद्दक्खाणं तहा रोओ॥
अंबरसहिओ वि जई सिज्झइ वीरस्स गब्भचारत्तं।
— Premi, op. cit., vv. 13-14, p. 8.

2. "At his (Nemesa's) left knee stands a small naked male, characterised by the cloth in his left hand as an ascetic and with uplifted right hand." — Bühler, *E.I.*, II., p. 316.

3. Ibid., p. 317.

Khaṇḍagiri Hills, says: "Only the Tīrthaṅkaras are represented nude, and even they are occasionally shown dressed, if the scene is intended to represent some scene of their human lives. Females, kings, *deva*s, arhats, *gandharva*s, attendants are generally represented dressed. In Mathurā sculptures the dancing girls, the centaurs, and some of the ascetics (Digambaras) are shown naked. Sometimes the females look naked, but a closer examination shows traces of a very thin fine cloth through which are perceptible the curves of the body."[1] In later history we find that Varāhamihira, in his *Bṛhat-Saṁhitā*, describes the Jaina *tīrthaṅkara*s in the following words: "The God of the Jainas is figured naked, young, handsome, with a calm countenance, and arms reaching down to the knees. . . ."[2]

Thus, though two distinct divisions had not come into existence till the beginning of the Christian era, it must be admitted that the traditions of Bhadrabāhu of the days of the great famine, and of Jinacandra and Śivabhūti of *c.* AD 80, are marked stages in the history of the great schism which, in our opinion, led to a final separation of the two parties by the time of the second great council at Vallabhī[3] under Devardhigaṇi, in the middle of the fifth century AD according to the traditional date of Mahāvīra's *nirvāṇa* in 527 BC.[4] It may be that the actual division took place a few days before this event, but the final fixing up and reduction into writing of the whole canonical literature of the Jainas at last brought about two distinct divisions before the Jaina community, with differences in matters of certain dogmas and beliefs, which may safely be termed the coincidences natural to a period when everything was to be put into black and white.

This period is confirmed also by James Bird for the great schism, who on the basis of his study of the caves of Western India comes to the following conclusion : "The reputed origin of the Digambara Jainas, about AD 436, harmonises with the date assigned for these caves. The *Śatruñjaya Māhātmya*

1. Chakravarti (Mon Mohan), *Notes on the Remains on Dhauli and in the Caves of Udayagiri and Khaṇḍagiri*, p. 2.
2. *Bṛhat-Saṁhitā*, chap. LIX., trans. by Kern in *J.R.A.S.* (New Series), VI., p. 328. Cf. Chakravarti (Mon Mohan), op. and loc. cit.
3. Cf. Premi, op. cit., p. 31.
4. "It seems certain that in AD 454 the whole canon was reduced to writing, and that a large number of copies were made, so that no monastery of any consequence should be without one." — Stevenson (Mrs), op. cit., p. 15.

or the legend of the Jaina temples Pālitānā, in Kathiawar, fixes also this period of the origin of the Digambara Jainas."[1]

In short, the history of this great schism may be summarized as follows in the words of Sir Charles Elliot: "It is therefore probable that both Digambaras and Śvetāmbaras existed in the infancy of Jainism, and the latter may represent the older sect reformed or exaggerated by Mahāvīra. Thus we are told that "the law taught by Vardhamāna forbids clothes but that of the great sage Pārśva allows an under and upper garment." But it was not until considerably later that the schism was completed by the constitution of the two different canons."[2]

In spite of such a complicated history behind this division in the Jaina community it must be conceded that there is little of real difference between the two parties. In matters of certain traditional beliefs and dogmas there is no doubt a great distance between the two, but most of the controversial points are unnecessary and indirect. This was more or less the feeling of Raichandji, the most righteous and highly respected Jaina of our days.[3] Intellectually too he was a great scholar, and his are the sentiments which are also shared by other.

"The Digambaras," says Dr Dasgupta, "having separated in early times from the Śvetāmbaras developed peculiar religious ceremonies of their own, and have a different ecclesiastical and literary history, though there is practically no difference about the main creed."[4] Thus the Jaina sub-sects did not differ much among themselves in philosophical speculation. Their differences were rather of a practical kind, and, as Wilson has rightly pointed out, their "mutual animosity is, as usual, of an intensity very disproportionate to the sources from whence it springs."[5]

Leaving aside the second great division in the Jaina community we come to the third and the last — viz. that of the non-idolatrous sect of the Śvetāmbara Jainas — very often known as the *Dhuṇḍhīā* or *Sthānakavāsī* sect of the Jainas. This division came very late in the history of the Jaina church, and to some extent it can safely be said that it was greatly a direct result of Mohammedan influence on the religious mind of India. "If one effect,"

1. Bird, *Historical Researches*, p. 72.
2. Elliot, op. cit., p. 112.
3. विवादसंबन्धीनि बहूनि स्थलानि तु अप्रयोजनायमानान्येव तयोः । — Raichandji, *Bhagavatī-Sūtra* (Jināgama Prakāśasabhā), Int., p. 6.
4. Dasgupta, op. cit., I., p. 170.
5. Wilson, op. cit., I., p. 340.

observes Mrs Stevenson, "of the Mohammedan conquest, however, was to drive many of the Jainas into closer union with their fellow idol-worshippers in the face of iconoclasts, another effect was to drive others away from idolatry altogether. No Oriental could hear a fellow Oriental's passionate outcry against idolatry without doubts as to the righteousness of the practice entering his mind.

"Naturally enough it is in Ahmedabad, the city of Gujarat that was most under Mohammedan influence, that we can first trace the stirring of these doubts. About AD 1452 the *Loṅkā* sect, the first of the non-idolatrous Jaina sects, arose, and was followed by the *Dhuṇḍhīā* or *Sthānakavāsi* about AD 1653, dates which coincide strikingly with the Lutheran and Puritan movements in Europe."[1]

Little more need we say about this division in the Jaina community. Speaking further on the various other splits in the Jaina church, suffice it to say that the Digambaras are divided into four principal sects,[2] the Śvetāmbaras into no less than eighty-four, and "at least eleven sub-sects amongst the Sthānakavāsi Jainas."[3] None of these is said to be dated earlier than the tenth century AD, and, except the Sthānakavāsī Jainas, most of them have practically died out, though some of them really exist, but hardly with any open bitterness or class-hatred amongst themselves as it is between the Digambara and Śvetāmbara sects of the Jainas.

It may be remarked here that a peculiarity of the Jaina church from the very days of Mahāvīra, and even earlier, is its mania for divisions. Whether it is also the case with the other religious communities in India or not we cannot say, but this much seems certain, that it is not to such an extent as it is with the Jainas. All the differences that have appeared in the life of the Jaina community during these more than two thousand years have generally originated from the following sources: there are some which have originated because of certain disagreement or misunderstanding about the very teachings of Mahāvīra; others because of certain peculiarities or characteristics (arising from the country or the class of people to which they originally belonged) of the people who were baptized to Jainism, and finally the remaining, who came into existence

---

1. Stevenson (Mrs), op. cit., p. 19.
2. दिगम्बराः पुनर्नाग्न्यलिङ्गाः पाणिपात्राश्च ।
   ते चतुर्धा, काष्ठासंघ-मूलसंघ-माथुरसंघ-गोप्यसंघभेदात् ।
   — Premi, op. cit., p. 44.
3. Cf. Stevenson (Mrs), op. cit., p. 13.

because of the Jaina clergy as a result of the peculiar fancy or idiosyncrasy of the particular *ācārya* or the head of a group of Jaina *sādhus*.[1]

With all these schisms and divisions in the Jaina church "it is remarkable that Jainism is still a living sect, whereas the Buddhists have disappeared from India."[2] This may sound strange at first sight, but to quote Mr Elliot, "Its strength and persistence are centred in its power of enlisting the interest of the laity and of forming them into a corporation.[3] But among the Buddhists the members of the order came to be regarded more and more as the true church and the laity tended to become (what they actually have become in China and Japan) pious persons who revere that order as something extraneous to themselves and very often only as one among several religious organisations. Hence when in India monasteries decayed, or were destroyed, active Buddhism was very little left outside them. But the wandering ascetics of the Jainas never concentrated the strength of the religion in themselves to the same extent; the severity of their rule limited their numbers; the laity were wealthy and practically formed a caste; persecution acted as a tonic. As a result we have a sect analogous in some ways to the Jews, Parsis and Quakers, among all of whom we find the same features — namely, a wealthy laity, little or no sacerdotalism and endurance of persecution."[4]

---

1. Just to illustrate all these we may take for the first the seven schisms and the Digambara-Śvetāmbara division in the Jaina church to which we have already referred; for the second we may mention the *Osvāl* and the *Śrīmāla* sects of the Jainas, of which the latter is called so "after the town of Śrimāla or Bhillamāla, the modern Bhimāl in the extreme south of Marvad" (*E.I.*, II., p. 41); and finally for the third we may refer to the 84 *gaccha*s or divisions of the Śvetāmbara Jainas, of which *tapa*, *kharatara* and *añcala* may be particularly mentioned here. Of these, *kharatara gaccha* is said to have originated under the following circumstances : "Jinadatta was a proud man, and even in his pert answers to others, mentioned by Sumatigaṇi, pride can be clearly detached. He was therefore called Kharatara by the people, but he gloried in the new appellation and willingly accepted it." — Hiralal (H.), op. cit., pt. II., pp. 19-20.
2. Elliot, op. cit., p. 122.
3. "Dr Hoernle is no doubt right in maintaining that this good organization of the Jaina lay community must have been a factor of the greatest importance to the church during the whole of its existence, and may have been one of the main reasons why the Jaina religion continued to keep its position in India, whilst its far more important rival, Buddhism, was entirely swept away by the Brahman reaction." — Charpentier, *C.H.I.*, I., pp. 168-69.
4. Elliot, op. cit., p. 122. The Buddhists had a similar organization of monks and laymen, but, as Smith has pointed out, they relied more on the *saṁgha* of ordained friars than on the laity. — Cf. Smith, *Oxford History of India*, p. 52. Among the Jainas the relations between the two sections were more balanced, and hence their social equilibrium was stable. Cf. Stevenson (Mrs), op. cit., p. 67 ; Macdonell, *India's Past*, p. 70.

The same feeling is entertained by other scholars also,[1] but besides this there are other reasons which cannot be overlooked when we are thinking of everything that contributed to the survival of Jainism to this day. If the fact of their having kept open the doors of the synod of their church to lay representatives contributed to the stability of Jainism, it may be said, side by side, that its adopting a less active missionary career than Buddhism, and preferring as its chief centres of worship more secluded sites, did more so.[2] This enabled the Jainas to resist more successfully the stress of the brāhmanical revival and Mohammedan persecution, under which Buddhism in India collapsed.[3] "The toleration extended to them by the brāhmaṇas, even though they were regarded as heretics, led large numbers of Buddhists to take refuge in their community in the days of the persecution."[4] Thus they were able to hold on till the period of the Mohammedan domination, "which, while it evidently contributed to the religious, political and social dismemberment of the nation, everywhere showed itself conservative of minorities, small associations, and small churches."[5]

According to Drs Charpentier and Jacobi what most enabled Jainism to weather the storms that in India wrecked so many of the other faiths was their more or less rigid fidelity or their everyday anxiety to stick to the doctrines that had come down to them since the days of Mahāvīra. "The

---

1. "Dr Hoernle's discussion of this subject in his Presidential address of 1898 before the Asiatic Society of Bengal was singularly luminous, emphasising as it did the place accorded from the very first to the lay adherent as an integral part of the Jaina organisation. In the Buddhist order, on the other hand, the lay element received no formal recognition whatsoever. Lacking thus any "bond with the broad strata of the secular life of the people," Buddhism, under the fierce assault on its monastic settlements made by the Moslems of the twelfth and thirteenth centuries, proved incompetent to maintain itself and simply disappeared from the land." — Stevenson (Mrs), op. cit., Int., p. xii. Cf. also Charpentier, op. cit., pp. 168-69; Hoernle, *Proceedings of the Asiatic Society of Bengal*, 1898, p. 53.
2. ". . . Jainism, less enterprising but more speculative than Buddhism, and lacking the active missionary spirit that in early times dominated the latter, has been content to spend a quiet life within comparatively narrow borders, and can show today in western and southern India not only prosperous monastic establishments but also lay communities, small perhaps, yet wealthy and influential." — Stevenson (Mrs), op. cit., Int., p. xii. "Never rising to an overpowering height but at the same time never sharing the fate of its rival Buddhism, that of complete extinction in its native land." — Charpentier, op. cit., pp. 169-70.
3. Cf. Crooke, *E.R.E.*, II., p. 496.
4. Tiele, op. cit., p. 141.
5. Barth, op. cit., p. 152.

inflexible conservatism of the small Jaina community in holding fast to its original institutions and doctrine has probably been the chief cause of its survival during periods of severe affliction; for, as Professor Jacobi has pointed out long ago, there can be little doubt that the most important doctrines of the Jaina religion have remained practically unaltered since the first great separation in the time of Bhadrabāhu, about 300 BC. And although a number of less vital rules concerning the life and practices of the monks and laymen, which we find recorded in the holy scriptures, may have fallen into oblivion or disuse, there is no reason to doubt that the religious life of the Jaina community is now substantially the same as it was two thousand years ago. It must be confessed from this that an absolute refusal to admit changes has been the strongest safeguard of the Jainas."[1]

It is doubtful if this conservative nature can any more help the Jaina community as it stands now. To a student of present-day contemporary religions it would seem otherwise. In conservatism he would see signs of intoleration, stagnation and religious hypocrisy. From dedicatory inscriptions and other records Sir Charles Elliot may conclude: "We learn from these records that the sect comprised a great number of schools and divisions. We need not suppose that the different teachers were necessarily hostile to one another, but their existence testifies to an activity and freedom of interpretation which have left traces in the multitude of modern sub-sects."[2] But one thing is certain, that these different teachers have, in trying to grind their own axes, disregarded the general good of the whole Jaina community.

Colonel Tod has rightly, remarked: "Tapa-Gaccha and Kharatara-Gaccha did much more harm than the Islamites to destroy all records of the past."[3] Well, the same thing may be said of the Digambara and the Śvetāmbara divisions of the Jainas. Their attitude towards each other, both in the past and as it is now, does in no way do any justice to the followers of Lord Mahāvīra. One need not be misunderstood if one were to express one's fears that if this aggressive attitude and mutual distrust amongst the existing divisions in the Jaina community were to go on at this rate a time may come when the Jainas may have to share the same fate as that of their brothers, the Buddhists.

---

1. Charpentier, op. cit., p. 169. Cf. Jacobi, Z.D.M.G., XXXVIII., pp. 17 ff.
2. Elliot, op. cit., p. 113.
3. Tod, *Travels in Western India*, p. 284.

CHAPTER III

Jainism in Royal Families
800-200 BC

I

IN our previous chapters we saw all that could be said about the Jaina church. That Pārśva could be historically identified and that Mahāvīra had blood-relations with some royal families of his time are facts that count much when we are out to investigate the circumstances under which "Jainism became the state religion of certain kingdoms, in the sense that it was adopted and encouraged by certain kings, who carried with them many of their subjects."[1]

This is nothing but ascribing the history of the Jainas of north India with all its legitimate historical background of that part of the country. In other words, the aim of this chapter is to draw, as far as possible, an exact picture of the Jainas of north India in their relations with the ruling dynasties of their times.

Taking first the times of Pārśva, we find that there is hardly any material available on which we can rely. Very "scanty is our knowledge of the life and teaching of Pārśva, in spite of the large body of literature which has clustered around his name."[2] As seen before, all that we know of any historical importance in connection with him is that he was born of King Aśvasena of Benares, who belonged to the Ikṣvāku race of the kṣatriyas,[3] and that he reached his final liberation, *nirvāṇa*, on the top of Mount Summeta in Bengal. In his marital relations he was connected with the royal family of King

---

1. Smith, op. cit., p. 55.
2. Charpentier, op. cit., p. 154.
3. . . . अनुगंगं नगर्यस्ति वाराणस्यभिधानतः ॥
तस्यामिक्ष्वाकुवंशोऽभूदश्वसेनो महीपतिः ।
— Hemacandra, *Triṣaṣṭi-Śalākā*, *Parva* IX, vv. 8, 14, p. 196.

Prasenajit, whose father, Naravarman, who designated himself as the lord of the universe and who had in his lifetime become a Jaina *sādhu*, was ruling at Kuśasthala, and whose daughter Prabhāvatī was married to Pārśva.[1]

It is difficult to say as to how far these facts can be taken as historically true. The trouble is that for all this we have got to wholly rely on whatever data the Jainas put before us, because there is no other historical monument or record which can be taken into consideration for the purposes of this history. But the same difficulty arises with the whole of Indian history of the days prior to Alexander the Great, and sometimes even later than that. Fortunately, as already remarked, looking to the great historical worth and the literary value attributed to the Jaina canonical and other literature of the centuries before the Christian era by some of the eminent scholars and historians of our day, it will not be too much to say that with the Buddhist and Hindu annals Jaina annals too have their place, and a due consideration should be extended to them also.

In the words of Dr Jacobi, "The origin and development of the Jaina sect is a subject on which some scholars still think it safe to speak with a sceptical caution, though this seems little warranted by the present state of the whole question; for a large and ancient literature has been made accessible, and furnishes ample materials for the early history of the sect to all who are willing to collect them. Nor is the nature of these materials such as to make us distrust them. We know that the sacred books of the Jainas are old, avowedly older than the Sanskrit literature which we are accustomed to call classical. Regarding their antiquity, many of those books can vie with the oldest books of the northern Buddhists. As the latter books have successively been used as materials for the history of Buddha and Buddhism, we can find no reason why we should distrust the sacred books of the Jainas as an authentic source of their history. If they were full of contradictory statements, or the dates contained in them would lead to contradictory conclusions, we should be justified in viewing all theories based on such materials with suspicion. But the character of the Jaina

---

1. पुरं कुशस्थलं नाम . . . ॥ तत्रासीन्नरवर्मेति . . . । . . . पृथिवीपतिः ॥ जैनधर्मे रतो नित्यं . . . । उपादत्त परिव्रज्यां सुसाधुगुरुसन्निधौ ॥ . . . राज्येऽभून्नरवर्मणः । सूनुः प्रसेनजिन्नाम . . . ॥ तस्य प्रभावती नाम . . . । . . . कन्यका ॥ . . . पार्श्वो . . . । . . . उदुवाह प्रभावतीम ॥ — Hemacandra, *Triṣaṣṭi-Śalākā*, *Parva* IX, vv. 58, 59, 61, 62, 68, 69, 210, pp. 198, 203.

literature differs little in this respect also from the Buddhist, at least from that of the northern Buddhists."[1]

Thus with the material that is at our disposal it is very difficult to historically identify the Aśvasena of Benares or Kāśī,[2] and the Prasenajit or his father Naravarman of Kuśasthala, but there are other historical and geographical coincidences from which we can deduce certain inferences which may be said to have some historical significance behind them.

Now, on the authority of Hemacandra's *Hemakośa,* Nundo Lal Dey has identified Kuśasthala with Kanauj or Kānyakubja,[3] and this is supported by other scholars also.[4] Furthermore, Dr Raychaudhuri tells us as to how the Pañcālas were connected "with the foundation of the famous city of Kānyakubja or Kanauj."[5] Again this fact of there existing side by side the kingdoms of Kāśī and Pañcāla is further supported by both the Buddhist and the Jaina literary traditions. From the Buddhist *Aṅguttara Nikāya* and the Jaina *Bhagavatī-Sūtra* we know that during this period (i.e. during the eighth century BC) "there were sixteen states of considerable extent and power known as the Soḷasa Mahājanapada."[6] Of these Kāśī, among others, is common to both, while Pañcāla is mentioned only by the former.[7]

Taking the history of Pañcāla we find that it roughly corresponds to Rohilkhaṇḍ and a part of the central Doāb. "The *Mahābhārata*, the *Jātakas* and the *Divyāvadāna* refer to the division of this state into northern and southern. The Bhāgirathī (Ganges) formed the dividing line. According to the Great

1. Jacobi, S.B.E., XXII., Int., p. ix. "We must leave to future researchers to work out the details, but I hope to have removed the doubts, entertained by some scholars, about the independence of the Jaina religion and the value of its sacred books as trustworthy documents for the elucidation of its early history." — Ibid., Int., p. xlvii. Cf. Charpentier, *Uttarādhyayana-Sūtra*, Int., p. 25.
2. "No such person as Aśvasena is known from Brahman record to have existed ; the only individual of that name mentioned in the epic literature was a king of the snakes (*Nāga*), and he cannot in any way be connected with the father of the Jaina prophet." — Charpentier, *C.H.I.*, I., p. 154. It may, by the way, be mentioned here that all his life Pārśvanātha was connected with snakes, and to this day the saint's symbol is a hooded serpent's head. Cf. Stevenson (Mrs), op. cit., pp. 48-49.
3. Dey, op. cit., pp. 88, 111.
4. "Kanyākubja was also called Gādhipura, Mahodaya and Kuśasthala." — Cunningham, *Ancient Geography of India* (ed. Mazumdar), p. 707.
5. Raychaudhuri, *Political History of Ancient India*, p. 86. "Kanauj . . . was primarily the capital of the kingdom of Pañcāla." — Smith, *Early History of India*, p. 391.
6. Raychaudhuri, op. cit., pp. 59, 60. Cf. Rhys Davids, *C.H.I.*, I., p. 172.
7. Raychaudhuri, op. cit., p. 60.

Epic, northern Pañcāla had its capital at Ahicchatra or Chatravatī (the modern Rāmnagar near Aonlā in the Bareilly District), while Southern Pañcāla had its capital at Kāmpilya, and stretched from the Ganges to the Chambal."[1]

Along with this background of the Pañcāla history we have direct references to it in the Jaina annals as well. The *Uttarādhyayana-Sūtra* mentions a great Pañcāla king named Brahmadatta, who was born of Culaṇī in Kāmpilya.[2] He meets Citta, his brother in a former birth, and who has become a śramaṇa in this. Brahmadatta is styled a universal monarch, and he is so fond of worldly pleasure that he does not care for the advice of his brother Citta and finally goes to hell.[3]

A further reference in this direction by the same *sūtra* is also to a king of Kāmpilya named Sañjaya, who "gave up his kingly power and adopted the faith of the Jinas in the presence of the venerable monk Gardabhāli."[4]

Thus it seems probable that Kāśī and Pañcāla, the two of the "sixteen states of considerable extent and power,"[5] were joined together on matrimonial grounds, and the probability becomes more of a certainty when we know from the dynastic lists prepared by Pargiter that there was some Senajit who was one of the rulers of Southern Pañcāla.[6] Doing away with

---

1. Raychaudhuri, op. cit., p. 85. Cf. also Smith, op. cit., pp. 391-92 ; Dey, op. cit., p. 145.
2. "Little is known about the history of Kāmpilya, apparently the modern Kampil in the Farrukabad District." — Smith, op. cit., p. 392.
3. चुलणीए बम्भदत्तो . . . ॥ कम्पिल्ले सम्भूओ चित्तो . . . । . . . धम्मं सोऊण पव्वइओ ॥ पंचालराया वि य बम्भदत्तो . . . तस्स वयणं अकाउं। . . . सो नरए पविट्ठो ॥ — *Uttarādhyayana-Sūtra*, Lecture XIII, vv. 1, 2, 34. Cf. Jacobi, S.B.E., XLV., pp. 57-61. The stories about Kitra (Citta) and Sambhuta (Brahmadatta) and the fate they underwent in many births are common to Brahmans, Jainas and Buddhists. Cf. ibid., pp. 56, 57 ; Raychaudhuri, op. cit., p. 86 ; Charpentier, *Uttarādhyayana*, pt. II., pp. 328-31.
4. कम्पिल्ले नयरे राया . . . ।
   नामेणं संजये . . . ॥
   संजओ चइउं रज्जं निक्खन्तो जिणसासणे।
   गद्दभालिस्स भगवओ अणगारस्स अन्तिए॥
   — *Uttarādhyayana-Sūtra*, Lecture XVIII, vv. 1, 19. Cf. Jacobi, op. cit., pp. 80, 82 ; Raychaudhuri, op. and loc. cit.
5. "The Jainas also afford testimony to the greatness of Kāśī, and represent Aśvasena, king of Benares, as the father of that Tīrthaṅkara Pārśva who is said to have died 250 years before Mahāvīra — i.e. in 777 BC" — Ibid., op. cit., p. 61. Taking 480-467 BC as the date of Mahāvīra's *nirvāṇa* we get 730-717 as the date of Pārśva's *nirvāṇa*.
6. Cf. Pargiter, *Ancient Indian Historical Tradition*, p. 146 ; Pradhan, *Chronology of Ancient India*, p. 103.

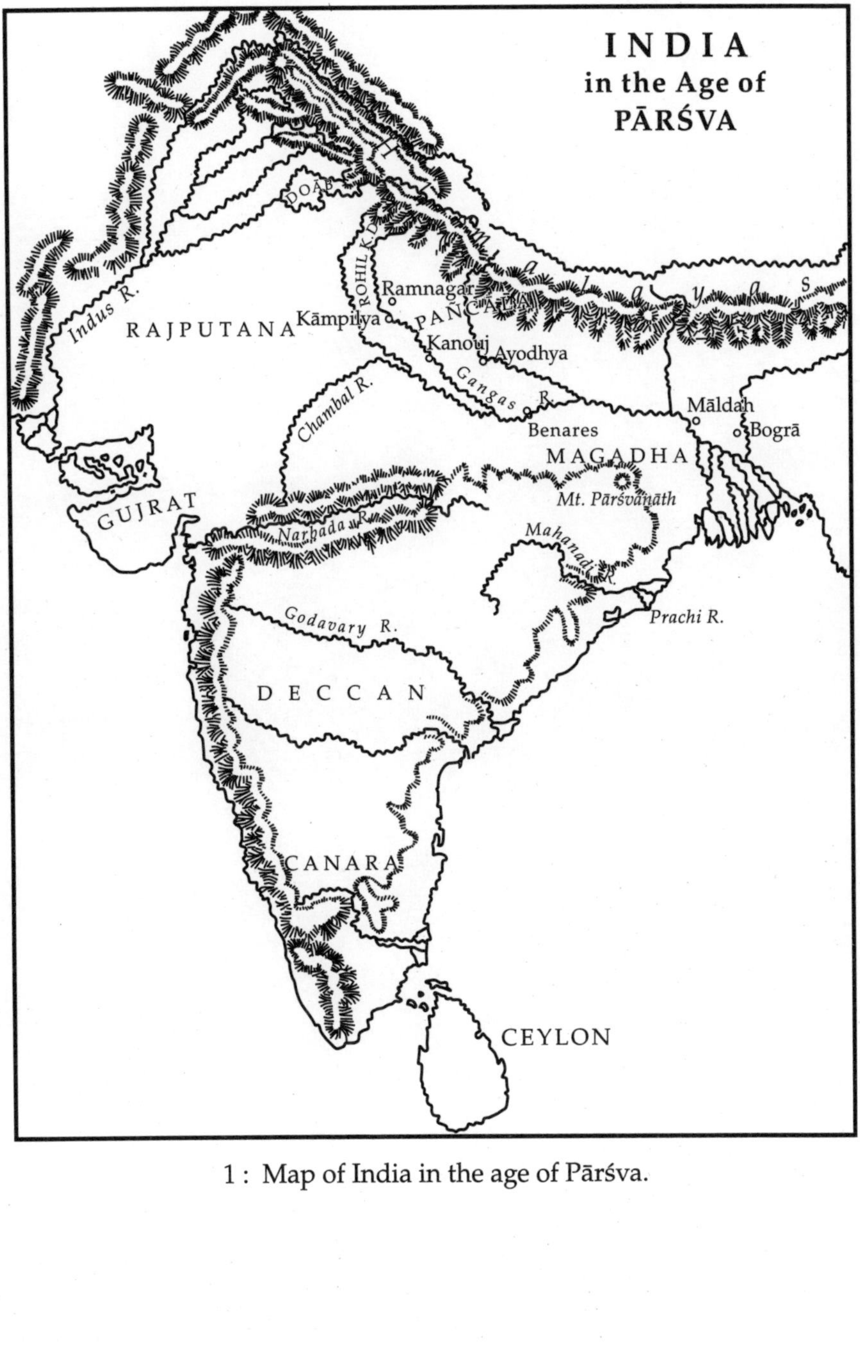

1 : Map of India in the age of Pārśva.

some superficial variations in names, this Senajit can with no historical fallacy be identified with Prasenajit, with whom we are here concerned.[1]

The most important and the only inference that we may draw from this is that Jainism in the days of Pārśva enjoyed no less royal patronage than in the days of Mahāvīra. The extent of his influence was in no way less extensive than during the career of his successor. He was a member of the royal family of Kāśī, son-in-law to that of Pañcāla,[2] and he died on the top of Mount Pārśvanātha in Bengal.[3] With this royal backing behind him it is natural that he must have had great influence on contemporary royalties and on his own subjects also. From *Sūtrakṛtāṅga* and other Jaina canonical books we know that even in the days of Mahāvīra there were followers of Pārśva round about Magadha.[4] As seen before, the very family of Mahāvīra was attached to the religion of Pārśva. In addition to this the reference made in the Jaina canonical books to the actual following of Pārśva in his own days confirms the fact that the Jaina community had spread well even in those early days throughout a great portion of north India, though it is not possible to put down any geographical limits.[5] As already mentioned,

1. "In other cases the first component is omitted . . . . Bhāgavata calls Prasenajit of Ayodhya Senajit." — Pargiter, op. cit., p. 127.
2. Mazumdar seems to be labouring under some confusion here. According to him Pārśva was a son-in-law of King Prasenajit of Oudh, and thus he connects the two dynasties of Kosala and Kāsī ; but we think he has wrongly identified him with the Prasenajit of the days of Mahāvīra, who was the father-in-law of King Bimbisāra, the great Śaisunāga, and one of the greatest royal supporters of Jainism. Furthermore he commits the same blunder when he says that Pārśva died at the age of seventy-two. We have already seen it was Mahāvīra who lived for seventy-two years, while Pārśva lived for one hundred. Cf. Mazumdar, op. cit., pp. 495, 551, 552 ; Mrs Stevenson also seems to be under the same misconception when she says, "Pārśvanātha . . . married Prabhāvatī, daughter of Prasannajita, king of Ayodhya." — Stevenson (Mrs), op. cit., p. 48.
3. ". . . he reached deliverance at last on Mount Sameta Śikhara in Bengal, which was thenceforth known as the Mount Pārśvanātha." — Ibid., p. 49.
4. "Outside of Rājagṛha, in a north-eastern direction, there was the suburb Nālandā, . . . and there in some house the venerable Gautama was staying. The venerable (man) was in the garden, and so was Udaka, the son of Pedhāla, a *Nirgrantha* and follower of Pārśva . . . ." — Jacobi, op. cit., pp. 419-20 ; जिणे पासि . . . तस्स . . . केसीकुमारसमणे . . . सावत्थिं पुरमागए . . . — *Uttarādhyayana-Sūtra*, Lecture XXIII, vv. 1-3. Cf. Jacobi, op. cit., pp. 119-20.
5. One does not know on what grounds Mazumdar tries to define geographically the limits of Jainism in the days of Pārśva. "His Jainism," observes the learned scholar, "prevailed from Bengal to Gujarat. The districts of Māldah and Bogrā were great centres of his faith. His converts were mostly from the depressed classes of the Hindus and Non-Āryans . . . . In Rajputana his adherents grew very powerful. . . ." — Mazumdar, op. and loc. cit.

there were 16,000 monks, 38,000 nuns, 164,000 lay-votaries, 327,000 female lay-votaries and a few thousands more belonging to the higher grade of religious qualification.[1]

From Pārśva to Mahāvīra there are no data of any historical worth. A period of two hundred and fifty years in Jaina history has to remain blank because of the absence of any historical records or monuments on which we can rely for purposes of history. Anyhow this much is certain, that though it is not possible at present historically to fill up the gap between the last two prophets of the Jainas, it may safely be said that throughout this period Jainism was a living religion.[2] As already seen, all along the Jaina clergy of Pārśva's school of thought were exerting their own influence, and Mahāvīra and some of his followers had regularly to face some representatives of that class just to win them over to the reformed church of the sixth century BC.

Coming to the days of Mahāvīra one seems to feel as if a better situation has to be met with, but here also, barring the canonical literature of the Jainas and the Buddhas and certain other traditions, there is hardly anything on which we can fall back upon.[3] Fortunately for us, the Jaina sacred books have preserved facts and comments which, though in bits and fragments, are yet sufficient to hold up before our eyes a living picture of this period of the Jaina history. Like Pārśva, Mahāvīra also had his blood-relations with the ruling dynasties of his age. His father, Siddhārtha, was a great nobleman himself, and he belonged to the clan of the *jñātṛ* kṣatriyas. His headquarters were at Kuṇḍapura or Kuṇḍagāma (Kuṇḍagrāma),[4] and from the way in

1. Cf. Jacobi, S.B.E., XXII., p. 274.
एवं विहरतो भर्तुः सहस्राः षोडशर्षयः।
अष्टात्रिंशत्सहस्राणि साध्वनो तु महात्मनाम्॥
. . . श्रावकाणां लक्षमेकं चतुःषष्टिसहस्रयुक्॥
श्राविकाणां तु त्रिलक्षी सहस्राः सप्तविंशतिः। . . .
— Hemacandra, op. cit., vv. 312, 314, 315, p. 219. Cf. *Kalpa-Sūtra, Subodhikā-Ṭīkā, sūt.* 161-64, pp. 130-31.

2. Cf. Hoernle, *Uvāsaga-Dasāo*, II., p. 6, n. 8.

3. "Early Indian history as yet resembles those maps of our grandfathers in which
Geographers for lack of towns
Drew elephants on pathless downs.
. . . though the Jainas have kept historical records of their own, it is very difficult to correlate these records with known facts in the world's history." — Stevenson (Mrs), op. cit., p. 7.

4. "It is another name for Vaiśālī (modern Besārh) in the district of Mozaffarpur (Tirhut); in fact Kuṇḍagāma (Kuṇḍagrāma), now called Basukuṇḍ, was a part of the ancient town of Vaiśālī, the latter comprising three districts or quarters : Vaiśālī proper (Besarh), Kuṇḍapur (Basukuṇḍ), and Vāniagāma (Bania)." — Dey, op. cit., p. 107.

which he is pictured in the Jaina sacred books it seems he was the head of the clan to which he belonged, and a ruler of some state, whether great or small.[1] As we shall see later on, it may be that he was one of the executive of the republic of which Kuṇḍapura was a leading division, but from the status that he enjoyed in society this much is certain, that Siddhārtha spent his life more or less as an independent ruler than as a mere petty chieftain under a sovereign state.[2]

Again referring to the sixteen *mahājanapada*s we find that the state of Vajji is also common to both the Buddhist and the Jaina lists. "The Vajjis," observes Dr Raychaudhuri, "according to Professor Rhys Davids and Cunningham, included eight confederate clans (*Aṭṭhakula*), of whom the Videhans, the Licchavis, the Jñātṛkas and the Vajjis proper were the most important. The identity of the remaining clans remains uncertain. It may, however, be noted here that in a passage of the *Sūtrakṛtāṅga* the Ugras, Bhogas, Aikshavākas and Kauravas are associated with the Jñātṛs and Licchavis as subjects of the same rulers and the members of the same assembly."[3]

On the other hand, on the authority of the Buddhist sources Dr. Pradhan adds one more member to this confederacy, and observes: "This confederacy consisted of nine clans, some of which were the Licchivis (or Licchavis), the Vṛjis (or Vajjis), the Jñātṛkas, and the Videhas. This confederacy of nine clans was known as the confederacy of the Vṛjis or of the Licchivis, as the Vṛjis and the Licchivis were the most important of the nine clans. These nine Licchivi

---

1. In the *Kalpa-Sūtra* the interpreters of the dreams of Triśalā, mother of Mahāvīra, are said to have come "to the front gate of Siddhārtha's excellent palace, a jewel of its kind." — Jacobi, op. cit., p. 245. At another place in the same *Sūtra* Siddhārtha is said to have celebrated the birthday of Mahāvīra by ordering his police authorities quickly to set free all prisoners in the town of Kuṇḍapura, to increase measures and weights, and so on. Cf. ibid., p. 252 ; Hemacandra, op. cit., *Parva* X, vv. 128, 132, p. 16.
2. Barnett, the *Antagaḍa-Dasāo* and *Aṇuttarovavāiya-Dasāo*, Int., p. vi. Dr Jacobi, in trying to expose the fond belief of the Jainas that "Kuṇḍagrāma was a large town and Siddhārtha a powerful monarch," seems to have gone to the other extreme when he observes : "From all this it appears that Siddhārtha was no king, nor even the head of his clan, but in all probability only exercised the degree of authority which in the East usually falls to the share of landowners, especially of those belonging to the recognised aristocracy of the country." — Jacobi, op. cit., Int., p. xii.
3. Raychaudhuri, op. cit., pp. 73-74. "The Ugras and Bhogas were Kṣatriyas. The former were, according to the Jainas, descendants of those whom Ṛshabha, the first Tīrthaṅkara, appointed to the office of Kotwals, or prefects of towns, while the Bhogas were descendants of those who Ṛshabha acknowledged as persons deserving honour." — Jacobi, S.B.E., XLV., p. 71, n. 2. Cf. Hoernle, op. cit., Appendix III, p. 58.

clans again federated themselves with the nine Mallaki clans and the eighteen Gaṇarājās of Kāsī-Kosala."[1] This statement of the learned scholar is also supported by the Jaina annals.[2]

"It is related," observes Dr. Jacobi, "that King Cetaka, whom Kūṇika, king of Campā, prepared to attack with a strong army, called together the eighteen confederate kings of Kāsī and Kosala, the Licchavis and Mallakis, and asked them whether they would satisfy Kūṇika's demands or go to war with him. Again on the death of Mahāvīra the eighteen confederate kings, mentioned above, instituted a festival to be held in memory of that event."[3]

From all this it seems highly probable that of all these confederate clans one common characteristic was that most of them had directly or indirectly come under the influence of Mahāvīra or his teaching. Whether all of them were Jainas by faith or not one cannot say, but this much is certain, that there was something more solid than mere lip-sympathy on their part.

Taking first the Videhans, we find that they "had their capital at Mithilā, which is identified by some scholars with the small town of Janakpur, just within the Nepal border. But a section of them may have settled in Vaiśālī. To this section probably belonged the princess Triśalā, also called Videhadattā, mother of Mahāvīra."[4] As already mentioned, we find scattered here and there direct references to Mahāvīra's relations with the Videhans in the Jaina *Sūtras*. Says the *Ācārāṅga-Sūtra*: "His (Mahāvīra's) mother had three names : Triśalā, Videhadattā and Prīyakāriṇi."[5]

"In that period, in that age, the venerable ascetic Mahāvīra, a Jñātṛ Kṣatriya, Jñātṛputra, a native of Videha, a prince of Videha, lived thirty years under the name of "Videha.""[6]

Coming next to the Kalpa-Sūtra: "The venerable ascetic Mahāvīra . . .; a Jñātṛ Kṣatriya, the son of a Jñātṛ Kṣatriya; the moon of the clan of the Jñātṛs;

1. Pradhan, op. cit., p. 215.
2. नव मल्लइ नव लेच्छइ कासीकोसलगा अट्ठारसवि गणरायाणो. . . . — *Bhagavatī, sūt*. 300, p. 316. Cf. Hemacandra, op. cit., p. 165.
3. Jacobi, S.B.E., XXII., Int., p. xii. Cf. ibid., p. 266 ; Law (B.C.), *Some Kṣatriya Tribes of Ancient India*, p. 11 ; Raychaudhuri, op. cit., p. 128 ; *Bhagavatī, sūt*. 300, p. 316 ; Hemacandra, op. and loc. cit. ; *Kalpa-Sūtra, Subhodhikā-Ṭīkā, sūt*. 128, p. 121 ; Pradhan, op. cit., pp. 128-29 ; Hoernle, op. cit., II., Appendix II., pp. 59-60.
4. Raychaudhuri, op. cit., p. 74 ; समणस्स णं भगवओ महावीरस्स माया . . . तिसला इ वा विदेहदिन्ना इ वा पीइकारिणी इ वा . . . — *Kalpa-Sūtra, Subodhikā-Ṭīkā, sūt*. 109, p. 89.
5. Jacobi, op. cit., p. 193.
6. Ibid., p. 194.

a Videha, the son of Videhadattā, a native of Videha, a prince of Videha — had lived thirty years in Videha when his parents went to the gods (i.e. died)."[1]

Thus from the Jaina *sūtras* themselves the following points are confirmed: that a section of the Videhans had settled in Vaiśālī, "the capital of Videha"[2]; that Princess Triśalā belonged to this section of the Videhans, and that Mahāvīra was closely connected with them. With all this the first point still needs some more elucidation. As Mahāvīra was a Videhan, even so according to Jacobi he was also a Vaisālika — i.e. a native of Vaiśālī. Thus Kuṇḍapura or Kuṇḍagrāma of King Siddhārtha cannot but be a prominent part of Vaiśālī, the capital of the reigning line of Videha.[3]

In addition to all these references confirming the close relationship that existed between Mahāvīra and the Videhans there are certain other indications in the sacered books of the Jainas which go to assert that the Videhans had a living interest in the Jaina church. Talking about Nami, the royal seer, the *Uttarādhyayana-Sūtra* says :

नमी नमेइ अप्पाणं सक्खं सक्केण चोइओ।
चइऊण गेहं च वेदेहि सामण्णे पज्जुवट्ठिओ॥

"Nami humbled himself; enjoined by Sakra in person, the king of Videha left the house, and took upon him Śramaṇahood."[4]

Besides this from the *Kalpa-Sūtra* we know that at Mithilā, the metropolis of Videha, Mahāvīra spent six rainy-seasons. This shows how far Mahāvīra was connected with the Videhans. In short, from what we have seen about them one thing is clear — that if not all, there was at least a section amongst the Videhans who were real Jainas.

Coming next to the Licchavis we find that they were a great and powerful people in eastern India in the sixth century before Christ. There is no use denying the fact that with the Jñātṛkas they must have come directly under

1. Jacobi, op. cit., p. 256.
2. Ibid., Int., p. xi.
3. "Kuṇḍagrāma, therefore, was probably one of the suburbs of Vaiśālī, the capital of Videha. This conjecture is borne out by the name Vesalie — i.e. Vaisālika — given to Mahāvīra in the *Sūtrakṛtāṅga,* 1, 3. The commentator explains the passage in question in two different ways, and at another place a third explanation is given. . . . Vaisālika apparently means a native of Vaiśālī : and Mahāvīra could be rightly called that when Kuṇḍagrāma was suburb of Vaiśālī, just as a native of Turnham Green may be called a Londoner." — Ibid.
4. *Uttarādhyayana-Sūtra,* Lecture IX, v. 61. Cf. ibid., v. 62 ; Lecture XVIII, v. 45 (trans Jacobi, S.B.E., XLV., pp. 41, 87). For a full description of the legendary tale of Nami see Meyer (J.J.), *Hindu Tales,* pp. 147-69.

the influence of the teaching of Mahāvīra. His mother Triśalā was sister to Ceṭaka, king of Vaiśālī,[1] who belonged to the Licchavi sect of the kṣatriyas, while on his father's side Mahāvīra was a Jñātṛka himself.

Here arises the difficulty that if Triśalā was the Licchavi princess there is no reason why she should be called Videhadattā.[2] The possible explanation that can be given for this is that she was so called because she belonged to that part of the country which was originally known as Videha, and, as we have just remarked, Vaiśālī was the capital of Videha. Furthermore, in the words of Dr. Raychaudhuri, "the Vajjian confederation must have been organised after the fall of the royal houses of Videha. Political evolution in India thus resembles closely the political evolution in the ancient cities of Greece, where also the monarchies of the Heroic age were succeeded by aristocratic republics."[3] Moreover, in confirmation with other traditions this leads to a further surmise — that after the fall of the Videhans a section of them might also have been called the Licchavis.[4]

Thus there is nothing unnatural or out of the way if Triśalā was called Videhadattā though she was a Licchavi princess. Now this Triśalā was married to Siddhārtha, who, according to the Jainas, was a follower of Pārśva, the predecessor of Lord Mahāvīra. This naturally leads one to infer that either the royal family of the Licchavis was Jaina by faith or that it was socially so situated that it could take a member of the other Jaina royal family as a bridegroom for its princess. This incident alone warrants the conclusion that the Licchavis had a distinct sympathy and respect for the Jainas, but the literary and the historical traditions of the Jainas do not stop with this solitary incident alone. We further know that Cellaṇā (also called Vedehi), the youngest of the seven daughters of King Ceṭaka,[5] was married to Bimbisāra, the great Śaiśunāga of Magadha, and that both Bimbisāra and Cellaṇā were great Jainas themselves.[6]

---

1. Jacobi, *Kalpa-Sūtra,* p. 113.
2. "In the opinion of several scholars Ceṭaka was a Licchavi. But the secondary names of his sister (Videhadattā) and daughter (Vedehi) probably indicate that he was a Videhan domiciled at Vesāli." — Raychaudhuri, op. cit., p. 78, n. 2.
3. Ibid., p. 76.
4. "In the time of Buddha, and for many centuries afterwards, the people of Vaiśālī were called Licchavis ; and in the *Trikaṇḍaśesha* the names of Licchavi, Videhi, and Tirabhukti have been given as synonymous." — Cunningham op. cit., p. 509.
5. वेसालिओ चेडओ . . . सत्त धूयाओ . . . — *Āyaśyaka-Sūtra*, p. 676.
6. "Bimbisāra had a son known as Vedehi-Putto Ajātśattū in the canonical Pāli texts, and as Kūṇika by the Jainas. The later Buddhist tradition makes him a son of the Kosala →

Besides Cellaṇā, Ceṭaka had six other daughters, out of whom one preferred to be a nun and the other five were married in one or the other royal family of eastern India. How far this fact can be taken as an historical truth we cannot say, but hardly with any exception almost all those ruling dynasties with whom the Licchavis were thus connected can be fully identified in the light of modern research. The names of these Licchavi princesses are Prabhāvatī, Padmāvatī, Mṛgāvatī, Śivā, Jyeṣṭhā, Sujyeṣṭhā and Cellaṇā.[1]

Of these, Prabhāvatī, the eldest, was married to King Udāyana of Vītabhaya, which has been identified at various places in the Jaina literature with a town of Sindhu-Sauvīra-Deśa.[2] But to what part of the country these literary evidences allude we cannot exactly say, because on the basis of various sources it has been identified with different places in the west and north-west of India. Cunningham identifies it with "the province of Badari or Eder, at the head of the Gulf of Cambay."[3] Dr Rhys Davids more or less agrees with Cunningham, and places Sauvīra in his map to the north of Kāṭhiāwār and along the Gulf of Cutch.[4] Alberuni identifies it with Multan and Jahrāvār, and this is also accepted by Mr. Dey.[5]

On the other hand the Jaina traditions are as follows :

Abhayadevasūri, in his commentary on the *Bhagavatī*, puts his interpretation in the following words: सिन्धुनद्या आसन्नाः सौवीरा-जनपदविशेषाः सिन्धुसौवीरास्तेषु . . . विगता ईतयो भयानि च यतस्तद्वीतिभयं विदर्भेति केचित्.[6]

The story of Udāyana translated by Meyer from the *Uttarādhyayana-Sūtra*

→ Devī ; the Jaina tradition, confirmed by the standing epithet of Vedehi-Putto, son of the princess of Videha, in the older Buddhist books makes him a son of Cellaṇā." — Rhys Davids, *C.H.I.*, I., p. 183.
देव्या चेल्लणया सार्धमपराह्णेऽन्यदा नृपः।
वीरं समवसरणस्थितं वन्दितुमभ्यगात्॥
वन्दित्वा श्रीमदर्हन्तं वलितौ तौ च दंपती।
— Hemacandra, op. cit., vv. 11-12, p. 86.

1. *Āvaśyaka-Sūtra*, p. 676 ; Hemacandra, op. cit., v. 187, p. 77.
2. सिंधुसोवीरेसु . . . वीतीभए नगरे . . . उदायणे नामं राया . . . तस्स . . . पभावती नामं देवी. — *Bhagavatī, sūt.* 491, p. 618. Cf. also *Āvaśyaka-Sūtra*, p. 676 ; Hemacandra, op. cit., v. 190, p. 77 ; सिन्धुसौवीर- देशेऽस्ति पुरं वीतभयाह्वयम्।. — Ibid., v. 327, p. 147 ; Meyer (J.J.), op. cit., p. 97.
3. Cunningham, op. cit., p. 569.
4. Rhys Davids, *Buddhist India*, map facing p. 320.
5. Sachau, *Alberuni's India*, I., p. 302. Cf. Dey, op. cit., p. 183.
6. *Bhagavatī, sūt.* 492, pp. 320-21.

mentions Vītabhaya as follows: "There was in a city in the countries of Sindhu and Sovīra, called Vīyabhaya, a king, Udāyana by name . . . ."[1]

"The *Śatruñjaya Māhātmya* places it in Sindhu or Sind."[2]

From all these identifications it seems that the country roughly corresponds to a portion of Sind on the east of the river Indus and of Rājpūtānā to the north-west of Mālwā. This is also confirmed by the fact that Udāyana went through the deserts of Marwar and Rājpūtānā, where his army began to die of thirst during the war which he had declared against the king of Avantī.[3]

Besides these identifications one thing we get about Sindhu-Sauvīra-Deśa from Varāhamihira's division of *Bhāratavarṣa* is this, that it formed one of the nine divisions into which the country was divided.[4] The historical and geographical importance accruing from this justifies the Jaina sources to some extent when they say that, along with Vītabhaya, Udāyana was the overlord of three hundred and sixty-three other towns.[5] Furthermore, from the life of Kumārapāla of the twelfth century AD we know that during his career he brought to Pattana[6] a Jaina idol[7] which, according to Hemacandra, had been lying underground at

1. Meyer (J.J.), op. cit., p. 97. For the story in the *Uttarādhyayana* see Laxmi-Vallabha's commentary (Dhanapatasiṁha's edition), pp. 552-61.
2. Cf. Dey, op. cit., p. 183.
3. उत्तरतां च मरूं स्कन्धावारस्तृषा मर्तुमारब्धः *Āvaśyaka-Sūtra*, p. 299. Cf. Meyer (J. J.), op. cit., p. 109. It may be mentioned here that, according to the Buddhist traditions, Roruka was the capital of Sauvīra. Cf. *C.H.I.*, I., p. 173 ; Dey, op. cit., p. 170. According to Cunningham, Roruka was "probably Alor, the old city of Sind." — Cunningham, op. cit., p. 700.
4. Varāhamihira calls each of the *nava-khaṇḍa*s a *varga*. He says : "By them (the *Vargas*) *Bḥāratavarsha* — i.e. half of the world — is divided into nine parts : the central one, the eastern one, etc." — Sachau, op. cit., p. 297. Cf. ibid., pp. 298-302 ; Cunningham, op. cit., p. 6. "According to this arrangement . . . Sindhu-Sauvīra was the chief district of the west . . . ; but there is a discrepancy between this epitome of Varāha and his details, as Sindhu-Sauvīra is there assigned to the south-west along with Ānarta." — Ibid., p. 7.
5. वीतभयादिनगरात्रिषष्टित्रिशतीप्रभुः — Hemacandra, op. cit., v. 328, p. 147. "This King Udāyana lived exercising the sovereignty over sixteen countries, beginning with Sindhu-Sauvīra, three hundred and sixty-three cities, beginning with Vītabhaya. . . ." — Meyer (J.J.), op. cit., p. 97.
6. "Aṇahila-Pattana, Virāwal-Pattana or Paṭṭaṇa, called also Northern Baroda in Gujarat, founded in Saṁvat 802 or AD 746, after the destruction of Valabhī by Banarāja or Vaṁśarāja. The town was called Aṇahilapattana, after the name of a cowherd who pointed out the site. . . . Hemacandra, the celebrated Jaina grammarian and lexicographer, flourished in the court of Kumārapāla, the king of Aṇahilapattana (AD 1142-73), and was his spiritual guide. He died at the age of eighty-four in AD 1172, in which year Kumārapāla became a convert to Jainism . . . but according to other authorities, the conversion took place in AD 1159. After the overthrow of Vallabhī in the eighth century Aṇahilapattana became the chief city of Gujarat, or western India, till the fifteenth century. . . ." — Dey, op. cit., p. 6.
7. Jayasiṁhasūri, *Kumārapāla-Bhūpāla-Caritra-Mahākāvya, Sarga* IX, vv. 261, 265, 266.

VIII : Guru Hemacandra and his royal disciple Kumārapāla.

Vītabhaya since the days of Udāyana.[1]

This much about Sindhu-Sauvīra-Deśa and its metropolis Vītabhaya. About its ruler, Udāyana, there are not many data wherefrom to infer historically. In the words of Dr Raychaudhuri "it is difficult to disentangle the kernel of historical truth from the husk of popular fables"[2]; but it must be admitted that there are a few facts about Udāyana which can be gleaned from the Jaina annals and which deserve some notice, howsoever little, on the part of historians. According to these annals Udāyana of Sauvīra-Deśa in an open fight defeated his dependent Canda Pradyota of Avantī,[3] who is an historical person, and about whom we shall see in detail in his relation as husband to Śivā, the fourth daughter of Ceṭaka. Besides this we know that Udāyana was succeeded by his nephew Keśī, in whose reign Vītabhaya went to wreck and ruin.[4] One cannot say if this is all a mere fiction or this is itself the reason why we have no traces of the history of this great part of the country, though we know on good authority that at one time it formed one of the "nine-*varga*s" of *Bhāratavarṣa*.

About Udāyana's and his wife Prabhāvatī's attitude towards the religion of the *jina*s we have ample proof, direct and otherwise, in the canonical literature of the Jainas, on which we can base our own inferences. At one place Prabhāvatī, the Licchavi princess, having performed the worship of a Jaina image, says : "The Arhat, Who is free from love, hatred and delusion, who knows everything, who is endowed with the eight miraculous powers, who wears the form of the supreme god of gods, may he grant me a sight of himself."[5]

This shows with what respect the queen of Sauvīra looked at the Jaina

1. उदायने शिवगते . . . । तदेव प्रतिमा . . . । भविष्यति . . . भूगता ॥ राज्ञः कुमारपालस्य . . . पुण्येन . . . । खन्यमानस्थले मंक्षु प्रतिमाविर्भविष्यति ॥ — Hemacandra, op. cit., vv. 20, 22, 83, pp. 158. 160.
2. Raychaudhuri, op. cit., p. 123. This war between the two, according to the legend, had taken place because Pradyota had run away with a servant girl and an image of *jina* which belonged to Udāyana. "Thereupon he sent a messenger to Pajjoya : "I care nothing for the servant girl. Send me the image." He did not give it. . . . Udāyana hurriedly took the field together with the ten kings (his vassals). . . . When Pajjoya descended he was bound (captured by Udāyana)." — Meyer (J.J.), op. cit., pp. 109-10. Cf. *Āvaśyaka-Sūtra,* p. 299.
3. उदायनो राजा . . . गत उज्जयिनीं . . . प्रद्योतो . . . बद्धो — Ibid., pp. 298-99. Cf. Hemacandra, op. cit., v. 578, p. 156.
4. तए णं से केसीकुमारे राया जाए . . . — *Bhagavatī-Sūtra, sūt.* 491, p. 619. "When he (Udāyana) died, a deity let a shower of dust fall. . . . Even to this day it lies buried." — Meyer (J.J.), op. cit., pp. 115-16.
5. Ibid., p. 105.

faith.[1] Moreover, from the *Uttarādhyayana* and other canonical literature we know that the king too was no less a believer in the religion of the *jina*,[2] though originally he was "devoted to Brahmanic ascetics."[3] He even went to the extent of renouncing the world,[4] and when the question of the succession of his son Abhii came before him he says to himself : "If I renounce the world after appointing Prince Abhii to royal power, then Abhii will become infatuated with royal power and royal dominion *down to* the country and with the enjoyment of human pleasures and will stray to and fro in the beginningless, endless tanglewood of the *Saṁsāra*. Therefore it is evidently better that I renounce the world after appointing my sister's son, Prince Kesi, to royal power."[5]

Thus the entire change in the heart of Udāyana is evident from this incident. This has made his renunciation proverbial with the Jainas. We find in the *Antagaḍa-Dasāo* a passage referring to Udāyana — viz. "Then King Alakkhe . . . withdrew from the world in the same way as King Udāyaṇe, save that he anointed his eldest son to *rule* over his kingdom."[6] It may be said here that in a note to this Dr Barnett has wrongly taken this passage to refer to Udāyana, "king of Kosambī and son of Sayāṇīe (Śatānīka) by Migāvaī, daughter of Ceḍaga, king of Vaiśāli."[7]

Furthermore, the treatment offered by Udāyana to the Avantī Pradyota, whom he had taken as a captive during the war, is illustrative of the fact that he strictly adhered to the "precept that during the *Paryushaṇāparvan* even the most deadly enmity should be given up."[8] It so happened that on the occasion of the *Paryuṣaṇāparvan*, although Udāyana himself observed a

1. प्रभावत्या . . . अन्तःपुरे चैत्यगृहं कारितं, . . . भक्तप्रत्याख्यानेन मृता देवलोकं गता. — *Āvaśyaka-Sūtra*, p. 298. Cf. Meyer (J.J.), op. and loc. cit. ; Hemacandra, op. cit., v. 404, p. 150.
2. "Udāyana, the bull of kings of Sauvīra, renounced the world and turned monk; he entered the order and reached perfection." — Jacobi, S.B.E., XLV., p. 87. In a note to this Jacobi writes : "He was contemporary with Mahāvīra." — Ibid.
3. Meyer (J.J.), op. cit., p. 103. स च तापसभक्तः — *Āvaśyaka-Sūtra*, p. 298 ; Hemacandra, op. cit., v. 388, p. 149.
4. तए णं से उदायणे राया . . . समणस्स भगवओ जाव पव्वइए. — *Bhagavatī, sūt.* 492, p. 620 ; Meyer (J. J.), op. cit., p. 114.
5. Ibid., pp. 113-14. एवं खलु अभीयीकुमारे . . . कामभोगेसु मुच्छिए . . . भाइणेज्जं केसिं कुमारं रज्जे ठावेत्ता . . . — *Bhagavatī, sūt.* 491, p. 619.
6. Barnett, op. cit., p. 96.
7. Ibid., p. 96, n. 2.
8. Bhandarkar, *Report for 1883-1884*, p. 142 ; *Pajjusaṇa* or *Paryuṣaṇa*, the sacred festival at the close of the Jaina year. Cf. Stevenson (Mrs), op. cit., p. 76 ; पज्जोसवियाणं . . . खमियव्वं खमावियव्वं . . . *Kalpa-Sūtra, Subodhikā-Ṭīkā, sūt.* 59, pp. 191-92.

fast he, notwithstanding, gave orders that Canda Pradyota be served with anything he liked. However the latter, from fear of being poisoned, did not wish to eat the food that was brought him, and said that he too had a fast to observe, being, as he was, of the same religion as Udāyana. This was reported to the king, and as a real Jaina he replied : "I know that he is a rogue, but while he is a captive my *Pajjusana* even does not become pure and auspicious."[1]

Coming next to Padmāvatī we find that she was married to King Dadhivāhana of Campā,[2] once a great centre of Jainism.[3] Haribhadra, in his commentary on the *Āvaśyaka-Sūtra*, clearly states that both the king and queen were great adherents of the Jaina church. Considering the historical importance that Campā enjoys in the Jaina annals there is nothing strange if one assumes on the authority of the Jaina literature that the family of Dadhivāhana had a living interest in the Jaina doctrines.[4]

"Jaina tradition places him in the beginning of the sixth century BC. His daughter Candanā or Candrabālā was the first female who embraced Jainism shortly after Mahāvīra had attained the Kevaliship."[5] Jaina narrative and other literature are full of references to this first female disciple of Mahāvīra. It was she who headed all the female lay and other worshippers of Vardhamāna in his own days.[6] The political significance connected with her life is that when "Śatānīka, king of Kauśāmbi, attacked Campā, the capital of Dadhivāhana, Candanā fell into the hands of a robber, but all along she maintained the vows of the order."[7] This statement of Dr Raychaudhuri is based on the Jaina

1. Cf. Bhandarkar, op. and loc. cit.; Meyer (J.J.), op. cit., p. 110-11 ; *Kalpa-Sūtra, Subodhikā-Ṭīkā, sūt.* 59, p. 192. अद्य पर्युषणा, राजोपोषितः, स भणति-अहमप्युपोषितः, ममापि मातापितरौ संयतौ, etc. — *Āvaśyaka-Sūtra*, p. 300.
2. दत्ता पद्मावती चम्पायां दधिवाहनाय — Ibid., pp. 676, 677. Cf. Meyer (J.J.), op. cit., p. 122.
3. Cf. Dey, op. cit., p. 44 ; Dey *J.A.S.B.* (New Series), X., 1914, p. 334.
4. Haribhadra tells us that, leaving the kingdom to their son Karakaṇḍū, both the king and the queen joined the order ; पद्मावती देवी . . . दन्तपुरे आर्याणां मूले प्रव्रजिता, . . . द्वे अपि राज्ये दधिवाहनस्तस्मै दत्त्वा प्रव्रजितः, करकण्डूर्महाशासनो जातः . . . — *Āvaśyaka-Sūtra*, pp. 716, 717, 718. It is further said that Karakaṇḍū also, like his father, finally joined the order. Cf. ibid., p. 719. For further reference about Karakaṇḍū and his parents see Meyer (J.J.), op. cit., pp. 122-36; Sāntyācārya, *Uttarādhyayana-Śiṣyahitā*, pp. 300-03; Laxmi-Vallabha, *Uttarādhyayana-Dīpikā*, pp. 254-59.
5. Raychaudhuri, op. cit., p. 69. Cf. Dey, op. cit., p. 321.
6. समणस्स भगवओ महावीरस्स अज्जचंदणापामुक्खाओ छत्तीसं अज्जियासाहस्सीओ . . . हुत्था — *Kalpa-Sūtra, Subodhikā-Ṭīkā, sūt.* 133, p. 123. Cf. Dey, op. and loc. cit.
7. Raychaudhuri, op. cit., p. 69. Cf. ibid., p. 84. "Campā was occupied and destroyed by Śatānīka II, the king of Kauśāmbī, a few years before Bimbisāra's annexation." — Pradhan, op. cit., p. 214.

sources, and the whole story of Candanā in short runs as follows: During the war between her father and King Śatānīka she was caught hold of by one of the enemy's army and was sold in Kauśāmbī to a banker named Dhanāvaha, who named her Candanā in spite of her already bearing the name Vasumatī as her family name. After a short time the banker's wife, Mūlā, felt jealous of her, and having cut her hair put her into custody. In this condition she once served a part of her food to Mahāvīra, and finally joined his ranks as a nun.[1]

Before we pass on to Mṛgāvatī, the third daughter of Ceṭaka, a few words about Campā in the light of Jaina history will not be out of place. The town of Campā seems to have been situated at a distance of a few miles in the neighbourhood of modern Bhāgalpur, and is known to us under some such names as Campāpurī, Campānagar, Mālinī and Campā-Mālinī.[2] Its importance in Jaina history is self-evident when we know that Mahāvīra spent three of his rainy-seasons in Campā, the capital of Aṅga, and its suburbs (Pṛṣṭha Campā), and that it is known to us as the place of both the birth and death of Vāsupūjya, the twelfth *tīrthaṅkara*. Again, as the headquarters of Candanā and her father it is remembered by the Jainas as a great centre of their religion. There are signs of old and new Jaina temples of both the Digambara and Śvetāmbara sects built for Vāsupūjya and other *tīrthaṅkaras* as the chief *jinas*.[3] The *Uvāsaga-Dasāo* and the *Antagaḍa-Dasāo* mention that the temple called Caitya Puṇṇabhadda existed at Campā at the time of Sudharman, one of the eleven disciples of Mahāvīra who succeeded as the head of the Jaina sect on his death.[4] "The town was visited by Sudharman, the head of the Jaina hierarchy, at the time of Kūṇika or Ajātaśatru, who came barefooted to see the Gaṇadhara outside the city where he had taken up his abode. Sudharman's

1. Cf. *Kalpa-Sūtra, Subodhikā-Ṭīkā, sūt.* 118, pp. 106-07 Cf. *Āvaśyaka-Sūtra*, pp. 223-25 ; Hemacandra, op. cit., pp. 59-62. For further references about Candanā see Barnett, op. cit., pp. 98-100, 102, 106.
2. Cf. Dey, *The Geographical Dictionary of Ancient and Mediaeval India*, p. 44 ; Cunningham, op. cit., pp. 546-47, 722-23. Now represented by the village of Campāpur on the Ganges, near Bhāgalpur; anciently it was the capital of the country of Aṅga, corresponding to the modern district of Bhāgalpur.
3. Dey, op. cit., pp. 44-45. "From the inscriptions on some Jaina images exhumed from the neighbourhood of an old Jaina temple at Ajmer it appears that these images, which were of Bāsupūjya, Mallinātha, Pārśvanātha and Vardhamāna, were dedicated in the thirteenth century AD — i.e. ranging from Saṁvat 1239-1247." — Ibid., p. 45. Cf. *J.A.S.B.*, VII., p. 52.
4. Hoernle, op. cit., II., p. 2, notes. "Verily, Jambū, in those days . . . there was a city named Campā . . . a sanctuary Punnabhadde. . . ." — Barnett, op. cit., pp. 97-98, 100. Cf. Dey, op. and loc. cit.

successor Jambū and Jambū's successor Prabhava also visited Campā, and Prabhava's successor, Sayambhava, lived at this city, where he composed the *Daśavaikālika-Sūtra*, containing in ten lectures all the essence of the sacred doctrines of Jainism."[1]

"After the death of Bimbisāra, Kūṇika or Ajātaśatru made Campā his capital, but after his death his son Udāyin transferred the seat of Government to Pāṭalīputra.[2] From the *Campaka-Śreshṭhi-Kathā*, a Jaina work, it appears that the town was in a very flourishing condition. In the opening lines the castes and the trades of the town are enumerated. There were perfumers, spice-sellers, sugar-candy sellers, jewellers, leather-tanners, garland-makers, carpenters, goldsmiths, weavers, washermen," etc.[3]

Coming to Mṛgāvatī, the third daughter of Ceṭaka, we find that she was married to King Śatānīka[4] of Kauśāmbī,[5] and was known also as the princess of Videha.[6] "Vinayavijayagaṇin, in his *Subodhikā* commentary to the *Kalpa-Sūtra*, draws from old Jaina sources, and says that when Mahāvīra visited the town of Kauśāmbi the king of that place was Śatānīka and the queen was Mṛgāvatī."[7] That both the king and the queen were devotees of Mahāvīra can be well established from the Jaina literature itself. Looking to the family atmosphere in which she was brought up it is natural that Mṛgāvatī could not be anything else than a Jaina.[8] Furthermore, the Jaina tradition tells us in particular that the king's *amātya* (minister) and his wife also were Jainas by faith.[9]

1. Dey, op. and loc. cit. अन्यदा श्रीगणधरः सुधर्मा . . . । जगाम चम्पां . . . ॥ तदा . . . कूणिकः . . . । त्यक्तपादुको . . . । सुधर्मस्वामिनं दृष्ट्वा दूरादपि नमोऽकरोत् ॥ — Hemacandra, *Pariśiṣṭaparvan*, Canto IV, vv. 1, 9, 33, 35.
2. Ibid., Canto VI, vv. 21 ff.
3. Dey, op. and loc. cit.
4. Śatānīka himself was styled also Parantapa. Cf. Rhys Davids, op. cit., p. 3.
5. "Kauśāmbi, Kauśāmbi-nagar or Kośam, an old village on the left bank of the Jamuna, about 30 miles to the west of Allahabad." — Dey, op. cit., p. 96.
6. "Śatānīka . . . married a princess of Videha, as his son is called Vaidehīputra." — Raychaudhuri, op. cit., p. 84. Cf. Law (B.C.), op. cit., p. 136.
7. Pradhan, op. cit., p. 257. ततः क्रमेण कौशाम्ब्यां गतस्तत्र शतानीको राजा मृगावती देवी. — *Kalpa-Sūtra, Subodhikā-Ṭīkā, sūt*, 118, p. 106.
8. Mahāvīra had been to Kauśāmbī during the years of his wanderings before he was endowed with *Kevala-Jñāna*. It so happened that during his stay there Lord Mahāvīra, owing to some vow that he had taken, did not accept any food for some days, and hence मृगावत्यपि . . . महता दुःखेनाभिभूता . . . तेन (राज्ञा) आश्वासिता-तथा करिष्यामि यथा कल्पे लभते . . . — *Āvaśyaka-Sūtra*, p. 223. Cf. Stevenson (Mrs), op. cit., p. 40.
9. सुगुप्तोऽमात्यो, नन्दा तस्य भार्या, सा च श्रमणोपासिका, सा च श्राद्धीति मृगावत्या वयस्या, . . . अमात्योऽपि सपत्निक आगतः स्वामिनं वन्दते, . . . — *Āvaśyaka-Sūtra*, pp. 222, 225. Cf. *Kalpa-Sūtra, Subodhikā-Ṭīkā, sūt*. 118, p. 106.

About Śatānīka's fight with Dadhivāhana we have already referred. The other fact of historical importance that we can get from the Jaina literature is this, that "his son and successor was the famous Udāyana, the contemporary of Bimbisāra."[1] "Again, the grandfather of Udāyana," observes Dr Pradhan, "is named Sahasrāṇīka by Bhāsa, and Vasudāman by the Purāṇas. Sahasrāṇīka was a contemporary of Bimbisāra and received religious instructions from Mahāvīra. The Jainas call him Sasānīka, which is evidently a softening of 'Sahasānīka,' the Prākr̥t equivalent of the Sanskrit from "Sahasrāṇīka." Sasānīka was probably the same as the Purāṇic Vasudāman and had his son Śatānīka II. Udāyaṇa was the son of Śatānīka II."[2]

In this the learned doctor is fully authorised by the *Bhagavatī-Sūtra*, the fifth *aṅga* of the Jainas.[3] We know further that Śatānīka's sister Jayantī was a staunch follower of Mahāvīra.[4] About Udāyana we shall speak at length a little later along with his father-in-law, Canda Pradyota, and his successors, but at present we need say this much only that by the Jainas he is claimed to have been a Jaina, and that "he was a great king who really made some conquests, and contracted matrimonial alliances with the royal houses of Avantī, Aṅga and Magadha."[5]

Taking Śivā, the fourth daughter of Ceṭaka, we find that she was married to Canda Pradyota of Ujjainī,[6] the capital of Avantī or ancient Mālwā.[7] He is known to us as Canda Pradyota Mahāsena — fierce Pradyota, the possessor of a great army,[8] and as the father-in-law of Udāyana of Kauśāmbī, the capital of the country of Vaṁsa or Vatśa.[9] "The king of Avantī in the Buddha's

1. Raychaudhuri, op. and loc. cit. Cf. Barnett, op. cit., p. 96, n. 2.
2. Pradhan, op. and loc. cit. "The *Kathā-Sarit-Sāgara* says that Śatānīka's son Sahasrāṇīka was the father of Udāyana. Thus the *Kathā-Sarit-Sāgara* reverses the order certainly wrongly." — Ibid. Cf. Tawney (ed. Penzer), *Kathā-Sarit-Sāgara*, I., pp. 95-96 ; Raychaudhuri, op. and loc. cit.
3. सहस्साणीयस्स रन्नो पोत्ते सयाणीयस्स रन्नो पुत्ते चेडगस्स रन्नो नत्तुए मिगावतीए देवीए अत्तए जयंतीए समणोवासियाए भत्तिज्जए उदायणे नामं राया होत्था, etc. — *Bhagavatī, sūt*. 441, p. 556.
4. तए णं जयंती समणोवासिया . . . पव्वइया जाव सव्वदुक्खप्पहगणा। . . . — Ibid,. *sūt*. 443, p. 558.
5. Pradhan, op. cit., p. 123.
6. Cf. *Āvaśyaka-Sūtra*, p. 677.
7. Cf. Dey, op. cit., p. 209.
8. Cf. Pardhan, op. cit., p. 230.
9. Cf. Raychaudhuri, op. cit., p. 83. "Kośāmbi-Nagar or Kośam . . . was the capital of Vaṁsadeśa or Vatsyadeśa, the kingdom of Udāyana. . . ." — Dey, op. cit., p. 96. Cf. ibid., p. 28.

time," observes Dr Rhys Davids, "was Pajjota the Fierce, who reigned at the capital Ujjeni. There is a legend about him which shows that he and his neighbour, King Udena of Kośāmbi, were believed to have been contemporary, connected by marriage, and engaged in war."[1] This "legend" is fully corroborated by Jaina sources. We know from these sources that the Vatsa king, Udāyana, was married to Vāsavadattā,[2] the daughter of Pradyota of Avantī.[3] Furthermore, to state in brief, Hemacandra tells us that Canda Pradyota had asked Queen Mṛgāvatī from Śatānīka, and on the refusal of the latter he had declared a war against him. It so happened that in the meantime Śatānīka died, and when Mahāvīra came down to Kauśāmbī Canda Pradyota was induced to give up his feeling of revenge and to allow Mṛgāvatī to become a nun, with a promise to make Udāyana the king of Kauśāmbī.[4]

This Udāyana, "the king of Vatsa, is the central figure in a large cycle of Sanskrit stories of love and adventure; and in these Pradyota, the king of Ujjain, the father of the peerless Vāsavadattā, plays no small part."[5] As just remarked, he is said to have contracted matrimonial alliances with the royal houses of Avantī, Aṅga and Magadha. From different sources, whether fully reliable or not, we know that Vāsuladattā or Vāsavadattā, the daughter of Pradyota, king of Avantī; Padmāvatī, the sister of Darśaka, the king of Magadha, and the daughter of Dṛḍhavarman, the king of Aṅga, were his queens.[6] Of these Vāsavadattā was the chief queen of Udāyana. Both Buddhist and Jaina literature "give a long and romantic story of the way in which Vāsuladattā, the daughter of Pajjota of Avantī, became the wife, or rather one of the three wives, of King Udena of Kośāmbi."[7] As to his attitude towards

1. Rhys Davids, *C.H.I.*, I., p. 185.
2. Cf. *Āvaśyaka-Sūtra*, p. 674 ; Hemacandra, *Triṣaṣṭi-Śalākā, Parva* X, pp. 142-45.
3. "Avantī roughly corresponds to modern Mālwā, Nimār and the adjoining parts of the central provinces. Prof. Bhandarkar points out that this *janapada* was divided into two parts : the northern part had its capital at Ujjain, and the southern part, called Avantī Dakshināpatha, had its capital at Mahāssatī or Māhiśmatī, usually identified with the modern Māndhāta on the Narmada." — Raychaudhuri, op. cit., p. 92.
4. Cf. Hemacandra, op. cit., v. 232, p. 107.
5. Rapson, *C.H.I.*, I., p. 311. Cf. Raychaudhuri, op. cit., p. 122 ; Pargiter, *Ancient Indian Historical Tradition*, p. 285.
6. Cf. Raychaudhuri, op. and loc. cit. ; Pradhan, op. cit., pp. 212, 246. "Tradition has preserved a long story of adventures of Udena and his three wives." — Rhys Davids, op. cit., p. 187.
7. Cf. Rhys Davids, *Buddhist India*, p. 4 ; *Āvaśyaka-Sūtra*, p. 674 ; Hemacandra, op. cit., pp. 142-45.

religion Udāyana had before him his mother, and also relatives like Bimbisāra, Cellaṇā and others, who were more or less the leading figures of the Jaina community of those days, and this naturally created in him respect and sympathy for the Jaina church.[1]

About the Avantī-Pradyota and his Queen Śivā's sentiments for the Jaina church Hemacandra tells us that he had his distinct sympathies for the Jaina faith, and that it was with his permission that his eight queens, Aṅgāravatī and others, along with Mṛgāvatī of Kauśāmbī, joined the order.[2] In his connection with Udāyana of Sauvīra we have already seen that Pradyota himself had declared that he also was traditionally a Jaina himself. No doubt the fierce and unscrupulous character of the lord of Avantī is known both to the Bauddhas and the Jainas,[3] but in this particular incident one cannot see for what earthly reason he should have falsely represented himself to be a Jaina. If he had his own suspicion he could as well have refused the food on some other ground than this. Whether a fact or a fiction, one thing is certain — that the moral of this particular incident is to show something else than the evil nature of this or that king. The leading idea is that though a great enemy of Pradyota as Udāyana was, he did not like to see a captive before him, whether a Jaina or not, during the days of his religious festival.[4]

Thus out of the seven daughters of Ceṭaka, Prabhāvatī, Padmāvatī, Mṛgāvatī, Śivā and Cellaṇā were married respectively to the lords of Sauvīra, Aṅga, Vatsa (Vaṁsa), Avantī and Magadha. Of these the last four are included both in the Buddhist and the Jaina lists of the sixteen *mahājanapadas*,[5] while nothing more can be said about the Sauvīra-Deśa. Of the remaining two daughters of Ceṭaka, Jyeṣṭhā was married to Nandivardhana, brother of Lord Mahāvīra and ruler of Kuṇḍagrāma,[6] while Sujyeṣṭhā joined the order of

---

1. सामी समोसड्ढे . . . । तए णं से उदायणे राया . . . पज्जुवासए। etc. — *Bhagavatī, sūt*. 442, p. 556.
2. सहागृह्णन्मृगावत्या प्रव्रज्यां स्वामिसन्निधौ।
   अष्टावंगारवत्याद्याः प्रद्योतनृपतेः प्रियाः॥
   — Hemacandra, op. cit., v. 233, p. 107.
3. Cf. Rhys Davids, op. and loc. cit. ; . . . सो धुत्तो . . . — *Āvaśyaka-Sūtra*, p. 300 ; Bhandarkar, op. and loc. cit. ; . . . धूर्त्तसाधर्मकि . . . — *Kalpa-Sūtra, Subodhikā-Ṭīkā, sūt*. 59, p. 192.
4. Cf. *Āvaśyaka-Sūtra*, p. 300 ; Meyer (J.J.), op. cit., pp. 110-11 ; *Kalpa-Sūtra, Subodhikā-Ṭīkā, sūt*. 59, p. 192.
5. Cf. Raychaudhuri, op. cit., pp. 59-60.
6. Cf. *Āvaśyaka-Sūtra*, p. 677 ; Hemacandra, op. cit., v. 192, p. 77.

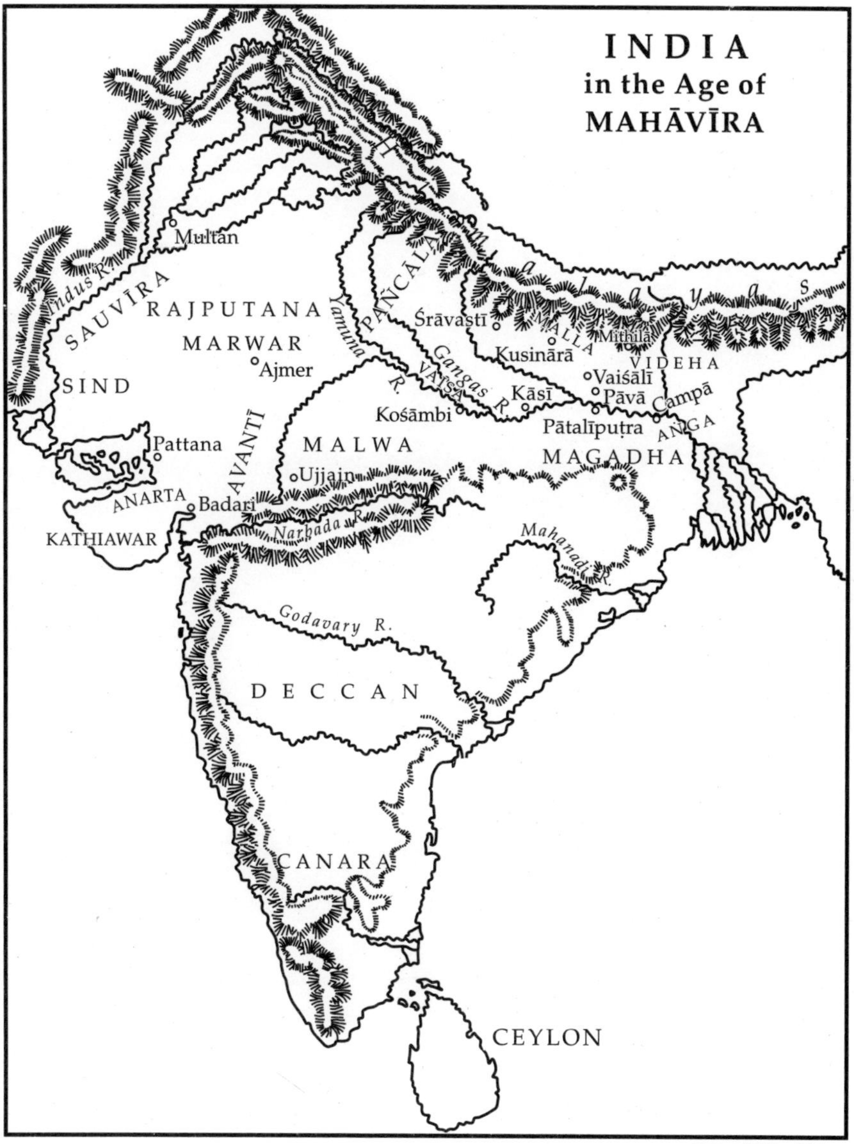

4.(b): Map of India in the age of Mahāvīra.

Mahāvīra's disciples.[1] All these facts combined go a long way to show how far Vardhamāna's influence reached through his mother Triśalā, the Licchavi princess. It is clear from this that at the time Mahāvīra lived and preached, the Licchavis were recognized as kṣatriyas, who held their heads very high on account of their high birth and with whom the highest born princes of eastern India considered it an honour to enter into matrimonial alliance.

In short, it was through the Licchavis, and thereby through the ruling dynasty of Vaiśālī, that the reformed church of Mahāvīra got a solid support from all directions in its early days.[2] It was through them that the religion of Mahāvīra had spread over Sauvīra, Aṅga, Vatsa, Avantī, Videha and Magadha, all of which were the most powerful kingdoms of the time. This is why the Buddhist works do not mention Ceṭaka, the king of Vaiśālī, though they tell us about the constitutional government of Veśālī.[3] To quote Dr Jacobi, "Buddhists took no notice of him, as his influence . . . was used in the interest of their rivals. But the Jainas cherished the memory of the maternal uncle and patron of their prophet, to whose influence we must attribute the fact that Vaiśālī used to be a stronghold of Jainism, while being looked upon by the Buddhists as a seminary of heresies and dissent."[4]

In addition to these there are other stray references to the Licchavis in the Jaina *sūtra*s which more or less confirm the fact that they were nothing short of Jainas themselves. Taking first the *Sūtrakṛtāṅga* we find that they were highly respected by the Jainas. According to it, "A Brāhmaṇa or Kshattriya by birth, a scion of the Ugra race or a Licchavi, who enters the order eating alms given by others is not stuck up on account of his renowned *Gotra*."[5]

Citing next the *Kalpa-Sūtra*: "In that night in which the Venerable Ascetic Mahāvīra died, ... freed from all pains, the eighteen confederate kings of Kāsī and Kosala, the nine Mallakis and nine Licchavis, on the day of new moon, instituted an illumination[6] on the . . . fasting day; for they said: "Since

1. Cf. *Āvaśyaka-Sūtra*, p. 685 ; Hemacandra, op. cit., v. 266, p. 80.
2. Cf. Dey, *Notes on Ancient Aṅga*, p. 322 ; Bühler, *Indian Sect of the Jainas*, p. 27.
3. Cf. Jacobi, S.B.E., XXII., Int., p. xii. See Turnour, *J.A.S.B.*, VII., p. 992.
4. Jacobi, op. cit., Int., p. xiii.
5. Jacobi, S.B.E., XLV., p. 321.
6. "The Jainas celebrate the *Nirvāṇa* of Mahāvīra with an illumination on the night of new moon in the month Kārttika." — Ibid., XXII., p. 266.

the light of intelligence is gone, let us make an illumination of material matter!" "[1]

Besides these two quotations from the Jaina *sūtras* there is something about a king, Jiyasattū, in the *Uvāsaga-Dasāo* which, if taken in the light of the interpretation of Dr Hoernle, is of the utmost importance when we are examining the relations that existed between Ceṭaka, the Licchavi king, and the Jainas. In the first of the ten lectures of this seventh *aṅga* of the Jainas we find in the reply of Sudharma[2] to the question of Jambū what was the purport of it — viz.

"Truly, Jambū, at that time and at that period, there was a city called Vāṇiyagāma. . . . Outside of the city of Vāṇiyagāma, in a north-easterly direction, there was a *Ceïya* called Dūipalāsa. At that time Jiyasattū was king over the city of Vāṇiyagāma. . . . There also lived then in Vāṇiyagāma a householder called Ānanda,[3] who was prosperous and without any equals.

"At that time and at that period, the *Samaṇa*, the blessed Mahāvīra arrived on a visit, and a company of people went out to hear him. Then King Jiyasattū also went out to hear him, just as King Kūṇiya had done on another occasion, and having done so . . . he stood waiting on him."[4]

The Jiyasattū mentioned here has rightly been identified by both Drs Hoernle and Barnett[5] with Ceṭaka or Ceḍaga, the maternal uncle of Mahāvīra, because Vāṇiyagāma, the city of Jiyasattū, was, as we shall see later on, either another name of Vaiśālī or some portion of it which was so called. To quote Dr Hoernle : "In the *Sūryaprajñapati* Jiyasattū is mentioned as ruling over Mithila, the capital of the Videha country. . . . Here he is mentioned as ruling over Vāṇiyagāma or Vesāli. On the other hand Ceḍaga, the maternal uncle of Mahāvīra, is said to have been a king of Vesāli and Videha. . . . It would seem that Jiyasattū and Ceḍaga were the same persons."[6] Furthermore, the King Kūṇiya, with whom Jiyasattū is compared

1. Jacobi, S.B.E., XXII., p. 266.
2. ". . . one of the eleven disciples (*Gaṇadhara*) of Mahāvīra, who succeeded him as head of the Jaina sect, being himself succeeded by Jambū, the last of the so-called Kevlī . . ." Hoernle, op. cit., p. 2, n. 5.
3. Ānanda is known to the Jainas as a typical example of a faithful lay-adherent of Jainism. Cf. Hemacandra, *Yoga-Śāstra*, chap. III., v. 151 ; Hoernle, op. cit., pp. 7 ff.
4. Ibid., pp. 3-7, 9.
5. Barnett, op. cit., Int., p. vi. For further references to Jiyasattū in the eighth and the ninth *aṅgas* of the Jainas see ibid., pp. 62, 113.
6. Hoernle, op. cit., p. 6, n. 9.

here, is none else but Ajātaśatru, the son and successor of Bimbisāra of Magadha. The comparison is quite appropriate when we know that Kūṇiya, like his father, was a great Jaina. Whether or not this was the state of things throughout his career we shall examine later on, but this much is certain, that he had his distinct sympathies for the Jaina church[1] and must have more than once come into personal touch with Lord Mahāvīra.

We have already seen that this Kūṇiya or Kūṇika had an occasion for an open fight with his grandfather, Ceḍaga, for an elephant with which his younger brother had run away to Vaiśālī. It appears from this that by way of rivalry with Ajātasattū (Ajātaśatru) Ceḍaga was called also Jiyasattū. Once again, to cite Dr Hoernle, "the name of Jiyasattū (Skr. Jitaśatru) he may have received, as has been suggested, by way of rivalry with Ajātasattū (Skr. Ajātaśatru), king of Magadha, who at first was also a patron of Mahāvīra, though afterwards he exchanged him for Buddha. To the Jainas Ajātasattū is known under the name of Kūṇiya, and under that name he is compared with Jiyasattū here and elsewhere."[2]

From all these traditions connected with the Licchavi kṣatriyas it is highly probable that, like the Videhans, they were also Jainas themselves.[3] If this is granted, the great and powerful dynasty of the Licchavis was really a valuable source of strength to the reformed church of Mahāvīra. Their very capital formed the headquarters of the Jaina community during the days of Mahāvīra. From the Jaina literature itself we know that Mahāvīra was very closely connected with the metropolis of the Licchavis. Vaiśālī claims the last prophet of the Jainas as its own citizen. The *Sūtrakṛtāṅga* says about Mahāvīra as follows: "Thus spoke the Arhat Jñātṛputra, the reverend, famous native of Vaiśāli, who possessed the highest knowledge and the highest faith, who possessed (simultaneously) the highest knowledge and faith."[4] "This passage is also repeated in another Jaina work, the *Uttarādhyayana-Sūtra*, with a slight variation.[5] Mahāvīra is spoken of as Vesalie or Vaisālika — i.e. a native of Vaiśālī. Moreover

---

1. तए णं से कूणिए राया . . . समणं भगवं महावीरं . . . वंदति णमंसति . . . — *Aupapātika-Sūtra* 32, p. 75.
2. Hoernle, op. and loc. cit.
3. For further facts about the strength of Jainism in Vaiśālī see Law (B.C.), op. cit., pp. 72-75. Jacobi, op. cit., p. 194.
4. Jacobi, S.B.E., XLV., p. 261.
5. Cf. *Uttarādhyayana-Sūtra*, Lecture VI, v. 17 ; Jacobi, op. cit., p. 27.

Abhayadeva, in his commentary on the *Bhagavatī*, 2, I.12, 2, explains Vaisālika by Mahāvīra, and speaks of Vaiśāli as *Mahāvīrajananī* or "the mother of Mahāvīra.""[1] In addition to this we know from the *Kalpa-Sūtra* that out of the forty-two rainy-seasons which he spent as a missionary during his later ascetic life Mahāvīra did not neglect the city of his birth, but passed no less than twelve years at Vaiśālī.[2]

Furthermore, the importance of this close relation between the last *tīrthaṅkara* of the Jainas and the Licchavis is greatly enhanced when we know from different sources that Vaiśālī, the capital of the Licchavis, was under a powerful dynasty which wielded considerable influence in both the political and social circles of its time. "Vaiśālī," observes Dr Law, "'the large city' *par excellence*, is renowned in Indian history as the capital of the Licchavi Rājās and the headquarters of the great and powerful Vajjian confederacy. This great city is intimately associated with the early history of both Jainism and Buddhism; it carries with itself the sacred memories of the founders of these two great faiths that evolved in north-eastern India five hundred years before the birth of Christ."[3]

One thing still remains to be considered, and that is about the relations that existed between Vaiśālī and Kuṇḍagrāma.[4] Considering the fact that Vaiśālī was the most flourishing town in India about five hundred years before the beginning of our era, one thing is certain — that Kuṇḍagāma, as has been already remarked, must have been a division of Vaiśālī. Taking both the Buddhist and the Jaina traditions, scholars like Hoernle,[5] Rockhill[6] and others agree to the fact that Vaiśālī was divided into three districts — namely, those of "Vesāli proper, Kuṇḍapura, and Vāṇiyagāma — occupying respectively the south-eastern, north-eastern and western portions of the

1. Law (B.C.), op. cit., pp. 31-32.
2. Jacobi, S.B.E., XXII., p. 264. Cf. Law (B.C.), op. cit., pp. 32-33.
3. Ibid., p. 31. "This was the capital of the Licchavi clan, already closely related by marriage to the kings of Magadha. . . . It was the headquarters of the powerful Vajjian confederacy. . . . It was the only great city in all the territories of the free clans who formed so important a factor in the social and political life of the sixth century BC. It must have been a great flourishing place." — Rhys Davids, op. cit., pp. 40-41 ; Charpentier, *C.H.I.*, I., p. 157.
4. "Under the name of Kuṇḍagāma the city of Vaiśālī is mentioned as the birthplace of Mahāvīra, the Jaina Tīrthaṅkara, who was also called Vesalie or the man of Vesāli. It is the Koṭigāma of the Buddhists." — Dey, *The Geographical Dictionary of Ancient and Mediaeval India*, p. 107.
5. Hoernle, op. cit., pp. 3-7.
6. Rockhill, *The Life of Buddha*, pp. 62-63.

area of the total city."[1] Moreover the fact that all three districts were closely connected with Vaiśālī is clear from the tradition that Mahāvīra was known as a native of Vaiśālī though he was born at Kuṇḍagrāma, and that the twelve rainy-seasons spent by Mahāvīra at Vaiśālī are put down in the *Kalpa-Sūtra* as follows : "Twelve in Vaiśālī and Vāṇijagrāma."[2] Both Hoernle and Nundo Lal Dey go a step farther than this and identify them at the outset with Vaiśālī, holding that the ancient town of Vaiśālī was known also as Kuṇḍapura or Vāṇijagrāma, but finally they nevertheless agree to the fact that both of them were separate divisions of Vaiśālī, the state of the Licchavis.[3]

Thus this much is certain, that Kuṇḍagrāma formed one of the three chief divisions of Vaiśālī, the government of which seems to have resembled that of a Greek state. The peculiar form of government, the free institutions, the manners and customs, and the religious views and practices of the time afford us glimpses of transitional India wherein the ancient Vedic culture was making a fresh development and undergoing a novel transformation under the influence of that speculative activity out of which emerged a new socio-religious order of things.

1. Hoernle, op. cit., p. 4. Cf. Law (B.C.), op. cit., p. 88 ; Dey, op. cit., p. 17. It may be mentioned here that in the *Uvāsaga-Dasāo* there is something in connection with Vāṇiyagāma to the following effect : वाणियगामे नयरे उच्चनीयमज्झिमाइं कुलाइं ("At the city of Vāṇiyagāma, to the upper, lower and middle classes"). — Hoernle, op. cit., I., p. 36. Curiously enough this agrees with the description of Vaiśālī given in the *Dulva*. — Rockhill, op. cit., p. 62. "There were three districts in Vesāli. In the first district were 7000 houses with golden towers, and in the middle district were 14,000 houses with silver towers, and in the last district were 21,000 houses with copper towers; in these lived the upper, the middle, and the lower classes according to their positions." — Cf. Hoernle, op. cit., II., p. 6, n. 8. Dey has taken the three districts or quarters, "Vaiśālī proper (Besarh), Kuṇḍapura (Basukunda), and Vāṇiagāmā (Bania)" as "inhabited by the Brahman, Kṣatriya and Baniā castes respectively." — Dey, op. cit., p. 107.
2. Jacobi, op. cit., p. 264.
3. "Vāṇiyagāmā, Skr. Vāṇijagrāma ; another name of the well-known city of Vesāli (Skr. Vaishālī), the capital of the Licchavi country. . . . In the *Kalpa-Sūtra* . . . it is mentioned separately, but in close connection with Vaiśālī. The fact is that the city commonly called Vesāli occupied a very extended area, which included within its circuit . . . besides Vesāli proper (now Besarh), several other places. Among the latter were Vāṇiyagāma and Kuṇḍagāma or Kuṇḍapura. These still exist as villages under the names of Baniya and Basukunda. . . . Hence the joint city might be called, according to circumstances, by any of the names of its constituent parts." — Hoernle, op. cit., II., pp. 3-4. "Bāniyagāma — Vaiśālī or (Besāḍ) in the district of Mozaffarpur (Tirhut); in fact, Bāniyagāmā was a portion of the ancient town of Vaisālī . . . ; Kuṇḍagāmā — it is another name for Vaiśālī (modern Besarh) in the district of Mozaffarpur (Tirhut) ; in fact, Kuṇḍagāma (Kuṇḍagrāma), now called Basukunda, was a part of the suburb of the ancient town of Vaiśālī." — Dey, op. cit., pp. 23, 107.

"It was," says Dr Hoernle, "an oligarchic republic; its government was vested in a senate composed of the heads of the resident Kṣatriya clans, and presided over by an officer who had the title of king, and was assisted by a viceroy and a commander-in-chief."[1] "The most important amongst the republics were the Vajjians of Vaiśālī and the Mallas of Kusinārā (Kusinagara) and Pāvā. As in Rome, so in Videha the overthrow of the monarchy was followed by the rise of a republic — the Vijjian confederacy."[2] Thus the monarchies of a former age were succeeded by aristocratic republics like that of Vaiśālī with the heads of the kṣatriya clans of Kuṇḍagāma and at other places. Looking at the great power that the Śaiśunāgas were wielding — in the political atmosphere of the country — such republic had doubtless a very short existence.

To quote Dr Law, "From the account of their political institutions that can be gleaned from the Pāli Buddhist canon we get an insight into the democratic ideas of statecraft and government that prevailed among the majority of the Āryan clans that peopled northern India before the imperialistic policy of the Mauryas grew and developed, as we have it on the authority of the great Brahman statesman whose policy and activity were responsible, in no little measure, for the foundation of the Maurya Empire."[3] For our purpose suffice it to say that Siddhārtha, as the head of the Nāta or Nāya clan, must have obtained some eminence in senate and state, which is amply borne out eventually by his marriage with Triśalā, the sister of this republican king.[4]

Taking next the Jñātṛkas[5] we find that they formed the clan which gave India one of its greatest religious reformers. Their importance as a kṣatriya tribe is self-evident when we already know that they formed one of the most important clans of the "Confederacy of the Vṛjis or of the Licchivis." They "were the clan of Siddhārtha and his son Mahāvīra the Jina. They had their seats at Kuṇḍapura or Kuṇḍagrāma and Kollāga,[6] suburbs of Vesāli.

1. Cf. Stevenson (Mrs), op. cit., p. 22; Raychaudhuri, op. cit., pp. 75-76.
2. Ibid., pp. 52, 116. Cf. Thomas (F.W.), *C.H.I.*, I., p. 491.
3. Law (B.C.), op. cit., pp. 1-2.
4. Cf. Stevenson (Mrs), op. cit., p. 22; Jacobi, op. cit., Int., p. xii.
5. The name of the clan is also given as the Nāya or Nātha clan. Cf. Law (B.C.), op. cit., p. 121 ; Hoernle, op. cit., p. 4, n.
6. The *Uvāsaga-Dasāo* says about Kollāga to the following effect : "Outside of the city of Vāṇiyagāmā, in a north-easterly direction, there was a suburb called Kollāga, which was large, strong . . . palatial, etc." — Hoernle, op. cit., p. 8. Cf. ibid., p. 4, n. "A suburb of Vaiśālī (Besar) in the district of Mozaffarpur (Tirhut) in which the Nāya-Kula Kṣatriyas resided. Mahāvīra, the Jaina Tīrthaṅkara, belonged to this class of Kṣatriya." — Dey, op. cit., p. 102.

Nevertheless they were known as "Vesalie" — i.e. inhabitants of Vesāli."[1]

Mahāvīra, the son of Siddhārtha and Triśalā, is undoubtedly the most noble scion of the Jñātṛka clan. A sidelight on the tremendous influence exercised by this remarkable man on his fellow-men is thrown by a passage occurring in the canonical literature of his bitter antagonists, the Buddhists. The passage may be translated thus : "He is the head of an order, of a following, the teacher of a school, well known and of repute as a sophist, revered by the people, a man of experience, who has long been a recluse, old and well stricken in years."[2]

We have already seen that Mahāvīra and his parents were the followers of the tenets of Pārśva, and hence with them it is highly probable that the whole clan of the Nāya kṣatriyas were also the followers of the same tenets. The Nāya clan seems to have supported a body of monks who followed the predecessor of Mahāvīra, and lastly, when he appeared, the members of his clan became his devoted followers.[3] The *Sūtrakṛtāṅga* tells us that those who followed the law proclaimed by Mahāvīra were "virtuous and righteous" and that they "confirmed each other in the law."[4]

Thus the Jñātṛkas, being of the clan of Mahāvīra, naturally were greatly affected by the doctrines of Nātaputta. The Jaina *sūtra*s give an idealized picture of the Jñātṛkas, and tell us that they avoided what was sinful and were afraid of sin.[5] For instance. the *Sūtrakṛtāṅga* observes :

"In compassion to all beings, the seers, the Jñātṛputras, avoid what is sinful; afraid of it, they abstain from food especially prepared for them. They abstain from wicked deeds, afraid of injuring living beings, and do no harm to any creature; therefore they do not partake of such food. This is a maxim of the monks of our creed."[6]

From the *Uvāsaga-Dasāo* we come to know that the Jñātṛkas possessed a Jaina temple outside their settlement at Kollāga, which bore the name of Dūipalāsa.[7] The term *ceïya* used here has been interpreted by Dr Hoernle to

---

1. Raychaudhuri, op. cit., p. 74. Cf. Barnett, op. cit., Int., p. VI ; Hoernle, op. and loc. cit.
2. Law (B.C.), op. cit., pp. 124-25.
3. Cf. Stevenson (Mrs), op. cit., p. 31 ; Law (B.C.), op. cit., p. 123.
4. Cf. Jacobi, S.B.E., XLV., p. 256.
5. Cf. Law (B.C.), op. cit., p. 122.
6. Jacobi, op. cit., p. 416. Dr Jacobi makes a note here that the term Jñātṛputras is used as the synonym for the Jainas. Cf. ibid.
7. Cf. Hoernle, op. cit., I., p. 2.

mean "properly the name of a Jaina temple or sacred shrine, but commonly applied to the whole sacred enclosure containing a garden, grove or park (*ujjaana, vana-saṇḍa* or *vana-khaṇḍa*), a shrine and attendants' houses."[1] This interpretation of the term *Ceïya* is quite appropriate, since, of course, the Jñātr̥kas as the followers of the religion of Pārśva ought to keep up a religious establishment for the accommodation of Mahāvīra on his periodical visits, with his disciples, to Kuṇḍapura or Vesāli. This becomes more of a certainty when we are informed that after Mahāvīra's assuming the vocation of a monk he used this *ceïya* for his accommodation whenever he visited the place of his birth.[2]

This much about the Jñātr̥kas and their attitude towards the religion propounded by one who was an ornament of their clan. "We may, however, mention the fact," observes Dr Law, "that it was he who brought the Jñātr̥kas into intimate touch with the neighbouring communities of Eastern India and developed a religion which is still professed by millions of Indians. Another celebrity of the Jñātr̥ka clan was Ānanda, a staunch follower of Mahāvīra. The Jaina work, *Uvāsaga-Dasāo*, mentions that he had with him a treasure of four *Kror* measures of gold deposited in a safe place. Again he is represented as a person whom many kings, princes and their dignitaries down to merchants found it necessary to consult on many matters requiring advice. He had a devoted wife, named Śivanandā."[3]

Taking next the Vajjis we find it very difficult to differentiate between them and the Licchavis. They "are often associated with the city of Vesāli, which was not only the capital of the Licchavi clan, but also the metropolis of the entire confederacy."[4] According to Dr Law "the Licchavis, or, to call them by their wider designation, the Vajjians, appear to have been imbued with a strong religious spirit and deep devotion. After Mahāvīra developed his doctrines and preached his faith of unbounded charity to all living beings in the Vajji land and in Magadha, the number of his followers among the Licchavis appears to have been large, and some men of the highest

1. Hoernle, op. cit., II., p. 2, n. 4.
2. Cf. ibid., I., p. 6 ; II., p. 9. In the *Kalpa-Sūtra* we do not get the *Ceïya* named Dūipalāsa, but the park of the Saṇḍavaṇa of the Nāya clan. — *Kalpa-Sūtra, Subodhikā-Ṭīkā, sūt*, 115, p. 95. Cf. Jacobi, S.B.E., XXII., p. 257 ; Hoernle, op. cit., pp. 4-5 ; Stevenson (Mrs), op. cit., p. 31.
3. Law (B.C.), op. cit., p. 125. Cf. Hoernle, op. cit., pp. 7-9.
4. Raychaudhuri, op. cit., pp. 74-75.

position in Vesālī appear to have been among them, as is seen from the Buddhist books themselves."[1]

Thus we have seen to what extent the Videhans, the Licchavis, the Jñātṛkas and the Vajjīs were connected with the Jaina church. It seems that the Vajjian or the Licchavi confederacy as a whole was a great source of strength to the reformed church of Mahāvīra. Taking next the Mallakins we find that they too had imbibed a feeling in them of respect and sympathy for the great prophet and his doctrines.

The country of the Mallas is spoken of as one of the sixteen "great countries" (*mahājanapadas*), and it is agreed to by both the Buddhists and the Jainas.[2] At the time of Mahāvīra they appear to have been divided into two confederacies — one with its capital at Pāvā, and the other at Kuśinārā.[3] Both the capitals are situated at a short distance from each other, and are known to the Jainas and Bauddhas as sacred places where their prophets reached their final liberation. We have already seen that Mahāvīra died here "while he was dwelling in the house of the scribe of King Hastipāla or, according to Stevenson's *Kalpa-Sūtra*, while he was spending the *Paryushaṇa* (*Pajjusaṇa*) at the palace of Shastipāla, King of Pāpā. There are four beautiful Jaina temples in an enclosure which marks the site of his death."[4]

The connections of the Jainas with the Mallas, though not as good as those with the Licchavis, seem to be good enough to get them their support for the progress of their church. According to Dr. Law we get ample proof for this even from the Buddhist literature. "Jainism," observes the learned scholar, "found many followers among the Mallas as among many other races of Eastern India. The accounts we get in the Buddhist literature of the schism that appeared in the Jaina church after the death of Mahāvīra

1. Law (B.C.), op. cit., pp. 67, 73.
2. Cf. Raychaudhuri, op. cit., pp. 59-60.
3. Cf. Law (B.C.), op. cit., p. 147 ; Raychaudhuri, op. cit., p. 79 ; Rhys Davids, *C.H.I.*, I., p. 175. "Pāpā is a corruption of Apāpapurī. Pāpā or Pāvā has been wrongly identified by General Cunningham with Padroana, which is the modern name of ancient Pāvā, where Buddha ate food at the house of Cuṇḍa. Pāvāpurī is the modern name of the ancient Pāpā or Apāpapurī, seven miles to the east of Bihar town, where Mahāvīra, the Jaina Tīrthaṅkara, died." — Dey, op. cit., pp. 148, 155. Kuśinārā or Kuśinagara is the place where Buddha died in 477 BC. It has been identified by Professor Wilson and others with the present village of Kasia, in the east of the Gorakhpur district, and it was also anciently known as Kuśāvatī. Cf. Raychaudhuri, op. cit., p. 79 ; Law (B.C.), op. cit., pp. 147-48 ; Dey, op. cit., p. 111.
4. Ibid., p. 148. Cf. Bühler, op. cit., p. 27 ; Stevenson (Rev.), *Kalpa-Sūtra*. p. 91.

amply prove this. At Pāvā the followers of Nigaṇṭha Nātaputta were divided after the death of their great *tīrthaṅkara*.[1] We find that there were both ascetics and lay-devotees among these Jainas, for we read that, on account of the disputations among the ascetics, "even the lay-disciples of the white robe, who followed Nātaputta, showed themselves shocked, repelled and indignant at the *nigaṇṭhas*." These lay-Jains appear from this passage to have been draped in white robes, just as the Śvetāmbaras are at the present day. The Buddha as well as Sāriputta, one of the principal disciples, seems to have taken advantage of the schism that appears to have overtaken the Jaina church on the death of their founder for the propagation of the rival faith. In the *Pāsādika Suttānts* we find that it is Cuṇḍa, the novice of Pāvā, who brings the news of the death of the great Tīrthaṅkara Mahāvīra, to Ānanda at Sāmagāma in the Malla country, and the latter at once saw the importance of the event and said : "Friend Cuṇḍa, this is a worthy subject to bring before the Exalted one. Let us go to him and tell him about it." They hastened to the Buddha, who delivered a long discourse.[2]

Moreover, from the Jaina sources we know that the Malla people were devotedly attached to Mahāvīra, the last prophet of the Jainas. As already remarked, we are informed by the *Kalpa-Sūtra* that, to mark the passing away of the Great *jina* along with the nine Licchavis, nine Mallakis or Malla chiefs also were among those who observed fast and instituted an illumination on the fifteenth day of the new month with the words "Since the light of the intelligence is gone, let us make an illumination of material matter."[3] Besides this it may be mentioned here that in the *Antagaḍa-Dasāo*, the eighth *aṅga* of the Jainas, we get a reference to the Mallakis, along with the Ugras, the Bhogas, the kṣatriyas and the Licchavis, who went to receive Ariṭṭhanemi or Ariṣṭanemi, the twenty-second prophet of the Jainas, when he went to the city of Bāravaī.[4]

Taking next the eighteen Gaṇarājās of Kāśī-Kośala we find that they too, like the Mallakis and the Licchavis, were devoted to Mahāvīra. They also observed fast and instituted an illumination to mark the passing away of the Great *jina*.[5] Furthermore, as we have already seen, the Jaina sources tell us

1. Cf. Bühler, op. and loc. cit.
2. Law (B.C.), op. cit., pp. 153-54. Cf. *Dialogues of the Buddha*, pt. III., pp. 203 ff., 203, 212.
3. Jacobi, op. cit., p. 266.
4. Barnett, op. cit., p. 36.
5. Cf. *Kalpa-Sūtra, Subodhikā-Ṭīkā, sūt.* 128, p. 121.

that along with the Mallaki chiefs these eighteen confederate kings of Kāśī-Kośala were also called by Ceṭaka when he came to know that Kūṇika had declared war against him.

Considering the Kāśī-Kośala confederacy we know from different sources that the Kāśīs — i.e. the people of Kāśī — were closely connected, both as foes and allies, with the people of Kośala and Videha.[1] "Of the sixteen *mahājanapadas* Kāsī was probably at first the most powerful," and it is accepted as such by both the Jaina and the Buddhist lists.[2] Its importance in connection with the Jaina history of the days of Pārśva we have already referred to. During his wanderings as a monk Mahāvīra also visited this place.[3] It may be mentioned here that in the *Antagaḍa-Dasāo* there is some reference to a king named Alakkhe of the city of Vārāṇasī who joined the order.[4]

Finally, considering Kośala of the Kāśī-Kośala confederacy we find that, like Kāsī, this also was one of the sixteen states, of considerable extent and power, and it also is found in both the Buddhist and the Jaina literature.[5] Geographically, Kośala roughly corresponds to the modern Oudh, and it seems to have contained three great cities — namely, Ayodhyā, Sāketa and Sāvatthī, or Śrāvastī — the first two of which are often supposed to be one and the same.[6] Of these Śrāvastī, "the capital of Kosala,"[7] was more than once visited by Mahāvīra, and all along he was well received there.[8] "Traditionally Śrāvastī, or, as it was called, Candrikāpurī or Candrapurī, was the birthplace of the third Tīrthaṅkara Sambhavanātha and the eighth Tīrthaṅkara Candraprabha of the Jainas. There is still a Jaina temple here dedicated to Śobhanāth, which is evidently a corruption of Sambhavanātha."[9]

---

1. Cf. Raychaudhuri, op. cit., p. 44.
2. Ibid., pp. 59, 60.
3. Cf. *Āvaśyaka-Sūtra*, p. 221 ; *Kalpa-Sūtra, Subodhikā-Ṭīkā*, p. 106.
4. Barnett, op. cit., p. 96.
5. Raychaudhuri, op. and loc. cit.
6. Ibid., pp. 62-63.
7. Pradhan, op. cit., p. 214. "Sāvatthī is the great ruined city on the south bank of Rapti called Saheth-Maheth, which is situated on the borders of the Gonda and Bahriah districts of the United Provinces." — Raychaudhuri, op. cit., p. 63. Cf. Dey, op. cit., pp. 189-90.
8. भगवं . . . सावत्थी . . . लोगो . . . वंदे ॥ — *Āvaśyaka-Sūtra*, p. 221. Cf. ibid., pp. 204, 214 ; *Kalpa-Sūtra, Subodhikā-Ṭīkā*, pp. 103, 105, 106 ; Barnett, op. cit., p. 93 ; Jacobi op. cit., p. 264.
9. Dey, op. cit., p. 190. "Śrāvastī is the Sāvatthī or Sāvatthīpura of the Buddhists and Candrapura or Candrikāpurī of the Jainas." — Ibid., p. 189.

We know from various sources that both the Kośalas and the Śaiśunāgas were also connected by matrimonial relations. Kośala-devī, the daughter of Mahākośala, had become one of the wives of Śreṇika with Cellaṇā, the foremost female disciple of Mahāvīra.[1] Besides this, certain Buddhist traditions tell us that Migara or Mr̥gadhara, the first minister of Prasenajit of Sāvatthī, the son of Mahākośala, was a sceptic and an adherent of the naked *tīrthakas* (i.e. *nirgrantha* ascetics).[2]

II

Taking into consideration all the facts that are laid down above, one thing that becomes fully evident is that practically all the most important sixteen *mahājanapadas* had, in one or the other capacity, come under the influence of the Jaina church.[3] Of the sixteen Great Powers we have as yet said hardly anything about Magadha; this is not because Magadha could not be combined with the other Great Powers, but because this pre-Norman Wessex of ancient India is going to be our centre from whence all further discussions about Jaina history shall proceed.

"The flourishing period of any of the sixteen *mahājanapadas*," observes Dr. Raychaudhuri, "ended in or about the sixth century BC. The history of the succeeding period is the story of the absorption of the states into a number of powerful kingdoms, and ultimately into one empire — namely, the empire of Magadha."[4] We need not enter into any direct details as to how this "one empire" of ancient India came to play the part of Prussia in the history of modern Germany. All that need be said is to show how far the different dynasties ruling over this empire were connected with the Jaina church. Beginning with the Śaiśunāgas, the Nandas and the Mauryas we shall come down to the times of Khāravela, who, as we shall see later on,

1. Cf. Pradhan, op. cit., p. 213 ; Raychaudhuri, op. cit., p. 99.
2. Cf. Hoernle, op. cit., Appendix III, pp. 56-57 ; Rockhill, op. cit., pp. 70-71 ; Ralston, *Schiefner's Tibetan Tales*, no. VII, p. 110 ; Pradhan, op. cit., p. 215.
3. The names of the sixteen Great Nations, according to the Buddhist traditions, are as follows : Kāśī, Kośala, Aṅga, Magadha, Vajjī, Malla, Ceītya (Cedi), Vaṁsa (Vatsa), Kuru, Pañcāla, Maccha (Matsya), Sūrasena, Assaka, Avantī, Gāndhāra, Kāmboja. The Jaina list in the *Bhagavatī* runs to the following effect : Aṅga, Baṅga, Magaha (Magadha), Malaya, Mālava, Accha, Vaccha (Vatsa), Koccha (Kaccha?), Pāḍha (Pāṇḍya), Lāḍha (Rāḍha), Bajji (Vajjī), Moli, Kāśī, Kośala, Avaha, Sambhuttar (Sumhotara?). Dr Raychaudhuri had made the following note to these lists : "It will be seen that Aṅga, Magadha, Vatsa, Vajjī, Kāśī and Kośala are common to both the lists. Mālava of the *Bhagavatī* is probably identical with Avantī of *Aṅguttara*. Moli is probably a corruption of Malla." — Raychaudhuri, op. cit., pp. 59-60.
4. Ibid., pp. 97-98. Cf. Law (B.C.)., op. cit., p. 161.

like Aśoka, enjoys the unique honour of being responsible for a distinct landmark in the history of the northern Jainas.

Before taking up the particular dynasties that had their sway over the Magadhan empire it will not be out of place to say something about the historical and geographical importance of Magadha proper, in the light of Jaina history. It roughly corresponds to the present Patna and Gayā, the districts of Bihar. Its earliest capital was Girivraja ("hill-surrounded") or old Rājagṛha, near Rājgīr among the hills near Gayā.[1] The capital seems to have been an impregnable city, being protected by five hills. "It is bounded on the north by Baibhāra-giri and Bipula-giri (the former on the western side and the latter on the eastern side); on the east by Bipula-giri and Ratnagiri or Ratnakūṭa; on the west by a portion of the Baibhāra-giri called Cakra and Ratnācala; and on the south by Udaya-giri, Sona-giri and Girivraja-giri."[2] These hills, one and all, enjoy a very important place in Jaina history even to this day. There are Jaina temples of Mahāvīra, Pārśva and other *tīrthaṅkara*s on the Baibhāra, Bipula, Udaya and Sonagiri hills.[3]

Besides this, Mahāvīra's personal connections with Magadha are self-evident when we know from the *Kalpa-Sūtra* that the greater part of his missionary life he spent in Rājagṛha and the suburb of Nālandā.[4] No less than fourteen rainy-seasons he was there,[5] and that too not only as an independent preacher but, as we shall see later on, as one who had the State behind him to directly patronize and sympathize with him in his great mission. Moreover, we know from the list of the *sthavira*s that the eleven *gaṇadhara*s of the venerable ascetic Mahāvīra died in Rājagṛha after a long religious fast.[6]

1. It is known by some other names also. For instance, the *Life of Hiuen-Tsiang* observes: "The old city of Rājagṛha is that which is called Kiu-she-kie-la-po-lo (Kuśāgarapura). This city is in the centre of Magadha, and in old times many rulers and kings lived in it." — Beal, *Life of Hiuen-Tsiang*, p. 113. Cf. Cunningham, op. cit., p. 529. Indian Buddhist writers gave still another name, Bimbasārapurī. Cf. Law (B.C.), *Buddhaghosha*, p. 87, n. 1 ; Raychaudhuri, op. cit., p. 70.
2. Dey, op. cit., p. 66. Cf. Cunningham, op. cit., p. 530.
3. Ibid., pp. 530-32.
4. Nālandā is identified with Bargaon, which lies seven miles to the north-west of Rājgīr in the district of Patna. Cf. Cunningham, op. cit., p. 536. It contains a beautiful Jaina temple of Mahāvīra, who appears to have dwelt at Nālandā, perhaps on the site of the present temple, while Buddha resided in the Pāvarika mango-orchard. — Dey, op. cit., p. 137.
5. Cf. Jacobi, op. and loc. cit.
6. Ibid., p. 287.

Coming to the different dynasties that ruled over Magadha since the days of Mahāvīra we shall begin with the Śaiśunāgas of the time of Bimbisāra, but before we do that we shall see if there is anything that can form a connecting link between Magadha and the Jaina church of the age previous to that of Vardhamāna. "The Jaina writers mention two early kings of Rājagṛha named Samudravijaya and his son Jaya.[1] Of these Jaya, the eleventh *Cakravartin*, or universal monarch, according to the *Uttarādhyayana*, "together with thousands of kings, renouncing the world, practised self-restraint. He reached perfection which has been taught by the Jainas."[2]

Leaving aside such uncorroborated facts of Jaina annals we shall enter into the realm of known facts, historical and others, and shall see how far the Jaina traditions are connected with them. Taking first Bimbisāra, the Śaiśunāga, we find that the Jaina annals are so overwhelming about this "lion of kings"[3] that, so far as they are concerned, it is no use denying the fact that he was a sincere follower of Nātaputta and his doctrines. However, before trying to enumerate a few of these details it is desirable to know from various sources what was the strength of the Magadhan empire during the Śaiśunāgas, because, after all, the progress of a church depends much on the strength of the people and the State whose patronage it enjoys.

For this we need not enter into a detailed description of the wars and the political feuds and intrigues that the Śaiśunāgas had to encounter until finally they developed into "one empire — namely, the empire of Magadha." We shall merely mention a few of the *mahājanapada*s that were openly defeated or that had indirectly accepted their sovereignty.

The early Buddhist texts throw a flood of light on the political condition of India during the time of Bimbisāra. There were, as Dr Rhys Davids observes, "besides a still surviving number of small aristocratic republics, four kingdoms of considerable extent and power."[4] In addition to these there were a number of smaller kingdoms and some non-Āryan principalities. As we have already

---

1. Raychaudhuri, op. cit., p. 72. Cf. Jacobi, S.B.E., XLV., p. 86.
2. अन्निओ रायसहस्सेहिं सुपरिच्चाई दमं चरे।
   जयनामो जिणक्खायं पत्तो गइमणुत्तरं॥
   — *Uttarādhyayana, Adhyayana* XVIII, v. 43. Cf. Jacobi, op. cit., pp. 85-87 ; Raychaudhuri, op. and loc. cit.
3. . . . रायसीहो . . . *Uttarādhyayana, Adhyayana* XX, v. 58.
4. Rhys Davids, *Buddhist India*, p. 1.

seen, the most important amongst the republics were the Vajjians of Vaiśālī, and the Mallas of Kuśinārā (Kuśinagara) and Pāvā. However the most important factors in the political history of the period were neither the republics nor the other principalities, but the four great kingdoms of Kośala, Vatsa, Avantī and Magadha, respectively ruled over by Prasenajit, Udāyana, Pradyota and Bimbisāra.[1]

Of these Bimbisāra or Śreṇika, the real founder of the Magadhan imperial power, strengthened his position by matrimonial alliances with the more powerful of the neighbouring states, having taken one consort from the royal family of Kośala, together with a village in the district of Kāśī producing a revenue of a hundred thousand for bath and perfume money,[2] and another from the influential Licchavi clan at Vaiśālī. We have referred to both these marriages before, and hence suffice it to say that they were of great importance for the history of Magadha. They paved the way for the expansion of Magadha both westwards and northwards. Thus disarming the hostility of his powerful western and northern neighbours by his shrewd policy, Bimbisāra could devote his undivided attention to the struggle with Aṅga, the capital of which — i.e. Campā — as we have seen, was occupied and destroyed by Śatānīka, the king of Kauśāmbī, a few years before Bimbisāra's annexation. The addition of Aṅga formed the first step taken by the kingdom of Magadha in its advance to greatness and the position of supremacy which it attained later on.[3] This is also confirmed by the Jaina sources, which tell us that Aṅga was governed as a separate province under Kūṇika, the Magadhan prince, with Campā as its capital.[4]

"Thus," observes Dr Raychaudhuri, "by war and policy Bimbisāra added Aṅga and a part of Kāśī to the Magadhan dominations, and launched Magadha in that career of conquest and aggrandisement which only ended when Aśoka sheathed his sword after the conquest of Kaliṅga. We learn from the *Mahāvagga* that Bimbisāra's dominions embraced 80,000 townships, the overseers (*Gāmikas*) of which used to meet in a great assembly."[5]

---

1. Cf. Raychaudhuri, op. cit., pp. 116, 120.
2. Cf. Pradhan, op. cit., p. 214 ; Raychaudhuri, op. cit., p. 124.
3. Cf. Smith, *Early History of India*, p. 33.
4. चम्पायां कूणिको राजा बभूव, . . . — *Bhagavatī, sūt*. 300, p. 316. Cf. Dey, *J.A.S.B.*, 1914, p. 322 ; Hemacandra, *Pariśiṣṭaparvan*, Canto IV, vv. 1, 9 ; Raychaudhuri, op. cit., p. 125 ; *Aupapātika-Sūtra, sūt*. 6.
5. Raychaudhuri, op. and loc. cit. Cf. Pradhan, op. cit., pp. 213-14.

With Ajātaśatru, also called Kūṇika or Kuṇiya, the successor of Śreṇika, Magadha reaches the high-water mark of the power of the Bimbisārian dynasty. He not only humbled Kośala and permanently annexed Kāśī, but, as the Jainas tell us, also absorbed the state of Vaiśālī.[1] As a result of his war with the Kośalas, like his father, Ajātaśatru was also given in marriage Vajirā, the princess of Kośala and the daughter of Prasenajit, with a part of the district of Kāśī as her dowry, and in all probability he won for Magadha a decided preponderance over its neighbour, Kośala. It is certain that the latter kingdom is not again mentioned as an independent power, and that later on it formed the integral part of the Magadhan empire.[2] However, Kūṇika's victory over Vaiśālī and its Mallaki and other allies, including the rulers of Kāśī-Kośala, was more decisive and highly fruitful from the point of view of the expansion of the Magadhan Empire.[3]

"It may be presumed," observes Smith, "that the invader carried his victorious arms to their natural limits, the foot of the mountains, and that from this time the whole region between the Ganges and the Himalayas became subject, more or less, directly to the suzerainty of Magadha."[4] He must have felt from the very beginning that the Licchavis formed the greatest bar to the realization of his idea of Magadhan expansion, and we find him taking the dreadful resolve, "I will root out these Vajjians, mighty and powerful though they be. I will destroy these Vajjians. I will bring these Vajjians to utter ruin."[5] Thus the Kośalan and the Licchavi or the Vajjian

---

1. वज्जी विदेहपुत्ते जइत्था, नवमल्लई नवलेच्छई कासीकोसलगा अट्ठारसवि गणरायाणो पराजइत्था ॥ . . . — *Bhagavatī, sūt.* 300, p. 315. Cf. *Āvaśyaka-Sūtra*, p. 684 ; Hemacandra, *Triṣaṣṭi-Śalākā, Parva* X, v. 290, p. 168 ; Raychaudhuri, op. cit., pp. 126-27.
2. Cf. Smith op. cit., p. 37 ; Raychaudhuri, op. cit., p. 67 ; Pradhan, op. cit., p. 215.
3. The *Bhagavatī* tells us that, in the war with Vaiśālī, Ajātaśatru is said to have made use of *mahāśilākaṇṭaka* and *rathamūsala*. The first seems to have been some engine of war of the nature of a catapult which threw big stones. The second was a chariot to which a mace was attached, and which, running about, effected a great execution of men. For a full description of these two wonderful engines of war see *Bhagavatī, sūt.* 300, 301, pp. 316, 319. Cf. Hoernle, op. cit., Appendix II, pp. 59-60 ; Raychaudhuri, op. cit., p. 129; Tawney, *Kathākoṣa*, p. 179.
4. Smith, op. and loc. cit. "Kūṇika-Ajātaśatru made protracted war on the confederacy of the Licchivis, the Mallakis and the eighteen *Gaṇarājās* of Kāsī-Kosala for more than sixteen years, and at last was able to effect their ruin, which it was his firm resolve to do, although his cause was unrighteous." — Pradhan, op. cit., pp. 215, 216. Cf. Hoernle, op. cit., Appendix I, p. 7.
5. S.B.E., XI., pp. 1, 2. Cf. Law (B.C.), *Some Kṣatriya Tribes of Ancient India*, p. 111. For a detailed description about Magadha and Vaiśālī conflict see ibid., pp. 111-16.

wars were probably not isolated events, but parts of a common movement directed against the establishment of the hegemony of Magadha.

The absorption of Vaiśālī, Videha, Kāśī and other territories as a result of these wars to a great extent brought the aspiring ruler of Magadha face to face with the equally ambitious sovereign of Avantī. We already know that the throne of Avantī was at this time occupied by Canda Pradyota Mahāsena. That he was a king feared by his neighbours is apparent from a statement of the *Majjhima Nikāya* that Ajātaśatru fortified Rājagṛha because he was afraid of an invasion of his territories by Pradyota.[1] This does not seem to be improbable in view of the fact that after the fall of Aṅga and Vaiśālī, and the discomfiture of Kośala, Avantī was the only important rival left for Magadha.

Thus by the end of Kūṇika's reign Magadha had absorbed almost all the kingdoms and republics of eastern India. During his son and successor Udāyin's period, as the Jaina traditions tell us, Magadha and Avantī were brought face to face with each other.[2] The *Sthavirāvali Carita* and other Jaina sources inform us that Udāyin was a very powerful king, and defeated and killed the king of a certain country in battle, and the son of that king went to Ujjayinī and there related the story of his distress to him. The deposed prince got into the favour of the Avantī lord, and with his help, having disguised as a monk, finally murdered Udāyin while asleep. If nothing else, this particular legend gives an insight into the spirit of rivalry that existed between Avantī and Magadha, both of whom tried to acquire the paramount power in northern India.[3]

Furthermore, from the equally aggressive policy of the Avantī ruler it seems clear that it was a contest between the two for the mastery of northern India. *Kathā-Sarit-Sāgara* and other Jaina traditions tell us that the kingdom of Kauśāmbī was at this time annexed to the realm of Pālaka of Avantī,[4] the son of Pradyota.[5] Thus the Avantī-Magadha contest which, as we have seen, began in the régime of Ajātaśatru seems to have continued during the reign of Udāyin. "The contest was finally decided in favour of Magadha under the leadership

---

1. Cf. Raychaudhuri, op. cit., p. 123 ; Pradhan, op. cit., p. 216.
2. अभूदसहनो नित्यमवन्तीशोऽप्युदायिनः — Hemacandra, *Pariśiṣṭaparvan*, Canto VI, v. 191. Cf. *Āvaśyaka-Sūtra*, p. 690. Cf. Pradhan, op. cit., p. 217.
3. Cf. Hemacandra, op. cit., vv. 189-190, 208 ; *Āvaśyaka-Sūtra*, op. and loc. cit.
4. Cf. Raychaudhuri, op. cit., p. 131.
5. उज्जयिन्यां प्रद्योतसुतौ द्वौ भ्रातरौ-पालको, etc. — *Āvaśyaka-Sūtra*, p. 699.

of Śaiśunāga, who, according to the *Purāṇas*, destroyed the prestige and influence of the descendants of Pradyota,"[1] though the Jaina sources tell us that Avantī now and then suffered defeat at the hands of Udāyin.[2]

Here arises the difficulty as to who was the real successor of Udāyin. But we need not at all enter, for the present, into any discussions about these controversial and still unsettled facts of Indian history. For our purpose suffice it to reiterate the fact that the contest between Magadha and Avantī was finally decided in favour of the former under the leadership of some Śaiśunāga,[3] who is known to us either as Śiśunāga or Nandivardhana, or whose full name may be, as Dr Pradhan suggests, Nandivardhana-Śiśunāga.[4]

Thus having seen the growth of the Magadhan Empire under the Śaiśunāgas we shall see in brief how far the Jaina church was connected with them. It may be stated here that whatever has been said up till now and whatever is going to be said from now about the different kings and dynasties that are claimed by the Jainas as their own or as those of their sympathizers has been claimed by the Buddhists also. There are reasons and reasons for this phenomenon of Indian history, but we need not enter at all into these details, because thereby it is not possible to fix a criterion in accordance with which we can say that such and such a king was a Buddhist or a Jaina by faith. Unless there are some inscriptional records or other sound historical documents it is not possible to put down anything as an historical fact. Nothing can be predicted as gospel truth where the source of information rests only with the canonical books and with some legendary and literary traditions of the people.

Taking first Bimbisāra or the Śreṇika of the Jainas it must be said that, whatever may be the claims of the Buddhists about him, looking to the nature of the evidence put forward by the Jainas it is certain that he was a great devotee of Mahāvīra. So much has been written about him and his successors by the Jainas that it is not possible to do anything but enumerate a few of the facts connected with their careers with a view to illustrate their relations with the Jaina church. The *Uttarādhyayana* tells us that King Śreṇika once laid the following point before Mahāvīra : "Though a young nobleman, you have

1. Pradhan, op. cit., p. 217. Cf. Raychaudhuri, op. cit., p. 132.
2. उज्जयिनी . . . राजा . . . बहुशः बहुशः परिभूयते उदायिना. — *Āvaśyaka-Sūtra*, p. 690.
3. Cf. Pradhan, op. cit., pp. 217, 220 ; Raychaudhuri, op. cit., pp. 133-34.
4. Cf. Pradhan, op. cit., p. 220 ; Raychaudhuri, op. cit., pp. 132-33.

entered the order; in an age fit for pleasure you exert yourself as a *śramaṇa*, O Ascetic; I want to hear you explain this."[1]

Hearing this, Nātaputta gave a lengthy explanation, and so convinced the king that he could not help giving vent to his feelings, as follows : "You have made the best use of human birth, you have made a true Jaina, O great sage, you are a protector (of mankind at large) and of your relations, for you have entered the path of the best Jinas. You are the protector of all unprotected beings, O Ascetic: I ask you to forgive me; I desire you to put me right. That by asking you I have disturbed your meditation, and that I invited you to enjoy pleasures, all this you must forgive me."[2]

Here the *Uttarādhyayana* rightly concludes : "When the lion of kings had thus, with the greatest devotion, praised the lion of the houseless monks, he, together with his wives, servants and relations, became a staunch believer in law, with a pure mind."[3]

We have already seen that this Bimbisāra was married to Cellaṇā, the daughter of Ceṭaka, the maternal uncle of Vardhamāna. With a few of her sisters as nuns and with her aunt Triśalā as mother of the prophet naturally Cellaṇā had come under the influence of Mahāvīra more than anybody else in the family of Bimbisāra.[4] This attitude of hers is particularly to be noticed when we know that she, as the mother of Ajātaśatru, the successor of Bimbisāra, must have been the chief queen of the Magadha lord. That is why the *Divyāvadāna* speaks, in one place, of Ajātaśatru as Vaidehīputra, and in another states, "At Rājagṛha reigns the King Bimbisāra. Vaidehī is his Mahādevī (or chief queen) and Ajātaśatru, his son and prince."[5]

Moreover, Cellaṇā is usually called "Vaidehī in the Buddhist books, and from her, Ajātaśatru is frequently designated as Vedehiputto or the

1. Jacobi, S.B.E., XLV., p. 101.
2. Ibid., p. 107.
3. एवं थुणित्ताण स रायसीहो
   अणगारसीहं परमाइ भत्तीए।
   — *Uttarādhyayana, Adhyayana* XX, v. 58. Cf. Jacobi, op. and loc. cit.
4. एकदा च प्रववृते शिशिरर्तुर्भयंकरः। . . . तदा . . .॥ देव्या चेल्लणया सार्धम् . . . नृपः। वीरं . . . वन्दितुमभ्यगात्॥
   — Hemacandra, *Triṣaṣṭi-Śalākā, Parva* X, vv. 6, 10, 11, p. 86. "Once upon a time, when a great stress of cold had fallen on the country, the king went with Queen Cellaṇā to worship Mahāvīra." — Tawney, op. cit., p. 175. For further references about this see ibid., p. 239.
5. *Rājagṛhe rājā Bimbisāro . . . tasya vaidehī mahādevī ajātaśatruḥ putraḥ*, Cowell and Neil, *Divyāvadāna*, p. 545. Cf. ibid., p. 55 ; Law (B.C.), op. cit., p. 107.

son of the Videha princess."[1] However "some of the commentaries — those for example on *Thusa* and *Tacchasūkara Jātakas* — state that Ajātaśatru's mother was a sister of the king of Kosala. Here the commentators have evidently made a confusion between the two queens of Bimbisāra."[2] There is no reason to doubt the Jaina belief that Kūṇika was one of the sons of Cellaṇā, and that, like Mahāvīra, he too was rightly called Vedehiputto.[3]

That, besides Cellaṇā and Kośaladevī, Bimbisāra had many other wives is borne out both by the Buddhist and the Jaina sources.[4] Accordingly, besides Kūṇika, Halla and Vehalla, the three sons of Cellaṇā,[5] he had many sons, all of whose names, whether they agree or not, are recorded by both the annals.[6] About these sons and wives of Śreṇika the Jaina claim is that most of them joined the order of Lord Mahāvīra and reached their salvation.[7] This claim of the Jainas, barring a few exaggerations here and there, is not based on absolutely false grounds. There is nothing strange or unbelievable if some of Mahāvīra's own kith and kin took a living interest in the great message that he put before suffering humanity. Leaving aside this question of close relationship between Mahāvīra and his royal followers, the literary and legendary traditions of the Jainas about Śreṇika are so varied and so well recorded that they are eloquent witnesses to the high respect with

---

1. Law (B.C.), op. cit., p. 106. Cf. *Saṁyutta Nikāya*, pt. II., p. 268 ; Raychaudhuri, op. cit., p. 124 ; Rhys Davids, *C.H.I.*, I., p. 183.
2. Law (B.C.), op. and loc. cit. Cf. Fausböll, *Jātaka*, III., p. 121, and IV., p. 342 ; Raychaudhuri, op. and loc. cit. ; Rhys Davids, op. cit., p. 183 ; Rhys Davids (Mrs), *The Book of Kindred Sayings*, pt. I., p. 109, n. 1.
3. कोणिकः, . . . चेल्लणाया उदरे उत्पन्नः. — *Āvaśyaka-Sūtra*, p. 678. . . . विदेहपुत्ते जइत्था. . . . — *Bhagavatī, sūt.* 300, p. 315 ; विदेहपुत्ते, ति कोणिकः, . . . — Ibid., *sūt.* 301, p. 317. Cf. Rhys Davids, *Buddhist India*, p. 3 ; Pradhan, op. cit., p. 212.
4. Cf. *Bhagavatī, sūt.* 6, p. 11 ; *Antagaḍa-Dasāo, sūt.* 16, 17, p. 25 ; Barnett, op. cit., p. 97.
5. Cf. *Āvaśyaka-Sūtra*, p. 679 ; Raychaudhuri, op. cit., p. 126. "Bimbisāra is said to have contracted marriage alliances with the kings of several states. These, we may be sure, were quite common in ancient India." — Beni Prasad, *The State in Ancient India*, p. 163.
6. Cf. *Āvaśyaka-Sūtra*, p. 679 ; *Aṇuttarovavāiya-Dasāo, sūt.* 1, 2, pp. 1-2 ; Barnett, op. cit., pp. 110-12 ; Raychaudhuri, op. and loc. cit. ; Pradhan, op. cit., p. 213.
7. सेणियभज्जाण . . . सिद्धा. — *Antagaḍa-Dasāo, sūt.* 16-26, pp. 25-32. Cf. Barnett, op. cit., pp. 97-107 ; *Āvaśyaka-Sūtra*, p. 687 ; Hemacandra, op. cit., v. 406, p. 171. Of the sons of Śreṇika, Halla, Vehalla, Abhaya, Nandisena, Meghakumāra and others are said to have joined the order of Mahāvīra. Cf. *Aṇuttarovavāiya-Dasāo, sūt.* 1, p. 1 ; ibid *sūt.* 2, p. 2 ; Barnett, op. cit., pp. 110-12 ; *Āvaśyaka-Sūtra*, pp. 682, 685.

which the Jainas held one of their greatest royal patrons,[1] whose historicity, fortunately, is past all doubts.

Taking next the Kūṇika of the Jainas we find that they are not so eloquent about him as about his father Śreṇika, though a lot of literature can be had which throws light on almost all the incidents connected with his life.[2] However, leaving this fact aside, there is one thing about his career that clearly brings out the attitude of this great monarch towards both the Buddhists and the Jainas.

This incident of Kūṇika's life is connected with his succession to the throne of Magadha. The Buddhists definitely tell us that "Bimbisāra made over the charge of government to his son Ajātaśatru when the latter was about to stab him with a dagger, but was seized upon by the officers. Ajātaśatru however starved him to death, and afterwards expressed repentance to Buddha for his sin."[3] The Jainas, on the other hand, have got something else to offer about this very incident. According to them no doubt the parricide Ajātaśatru of the Buddhists imprisoned his father and greatly ill-treated him, but the death of Śreṇika took place under circumstances which would draw our sympathy rather than our hatred for both the father and the son — for the former for his untimely death, and for the latter for his good motives being misunderstood by the victim of this incident.

The Jaina account of this tradition in brief runs as follows. Though Śreṇika had made up his mind that he would make Kūṇika his successor, the latter felt a bit impatient and suspicious, and on the advice of his brothers Kāla and others imprisoned his father. During his imprisonment Bimbisāra

1. For Śreṇika's attachment towards Mahāvīra see सेणिए राया, चेल्लणा देवी ॥ . . . परिसा निग्गया, धम्मो कहिओ. — *Bhagavatī, sūt*. 4, 6, pp. 6, 10 ; मेहस्स कुमारस्स अम्मापियरो . . . समणं भगवं महावीरं . . . वंदंति नमंसंति एवं वदासी . . . — अम्हे णं देवाणुप्पियाणं सिस्सभिक्खं दलयामो. — *Jñātā-Sūtra, sūt*. 25, p. 60. Cf. *Kalpa-Sūtra, Subodhikā-Ṭīkā*, p. 20. (श्रेणिकः) राजा भणति — अहं युष्मासु नाथेषु कथं नरकं गमिष्यामि? — *Āvaśyaka-Sūtra*, p. 681. In this way many more such references about Śreṇika can be gathered from the Jaina canonical books, but for our purpose suffice it to say that the Jainas respect him as the first *tīrthaṅkara* of the coming age. श्रेणिकराइजीवः पद्मनाभो जिनेश्वरः. — Hemacandra, op. cit., v. 189, p. 179. Cf. Tawney, op. cit., p. 178.

2. About the whole of *Aupapātika*, the first *Upāṅga* of the Jainas, deals with Ajātaśatru. Besides this we get references about him in the *Bhagavatī*, the *Uvāsaga-Dasāo*, the *Antagaḍa-Dasāo*, and many other places. Kūṇika has been fully dealt with by the Jainas.

3. Pradhan, op. cit., p. 214. Cf. Rockhill, op. cit., pp. 95 ff. ; Rhys Davids, *Dialogues of the Buddha*, pt. I., p. 94 ; Raychaudhuri, op. cit., pp. 126-27 ; Rhys Davids (Mrs), op. cit., pp. 109-10.

was no doubt very badly treated by his son, but his comforts were very keenly looked after by his wife Cellaṇā, the mother of Kūṇika. Once it so happened that while he was taking his food with his son Udaya in his lap, the child's urine fell into his dishes, but without taking any notice of this he went on taking his food. After a short while he asked his mother, who was sitting near him : "Mother, did anybody ever love his son so much?" His mother replied : "You monstrous criminal, listen! When you were born I abandoned you in an enclosure of Aśoka-trees, saying that you were a villain. When your father came to know about this he himself went to the enclosure and brought you back; so you were named Aśokacandra. Then a cock tore your finger. It became a whitlow. So all gave you the name of Koṇika. When the swelling on your finger ripened you suffered a good deal of pain from it. Your father held that finger in his mouth, though streaming with matter, so you did not cry. To this extent did he love you." When Kūṇika heard this he was full of remorse. He said : "A sorry return I have made to my father." So he immediately went off in person with an iron club to break the fetters of his father. In the meanwhile the guards said to Śreṇika : "Koṇika is coming in a very impatient mood, with an iron club in his hand; it is not known what his object is." Hearing this, Śreṇika felt that he would be put to death by some painful execution, so he took *tālapuṭa* poison and died then and there, before Kūṇika could come over to break his father's fetters. When Kūṇika came to know about this sad coincidence he was very much afflicted at the loss of his father. Though admonished by his nobles he would not bathe or take food. Then, being unable to endure his sorrow for his father, he left Rājagṛha, and made Campā the seat of his rule.[1]

This incident of Kūṇika's life as laid down by the Jainas makes at least this much clear — that it was not he who murdered or starved Śreṇika to death. This is because there is nothing in this account that is unnatural or cannot be believed. It further shows that the Jainas were in the good books of Kūṇika, because if otherwise they would, like the Buddhists, have given a crude version of this unfortunate happening of his life.[2]

1. Cf. *Āvaśyaka-Sūtra,* pp. 682-83 ; Hemacandra, op. cit., pp. 161-64 ; Tawney, op. cit., pp. 176-78.
2. "It is probable, however, that the story is the product of *odium theologicum,* or sectarian rancour, which has done so much to falsify the history of ancient India. . . . Later when, in consequence of Aśoka's patronage, Buddhism became pre-eminent in Northern India, leanings towards Jainism became criminal in the eyes of ecclesiastical chroniclers, who were ready to blacken the memory of persons deemed heretical with unfounded accusations of the gravest character." — Smith, op. cit., pp. 33, 37.

This surmise of ours is greatly strengthened when we read from the Buddhist sources themselves of Ajātaśatru being incited to get his father slain by Devadatta, "the quondam disciple and bitter foe of the Buddha," and hence "the Judas Iscariot of the Buddhist story."[1] Furthermore, commenting on the Buddhist tradition of Kūṇika's having repented before Buddha for his sin, Dr Rhys Davids observes : "At the close of the discourse the king is stated to have openly taken Buddha as his guide in future, and to have given expression to the remorse he felt at the murder of his father. But it is also distinctly stated that he was not converted. There is no evidence that he really, after the moment when his heart was touched, continued to follow the Buddha's teaching. He never, so far as we know, waited again either upon the Buddha or upon any member of the order to discuss ethical matters, and we hear of no material support given by him to the order during the Buddha's lifetime."[2]

What Buddha and Ajātaśatru thought of each other is clear from the following two passages from the Buddhist literature : "Then Devadatta went to Prince Ajātaśatru and said: "Give such order, O King, to our men that I may deprive the *samana* Gotama of life"; and Ajātaśatru the prince gave orders to his men: "Whatsoever the worthy Devadatta tells you, that do!""[3]

The above passage clearly shows the nature of Kūṇika's repentance before Lord Buddha. The following one, moreover, manifests the estimate in which the latter held the former : "Almsmen, the king of Magadha, Ajātaśatru, son of the accomplished princess, is a friend to, an intimate of, mixed with, whatever is evil."[4]

On the other hand the *Aupapātika* and other Jaina sources tell us that Kūṇika used to go with his queens, now and then, accompanied with a great

1. Rhys Davids, *Buddhist India*, pp. 13-14. Cf. Rhys Davids and Oldenberg, S.B.E., XX., pp. 238-65. And Devadatta went to Ajātaśatru the prince and said to him : "In former days, Prince, people were long-lived, but now their term of life is short. It is quite possible, therefore, that you may complete your time while you are still a prince. So do you, Prince, kill your father and become the *Rājā*, and I will kill the blessed one and become Buddha." — Ibid., p. 241.
2. Rhys Davids, op. cit., p. 15.
3. Vinaya Texts, pt. III., p. 243.
4. Rhys Davids (Mrs), op. cit., p. 109.

retinue, to pay his respects to Nātaputta. In connection with the Vaiśālī king, Ceṭaka, and Campā, the capital of Dadhivāhana, we have seen that more than once he had come in touch with Mahāvīra, and that he looked with great respect and honour towards all those who were connected with the Jaina church.[1] His love for Mahāvīra and his faith in the doctrines propounded by the *jina* are clear when he openly confessed before Vardhamāna and his followers to the following effect : "O Lord! you have said the right thing. The path of true religion has been made clear to us by your honour. Yours is a unique message of renunciation, peace," etc.[2]

Coming to Udaya or Udāyin, the successor of Kūṇika, we find that both the Buddhists and the Jainas hold him as such in the teeth of various other traditions. Referring to this Dr Raychaudhuri observes: "Ajātaśatru was succeeded according to the Purāṇas by Darśaka.[3] Professor Geiger considers the insertion of Darśaka after Ajātaśatru to be an error, because the Pāli canon indubitably asserts that Udāyibhadda was the son of Ajātaśatru, and probably also his successor.[4] Though the reality of the existence of Darśaka, as king of Magadha, is established by the discovery of Bhāsa's *Svapna-Vāsavadatta*, yet in the face of the Buddhist and Jaina evidence it cannot be confidently asserted that he was the immediate successor of Ajātaśatru."[5]

The Jaina evidence of which the learned scholar speaks about is based mostly on the *Āvaśyaka* commentary of Haribhadra,[6] the *Triṣaṣṭi-Śalākā* and the *Pariśiṣṭaparvan* of Hemacandra[7] and the *Kathākośa* of Tawney.[8] Further than this the traditions recorded in these books do not seem to agree with those in the Pāli canon. To quote Dr Pradhan : "Ajātaśatru was, according to

1 Cf. *Aupapātika, sūt.* 12, 27, 30, pp. 24, 25, 57, 58, 59, 63, 64 ; Stevenson (Mrs), op. cit., p. 40; Hemacandra, *Pariśiṣṭaparvan,* Canto IV, vv. 1, 9, 33, 35 ; *Āvaśyaka-Sūtra*, pp. 684, 687; Hoernle, op. cit., II., p. 9.

2. तए णं कूणिए राया . . . महावीरं . . . वंदति . . . एवं वयासी–सुअक्खाए ते भंते ! etc. — *Aupapātika, sūt*. 36, p. 83.

3. Cf. Pargiter, *Dynasties of the Kali Age*, pp. 21, 69 ; Pradhan, op. cit., p. 217.

4. Cf. Geiger, *Mahāvaṁsa, Paricchedo* IV, vv. 1-2.

5. Raychaudhuri, op. cit., p. 130. "The order of succession in the *Vishṇu* which inserts Darśaka between Ajātaśatru and Udāyaśva must be rejected. . . ." — Pradhan, op. and loc. cit. Darśaka may be one of Bimbisāra's many sons who managed the State affairs during the lifetime of his father. Cf. ibid., p. 212.

6. कोणिकः . . . मृतः . . . तदा राजान उदायिनं स्थापयन्ति, . . . — *Āvaśyaka-Sūtra*, p. 687.

7. Hemacandra, op. cit., v. 22. Cf. *Triṣaṣṭi-Śalākā, Parva* X, v. 426, p. 172.

8. Cf. Tawney, op. cit., p. 177.

the *Mahāvaṁsa*, murdered by his son Udāyibhadra,[1] but the *Sthavirāvali-Carita* informs us that Udāyin was overpowered with sorrow at the death of his father Ajātaśatru, and transferred his capital from Campā to Pāṭalīputra."[2]

This part of the Jaina tradition is confirmed by the testimony of the *Vāyu Purāṇa*, according to which Udāyi built the city of Kusumapura (Pāṭalīputra[3]) in the fourth year of his reign,[4] and hence it seems almost certain that Udāyin was in no way connected with the death of his father. It is not possible to say why the Buddhists have pictured him, like his father, as a man whose greed for power and position did override even the natural instinct of regard for his father's life. If the Buddhist tradition of the *Mahāvaṁsa* had any ground at its back the Jaina writers would have at least taken a note of it, as they have done in the case of Kūṇika.

The Jainas, on the other hand, tell us that he was a devout Jaina. By his order a fine Jaina temple was built in the centre of his new capital, Pāṭalīputra.[5] That the Jaina monks had free access to him is clear from the fact, as related before, that he was murdered by some prince, whose father had been dethroned by him, in the disguise of a monk. Furthermore, from this very incident we can infer that, like an orthodox Jaina, he was regularly observing the monthly religious festivals, because it was on a *paushadha* day that the *Sūri*, accompanied by the novice who carried a concealed weapon about him, went to the palace and preached to the king.[6]

This is, in short, what the Jainas have to say about the Śaiśunāgas, under whom the Magadhan Empire took a definite form. Let it be clear that we have not entered into any details while dealing with them in their relations with the Jaina church, and that we do not mean doing so in the case of

1. Cf. Geiger, op. cit., v. 1.
2. Pradhan, op. cit., p. 216. Cf. ibid., p. 219. "The Ceylonese chronicles state that all the kings from Ajātaśatru were parricides." — Raychaudhuri, op. cit., p. 133; Hemacandra, *Pariśiṣṭaparvan*, Canto VI, vv. 32-180. Cf. *Āvaśyaka-Sūtra*, pp. 687, 689.
3. "The choice of Pāṭalīputra was probably due to its position in the centre of the realm, which now included North Bihar. Moreover, its situation at the confluence of two large rivers (the Ganges and the Son) was important from the commercial as well as the strategic point of view. In this connection it is interesting to note that Kauṭilya recommends a site at the confluence of rivers for the capital of a kingdom." — Raychaudhuri, op. cit., p. 131.
4. Cf. Pargiter, op. cit., p. 69 ; Pradhan, op. cit., p. 216 ; Raychaudhuri, op. and loc. cit.
5. नगरनाभौ चोदायिना चैत्यगृहं कारितं, . . . — *Āvaśyaka-Sūtra*, p. 689. Cf. Hemacandra, op. cit., v. 181.
6. स राजाऽष्टमीचतुर्दश्योः पौषधं करोति. — *Āvaśyaka-Sūtra*, p. 690. Cf. Hemacandra, op. cit., v. 186; ibid., vv. 186-230 ; Charpentier, *C.H.I.*, I., p. 164.

other dynasties that are mentioned in this chapter. It need not, however, be understood that all these details are superfluous, but that it is neither possible nor desirable to enter into them while taking a general historical review of the northern Jainas.

Coming to the successors of Udāyin we find that, according to the Buddhist traditions, he was succeeded by Aniruddha, Muṇḍa and Nāga-Dāsaka. The traditions tell us further that all these were parricides, and that "the people became angry, banished the dynasty and raised an *amātya* named Śusu-Nāga (Śisunāga) to the throne."[1] However, the Jaina and Purāṇic traditions omit or forget the weaklings Aniruddha and others, and put down some Nanda or Nandivardhana as the successor of the Udāyibhadda of the Buddhists.[2]

The Jainas say that on the death of Udāyin, who left no heirs, the five royal insignia — viz. the State elephant, the horse, the parasol, the pitcher and the chowries — were anointed by the ministers and led through the streets, and this procession met the marriage procession of a man named Nanda, the son of a courtesan by a barber, and the five royal insignias themselves pointed out Nanda as the king of Magadha. He was accordingly proclaimed king, and ascended the throne sixty years after the *nirvāṇa* of Mahāvīra.[3]

In connection with the date of Mahāvīra's *nirvāṇa* we have seen that the Mauryas came to the imperial throne of Magadha one hundred and fifty-five years after the death of Vardhamāna, and thus the Jainas allot ninety-six years to Nanda and his descendants. "This," observes Dr Pradhan, "agrees fairly well with the Purāṇic tradition that the Nandas ruled for about a hundred years. The Purāṇas probably borrowed the information from the ancient Jaina sources."[4]

He says further: "Hemacandra who has, on account of the similarity of names, not only confounded Nandi-(a)-Vardhana with Nanda (=Mahāpadma),

---

1. Raychaudhuri, op. cit., p. 133. Cf. Geiger, op. cit., vv. 2-6 ; Pradhan, op. cit., pp. 218-19 ; Smith, op. cit., p. 36 ; Rapson, *C.H.I.*, I., pp. 312-13.
2. Cf. *Āvaśyaka-Sūtra*, pp. 690 ff. ; Hemacandra, op. cit., v. 242 ; Pargiter, op. cit., pp. 22, 69.
3. नापितदास . . . राजा जातः — *Āvaśyaka-Sūtra*, p. 690. Cf. Hemacandra, op. cit., vv. 231-243.
4. Pradhan, op. cit., p. 218. Cf. Pargiter, op. cit., pp. 26, 69.

but has practically supported the wrong tradition that Nanda (=Mahāpadma) ruled for about a hundred years (95 years according to the *Sthavirāvalicarita*)."[1]

But there is no such confounding of names on the part of Hemacandra at all. Both Haribhadra and Hemacandra have taken into consideration Nine Nandas, the first of whom really was of base origin.[2] It is not correct to say that "Hemacandra has confounded Nandi-(a)-Vardhana with Nanda (=Mahāpadma)," because if at all the identity of Nandivardhana or Nandavardhana is to be accepted he must go along with the Śaiśunāga dynasty as one of those who succeeded Udāyin. This is clear from all sources — both ancient and modern. "The Purāṇas and the Ceylonese authorities," observes Dr Raychaudhuri, "know of the existence of only one Nanda line. Those works represent Nandivardhana as a king of the Śaiśunāga line, a dynasty which is sharply distinguished from the Nandas."[3]

Thus it is clear that there is no confusion in what has been laid down by the Jainas when they definitely say that Udāyin had no successor, and that the Magadhan empire went into the hands of the Nandas. We are not concerned with the circumstances under which the Śaiśunāgas were supplanted by the Nandas. It may be, as we have seen, that Udāyin was succeeded by some weaklings, and that Mahānandin, the last of the dynasty, as Smith observes, "had by a śūdra, or low caste, woman a son named Mahāpadma Nanda, who usurped the throne, and so established the Nanda family or dynasty."[4]

This observation of the learned historian essentially agrees with the Jaina tradition that Nanda was born of a courtesan by a barber. This is also corroborated by the Purāṇas and the Greek accounts of the father of Alexander's Magadhan contemporary. The Purāṇas describe him as śūdra-*garbha-udbhava* — i.e. born of a śūdra mother.[5] The Jaina tradition is strikingly confirmed by the classical accounts, though according to them the Nandas retained possession of the throne for only two generations, and their duration

1. Pradhan, op. cit., p. 220. Cf. ibid., p. 225.
2. . . . नवमे नन्दे . . . — *Āvaśyaka-Sūtra*, p. 693. Cf. Hemacandra, op. cit., Canto VII, v. 3.
3. Raychaudhuri, op. cit., p. 138. Cf. Pargiter, op. cit., pp. 23, 24, 69 ; Smith, op. cit., p. 51.
4. Ibid., p. 41.
5. Cf. Pargiter, op. cit., pp. 25, 69 ; Raychaudhuri, op. cit., p. 140 ; Pradhan, op. cit., p. 226 ; Smith, op. cit., p. 43 ; Rapson, op. cit., p. 313.

was for only fifty-five years,[1] Curtius says : "His father (i.e. Agrammes' or Xandrammes' father — i.e. the first Nanda — i.e. Mahāpadma Nanda) was, in fact, a barber, scarcely starving off hunger by his daily earnings, but who, from his being not uncomely in person, had gained the affections of the queen, and was, by her influence, advanced too nearer a place in the confidence of the reigning monarch. Afterwards, however, he treacherously murdered his sovereign, and then, under the pretence of acting as the guardian to the royal children, usurped the royal authority, and having put the young princes to death begot the present king, who was detested and held cheap by his subjects, as he rather took after his father than conducted himself as the occupant of a throne."[2]

Besides this agreement between the Jaina and other source about the non-kṣatriya origin of the Nandas we see that chronologically also Jainas are right if, according to Smith, "this even may be dated in or about 413 BC."[3] This is because, as we have seen, the suzerainty of Magadha passed from the hands of the Śaiśunāgas to those of the Nandas sixty years after the *nirvāṇa* of Mahāvīra, which we have put down between 480-467 BC. It may be repeated here that the duration of the Nandas as put down by the Jainas is ninety-five years, and this agrees with the Purāṇic traditions. Taking into consideration the tradition based on Merutuṅga and others, Vincent Smith remarks that "the Jainas, doing still greater violence to reason, extend the duration of the dynasty to 155 years."[4] According to the chronology relied upon by us the period of one hundred and fifty-five years thus alluded to by the great historian does not obtain to the dynasty of the Nandas, but, as already remarked, it is the duration between the death of Mahāvīra and the accession of Candragupta. As it is, our period seems to be acceptable to him, seeing that a period of ninety-one years has been assumed by him as "fitting into a definite chronological scheme."[5]

Thus about the baṣe origin, the date of the succession, and the duration of the Nandas the Jaina traditions are confirmed by other sources also. Before we enter into the details as to where the Jainas stood in their relations

---

1. Cf. McCrindle, *The Invasion of India by Alexander the Great*, p. 409.
2. Ibid., p. 222. Cf. ibid., p. 282 ; Raychaudhuri, op. and loc. cit.; Pradhan, op. and loc. cit.; Smith, op. cit., pp. 42-43 ; Jayaswal, *J.B.O.R.S.*, I., p. 88.
3. Smith, op. cit., p. 43.
4 Ibid., p. 42.
5. Ibid., p. 44.

with the ruling dynasty it may be seen whether Magadha remained the premier state of India during the period of the Nandas. What we can glean from various sources is that it not only remained an empire, but its boundaries were spread far and wide, so that it remained for Candragupta to extend the imperial dominion by the annexation of the north-western region — which for a few years had owned the sway of Alexander the Great and his Satraps — and for Aśoka to re-establish his authority over Kaliṅga.

The Purāṇas call Mahāpadma, or Nanda I, the destroyer of all the kṣatriyas — like a second Paraśurāma — and sole monarch of the earth, which was under his undisputed sway.[1] This Purāṇic account of the unification of a considerable portion of India under Nanda's sceptre is corroborated by the classical writers, who speak of the most powerful peoples who dwelt beyond the seas in the time of Alexander as being under one sovereign who had his capital of Pālibhotra (Pāṭalīputra). Curtius tells us that Agrammes, king of Ganjaridae and Prassi, "kept in the field for guarding the approaches to his country 20,000 cavalry and 200,000 infantry, besides 2000 four-horsed chariots, and, what was the most formidable force of all, a troop of elephants, which he said ran up to the number of 3000."[2] Besides this, the inclusion of Kośala within Nanda's dominions seems to be implied by a passage of the *Kathā-Sarit-Sāgara* which refers to the camp of the King Nanda in Ayodhyā.[3] More important is the evidence of the Hāthīgumphā inscription of Khāravela, which, as we have seen, mentions Nandarāja in connection with an aqueduct of Kaliṅga, and this naturally seems to imply that Nandarāja held sway in Kaliṅga.[4] To quote Dr Raychaudhuri : "In view of Nanda's possession of Kaliṅga, the conquest of regions lying farther south does not seem to be altogether impossible. The existence on the Godaveri of a city called *Nau Nand Dehra* (Nander)[5] also suggests that the Nanda dominions embraced a considerable portion of the Deccan."[6]

Besides this, as we shall see in the following chapter, the second passage

---

1. Cf. Pargiter, op. cit., pp. 25, 69.
2. McCrindle, op. cit., pp. 221-22. Cf. ibid., pp. 281-82 ; Smith, op. cit., p. 42 ; Raychaudhuri, op. cit., p. 141.
3. Cf. Tawney (ed. Penzer), *Kathā-Sarit-Sāgara*, I., p. 37 ; Raychaudhuri, op. and loc. cit.
4. Cf. Rapson, op. cit., p. 315.
5. Cf. Macauliffe, *The Sikh Religion*, V., p. 236.
6. Raychaudhuri, op. cit., p. 142.

in the inscription seems to state that Nanda carried away as trophies the image of the *jina* of Kaliṅga as well as other treasures of the Kaliṅga kings to Magadha. This statement of the Khāravela inscription finally brings us to the discussion of the relations of the Nandas with the Jaina church. The difficulty that arises in connection with this and the other passage referring to Nandarāja is about the identification of this Nandarāja. While considering the *nirvāṇa* date of Mahāvīra we have seen that there is no reason why this Nandarāja should be identified with Nandivardhana, as Jayaswal, Banerji, Smith and others have done. Besides the authority of Charpentier, to which reference has been already made, as Professor Chanda points out, "there is nothing in the Purāṇas, our only source of information for Nandivardhana, to show that he ever had anything to do with Kaliṅga. On the contrary we are distinctly told in the Purāṇas that when the kings of the Śaisunāga dynasty and their predecessors were reigning in Magadha, thirty-two Kaliṅgas — that is to say, thirty-two kings — reigned in Kaliṅga in succession synchronously.[1] It is not Nandivardhana but Mahāpadma Nanda who is said to have brought "all under his sole sway" and "uprooted all Kṣatriyas," or the old reigning families. So we should identify Nandarāja of the Hāthigumphā inscription who held possession of Kaliṅga either with the all-conquering Mahāpadma Nanda or one of his sons."[2]

In short, the Nandarāja of the Khāravela inscription is none else but Nanda I of the Jainas or Mahāpadma Nanda of the Purāṇas, because of the later Nandas both the Jaina and the Purāṇic traditions have nothing to say which can claim for any one of them the triumphant career of the first Nanda. It may be remarked here that though the Purāṇic and the Jaina traditions confirm each other to a great extent, the Khāravela inscription rightly supports the latter by calling this Nanda king simply Nandarāja, and not Mahāpadma Nanda, as the Purāṇas have done.

As to the relations of the Jainas and the Nandas, the above reference to the Hāthīgumphā inscription tells us that some Jaina image was taken away by King Nanda as a trophy, and this, according to Jayaswal, as we shall see in the next chapter, proves that Nanda was a Jaina, and that Jainism was introduced

---

1. Cf. Pargiter, op. cit., pp. 24, 62.
2. Chanda, *Memoirs of the Archaeological Survey of India*, no. I, pp. 11-12. Cf. Raychaudhuri, op. cit., p. 138.

in Orissa very early.[1] This is because, according to him, "carrying away idols of worship as a mark of trophy and also showing respect to the particular idol is known in later history."[2] This is also confirmed by scholars like Smith and Charpentier.[3] To quote the former, "The Nanda dynasty exercised dominion over Kaliṅga for a long time. The Jaina religion, if not predominant, as it may have been, certainly occupied a position of high honour both in the days of the Nandas and in those of Khāravela. I may mention that I had come independently to the opinion that the Nandas were Jainas."[4]

Looking to the anti-Brāhmanical origin of the Nandas it is not strange to find that they were Jainas.[5] Besides their origin the Jainas have nothing to say against the Nandas, as is the case with the Buddhists. According to Dr Charpentier "this fact seems to suggest that the Nanda kings were not unfavourably inclined towards the Jaina religion."[6] This is further supported by the Jaina tradition that the Nanda dynasty as such had a line of Jaina ministers beginning with Kalpaka,[7] who was perforce made to accept the ministership.[8] It was with the help of this minister that King Nanda uprooted all the reigning kṣatriya dynasties,[9] and, as the Jainas tell us, all the ministers of the Nandas were his descendants.[10] The minister of the ninth Nanda was Śakaṭāla, who had two sons. The elder was Sthūlabhadra and the younger son was called Śrīyaka. After the death of Śakaṭāla, Nanda offered the ministership to his elder son Sthūlabhadra, but the latter refused and, perceiving the vanity of the world, took *dīkṣā*, or joined the order under Sambhūtavijaya,[11]

1. "Kaliṅga culture was a complex compound of animism, Brahmanism, Buddhism and Jainism. Curiously enough none of them was completely superseded at any time." — Subrahmanian, *A.H.R.S.*, I., p. 50.
2. Jayaswal, *J.B.O.R.S.*, XIII., p. 245.
3. Charpentier, op. cit., p. 164.
4. Smith, *J.R.A.S.*, 1918, p. 546.
5. "Some would make us understand that Kaliṅga was Jaina, as it was long under the anti-Brāhmanical Nandas, whose Jaina remains probably are found now in Nandapur in Jeypore. . . ." — Subrahmanian, op. and loc. cit.
6. Charpentier, op. cit., p. 174.
7. *Āvaśyaka-Sūtra*, p. 692 ; Hemacandra, op. cit., vv. 73-74, 80.
8. Cf. *Āvaśyaka-Sūtra*, pp. 691-92 ; Hemacandra, op. cit., vv. 1-74.
9. दर्शितः सन् कल्पक इति ते (राजानः) भीताः . . . नष्टाः. — *Āvaśyaka-Sūtra*, p. 693 ; Hemacandra, op. cit., vv. 84, 105-37. Cf. Pradhan, op. cit., p. 226.
10. कल्पकस्य वंशो नन्दवंशेन सममनुवर्तते, . . . — *Āvaśyaka-Sūtra*, p. 693 ; Hemacandra, op. cit., Canto VIII, v. 2.
11. शकटालमन्त्रि पुत्रः श्रीस्थूलभद्रो . . . पितरि मृते नन्दराजेनाकार्य मन्त्रिमुद्रादानायाभ्यर्थितः सन पितृमृत्युं स्वचित्ते विचिन्त्य दीक्षामादत्त. — *Kalpa-Sūtra, Subodhikā-Ṭīkā*, p. 162. Cf. *Āvaśyaka-Sūtra*, pp. 435-36, →

the sixth pontiff of the Jaina church.[1] The ministership was finally given to his brother Śrīyaka, who was already in the king's office.[2]

This is how the relationship between the Nandas and the Jainas stands. That the Jainas were powerful in the days of the Nandas is also clear from the Sanskrit play *Mudrārākṣasa*, which dramatises the story of Candragupta's accession, and tells us that "Jainas held a prominent position at the time," and that Cāṇakya, "who was the prime agent in the revolution, employs a Jaina as one of his chief emissaries."[3]

Unlike the Śaiśunāgas the Jaina records do not throw any particular light upon the political power of the Nandas. They inform us only in a very vague manner that, with the help of the Jaina minister Kalpaka, King Nanda subdued many kings, and that, as we shall see later on, the last Nanda had to throw himself at the mercy of Cāṇakya, who, being insulted at his court, had taken a vow to dethrone him and to destroy his power. However it must be remembered that this is not the case with the Jaina annals alone. As Dr Charpentier remarks, "The reign of the Nandas is one of the darkest even of the many hopelessly dark epochs in the history of ancient India."[4]

The Nandas are followed by the Mauryas. Why and wherefore the Nandas were supplanted by the Mauryas is not yet clearly known, but this much is certain, that it is in connection with this landmark in Indian history that we get Cāṇakya, "the first economist of India, if not of the world."[5] It is strange that no detailed account of the dynastic revolution has survived. However from the classical accounts we have seen that the last Nanda "was detested and held cheap by his subjects." Furthermore, the vast standing army of the Nandas which has been mentioned by these accounts and the

---

→ 693-95 ; Hemacandra, op. cit., vv. 3-82. Smith has wrongly put him down as "Mantrin of the ninth Nanda." — Smith, *Early History of India*, p. 49, n. 2.

1. "Sudharman, the first pontiff, had died twenty years after his master, leaving the mitre to Jambū, who held his high office for forty-four years, dying at a time nearly coincident with the accession of the Nandas. After him passed three generations of pontiffs ; and in the time of the last Nanda the Jaina church was governed by two high priests, Sambhūtavijaya and Bhadrabāhu. . . ." — Charpentier, op. cit., p. 164 ; Jacobi, S.B.E., XXII., p. 287.
2. . . . श्रीयकः स्थापितः, . . . — *Āvaśyaka-Sūtra*, p. 436 ; Hemacandra, op. cit., vv. 10, 83, 84.
3. Cf. Narasimhachar, *E.C.*, II., Int., p. 41 ; Rice (Lewis), *Mysore and Coorg*, p. 8 ; Smith, *Oxford History of India*, p. 75.
4. Charpentier, op. and loc. cit.
5. Sammadar, *The Glories of Magadha*, p. 2.

traditional facts of the vast treasures of the Nandas naturally imply a good deal of financial extortion.[1] Nevertheless the Jainas have no such complaint to make against any of the Nandas.

The Jaina tradition in brief runs as follows :

Cāṇakya, who was born of Caṇeśvarī, the wife of the brāhmaṇa Caṇin, a devout Jaina, hearing that Nanda was accustomed to liberally reward renowned brāhmaṇas, went to Pāṭalīputra to make money. There at the king's court he felt he was insulted, and since then became the enemy of the last Nanda. He then went to Himavatkūṭa and entered into an alliance with Parvataka,[2] the king of that place, promising him half of Nanda's country if he would aid him to subdue Nanda. They opened the campaign by reducing the outlying provinces, and finally, having devastated the country, the allies laid siege to Pāṭalīputra, and at last forced the enemy to capitulate. Nanda, throwing himself on the mercy of Cāṇakya, was permitted to leave his kingdom, carrying with him all that he could place on one car. Accordingly he put his two wives and a daughter on his carriage, and loading it with treasures he drove off. Meeting Candragupta on the road, the princess instantly fell in love with him, and on her father's advice selected him for her husband by the rite of *svayaṁvara*. She got down at once and began to climb into Candragupta's carriage, in doing which, however, nine spokes of the wheel broke. Candragupta would have turned her out, but Cāṇakya prevented him, saying that the new dynasty would flourish during nine generations.[3]

This is what the Jainas say about the fall of the Nandas and the rise of the Mauryas. About the ally Parvata of Himavatkūṭa it so happened that by some unhappy coincidence he died, and thus Candragupta got possession of Nanda's and Parvata's kingdom.[4] This, as seen before, happened one hundred and fifty years after the *nirvāṇa* of Mahāvīra.

1. "The *Mahāvaṁsa*, when it dubs the last Nanda by the name of Dhana, or 'riches,' seems to hint at an imputation of avariciousness against the first Nanda ; and the Chinese pilgrim Hiuen-Tsiang also refers to the Nanda Rāja as the reputed possessor of great wealth." — Smith, *Early History of India*, p. 43. Cf. Raychaudhuri, op. cit., p. 143.
2. गतो हिमवत्कूटं, पार्वतिको राजा, तेन समं मैत्री जाता. — *Āvaśyaka-Sūtra*, p. 434 ; Hemacandra, op. cit., v. 298. Jacobi makes a note of this in his edition of the *Pariśiṣṭaparvan*, as follows: In the list of the kings of Nepal, according to the Bauddha Pārvatīya Vaṁśāvalī, the eleventh king of the third dynasty, that of the Kirātas, is Parba — apparently our Parvata ; for in the reign of the seventh king, Jitedāsti, is placed Buddha's visit to Nepal, and in that of the fourteenth, Sthuṅka, Aśoka visited the country. — Jacobi, *Pariśiṣṭaparvan*, p. 58. Cf. Bhagawanlal Indraji, *I.A.*, XIII., p. 412.
3. Cf. *Āvaśyaka-Sūtra*, pp. 433, 434, 435 ; Jacobi, op. cit., pp. 55-59.
4. द्वे अपि राज्ये तस्य जाते. — *Āvaśyaka-Sūtra*, p. 435. Cf. Hemacandra, op. cit., v. 338.

Here arise two difficulties : that if, as the Jaina and other sources inform us,[1] it was Cāṇakya alone who was at the back of the fall of the Nandas, what was the ancestry of Candragupta? And again, how is it that Cāṇakya did not proclaim himself the Emperor of Magadha? Of the two the problem of the ancestry of Candragupta is insoluble. The Jaina tradition represents him as the son of a daughter of the chief of the village of the feeders of the king's peacocks (*mayūra-poṣaka*).[2] According to Smith the dynasty founded by Candragupta is said to be a derivative from Murā, his mother's or grandmother's name.[3] The Hindus connect the Mauryas with the Nandas. *Kathā-Sarit-Sāgara* refers to Candragupta as a son of the Nandas.[4] The *Mahāvaṁsa* calls him a scion of the Moriya clan.[5] In the *Divyāvadāna* Bindusāra, the son of Candragupta, claims to be a kṣatriya *mūrdhābhiṣikta*. In the same work Aśoka, the son of Bindusāra, calls himself a kṣatriya.[6] In the *Mahāparinibbāṇa Sutta* the Moriyas are represented as the ruling clan of Pipphalivana, and as belonging to the kṣatriya caste.[7]

Taking into consideration all these facts, Dr Raychaudhuri observes : "It is, therefore, practically certain that Candragupta belonged to a kṣatriya community — viz. the Moriya (Maurya) clan. In the sixth century BC the Moriyas were the ruling clan of the little republic of Pipphalivana. They must have been absorbed into the Magadhan Empire along with the other states of eastern India. During the inglorious reign of Agrammes, when there was general disaffection amongst his subjects, the Moriyas evidently came into prominence, probably under the leadership of Candragupta. With the help of Kauṭilya, also called Cāṇakya or Viṣhṇugupta, son of a brāhmaṇa of Taxila,[8] he overthrew the infamous Nanda."[9]

1. "We learn from Kauṭilya's *Arthaśāstra*, Kāmaṇḍaka's *Nitisāra*, the Purāṇas, the *Mahāvaṁsa* and the *Mudrārākshasa* that the Nanda dynasty was overthrown by Kauṭilya, the famous minister of Candragupta Maurya." — Raychaudhuri, op. and loc. cit. "A Brahman Kauṭilya will uproot them all ; and after they have enjoyed the earth 100 years, it will pass to the Mauryas." — Pargiter, op. cit., p. 69.
2. Cf. *Āvaśyaka-Sūtra*, pp. 433-34 ; Hemacandra, op. cit., v. 240.
3. Cf. Smith, op. cit., p. 123.
4. Cf. Tawney (ed. Penzer), op. cit., I., p. 57.
5. "*Moriyānaṁ Khattiyānaṁ vamse* . . . etc." — Geiger, op. cit., p. 30.
6. "*Ahaṁ rājā kshatriyo mūrdhābhishiktaḥ*. . . ." — Cowell and Neil, *Divyāvadāna*, p. 370.
7. Rhys Davids, S.B.E., XI., pp. 134-35.
8. According to the Jainas Cāṇakya was a native of Caṇaka, a village of the Golla district. Cf. Jacobi, op. cit., p. 55 ; *Āvaśyaka-Sūtra*, p. 433.
9. Raychaudhuri, op. cit., pp. 165-66.

This much about the ancestry of Candragupta. The question as to why Cāṇakya did not usurp the Magadhan Empire for himself is more or less made clear in the above statement of Dr Raychaudhuri. It seems highly probable that Candragupta himself was, as the Greeks tell us, "prompted to aspire to royalty by an omen significant of an august destiny."[1] Like the other sources of Jaina history the Greek annals also throw comparatively little light on real history. They tell us about Candragupta's having escaped from the death sentence passed upon him by the Nanda king, about a lion having licked the sweat oozing from his body while he was sleeping, about his being inspired from this prodigy with the hope of winning the throne, and about a wild elephant having submissively knelt before him.[2] When such annals, which rank as contemporary witnesses reported at second-hand, throw such light on the period of Candragupta, it is no wonder that the Jaina interpretation, in short, runs as follows : Cāṇakya had all his teeth complete on being born.[3] The monks being informed of this marvellous circumstance foretold that the boy would become a king, but the father being of a religious turn of mind desired to spare his son a lot which he considered dangerous to the well-being of the inner man. Accordingly to remove the omen he broke out the boy's teeth. Upon which the monks foretold that Cāṇakya would govern by proxy. Further on, after the defeat of the Nanda king, we are told that his treasures were divided by Candragupta and Parvata between themselves.[4]

Leaving aside these uncorroborated facts of Indian history we shall see in brief what was the strength of the Magadhan Empire during the Mauryas. It may safely be said that the high-water mark of its power and extension was reached during the days of Aśoka. The real conquests and annexations were begun and accomplished during the days of Candragupta and not in the days of Aśoka. Politically the latter was a Quaker, and was better fitted to fill the chair of an abbot than of an emperor. What he did was to reconquer or re-establish the authority of the Magadhan over the Kaliṅgas.

1. McCrindle, op. cit., p. 327.
2. Ibid., pp. 327-28. Cf. Smith, op. cit., p. 123, n. 1.
3. About this incident of Cāṇakya's life Jacobi makes a note as follows : "The same circumstance is told of Richard III :
'Teeth hadst thou in thy head when thou wast born
To signify thou comest to bite the world.' "
— Jacobi, op. and loc. cit.
4. Cf. *Āvaśyaka-Sūtra*, p. 435 ; Hemacandra, op. cit., v. 327.

To quote Rev. Heras : "The greatest monarch of Hindustan during the Hindu period was Candragupta. His grandson Aśoka's glory is based upon intellectual grounds. He was a philosopher rather than a sovereign; he was a teacher of morals rather than an administrator."[1]

Nevertheless the limits of the enormous Mauryan Empire in Magadha were extensive. Nearly the whole of Northern India, except the Punjab, Sind and Northern Rājpūtāna, had passed under the Nandas. To this vast empire were undoubtedly added the Punjab, Sind, Baluchistan, Afghanistan and presumably, as we have seen in a note to the Parvata of Himavatkūṭa, Nepal and Kashmir during the days of Candragupta.[2] Events in the north itself were so crowded that there was no possibility of his having diverted his attention to the south. As Smith observes : "It is difficult to believe that he could have found time to do more than climb from obscurity to power, expel the Macedonian garrisons, repel the attack of Seleukos, effect a revolution and establish a dynasty at Pāṭalīputra, annex a large part of Ariāna, and extend his dominion from the Bay of Bengal to the Arabian Sea."[3]

The conquest of the south can be affirmed from various sources to have been effected by Bindusāra, the son and successor of Candragupta. He was guided also by his father's minister Cāṇakya.[4] The Deccan, or Peninsular India, down to approximately the latitude of Nellore, must therefore, apparently, have been subjugated by Bindusāra, because it was inherited from the latter by Aśoka, whose only recorded war was the conquest of Kaliṅga.[5] As to the later Mauryas, their contribution to the growth of the Mauryan Empire is next to nothing. Really speaking, with the close of Aśoka's reign began the decline of the Maurya rule, and ended with Bṛhadratha, who, as we shall see in our next chapter, was murdered by his commander-in-chief, Puṣyamitra, who established a new dynasty, known as that of the Śuṅgas.[6]

Having thus seen in a connected form the growth of the Magadhan Empire during the Mauryas we shall now examine them in their relations with the Jaina church. Jaina tradition avers that Candragupta, the founder of the

---

1. Heras, *Q.J.M.S.*, XVII., p. 276. Cf. Jayaswal, *J.B.O.R.S.*, II., p. 83.
2. Cf. ibid., p. 81.
3. Smith, op. cit., p. 156. Cf. Jayaswal, op. and loc. cit.
4. *Āvaśyaka-Sūtra*, op. cit., p. 184.
5. Cf. Jayaswal, op. cit., pp. 82-83 ; Smith, op. cit., p. 157 ; Schiefner, op. cit., p. 89.
6. Cf. Smith, op. cit., p. 204.

dynasty, the conqueror of the Greeks and the first known Emperor of India, was a Jaina. To state briefly the tradition, it is as follows:

When King Candragupta was ruling over north India (either from Ujjain or from Pāṭalīputra) a great twelve years' famine was foretold by the *śrutakevalin* Bhadrabāhu, who, as we have seen, was one of the high priests during this period. As a result of this prophecy a large body of Jainas (numbering about 12,000) came to the south, where several of them (including Bhadrabāhu?) died by the holy vow of *sallekhanā*, or the total rejection of food unto death. This event took place at Śravaṇabeḷgoḷa, in Mysore. Candragupta, who followed the *saṁgha*, renouncing everything, remained (?) for twelve years at Beḷgoḷa, worshipping the footprints of his departed preceptor Bhadrabāhu, and finally himself died by the same rite.

The parentheses and interrogations in the above summary indicate the different versions of a single legend, agreeing in its fundamentals and differing only in details of lesser importance. We have seen that this tradition also forms one of the links connected with the great Digambara-Śvetāmbara schism in the Jaina church, and that it is not acceptable to the Śvetāmbaras, who agree only with the fact of the great famine which lasted for twelve years, and tell us that *ācārya* Suṣṭhita, who lived in Candragupta's capital, was forced to send his *gaṇa* to some other country.[1] Our interest in this tradition lies only so far as it shows that Candragupta was a Jaina. A detailed examination of it must be left to a student of Jainism in south India. However, it may be mentioned here that it has been dealt with at some length by scholars like Narasimhachar of Mysore, Fleet and others.[2]

The earliest literary form of the tradition is found in the *Bṛhat-Kathā-Kośa* by Harisena, dating from about AD 931.[3] An inscription at Śravaṇabeḷgoḷa, which has been roughly assigned to *c.* AD 600, is supposed to be the basis of this entire account.[4] Some of the modern scholars of great repute and

---

1. Cf. Hemacandra, op. cit., vv. 377-78. In the list of the *sthaviras* Suṣṭhita comes after Sthūlabhadra, who is the eighth pontiff of the Jaina church. Cf. Jacobi, S.B.E., XXII., pp. 287-88.
2. Narasimhachar, op. cit., Int., pp. 36-42 ; Fleet, *I.A.*, XXI., pp. 156-60.
3. ". . . the *Bṛihat-Kathā-Kośa*, a Sanskrit work written by Harisena in 931, says that Bhadrabāhu, the last of the *Śrutakevalins*, had the King Candragupta as his disciple." — Narasimhachar, op. cit., Int., p. 37. Cf. Rice (Lewis), op. cit., p. 4.
4. Cf. Narasimhachar, op. cit., Int., p. 39; ibid., Translation, pp. 1-2 ; Rice (Lewis), op. cit., pp. 3-4.

authority have come to the conclusion that Candragupta can safely be called a Jaina on the authority of this tradition. "The Jaina books (fifth century A.C.) and later Jaina inscriptions," observes Jayaswal, "claim Candragupta as a Jaina imperial ascetic. My studies have compelled me to respect the historical data of the Jaina writings, and I see no reason why we should not accept the Jaina claim that Candragupta at the end of his reign accepted Jainism and abdicated, and died as a Jaina ascetic."[1]

To quote Smith, who has ultimately leaned towards it : "The only direct evidence throwing light on the manner in which the eventful reign of Candragupta Maurya came to an end is that of Jaina tradition. The Jainas always treat the great Emperor as having been a Jaina like Bimbisāra, and no adequate reason seems to exist for discrediting their belief. The Jaina religion undoubtedly was extremely influential in Magadha during the time of the later Śaisunāgas, the Nandas and the Mauryas. The fact that Candragupta won the throne by the contrivance of a learned brāhmaṇa is not inconsistent with the supposition that Jainism was the royal faith. Jainas habitually employ brāhmaṇas for their domestic ceremonies, and in the drama cited above (*Mudrā-Rākshasa*) a Jaina ascetic is mentioned as being a special friend of the minister Rākṣasa, who served first the Nanda and then the new sovereign.

Once the fact that Candragupta was or became a Jaina is admitted, the traditions that he abdicated and committed suicide by slow starvation in the approved Jaina manner become readily credible. It being certain that Candragupta was quite young and inexperienced when he ascended the throne in or about 322 BC, he must have been under fifty when his reign terminated twenty-four years later. His abdication is an adequate explanation of his disappearance at such an early age. Similar renunciations of royal dignity are on record, and the twelve years' famine is not incredible. In short, the Jaina tradition holds the field, and no alternative account exists."[2]

Besides these two eminent scholars there are others also who are of the same opinion. Both Rice and Narasimhachar, who have studied the Jaina

---

1. Jayaswal, *J.B.O.R.S.*, III., p. 452.
2. Smith, *Oxford History of India*, pp. 75-76. "I am disposed to believe that . . . Candragupta really abdicated and became a Jaina ascetic." — Smith, *Early History of India*, p. 154. Hemacandra informs us that Candragupta समाधिमरणं प्राप्य दिवं ययौ . . . . — Hemacandra, op. cit., v. 444.

inscriptions of Śravaṇabeḷgoḷa thoroughly, give a verdict in favour of it.[1] Of the older scholars we have Edward Thomas, who has taken into consideration the Greek accounts and comes to the same opinion.[2] Besides this, as Dr Jacobi tells us, "the date of Bhadrabāhu's death is placed identically by all Jaina authors — from Hemacandra down to the most modern scholiast — in the year 170 A.V."[3] And this, according to our calculation, falls in about 297 BC. This date of the great pontiff's *nirvāṇa* exactly coincides with that of Candragupta, who reigned from 321-297 BC.[4]

Besides this tradition there are also other references in the Jaina literature which go to show that Candragupta was or had become a Jaina,[5] but we need not now enter more into all these literary sources. However, before we pass on to the successors of Candragupta, a few words regarding the importance of the Jaina migration to the south and about the religion followed by Cāṇakya will not be out of place. As to the first, it gives us a definite starting point in the history of Jainism in south India. Besides, its value in general to south Indian history is not less; for we know of no other earlier event of equal moment in the annals of south India. The age of Candragupta which Smith, rightly or wrongly, considers to lead the historian "from darkness to light" in north India[6] is thus seen to open a new era in south Indian history as well. It is of not less interest to note that the religion which was to give south India her earliest, if not her best, literature also gave her first reliable historical tradition.

Coming next to the faith of Cāṇakya we find that the Jainas believe that he was also a Jaina, favoured Jaina teachers, and in his old age tried to starve

---

1. Rice (Lewis), op. cit., pp. 3-9. "We are therefore not without warrant for assuming that Candragupta was a Jaina by creed." — Ibid., p. 8. "A dispassionate consideration of the above-mentioned facts leads one to the conclusion that the Jaina tradition has some basis to stand upon." — Narasimhachar, op. cit., Int., p. 42.
2. "That Candragupta was a member of the Jaina community is taken by their writers as a matter of course, and treated as a known fact, which needed neither argument nor demonstration. . . . The testimony of Megasthenes would likewise seem to imply that Candragupta submitted to the devotional teaching of the Sermānes, as opposed to the doctrines of the Brahmans." — Thomas (Edward), op. cit., pp. 23-24. For references to Jainism in the Greek annals see Rice (Lewis), op. cit., p. 8.
3. Jacobi, *Kalpa-Sūtra*, Int., p. xiii. According to the Digambaras he died in 162 A.V. Cf. Narasimhachar, op. cit., Int., p. 40.
4. Cf. Rice (Lewis), op. cit., p. 7 ; Smith, op. cit., p. 206 ; Narasimhachar, op. cit., Int., p. 41.
5. Cf. Jacobi, *Pariśiṣṭaparvan*, pp. 61-62.
6. Cf. Smith, *Oxford History of India*, p. 72.

himself to death like a true Jaina saint.[1] Tradition represents the "wicked minister" as having repented and retired to *Shookul Tīrtha*, on the banks of the Narbada, where he died, and Candragupta is also supposed to have accompanied him.[2] "*Shookul Tīrtha*" is the exact equivalent of "Beḷgoḷa," which in Kanarese means "white pond." In the inscriptions it is also called धवल सरस्, which means "white lake."[3] This coincidence, even if it were merely accidental, is certainly significant. Apart from minor details, this coincides with the opinion of Rhys Davids that "the linguistic and epigraphical evidence so far available confirms in many respects the general reliability of traditions current amongst the Jainas." He has also remarked : "It is certain that in the extant priestly literature Candragupta is completely ignored for about ten centuries."[4] It seems not a little likely that this silence of brāhmanical writers was due in no small measure to the Mauryan Emperor's acceptance of the Jaina religion towards the end of his earthly career.

Finally, taking the successors of Candragupta, we have before us Bindusāra, Aśoka, Kunāla and Samprati, according to the Jaina tradition. As with the Śaiśunāgas and the Nandas so also in the case of the Mauryas there are differences and discrepancies in the lists put forth by various traditions. However, as far as Aśoka is concerned there is no trouble. It is agreed to by all that Candragupta left behind him his son and successor, Bindusāra, who was in turn followed by his son Aśoka. As to the relations of these two Mauryas with the Jainas this much is certain, that their literary traditions are not so eloquent about them as is the case with their predecessor Candragupta and their successor Samprati. Nevertheless there are grounds before us to infer that both of them must have been favourably inclined towards the Jaina church. About Bindusāra, the predecessor of Aśoka, we know practically little beyond the fact that he sent an embassy to Antiochos Soter requesting

1. Cf. Jacobi, op. cit., p. 62 ; Jolly, *Arthaśāstra of Kauṭilya*, Int., pp. 10-11. For the mutual relations between the *Arthaśāstra* and Jaina literature see ibid., p. 10. We have seen that the Jaina tradition puts Cāṇakya's father as supposed to have been both a brāhmaṇa and a devout Jaina. This looks like the brāhmaṇa-Christians of our days. This means that Cāṇakya's family was of brāhmaṇa origin by birth or heritage, and Jaina by faith. To quote Edward Thomas : "But though our king-maker was a Brahman, he was not necessarily, in the modern acceptation of the term, "Brahmanist."" — Thomas (Edward), op. cit., pp. 25-26.
2. Cf. Smith, op. cit., p. 75, n. 1.
3. Cf. Narasimhachar, op. cit., Int., p. 1.
4. Rhys Davids, *Buddhist India*, pp. 164, 270.

him to send him a Greek philosopher; and also the inference, from the known extent of his conquests and his father's empire, that he must have extended his dominions so as to cover at least some portions of Mysore.[1] Both these facts are not without their significance to us, inasmuch as the first explains to some extent the philosophic eclecticism of Bindusāra, and the second the distribution of Aśoka's edicts in south India. It may not be unlikely that, in addition to the kṣatriya ambitions of mere conquest, Bindusāra might have been actuated by filial motive in acquiring Mysore, a place rendered sacred by the last days of his father Candragupta.

The Ceylonese traditions, however, assert that Bindusāra was Brāhmanical. About the father of Aśoka the *Mahāvaṁsa* informs us that he being of the Brāhmanical faith maintained sixty thousand brāhmaṇas[2]; but, as Edward Thomas observes, "their testimony would not carry much weight in the argument about other lands and other times, and it is, moreover, a critical question as to how much they knew about brāhmanism itself, and whether the use of the word "brāhmaṇa" does not merely imply, in their sense, a non-Buddhistic or any religion opposed to their own. We may conclude, for all present purposes, that Bindusāra followed the faith of his father, and that, in the same belief — whatever it may prove to have been — his childhood's lessons were first learnt by Aśoka."[3]

Besides this it is not possible to say anything more about the shadowy figure of Bindusāra. That, like his father, he also was under the influence of Cāṇakya we have already remarked. The Jaina tradition tells us that during his period the brāhmaṇa minister incurred the king's displeasure and was supplanted by some Subandhu.[4] Coming to Aśoka, his son and successor, it need not be said that his is not the shadowy figure of his father. There is ample material to show how far he kept his relations with the *Nigganṭha* church, though there is a great difference of opinion with regard to the one faith which Aśoka might have followed throughout his career. What we are most immediately concerned with is Aśoka's attitude towards Jainism, which, apart from his hereditary affinities towards eclecticism, we venture to think

1. Cf. Smith, *Early History of India*, pp. 155-56.
2. *Pitā saṭṭhisahassāṁ brāhmaṇe brahmapakkhike bhojesi.* — Geiger, op. cit., *Paricchedo*, V, v. 34.
3. Thomas (Edward), op. cit., p. 29.
4. For the circumstances under which Cāṇakya lost the goodwill of his master see Hemacandra, op. cit., vv. 436-59.

must have been influenced to no small extent by its having been the faith of his grandfather Candragupta, though the *Mahāvaṁsa* tells us that, like his father, Aśoka also bestowed alms on the brāhmaṇas for three years.[1] His edicts are very broad-based, and indicate equal tolerance of all sects. Yet the genesis of this psychology might have been as suggested.

The fact of Aśoka's having been influenced in his early years by the faith of his grandfather Candragupta gathers strength on the testimony of Edward Thomas that in his *Āīn-i-Akbarī* Abu-l-Fazl, the accomplished minister of Akbar, has retained in his notice of the kingdom of Kashmir three very important entries, of which the first establishes "that Aśoka himself first introduced "Jainism," *eo nomine*, into the kingdom of Kashmir."[2] Emphasizing the same point the learned scholar further observes that "the leading fact of Aśoka's introduction or recognition of the Jaina creed in Kashmir does not, however, rest upon the sole testimony of the Muhammadan author, but is freely acknowledged in the brāhmanical pages of the *Rāja Taraṅgiṇi* — a work which, though finally compiled and put together only in AD 1148, relies, in this section of its history, upon the more archaic writings of Padma Mihira and Śrī Chavillākāra."[3]

With all this the learned scholar is conscious that Aśoka was not a Jaina throughout his career, otherwise, as he observes, he would have reasonably been claimed by the Jainas as a potent upholder of their faith.[4] According to Edward Thomas by and by he became a pervert and ultimately leaned towards Buddhism.[5] However, this idea of Aśoka's actual perversion to the Buddhist faith is not easily acceptable. What we venture to suggest is this, that as years went on Aśoka came more and more under the influence of the teaching of Buddha, became less and less of a sectarian, and tried to inculcate in his subjects the *dharma* which embraced the moral precepts and dogmatic tenets common to other religions, though, as Rev. Heras rightly observes, he was "especially influenced by the Jaina doctrines as regards sacredness and inviolability of life."[6]

1. . . . *so pi te yeva tīṇi vassāni bhojayi.* — Geiger, op. and loc. cit.
2. Cf. Thomas (Edward), op. cit., pp. 30-31. "When the succession devolved on Aśoka, the son of Janaka's paternal uncle, he abolished the Brāhmanical religion and established the Jaina faith." — Jarrett, *Āīn-i-Akbarī*, II., p. 382 ; Wilson, *A.R.*, XV., p. 10.
3. Thomas (Edward), op. cit., p. 32. Cf. Wilford, *A.R.*, IX., pp. 96-97.
4. Thomas (Edward), op. cit., p. 24.
5. Cf. ibid.
6. Heras, op. cit., p. 272. Cf. Rock Edicts (I, B), (III, D), (IV, C), (XI, C), etc.; Hultzsch, *C.I.I.*, I., pp. 2, 5, 8, 19, etc. (new edn.).

The statement that Aśoka's *dharma* was not Buddhistic is not a new one. Wilson,[1] Macphail,[2] Fleet,[3] Monahan[4] and Rev. Heras[5] have affirmed this prior to us. Even Dr Kern says that "his inscriptions, with a few exceptions, contain nothing particularly Buddhistic."[6] Senart, after having said that in the *dharma* "there is nothing exclusively Buddhist," makes the following statement: "In my opinion our monuments (Aśoka's inscriptions) are witnesses of a stage of Buddhism, sensibly different from that which is developed in later times."[7] This is a guess without any foundation. The same contradiction is also made by Hultzsch. He says that all his moral proclamations "do not characterize him as a Buddhist reformer"; but he adds, "If we turn to an exaimination of what he tells us about the nature of his *dharma*, it appears that the latter is in thorough agreement with the picture of Buddhist morality which is preserved in the beautiful anthology entitled *Dhammapada* — i.e., 'words of morality.'"[8] The statements of both Senart and Hultzsch seem to have been elicited in compliance with the statements of those who style Aśoka the great Buddhist missionary.[9]

Having thus seen, mainly on the authority of various scholars, that the Pillar Edicts and inscriptions of Aśoka do not *ipso facto* mean that he was or had become a Buddhist, we shall now examine his own writings as to how far he was under the influence of *nirgrantha* doctrines. "There is no country," says Aśoka, "where these (two) classes, (viz.) the Brahmanas and *Śramaṇas*, do not exist, except among the *Yonas*."[10] But who were these "Śramaṇas"? Hultzsch takes them to

1. "In the first place, then, with respect to the supposed main purport of the inscriptions, proselytism to the Buddhist religion, it may not unreasonably be doubted if they were made public with any such design, and whether they have connection with Buddhism at all." — Wilson, *J.R.A.S.*, XII., p. 236. Cf. ibid., p. 250.
2. Cf. Macphail, *Aśoka*, p. 48. "*Dharma*, the colloquial for *Dharma*, is the word used. In the edicts it does not stand for Buddhism, but for the simple piety which Aśoka wished all his subjects of whatever faith to practise." — Ibid.
3. Cf. Fleet, *J.R.A.S.*, 1908, pp. 491-92. ". . . The distinct object of both the Rock and the Pillar Edicts was not to propagate Buddhism or any other particular religion, but to proclaim the determination of Aśoka to govern the realm righteously and kindly in accordance with the duty of pious kings, and with considerations for all forms of religious belief . . ." etc. — Ibid., p. 492.
4. "The doctrines of Aśoka's major Rock and Pillar Edicts cannot be called distinctively Buddhist," etc. — Monahan, *Early History of Bengal*, p. 214.
5. "Buddhist chronicles of the fourth, fifth and sixth centuries have deceived many scholars. . . . There is not the least mention of any Buddhist deep principle." — Heras, op. cit., pp. 255, 271.
6. Kern, *Manual of Indian Buddhism*, p. 112.
7. Senart, *I.A.*, XX., pp. 260, 264-65.
8. Cf. Heras, op. cit., p. 271.
9. Hultzsch, op. cit., Int., p. xlix.
10. Hultzsch, op. cit., p. 47 (J).

mean "Buddhist monks,"[1] though there is no special reason why such a restriction should be made.

"*Śramaṇa*" simply denotes an ascetic or monk, and the Jainas used the term even befor the Buddhists appropriated it. It has been used so in the Greek annals, and this has been, as seen before, confirmed by other scholars also.[2] Thus an ancient vow of the Jaina runs : "I take the twelfth vow, the *Atithi saṁvibhāga vṛata*, by which I promise to give *Śramaṇa* or *Nirgrantha* any of the fourteen things which they can accept without blame," etc.[3] Likewise the *Kalpa-Sūtra* speaks of "the *Nirgrantha Śramaṇas* of the present time."[4] Kundakundācārya as well, the earliest Digambara writer of the south, uses the term to signify the monks of his own sect.[5] But over and above all the Buddhists themselves applied the term *Śramaṇa* to the *nirgranthas*. For the *Aṅguttara Nikāya* says : "O Viśākha, there is a class of *Śramaṇas* who are called *Nirgranthas*."[6] That the Jainas used the term prior to the Buddhists is also conclusively proved by the fact that the latter styled themselves "*Sākyaputtiya Samaṇas*" as distinguished from the already existing "*Nigganṭha Samaṇas*."[7]

On the other hand, however, when Aśoka wanted to speak of Buddhists alone, he has always used the word *saṁgha*. For instance, in Pillar Edict VII, he says : "Some (*Mahāmātras*) were ordered by me to busy themselves with the affairs of the *Saṁgha*; likewise others were ordered to busy themselves with the Brahmanas (and) *Ājīvikas*; others were ordered by me to busy themselves also with the *Nirgranthas*; others . . . with various (other) sects."[8]

The independent mention of brāhmaṇas, *ājīvikas* and *nirgranthas* shows that these were distinct entities altogether different from the *saṁgha*. In all other places the *śramaṇas* are invariably mentioned together with the brāhmaṇas.[9] The omission of *śramaṇas* in this passage can be explained only

1. Hultzsch, op. cit., Int., p. 1.
2. Cf. Rice (Lewis), op. cit., p. 8.
3. Stevenson (Mrs), op. cit., p. 218.
4. Jacobi, S.B.E., XXII., p. 297.
5. Cf. Bhandarkar, op. cit., pp. 97-100.
6. Cf. Jacobi, S.B.E., XLV., Int., p. xvii. Read also Kamta Prasad Jain's interesting article on "The Jaina References in the Buddhist Literature," *I.H.Q.*, II., pp. 698-709.
7. Cf. Rhys Davids, op. cit., p. 143.
8. Delhi-Topra Pillar Edict VII ; Cf. Hultzsch, op. cit., p. 136 (Z).
9. See Rock Edicts (III, D), (IV, C), (IX, G), (XI, C), (XIII, G), and Pillar Edict VII (H H) ; Cf. Hultzsch, op. cit., Int., p. 1.

by the substitution of *ājīvikas* and *nirgranthas*, both of whom, as already seen, can be distinguished from the *saṁgha*.

As to the attitude of Aśoka towards Jainism, or in fact towards any such other faith, it is indicated in the following words : "All men are my children. As on my behalf of (my own) children I desire that they may be provided with complete welfare and happiness in this and in the other world, even so is my desire on behalf of all men."[1] Likewise, more specifically, he states : "In the same manner I am directing my attention to all classes. And all the sects have been honoured by me with honours of various kinds."[2]

Aśoka had his *Dharma-Mahāmātra* in the north as well as in the south "to supervise Buddhists, Brahmanas and *Ājīvikas*, *Nirgrantha* and other sects."[3] His non-sectarian policy is perhaps nowhere better in evidence than in the following :

"Whosoever," says the Emperor, "praises his own sect or blames other sects — all (this) out of devotion to his own sect — if he is acting thus, he rather injures his own sect very severely."[4]

Speaking of the Barābar cave inscriptions Smith writes : "These records are chiefly of interest as a decisive proof that Aśōka was sincere in his solemn declaration that he honoured all sects."[5] This is no less true of Aśoka's other inscriptions, and although we have no direct evidence as to the state of Jainism in north India under his benevolent rule, the above observations at least serve to reveal the attitude of Candragupta's greatest successor towards the religion he himself had adopted—at least in the evening of his glorious career, if not earlier.

Our hypothesis of the hereditary influence of this tradition is also supported by the conversion of Aśoka's grandson, Samprati, by Suhastin to the Jaina faith.[6] Before entering into any further discussion about Samprati's enthusiasm for Jainism it may be şeen who were the successors of Aśoka. Unfortunately, to quote Dr Raychaudhuri, "No Kauṭilya or Megasthenes has left any account of the later Mauryas. It is impossible to reconstruct a detailed

---

1. Separate Rock Edicts : Jaugada, I (F.G.), II (E.F.) ; Cf. Hultzsch, op. cit., pp. 114-17.
2. Delhi-Topra Pillar Edict VI (D.E.) ; Cf. Hultzsch, op. cit., p. 129 ; Int., p. xlviii.
3. Ibid., Int., p. xl.
4. Girnar Rock Edict XII (H) ; Cf. Hultzsch, op. cit., p. 21.
5. Smith, op. cit., p. 177. Cf. Hultzsch, op. cit., Int., p. xlviii.
6. Cf. Jacobi, *Pariśishṭaparvan*, p. 69 ; Bhandarkar, op. cit., p. 135.

history of Aśoka's successor from the scanty data furnished by one or two inscriptions and a few brāhmanical, Jaina and Buddhist works."[1]

The Purāṇas themselves do not agree as to who was the successor of Aśoka. It is not an easy task to reconcile the divergent versions of different authorities. However, the reality of Kunāla the son of Aśoka is established by the combined testimony of all,[2] but as to his succession the tradition is not unanimous. Hemacandra tells us under what unhappy circumstances he became blind, and was rendered "unfit to carry on the work of government which was presumably entrusted to his favourite son Samprati, the Jaina Aśoka, who is described by the Jaina and Buddhist writers as the immediate successor of Aśoka."[3]

The only difficulty that lies in our way in accepting Samprati as the successor of Aśoka is the reality of Daśaratha, whom we have already seen in connection with the Nāgārjunī Hills bestowed by him upon the *ājīvikas*. The only possible explanation of the difficulty seems to be this, that as the grandsons of Aśoka either both of them ruled at the same time with Samprati as the successor of Aśoka or that Daśaratha has been omitted by both the Buddhist and the Jaina annals. Of the two the first presumption seems to be more correct, considering the unanimous inclusion of Samprati in the Magadhan list.[4]

Thus there is no doubt about the fact that Samprati was one of the Maurya emperors who was great enough to be mentioned by all. As to his enthusiasm for the Jaina church, it can safely be opined that he is one of the leading stars of the Jaina history in the north. In the matter of propagation of the Jaina faith Jaina records speak as highly of Samprati as the Buddhist records do of Aśoka. Smith observes : "He (Samprati) is reputed to have been as zealous in promoting the cause of Jainism as Aśoka had been in propagating the religion of Gautama."[5]

1. Raychaudhuri, op. cit., p. 220.
2. Cf. Pargiter, op. cit., pp. 28, 70 ; Cowell and Neil, op. cit., p. 430 ; *Kalpa-Sūtra, Subodhikā-Ṭīkā, sūt*. 163 ; Raychaudhuri, op. cit., p. 221.
3. Cf. Jacobi, op. cit., pp. 63-64 ; Cowell and Neil, op. cit., p. 433 ; Raychaudhuri, op. and loc. cit. ; Bhandarkar, op. and loc. cit.
4. Both the Buddhist and the Jaina traditions about Samprati have been referred to by us in the previous note. For the Purāṇic see Pargiter, op. cit., pp. 28, 70. Cf. Raychaudhuri, op. cit., p. 220. "Perhaps the empire was divided between his grandsons, Daśaratha . . . and Samprati. . . ." — Smith, op. cit., 203.
5. Smith, *Oxford History of India*, p. 117, and n. 1. Cf. Bhandarkar, op. and loc. cit. ; सम्प्रति . . . पितामहदत्तराज्यो रथयात्राप्रवृत्तश्रीआर्यसुहस्तिदर्शनाज्जातजातिस्मृतिः . . . जिनालय सपादकोटि . . . अकरोत. — →

About Samprati's zeal for the Jaina church Hemacandra briefly observes as follows : "He showed his zeal by causing Jaina temples to be erected over the whole of *Jambūdvīpa*. During Suhastin's stay at Ujjaini, and under his guidance, splendid religious festivals and processions in honour of the *Arhat* were celebrated, and great was the devotion manifested by the king and his subjects on this occasion. The example and advice of Samprati induced his vassals to embrace and patronise his creed, so that not only in his kingdom but also in adjacent countries the monks could practise their religion."[1]

What is more important for us to know in connection with Samprati is this — that he sent Jaina missionaries to south India, and that these were of the Śvetāmbara persuasion.[2] To quote Hemacandra : "In order to extend the sphere of their (Jaina monks) activities to uncivilised countries, Samprati sent there messengers disguised as Jaina monks. They described to the people the kind of food and other requisites which monks may accept as alms, enjoining them to give such things instead of the usual tax to the revenue collector who would visit them from time to time. Of course these revenue collectors were to be Jaina monks. Having thus prepared the way for them, he induced the superior to send monks to those countries, for they would find it in no way impossible to live there. Accordingly missionaries were sent to the Āndhras and Dramilas, who found everything as the king had told. Thus the uncivilised nations were brought under the influence of Jainism."[3]

The importance of the Jaina missionaries sent by Samprati to uncivilized countries, as Hemacandra tells us, lies in this — that it is the earliest reference, so far as we know, to contact of the Śvetāmbaras with the south. Hence it is as important as the great migration dealt with in this and the preceding chapter. We particularly call it the Śvetāmbara contact because, as seen before, the Śvetāmbara-Digambara schism in the Jaina church is connected with both the migration and the Suhastin-Mahāgiri tradition.

→ *Kalpa-Sūtra, Subodhikā-Ṭīkā, sūt.* 6, p. 163. "Almost all ancient Jaina temples or monuments of unknown origin are ascribed by the popular voice to Samprati, who is in fact regarded as a Jaina Aśoka." — Smith, *Early History of India*, p. 202.

1. Jacobi, op. cit., p. 69.
2. Cf. Bhandarkar, op. and loc. cit. About this the *Pāṭalīputrakalpa* of Jinaprabhasūri observes : "In Pāṭalīpustra flourished the great King Samprati, son of Kunala, lord of Bharata with its three continents, the great Arhanta who established *Vihāras* for *Śramaṇas* even in non-Āryan countries." — Cf. Raychaudhuri, op. cit., p. 222.
3. Cf. Jacobi, op. and loc. cit.

That Suhastin was a Śvetāmbara is also evident from the fact that the Digambara *paṭṭāvalīs*, or genealogies of teachers, do not mention him.[1] We are further informed that when Āryamahāgiri saw that Samprati was converted by Suhastin, he withdrew himself to Daśārṇabhadra, seeing that, "all his hopes of winning the monks to lives of sterner asceticism" were at an end.[2] Thus the Śvetāmbara rule triumphed at the court of Samprati.

Here ends the importance of Magadha as seen in the light of Jaina history. With the end of the Mauryas and the consequent beginning of the Śuṅgas Kaliṅga becomes the centre of our history. With the fall of the sovereign power in Magadha, Kaliṅga more or less succeeds in taking its place. Magadha learned to her cost what the powerful Kaliṅga meant in the time of Khāravela. Fortunately enough, though for a very short time, it also plays an equally important part in the history of the Jaina church. That after Samprati the Mauryas did not survive long is certain, and whatever survival they must have had seems to be highly shadowy and positively degrading — that the last of them, as seen before and as we shall see in the next chapter, was grievously murdered by his own commander-in-chief.

However at present we need not enter into the why and wherefore of the fall of the powerful Mauryas. Suffice it to say that the reconquest of Kaliṅga by the Maurya Aśoka was a great landmark in the history of Magadha and of India. It completed the unification of non-Tamil India under the hegemony of Magadha. It marked the close of that career of conquest and aggrandisement which was ushered in by Bimbisāra's annexation of Aṅga. It opened a new era — an era of peace, of social progress, of religious propaganda and at the same time of political stagnation and, perhaps, of military inefficiency, during which the martial spirit of imperial Magadha had died out for want of exercise. The era of Digvijaya was over, the era of Dharmavijaya had begun, and this finally resulted in the disappearance of the Maurya sovereignty over the Magadhan Empire.

---

1. Cf. Hoernle, *I.A.*, XXI., pp. 57-58, and Klatt, ibid., XI., p. 251.
2. Stevenson (Mrs.), op. cit., p. 74. Cf. Barodia, *History and Literature of Jainism*, p. 55.

CHAPTER IV

Jainism in Kaliṅga-Deśa

THE expression "Jainism in Kaliṅga-deśa," in the main, embraces the history of the religion during the times of Khāravela. This does not mean that Jainism in Kaliṅga cannot be traced farther than Khāravela. On the other hand, that would be denying what can be clearly deduced from such historical data as the Hāthīgumphā inscription, the architectural and sculptural similarity of the monuments standing there to those of the fourth and fifth century BC, and the most sacred of the Jaina canonical works. With all this it must be admitted that but for the inscription of Khāravela in the Hāthīgumphā and of his wife in the Swargapurī cave there is no other decisive ground on which we can base our inferences.[1]

As already seen, after Mahāvīra we have kings of the Śaiśunāga, Nanda, Maurya and other dynasties, most of whom were, according to Jaina traditions and history, the followers or supporters of Jaina religion during their régime. No doubt these traditions and history are confirmed by many Jaina and non-Jaina writers, but from the standpoint of a purely historical proof none of these, excepting perhaps Candragupta, can be compared with that great Cedi[2] king, Khāravela, who was, as stated in one of his own inscriptions, a Jaina.

The chief historical proof as to when and how far and how long the Emperor Khāravela ruled, and as to whether he was a Jaina or not, lies in the Hāthīgumphā inscription of his time. That he was a great Kaliṅga king

1. Let it be clear from the very beginning that it is really not desirable and practically impossible to trace out chronologically the progress of Jainism in Kaliṅga. All that is required is to lay our hands on whatever historical monuments, small or great, ancient or modern, that are available at present, and draw our inferences from them, keeping in view as far as possible the contemporary historical atmosphere of the time.
2. We know the Cedis as the well-known Vedic and classical ruling family which seems to have migrated into Orissa from Mahākośala, where they are also found in later history. "It is certain that one of the seats of the Cedis was near about Orissa in very ancient times." — *J.B.O.R.S.*, XIII., p. 223.

is a fact which cannot be denied, but it is not possible to fix accurately the limits of Kaliṅga country. It was under him that on the downfall of the Mauryan Empire Kaliṅga revolted and became an independent kingdom. The boundaries of Kaliṅga, the territory under the Eastern Ghāṭs lying along the coast of the Bay of Bengal on the north of Teleṅgānā, seem to have been uncertain.[1] The strip of land that fringes the Bay of Bengal, extending from the Godāvarī towards the north, was anciently known as Kaliṅga. Roughly speaking, it may be taken as comprising the part of the country which we now call Orissa and Gañjam.

Khāravela's inscription "is one of the most celebrated and also one of the most perplexing of all the historical monuments in India."[2] Among the followers of Lord Mahāvīra, Khāravela's is the most ancient name of a ruling potentate that can be found in an inscription. Considering the chronology of post-Mauryan times and the ancient glory of Jainism his is the most important, and the only inscription yet discovered in the country. No doubt it is unparalleled from the viewpoint of Jaina history, but unquestionable is its importance from even the standpoint of the political history of India.

In the words of Sir Ashutosh Mookerji: "In the region of epigraphy, that branch of historical research which has removed (the impression of) the seals written in forgotten and mysterious letters and unlocked the gates of the past, our attention is arrested by the Hāthigumphā inscription of Emperor Khāravela. The inscription, which was recorded in the second century before the Christian era, embodies a biography of the king of Orissa from his infancy to the thirteenth year of his reign and the thirty-seventh year of his life. The inscription is chiselled on the face of a rock, which has been known and studied for a century since its first discovery by Sterling in 1825; and the numerous historical data furnished thereby have been recognized as of first-rate importance, as they include references to the contemporary king of Magadha, the Greek king of Mathura, the fortresses of Gorathagiri (Barābar Hills) and Rājagṛha, the Gangetic places at Pāṭalīputra and King Sātakarṇi of the Deccan. Numerous and fruitful have been the consequential studies based on this reinvestigation of what, in the long array of Brāhmī inscriptions, can be placed, next to the edicts of Aśoka, in the same category only with the fourth-century inscription of Samudragupta."[3]

1. *C.H.I.*, I., p. 601.
2. Ibid., p. 534.
3. *J.B.O.R.S.*, X., pp. 9-10.

In India, Benares and Purī are the two most important places of pilgrimage, famous alike from sanctity and historic associations treasured up in the nation's undying remembrance. It is here that the whole nation's fervent devotion has manifested itself in many a form; it is here that the heart and intellect of the nation have proceeded on parallel lines.

We have reason to believe that Orissa, now "the garden of Hinduism, with Jagannath its Jerusalem,"[1] was an important seat of Buddhist and Jaina influence from the third century BC to the eighth or ninth century AD. Buddhism began to exercise its influence at the conquest of Kaliṅga by Aśoka, the great Maurya king in 262 BC[2]; but with his death the Mauryan Empire rapidly declined, and Puṣyamitra, the royal chaplain (*purohit*) to the Mauryas and the mighty champion of the Brāhmanical reaction which set in after the triumph of Buddhism during Aśoka's rule, usurped the royal throne and gave a severe blow to the Buddhist faith in India.[3] With all this he could not enjoy his dominions unchallenged. Side by side with the great Āndhra dynasty in the south another great power that arose in the wake of the Mauryan Empire was the illustrious Cedi dynasty under Mahāmeghavāhana Khāravela, with its home in the lowlands of the eastern coast. This dynasty proved a good set-back to the Brāhmanical reaction of the north.[4]

Thus in the second century BC all the three religions — Brāhmanism, Jainism and Buddhism — were represented by Kaliṅga, while the middle one enjoyed the privilege of being the State religion. Hiuen-Tsiang, the Chinese pilgrim who visited Kaliṅga some time between AD 629 and 645, testifies to the numerical strength of Jainism, and describes the territory as a stronghold of the Jaina faith. He tells us that there were "very many unbelievers of different sorts, the most numerous being the *Nirgranthas* (Ni-kin followers)."[5]

This is a clear advance of the Jaina faith from Magadha, the land of its birth, into south-eastern India as far as Kaliṅga. This progress of the Jainas can be traced out, and can be proved as a matter of fact, from two documents at Khaṇḍagiri in Orissa of the great King Khāravela and his wife. He governed

---

1. *J.A.S.B.*, XXVIII., nos. I to V (1859), p. 186.
2. Ganguly, *Orissa and her Remains — Ancient and Mediaeval*, p. 17.
3. Mazumdar, *Hindu History*, p. 636 (2nd edn.).
4. *C.H.I.*, I., pp. 518, 534.
5. Beal, *Si-Yu-Ki*, II., p. 208.

the east coast of India from *c.* 183 BC to *c.* 152 BC — that is, in the first half of the second century BC.[1] This is also confirmed by certain other caves and ruins of temples lying on either Udayagiri or Khaṇḍagiri Hills. Both these hills are situated at a distance of about five miles to the north-west of Bhubaneśvara, and are separated by a ravine forming a continuous line with the road from Bhubaneśvara. Furthermore the hill tribes, who now occupy a degraded position among the servile castes, are mentioned in several places in the *aṅga*s and the *upāṅga*s, the oldest sacred literature of the Jainas, where their language is referred to as one of the tongues of the barbarians (*mleccha*).[2]

Of the documents just mentioned the first and the largest is the inscription of Khāravela, which opens with the usual benedictory formula of the Jainas. It proves that Jainism entered Orissa and probably became the State religion within one hundred years from its last prophet, Mahāvīra. The second and the smaller one in the Swargapurī cave asserts that Khāravela's chief queen caused a temple and a cave to be prepared for the *śramaṇa*s of Kaliṅga.

Before we take up a detailed review of the Hāthīgumphā inscription we shall first see what little can be had from the neighbouring ruins. According to the *District Gazetteer* it seems certain, that during the rule of the Emperor Aśoka a number of Jainas settled in the district, for the sandstone hills of Udayagiri and Khaṇḍagiri are covered with their hermitage caves, some of which bear inscriptions in the Brāhmī character of the Maurya age. They all appear to have been made for the religious use of the Jainas, and to have been used by Jaina monks for many a century.[3]

It may be noticed here that both the Buddhist and the Jaina period of architectural growth in Orissa is characterized by cave temples.[4] We say both the Buddhist and the Jaina influence because some of the Khaṇḍagiri caves, like the Rānīgumphā and the Anantagumphā, are conspicuous for Buddhist symbols like the Bo-tree, a Bauddha *triśūla*, a votive *stūpa*, the characteristic *swastika* mark, and so on.[5]

---

1. *J.B.O.R.S.*, XIII., p. 244.
2. They have been identified with Suari of Pliny and Sabarai of Ptolemy. For the reference of the Jaina literature see Weber, *I.A.*, XIX., pp. 65, 69 ; XX., pp. 25, 368, 374.
3. *B.D.G.P.*, p. 24.
4. Ganguly, op. cit., p. 31.
5. Ibid., pp. 40, 57.

This influence is noticeable from the fifth century BC down to the fifth or sixth century AD. This is well corroborated by the fact that both the Khaṇḍagiri and Udayagiri Hills, otherwise called Khaṇḍagiri, are honeycombed with caves or cells, of which forty-four are in Udayagiri, nineteen in Khaṇḍagiri and three in Nilgiri.[1] Their number, age and carvings make these caves the most interesting in eastern India. They were inhabited in ancient times by the Bauddha and Jaina hermits, or *śramaṇas*, and many of them appear from palaeographic grounds, to have been excavated in the second or third century BC. As Mr Ganguly says: "We think we shall not be far from the truth in dating some of the caves even in the 4th or 5th century BC — that is, before the period of the Hāthigumphā inscription — for the locality where the caves were excavated must have had some sort of previous sanctity preserved in the eyes of the co-religionists."[2]

It is almost a hopeless task to fix with certainty any dates for the caves, and intermingling of Buddhist and Jaina influences has rendered it more so. On the walls of the cells are usually carved the figures of Buddhist legends and of the Jaina *tīrthaṅkaras* in *basso-rilievo*. Elaborate pillars are noticed in the Jaina Gumphā on Khaṇḍagiri Hill. The peculiarity of almost all these caves is that a bench runs round the three sides of the front verandah, the height varying from 1 ft to 1 ft 6 inches. The two walls of the verandah are so hollowed out on the top as to look like cupboards. These were meant to hold the scanty necessaries of life of the Buddhist or Jaina monks. Further details on the architectural side of the caves we shall note in the chapter entitled "Jaina Art in the North." For the present we shall stop with a remark of Mr Ganguly that "the caves present a very simple, though massive face, consistent with the lives of their past inmates."[3]

Among the Khaṇḍagiri caves the Satghara or Satbakhra, Navamuni and Ananta are the most important. The first two bear evident traces of Jaina influences,[4] and the last of Bauddha, because of the *svastika*s and pointed *triśūla*s carved on its back wall. Anyhow, below the first *svastika* there is a small standing image, now much worn out, which, according to the *District Gazetteer*, probably represents Pārśvanātha, the twenty-third *tīrthaṅkara* of

1. *B.D.G.P.*, p. 251.
2. Ganguly, op. cit., p. 32.
3. Ibid., p. 34.
4. Cf. Chakravarti (Mon Mohan), *Notes on the Remains in Dhauli and in the Caves of Udayagiri and Khaṇḍagiri*, p. 8.

the Jainas.[1] Moreover, the courtyard of the cave is formed by levelling the northern portion of the higher ledge, which contains images of Jaina saints and deities, and the mass of carvings has every arch enfolded within two big serpent-hoods, the symbols of Pārśva. The space between the arches and the side walls is filled with *vidyādharas* flying with offerings in their hands.

The Satghara cave is noted for the figures of Jaina *tīrthaṅkaras* with their characteristic symbols, or *lāñchana*, sculptured on the antechamber walls of the southern portion,[2] while the Navamuni, or the cave of the nine saints, is an ordinary cave, consisting of two rooms with a common verandah. It contains images in moderate relief of ten *tīrthaṅkaras* about a foot high, with their Śāsana-devīs, or consorts, below them. Pārśvanātha, who is easily recognized by his serpent-hoods, is the most honoured, for he is carved twice.[3]

Furthermore, this cave is noted for two inscriptions, one of them being of "the year 18 of the increasing and victorious reign of the illustrious Uddyotakeśarideva,"[4] and both referring to the Jaina *śramaṇa* Śubhacandra, "the disciple of the lord of the illustrious Kulacandra, the *Ācārya* of the *Deśigaṇa* derived from *Graha Kula*, belonging to the illustrious *Ārya Saṁgha*."[5] Both the inscriptions seem to belong to the same date — about the tenth century AD.[6]

Beyond this cave lies the Bārabhujī, or the twelve-handed cave, so called because of the figure of a female with twelve hands carved on the left wall of the verandah. Like the Navamuni cave, here also are carved in moderate relief seated *tīrthaṅkaras* or Jaina saints with their Śāsana-devīs, and on the back wall is a standing Pārśvanātha, canopied by a seven-hooded serpent and without any Devīs. The saints and their wives are shown with their different symbols, and are nearly of equal size — 8 to 9½ inches each — but the figure of Pārśva is 2 ft 7½ inches high, from which he would appear to have had special honour.[7]

---

1. *B.D.G.P.*, p. 263.
2. The sculptures are the Jaina *tīrthaṅkaras* with all their Śāsana-devīs, and do not resemble Bauddha symbols as believed by the editor of *The Archaeological Survey Report*, XIII., p. 81.
3. *B.D.G.P.*, p. 262.
4. *E.I.*, XIII., p. 166.
5. Ibid.
6. Ganguly, op. cit., p. 60.
7. *B.D.G.P.*, op. and loc. cit.

Adjoining this on the south is the *triśūla* cave, so called from a rude carving on the verandah wall, which is unique in having the inside benched. Above the benches is carved a series of twenty-four *tīrthaṅkaras*, including Pārśva, under the seven hoods of a snake, and ending with Mahāvīra. In this group too, Pārśva, instead of being placed before Mahāvīra as the twenty-third saint, is given a position of honour in the centre of the back wall. The base of the fifteenth saint is hidden by a masonry structure rising from the floor, on which are placed three well-carved steatite images of Ādinātha. The general execution of the images in this group is finer than in the adjoining cave.[1]

Of the same date as the Navamuni cave we gave an inscription of Uddyotakeśari in Lālatenḍu-keśari's cave or lion gate. According to the *District Gazetteer* it is a two-storeyed cave called after King Lālatenḍu Keśari, and the rooms on the first floor contain some carvings of Jaina saints, of whom Pārśvanātha is the most important.[2] It is incised on the back wall of the cave, at a height of about 30 or 40 ft from the floor of the cave, above a group of images of the Digambara sect.[3]

The inscription does not seem to be well preserved, and hence a few words are missing in the last line. As it is, it tells us that "in the year five of the victorious reign of the illustrious Uddyotakeśarī, on the illustrious Kumāra mountain,[4] decayed tanks and decayed temples were caused to shine, (and) at that place the images of the twenty-four Tīrthaṅkaras were set up. At the time of the dedication . . . Jasanandi . . . in the place (temple ?) of the illustrious Pāraśyanātha (Pārśvanātha)."[5]

It becomes apparent from what is laid down in the inscription that Uddyotakeśarī was either a Jaina by religion or at least a great protector of the Jaina faith. We have no certain grounds to identify this Uddyotakeśarī of

1. *B.D.G.P.*, op. and loc. cit.
2. Ibid. Cf. Chakravarti (Mon Mohan), op. cit., p. 19.
3. It may be that at the time of Khāravela the great schism, which was followed by the division of the Jaina community into the Digambaras and Śvetāmbaras, had not fully manifested itself, but, as we have seen before, in later history the former were predominant in the south. This is clear from the Jaina caves at Ellorā, Bādāmī and such other places.
4. We learn from line two of the inscription that the ancient name of Khaṇḍagiri is Kumāraparvata. The Hāthīgumphā inscription of Khāravela mentions Kumāraparvata as the ancient name of Udayagiri. The twin hills seem to have been known as the Kumāra-Kumārī-parvata up to the tenth or eleventh century AD.
5. *E.I.*, XIII., p. 167.

the inscription with any historical personage. It may safely be said that the history of Orissa is wrapped in darkness, more or less, from AD 200 — i.e. the time of the Āndhras to the beginning of the seventh century AD.

However, according to the Mādalā Pāñjī, or palm-leaf chronicles of the temple of Jagannātha, Orissa was under the Keśarī or Lion dynasty from the seventh to the twelfth century AD[1]; but it would be going beyond our period to trace in detail the Keśarī dynasty. Nevertheless the number and magnificence of the remains at Bhubaneśvara and elsewhere are evidence of a wealthy and highly civilized kingdom. These stately temples show the hold which Hinduism had obtained in Orissa by this time, and no further trace is found of Buddhism, which according to tradition was introduced a few centuries earlier. At the same time Jainism appears to have continued to retain its hold on the affections of the people or to have had a rival, for in the cave at Khaṇḍagiri and Udayagiri we find inscriptions and rock-cut images of Jaina saints or deities dating back to the same period.

Coming to the caves in the Udayagiri Hills we find that they are the most important caves in Orissa from the point of view of architecture and sculpture, and of them the Rānīgumphā or the Rānī Nūr is the best known. It is the most important of all, and in it elaborately carved friezes represent various scenes of human activities. The three friezes and the carvings on the lower-storey rooms naturally attract special attention. According to the *District Gazetteer*, "the scenes, though mostly mutilated, clearly indicate the procession of a saint through a town during some religious festival, when persons would be looking out from their houses for a glimpse of him, when horses would be led, elephants be ridden and guards be in attendance, while the people, both male and female, would follow the saint with folded hands, and women standing or kneeling would present him with fruits or cakes on plates and ask his blessing."[2]

The frieze on the upper main wing, which is nearly 60 ft long, is the most interesting. In fact no frieze in Indian caves has excited more discussion among archaeologists. Various explanations have been given of these scenes, which are also briefly repeated in the Gaṇeśa cave. The editor of the *District Gazetteer* believes that in this Pārśvanātha appears to be the most honoured of the *tīrthaṅkaras*.[3] Taking just a brief survey of the life of Pārśva from such

1. Cf. *B.D.G.P.*, p. 25.
2. Ibid., p. 254.
3. Ibid., Cf. Chakravarti (Mon Mohan), op. cit., pp. 9-10.

IX : Jaina *Gumphā*, Khaṇḍagiri
(From Mitra, *The Antiquities of Orissa*)

X : Portion of a frieze in the upper verandah of the Rānigumphā, Udayagiri
(from Mitra, *The Antiquities of Orissa*)

XI : Swargapurī Caves, Udayagiri
(from Mitra, *The Antiquities of Orissa*)

XII : Jaina Temple at Khaṇḍagiri
(from Mitra, *The Antiquities of Orissa*)

sources[1] as the *Pārśvanātha-Carita* of Bhāvadeva Sūri, the *Kalpa-Sūtra* and the list of the *sthaviras*, the editor concludes that the mediaeval Jaina legends connect Pārśva, the twenty-third *tīrthaṅkara*, with eastern India (including Kaliṅga)[2]; and it is not unreasonable therefore to suggest that the elephant scene introduces Pārśva's future wife Prabhāvatī, with her relatives and attendants, that in the next scene she is abducted by the Kaliṅga king, that in the fourth scene she is rescued by Pārśva in a forest while hunting, that the following scene depicts the wedding feast, the seventh scene the consummation of marriage, and the eighth scene in the lower wing may represent Pārśvanātha as a *tīrthaṅkara*, his wanderings and the honour shown to him.[3] It may therefore be conjectured that the scenes are somehow connected with Pārśva or some revered disciple of his, though it seems too far-fetched to the learned author of *The Remains of Orissa, Ancient and Medieval*,[4] from its being an eminently Buddhist cave because of certain considerations which have been already marked.

The same confusion also arises in the case of the Gaṇeśagumphā. Because of the occurrence of kilted soldiers in the frieze sculpture of this cave like the Rānī Nūr the editor of the *District Gazetteer* comes to the conclusion that this scene refers to a mediaeval legend of the abduction of Prabhāvatī by the Yavan king of Kaliṅga,[5] and her subsequent rescue by Pārśvanātha, the twenty-third *tīrthaṅkara* of the Jainas.[6] This conclusion is specially strengthened when we see that the kilted soldiers probably look like foreigners, and thus to some extent corroborate the mediaeval legend that Pārśva rescued a princess from some Yavan king. However, Mr Ganguly differs from the editor, in taking the cave for a Buddhist one. According to him the sculpture unmistakably indicates a Bauddha origin.[7] With all this it is quite natural that the Jaina monks may have carved in their cells episodes of the life of their venerable saint.

Next in order of importance, from the architectural point of view, come

1. See also Hemacandra, *Triṣaṣṭi-Śalākā*, *Parva* IX, pp. 197-201.
2. तत्राज्ञासीत् कलिङ्गादिदेशानामेकनायकः ।. — Ibid., v. 95, p. 199.
3. *B.D.G.P.*, p. 256.
4. Ganguly, op. cit., p. 39.
5. यवनो नाम दुर्दान्तः — Hemacandra, op. and loc. cit.
6. *B.D.G.P.*, op. and loc. cit. "This scenic frieze appears to be the early story of that developed in the upper storey in the Rāni Gumphā." — Chakravarti (Mon Mohan), op. cit., p. 16.
7. Ganguly, op. cit., p. 43.

the Jayavijaya, the Swargapurī, the Tiger and the serpent caves. Except the Swargapurī cave none of these is of any great historical importance but for the fact that the Tiger cave has a Buddhist inscription, and that, according to Drs Fergusson and Burgess, both the Tiger and the Serpent caves are "the oldest of the sculptured caves in these hills."[1] By the by, it may be mentioned that the Sarpagumphā or the Serpent cave, which is to the west of the Hāthīgumphā, has its verandah so carved as to resemble the head of a serpent with three hoods, the symbol of Pārśva.[2]

In the Swargapurī cave there are three inscriptions, one of which, the first one, speaks of the chief queen of the illustrious Khāravela, the overlord of Kaliṅga. It seems from this that in the noble task of serving the Jaina church he always associated himself with his chief queen. The memory of this noble and pious lady, who was the daughter of Lālāka, is associated, as we shall see later on, with a cave which bears a short inscription mentioning a Jaina temple and a cave built by her.

According to Mr Banerji in the plan printed with the Purī volume of the *Bengal District Gazetteer* this is called the Mañcapurī cave, and some time ago it was known as Swargapura.[3] It was called Vaikuṇṭhagumphā by Prinsep,[4] Vaikuṇṭhapura by Mitra.[5] Speaking on this variety of names Mr Banerji says: "I have found that the local names of these caves vary with each generation. As one name is forgotten a new one is immediately invented. This cave is in reality the upper storey of a cave with two storeys and a side wing, but the local people very often give different names to different parts."[6]

The first inscription is incised on the raised space between the second and the third doorways in front. It consists of three lines, and tells us that "a temple of Arhats and a cave for the *Śramaṇa*s of Kaliṅga had been made by the chief queen of Khāravela, who was the daughter of King Lālāka, the grandson of Hastisāhasa (or Hastisāha)."[7]

The second and the third record merely mention two caves, one of them

1. Fergusson and Burgess, *Cave Temples of India*, p. 68.
2. *B.D.G.P.*, p. 260.
3. *E.I.*, XIII., p. 159.
4. *J.A.S.B.*, VI., p. 1074.
5. Mitra, *Antiquities of Orissa*, II., pp. 14-15.
6. *E.I.*, XIII., op. and loc. cit.
7. अरहंतपसादायं कालिङ्गानं समनानं लेणं . . . सिरि-खारवेलस अगमहिसिना कारितम्. — Ibid.

being in the name of Kūḍepsīrī, "the king, master of Kaliṅga,"[1] and the other in the name of the Prince Vaḍukha.[2] The first is incised on the front wall, while the other is on the side wall of the lower storey. According to Mr Banerji the characters of all the three inscriptions "are slightly later than those of the Hāthīgumphā inscription of Khāravela."[3]

These fragmentary evidences tend to prove the existence of an influential Jaina dynasty which ruled over Kaliṅga. It is not known how long this dynasty lasted or by what other dynasty it was succeeded, but according to the *District Gazetteer* "it is possible that in the 2nd century AD Kaliṅga, including Orissa, acknowledged the suzerainty of the Āndhras, to whose active influence the introduction of Buddhism may perhaps be ascribed. The Tibetan chronicles have preserved a tradition that the king of Otisha was converted to Buddhism, with 1000 of his subjects, by Nāgārjuna, who is believed to have flourished about AD 200 at the court of the Āndhras. The conversion of the people must naturally have been facilitated by this royal example."[4]

With these historical monuments at our disposal it will not be too much to say that the family of the great queen on her father's side also must have been under the Jaina church. As we shall see later on, the party with whom Khāravela, the mighty emperor, joined hands on matrimonial grounds must have been one belonging to the family of a great ruler of those days.

From all that we have seen up till now one thing is very characteristic of these hills, and this must be duly emphasized. In the words of the *District Gazetteer*, "several caves in Khaṇḍagiri contain images of Tīrthaṅkaras which, even if of a later date than the caves, are interesting as examples of mediaeval Jaina hagiology, while if contemporaneous, they are the oldest existing specimens of Jaina Tīrthaṅkaras and their consorts. The prominence given to Pārśva, whether among the images or by the use of his symbol, the serpenthood, is curious, for in other existing remains Mahāvīra is the greatest of all the saints. The preference for Pārśva may point to the early age of the remains, and if so, they are unique specimens of Jaina iconography. So little is known about this great preacher who lived, according to Jaina chronicles, 200 years earlier than Mahāvīra, or about 750 BC, and whose law

1. *E.I.*, XIII., p. 160.
2. Ibid., p. 161.
3. Ibid., p. 159.
4. *B.D.G.P.*, p. 25.

recognized but four vows and allowed an under and upper garment, that the sculptured record contained in these caves, scanty as it is, cannot but be welcome to the antiquarians."[1]

This is what we can glean from the sacred remains of the country which has been spoken of as the land of the "blessed adorned with all the virtues,"[2] and as "the bestower of heaven and salvation."[3] It was here that, long before the Christian era, Jainism and Buddhism gained ascendancy, and exercised a great influence on Hinduism or, properly called, Brahmanism. It is this very land of the *ṛṣis* which experienced alternate cycles of the Jaina or the Buddhist predominance, and hence it seems difficult and sometimes impossible to lay down with absolute certainty that such and such cave is of Jaina or Bauddha origin on the flimsy grounds of certain symbols or some characteristic architectural designs. This becomes specially so when, in those days both the faiths had many a similar symbol — namely, "a *svastika*," "a tree," and so on. After all, whatever may be the nature of such historical data, it is certain that the union of Brāhmanism with Buddhism and Jainism is marked by a great upheaval in every department of thought and art, and architecture, with sculpture, could not escape its influence.

With these preliminary remarks we shall pass on to the Hāthīgumphā inscription, but before we do that a passing reference to the Jaina temple built on the summit of the Khaṇḍagiri Hill by the Mahrattas will not be out of place. The temple is about a century old and was built towards the close of the eighteenth century.[4] As usual with other Jaina temples, it occupies a grand site and commands a beautiful view. Referring to this small temple the learned author of *The Antiquities of Orissa* says: "The sanctuary contains a standing figure of Mahāvīra in black stone, placed on a wooden chair. The temple was built by Manju Chaudhuri and his nephew, Bhavāni Dādu of Cuttack, a Jaina merchant of the Digambara sect."[5] Within the sanctuary there is also a masonry platform, with a small raised wall behind, in which are embedded five images of Jaina saints. Behind the temple at a slightly lower level there is another terrace, on which lie scattered scores of votive *stūpas*, indicating the existence of an older temple.[6]

---

1. *B.D.G.P.*, p. 266.
2. *Brahma Purāṇa*, 26th chapter.
3. *Vana Parva*, sec. 114, vv. 4-5.
4. Mitra, op. cit., p. 35.
5. Ibid.
6. *B.D.G.P.*, p. 264.

Finally coming to the Hāthīgumphā we find that it is a natural cavern, very little improved or enlarged by art. It is on the southern face of the Udayagiri Hills, which is the northern part of that low range of hills called Khaṇḍagiri, situated at a distance of about three miles from Bhubaneśvara, in the Purī district of Orissa. Though not important from an artistic and architectural point of view, it is the most important of all the caves in the locality by reason of its containing a long inscription recording the autobiography of a king of Kaliṅga "on the overhanging brow of the cavern."[1]

The record is incised partly in front and partly on the roof of the cave. It throws considerable light on the history of India in the second century BC, "when the empire of Candragupta and Aśoka had crumbled into decay, when the usurper Pushyamitra was ruling over the fragments of the Mauryan empire, and the Āndhras of Southern India, having acquired power, had advanced northwards and had perhaps conquered Malva."[2]

The inscription begins with an invocation to the *arhat*s and the *siddha*s in the Jaina style.[3] As believed by Fleet,[4] it is not a version of the acts done by Khāravela for the promotion of the Jaina faith, but it is, after all, a secular record, and records all performances of King Khāravela, who belonged to the Jaina faith up to the thirteenth year of his reign or thirty-seventh year of his life.

Following the inscription as it is, we find that its language may be described as Apabhraṁśa Prākṛt, with traces of Ardha-Māgadhī and Jaina Prākṛtisms, and that it was incised in the thirteenth year of Khāravela's reign. This thirteenth year of his reign coincides with the thirty-seventh year of his life, because, after completing his fifteenth year, Khāravela became a *yuvarāja* and performed the Vedic coronation called the *mahārājya-abhiṣeka* as soon as he completed his twenty-fourth year. The *abhiṣeka* of Khāravela shows that Jainism did not interfere with the national constitutional rites of the orthodox type.[5]

Over and above the exact information that this inscription gives us about Khāravela, and about some of the principal events of his political career, it gives us a clue to more or less accurately fix the date of this great emperor. But for this inscription there is nothing of any historical or even non-historical value that can so well enlighten us on this chronological point of Indian history.

---

1. Ganguly, op. cit., p. 47.
2. *J.B.O.R.S.*, III., p. 488.
3. नमो अराहंतानं नमो सवसिधानं . . . etc. — Ibid., IV., p. 397, and XIII., p. 222.
4. *J.R.A.S.*, 1910, p. 825.
5. *J.B.O.R.S.*, III., pp. 431, 438.

As laid down in the footnote,[1] until recently it was believed by certain scholars, as against Fleet and others, that in line sixteen of the inscription there was a reference to a date of the Maurya era, and that it formed the sole basis for fixing this important period of Kaliṅga history. Mr Jayaswal, once the foremost advocate of this theory

1. This note gives, more or less in a chronological order, the names of different scholars who touched this inscription from one or other point of view. Mr A. Sterling first discovered it, and with the help of Colonel Mackenzie took a facsimile of this interesting document in 1820 and published it, without translation or transcript, in 1825 with his most valuable article on *An Account, Geographical, Statistical and Historical, of Orissa proper or Cuttack* (*A.R.*, XV., p. 313 ff., and plate); then James Prinsep published it for the first time in 1837 on the basis of the correct facsimile of Lieutenant Kittoe, and according to him the date of the inscription could not be earlier than 200 BC (*J.A.S.B.*, VI., pp. 1075 ff., and Plate LVIII).

A further lithograph of the inscription we find by Cunningham in *C.I.I.*, I., (1877), pp. 27 ff., 98-101, 132 ff., and Plate XVII ; but it appears that Prinsep's interpretation drew the attention of Oriental scholars to its importance and historic worth. Rajendralal Mitra copied his transcripts and translations and published it in a revised form, in his great work on *The Antiquities of Orissa*, in 1880, p. 16 ff., with a facsimile; and the date of the inscription, according to him, ought to be between 416-316 BC. A few years after Dr Mitra, the late Pandit Bhagwanlal Indraji, published for the first time a workable version of this important inscription, in the *Proceedings of the Sixth International Congress of Orientalists, held at Leyden in 1885*, and according to him the date of the inscription is 165 Maurya era or 157 BC (*Actes Six. Congr. Or. à Leide*, pt. III., sec. II., pp. 152-77, and plate). This was followed by Bühler in 1895 and 1898 in *Indian Studies*, no. III, p. 13, and in *On the Origin of the Indian Brahma Alphabet*, p. 13 ff., respectively but he merely proposed certain corrections. This fixing of the date by the late Pandit, on the basis of a reference to some Mauryan date in line sixteen of the inscription, had been accepted up till now by most of the modern school of antiquarians, headed by Vincent Smith, K.P. Jayaswal, R.D. Banerji and others; but it was Fleet and a few others after him that protested against such a reading of the said line, though he accepted that not a single voice had been raised against the interpretation of Pandit Indraji (see Smith, *Early History of India*, p. 44, n. 2 (4th ed.), and also in *J.R.A.S.*, 1918, p. 544 ff.; Jayaswal, *J.B.O.R.S.*, I., p. 80, n. 55, III., pp. 425-85, IV., p. 364 ff.; Banerji (R.D.), *J.B.O.R.S.*, III., p. 486 ff.; Dubreuil, *Ancient History of the Deccan*, p. 12; Jinavijaya, *Prācin Jaina Lekha Saṁgraha*, I., which wholly deals with Khāravela and agrees with the school of Jayaswal; and Konow, *A.S.I.*, 1905-1906, p. 166. According to him the inscription contained a date in the Maurya era). Reviewing this volume in his first note in the *J.R.A.S.*, 1910, p. 242 ff., Dr Fleet says : "In the course of his remarks Dr Konow has mentioned the Hāthigumphā inscription of Khāravela, and has observed, as an *obiter dictum*, that "It is dated in the year 165 of the Maurya era." We may take the opportunity of saying that it is a mistake, and has no basis except in Pandit Bhagwanlal Indraji's treatment of a passage in line 16th of the record."

Now we shall refer to Fleet and others of his class. In 1910 Professor H. Lüders published in *E.I.*, X., Lüders' list, No. 1345, p. 160, a summary of the inscription, and stated that there was no date in the record. This was followed by two short notes from the late Dr J.F. Fleet in *J.R.A.S.*, 1910, pp. 242 ff. and 824 ff. As we saw above, Dr Fleet had his own doubts

→

in the light of fresh researches then made by him, has, with all the broadmindedness worthy of a real scholar, to a great extent allowed himself to agree with Mr Fleet and others that there is no such reference in the line referred to, or even anywhere else in the body of the inscription.[1]

No doubt in the sixth line of the inscription there is a reference to the era of Nanda, but this reference hardly helps us in fixing the date of Khāravela.[2] For fixing the date of the inscription and of the great Cedi king recourse to certain other facts laid down by the inscription is necessary. These facts are to be interpreted and understood in the light of whatever contemporary historical gleanings are at our disposal to fix as accurately as possible the date of the inscription.

According to the new reading and interpretation of Mr Jayaswal a certain portion of the eighth line of the inscription, which speaks of the eighth year of Khāravela's reign, reads as follows: घातापयिता राजगहं उपपीडापयति एतिना च कम्मापदाण संनादेन संबइत-सेन-वाहनो विपमुंचितुं मधुरां अपयातो यवन-राज-डिमिट यच्छति-वि-पलव, [3] and which mean, "on account of the report (uproar) occasioned by the acts of

→ about the existence of a date in the Maurya era in this record. He tried to prove that the passage in the sixteenth line of the Hāthigumphā inscription does not contain any such date, but on the other hand that it refers to a certain canonical text of the Jainas which went out of use during the reign of the Mauryas. See also Ramesh Chandra Mazumdar (*I.A.*, XLVII., 1918, p. 223 ff., and XLVIII., 1919, p. 187 ff.). According to him line sixteen is far from being clear and positive, and he contested many of the conclusions of Messrs Jayaswal and Banerji (Ramaprasad Chanda) (*J.R.A.S.*, 1919, p. 395 ff.). He agreed with Fleet and Lüders in denying the existence of any date in the Hāthīgumphā inscription. However now to our satisfaction we find that Mr Jayaswal and others of his school more or less agree with those of the opposite school about this crucial point, and hence the reading of line sixteen of the record, which is the keystone of the whole structure, is now to a great extent fully agreed to by all (see Jayaswal, *J.B.O.RS.*, XIII., p. 221 ff., and XIV., pp. 127-28 and 150-51).

Over and above these researches we have references to scholars like Ganguly, Fergusson and Burgess, and Professor K.H. Dhruv. Mr Mono Mohan Ganguly places the inscription on principles based on architectural and sculptural considerations towards the close of the third century BC — that is, before Aśoka came to the throne of Magadha (see Ganguly, op. cit., pp. 48-50). According to Drs Fergusson and Burgess "300 BC or thereabouts is the most probable date for this inscription." They add that "with his (of Aśoka) reign the fashion of chiselling cells out of the living rock commenced, and was continued with continually increasing magnificence and elaboration for nearly 1000 years after his time" (Fergusson and Burgess, op. cit., pp. 67-68). Professor Dhruv talks of Khāravela and the antiquity of Jainism in connection with Puṣyamitra Śuṅga and other ruling dynasties of the time in the preface of his Gujarātī drama, *Sāchuṁsvapna* — the Gujarātī rendering of the Sanskrit drama, *Svapnavāsavadattā* of Bhāsa.

1. *J.B.O.R.S.*, XIII., p. 236. 2. नंदराज-ति-वस-सत-ओघाटितं . . . etc. — Ibid., IV., p. 399.
3. Ibid., and xiii., p. 227.

valour (i.e. the capture of Gorathagiri fortress and the siege of Rājagṛha, with which we shall deal later on) the Greek king Demet(rios), drawing in his army and transport, or covering himself with his army and vehicles, retreated to abandon Mathura."[1] This is according to the latest researches made by Mr Jayaswal, the identification being accepted by Mr Banerji and Dr Konow.[2] This is what the most modern methods in estampage and historical research can give us, and hence, taking it as the sole clue to Khāravela's period, we evidently find that the Greek king had captured Mathura, and had advanced eastwards, probably as far as Sāketa. This is corroborated by the information given by the *Gārgī Saṁhitā* that the Yavanas, after taking Sāketa, Pañcāla and Mathura, were marching towards Kusumadhvaja (Pāṭalīputra) at the close of the Maurya period.[3]

Emphasizing the same point Mr Jayaswal states: "When Patañjali was writing his commentary on Sanskrit Grammar the king of Magadha (Pushyamitra) had undertaken a long sacrifice not yet finished. Two *Aśvamedhas* were performed by that Magadha king, according to the new Ayodhya inscription. Evidently while an *Aśvamedha* was in progress Patañjali records that a Yavana king besieged Sāketa and Madhymikā. Kālidāsa mentions an imperial victory on a river which is near the Madhymikā territory during an *Aśvamedha* by Pushyamitra. We thus have definite evidence that in the reign of Pushyamitra there was an unsuccessful Greek invasion. Now we have in Khāravela's inscription a contemporary Greek invader who had to retreat and give up Mathura. This occurred in the reign of Bṛhaspati-Mitra, who was a predecessor of Agni-Mitra, on the evidence of coins. The conclusion is irresistible that the invasion is identical with one mentioned by the *Gārgī Saṁhitā* and Patañjali."[4]

For all this there arises another difficulty — whether this Greek king is Demetrios or Menander. Now, according to Gardner, Menander's time is about the beginning of the second century BC[5] and according to Vincent Smith about 155 BC.[6] Furthermore, Menander is not said to have crossed the

1. Ibid., p. 229.
2. *J.B.O.R.S.*, XIII., p. 228.
3. In the *Yuga Purāṇa*, one of the chapters of the *Gārgī Saṁhitā*, there is described that "the viciously valiant Greeks" after reducing Sāketa (in Oudh), the Pañcāla country (in the Doab between the Jumna and the Ganges) and Mathura (Muttra), reached Pushpapura (Pāṭalīputra); but that they did not remain in the midland country because of a dreadful war among themselves which broke out in their own country (Kern, *Bṛhat Saṁhitā*, p. 37) — an evident allusion to the internecine struggle between the houses of Euthydemus and Eucratides.
4. *J.B.O.R.S.*, XIII., pp. 241, 242.
5. Cf. Gardner, *Catalogue of Indian Coins, Greek and Sythic*, Int., pp. xxii, xxiii.
6. Smith, *Early History of India*, p. 239.

Isamos (Yamunā?), while he is said to have gone beyond the Hypanis (Biās),[1] and the classical passage which refers to both Demetrios and Menander has been interpreted by the best authorities to apply to Demetrios in respect of the extensive conquests.[2] Above all, the retreat of Demetrios from India to oppose his rival Eucratides in Bactria is a fact that largely helps the identification, because, according to our inscription, the Greek king, without any action on the part of Khāravela against him, retreated and left Mathura. Thus it seems to be certain that Khāravela's time is between Demetrios and Menander.

Coming to the Greek history we find that the very success of Demetrios appears to have caused his downfall. As a direct consequence of his victories the centre of his dominions was shifted beyond the borders of Bactria proper. The homeland, however, was not content to degenerate into a mere dependency. A revolt ended in the establishment of a separate kingdom under Eucratides, a leader of great vigour and ability, about whom written history has hardly anything to say.[3] His recognition as king took place with the accession of Mithradates I to the throne of Parthia. As Mithradates succeeded his brother Phraates I about 171 BC we may accept Von Gutschmid's date of 175 BC as approximately correct for Eucratides.[4] The beginning of his reign was stormy. Demetrios, who was now king of India — i.e. of the country round about the Indus — not of Bactria, and who was therefore one of his most natural foes, had to retreat from India on account of the troubles raised in Bactria by the rival Eucratides. This retreat of Demetrios is placed by the historians of Bactria about 175 BC,[5] and this, with the siege of Gorathagiri and Rājagṛha, coincides with the eighth year of Khāravela — *c.* 175 BC. The first year of Khāravela would thus be *c.* 183 BC, and the date of the inscription about 170 BC.

Leaving aside this reference to the Greek king, Demetrios, there is another ground on which we can approximately fix the date of Khāravela. An Āndhra king, Sātakarṇi, the Lord of the West, is actually mentioned in the inscription as Khāravela's rival,[6] and he can safely be identified with the Sātakarṇi of the Nānāghāṭ inscriptions, because on epigraphical grounds

1. Gardner, op. cit., Int., p. xxxvii.
2. See Meyer (Eduard), *E.B.*, VII., p. 982 (11th edn.) ; and Rawlinson, *Parthia* (The Story of the Nations), p. 65.
3. *C.H.I.*, I., p. 446.
4. Ibid.
5. Meyer (Eduard), op. cit., IX., p. 880.
6. Cf. *J.B.O.R.S.*, IV., p. 398, and XIII., p. 226.

both the Nānāghāṭ inscription of Nāganikā, the queen of Sātakarṇi, and the Hāthīgumphā inscription of Khāravela belong to the same period as the Nāsik inscription of Kṛṣṇa.[1] Now the Nānāghāṭ inscriptions of the early Sātavāhanas are "a little, not much, later than Aśoka's and Daśaratha's edicts," and on epigraphical grounds "they are of the time of the last Mauryas or the earliest Suṅgas — that is, the beginning of the second century BC.[2] Even therefore if it must be admitted that the Hāthīgumphā inscription is undated, there is still reason to believe that the date of Khāravela would fit in with the dates of Demetrios and Sātakarṇi in the first half of the second century BC. Moreover, as the rise of both the Āndhra and Kaliṅga dynasties must no doubt date from the same period, when the Maurya power began to decline, the probability that these two kings were contemporary is great indeed.

Having thus approximately fixed the date of the inscription we shall now examine its contents and see what information we can gather about this great patron of Jainism, and the extent of his political career, which makes him one of the most important figures of Indian history.

The first line of this inscription as laid down above begins with an invocation of the *arhat*s and the *siddha*s in the Jaina style, which corresponds to the beginning of the fivefold form of homage still used among the Jainas.[3] It is here that we came to know that Khāravela belonged to the Cedi dynasty, and that the term *aira* formed one of the titles of the kings of this family.[4] According to Mr Jayaswal this is to be taken as a term denoting the descent of the Cedi kings — *aira*, a descendant of *irā* or *Iḷā* — and he proposes "to identify it with the Purāṇic *Ailā*,[5] one of the main dynastic divisions to which the Cedis belong according to the Purāṇas."[6]

The second line says that for fifteen years Khāravela enjoyed his princely life, and during that period, having accomplished various *vidyā*s (arts), he, "who was having conquests as large as those of King Vena," ruled as *yuvarāja* for many years.[7]

---

1. See Bühler, *A.S.W.I.*, V., p. 71, and *Indische Paleographie*, p. 39.
2. Bühler, *A.S.W.I.*, V., p. 71 ff.
3. णमो अरिहंताणं णमो सिद्धाणं णमो आयरियाणं णमो उवज्झायाणं णमो लोए सव्वसाहू णं, एसो पंचणमुक्कारो, . . . — *Kalpa-Sūtra*, *sūt*. 1.
4. Cf. *J.B.O.R.S.*, IV., p. 397, and XIII., p. 222.
5. Pargiter, *J.R.A.S.*, 1910, pp. 11, 26.
6. *J.B.O.R.S.*, XIII., p. 223.
7. Cf. ibid., IV., p. 397, and XIII., p. 224.

This King Vena is a Vedic personality,[1] and according to Manu[2] King Vena had the whole earth (country) under his rule. Speaking about him Mr Jayaswal says: "It is noteworthy that the *Padma Purāṇa* also says that Vena began his rule well, but subsequently he became a Jaina. From the Hāthigumphā inscription we get an indirect confirmation of the *Padma Purāṇa*, in so much that Vena, who has not got throughout a good reputation in the Brāhmanical tradition, had a good reputation amongst the Jainas as an ideal king. If amongst the Jainas at the period when the inscription was written Vena had been regarded as a bad king towards the end of his career, the comparison would not have been adopted in praise of Khāravela. It is significant that the only defect in Vena, the Brahmins found, was of Jaina characteristics — that is, he did not recognise caste. Presumably the tradition disparaging Vena is later and post-Jainism."[3]

Coming to the third line we find, as already stated, that after the twenty-fourth year was complete Khāravela obtained "Māhārājābhiṣecanam" in the third generation of the Kaliṅga dynasty, and with many other repairs got an embankment made to the lake of Khibīra *R̥ṣi* in the capital of Kaliṅga.[4]

With the fourth line of the inscription begins the political life of Khāravela. In the beginning of the line it is said that Khāravela tried to please his teeming population of three and a half millions.[5] There is nothing particular to wonder at this figure. We know from Aśoka's Rock Edict XIII that against Aśoka's forces Kaliṅga lost 150,000 soldiers as captives of war, 100,000 were slain and "many times as many died."[6] This comes to about two and a half lakh as the total number of casualties. Now according to Scharnhorst's estimate every fifteenth soul of the population could take up arms against a foreign invasion, and hence the population of Aśoka's time comes to about thirty-eight lakhs.[7] A century after this, in the time of Khāravela, it is quite likely that it was three and a half millions after the loss occasioned by the Maurya conquest and rule. Accepting the same figure Mr Vincent Smith says: "Knowing as we

1. *Rigveda*, X., 123.
2. Manu, chap. IX., 66-67.
3. *J.B.O.R.S.*, XIII., pp. 224, 225.
4. Cf. ibid., IV., pp. 397-98, and XIII., p. 225.
5. Cf. ibid., IV., p. 398, and XIII., p. 226.
6. Bühler, *E.I.*, II., p. 471.
7. Cf. *J.B.O.R.S.*, III., p. 440.

do that the Mauryas and their predecessors maintained a permanent census, there is no reason to distrust the figures."[1]

Before we go any further a peep into the history of the times will not be out of place here. In the words of Dr Barnett: "After the death of Aśoka the Maurya empire rapidly decayed, and the neighbouring rulers were left free to indulge in their ambition and enlarge their boundaries. Among these was a certain Simuka, who in the last quarter of the third century BC established the powerful Sātavāhana or Sātakarṇi dynasty, which ruled the Telugu country for nearly five centuries. In his reign or in the reign of his immediate successor, his younger brother Kṛṣṇa (vernacularly Kaṇha), the Āndhra empire spread westward to at least 74' longitude, and possibly even to the Arabian Sea.[2] Under these early Sātavāhana kings the boundaries of the Āndhra dominions were enlarged so as to include a great part, if not the whole, of Vidarbha (Berar), the central provinces and Hyderabad."[3]

"But the Suṅgas and the Āndhras were not the only powers which at this period were contending for mastery in the region now known as Central India. The Hāthigumphā inscription shows that *c.* 180 BC Khāravela, king of Kaliṅga, appeared in the field as a new combatant."[4]

Khāravela's ambition to secure his country a dictating voice in the political affairs of his times brought him into conflict with his neighbours, who were a paramount power in the Deccan. In his second year he sent a large army to the west in defiance of Sātakarṁi, the Āndhra monarch.[5] This monarch was a king of the dynasty called the Sātavāhanas according to the inscriptional records of the family themselves, and the Āndhras (Āndhrabhṛtyas) according to the Purāṇas.[6] These were the unsubdued peoples on the southern borders of the Mauryan dominions, and their home was on the coastal region of the Madras Presidency, between the rivers Godāvarī and Kṛṣṇā.

1. Smith, *J.R.A.S.*, 1918, p. 545.
2. This is indicated by the inscriptions at Nasik (No. 1144) and at Nānāghāṭ, fifty miles north-west of Poona (No. 1114).
3. *C.H.I.*, I., pp. 599, 600.
4. Ibid., p. 600.
5. The Āndhra king alluded to can only be Śrī-Sātakarṇi, No. 3 of the Purāṇic list, who is commemorated by a defaced but happily inscribed relief image at Nānāghāṭ, a pass leading from the Koṅkaṇ to the ancient town of Junar in the Poona district, Bombay. — Bühler, *A.S.W.I.*, V., p. 59.
6. Pargiter, *Dynasties of the Kali Age*, p. 36 ff.

Talking about the original home and the caste of the Sātavāhana princes Mr Bakhle says: "In the inscription of Khāravela the Sātavāhanas are said to be in the west of Kaliṅga; in the Jaina legends Paiṭhān, in the Naizam's dominions, is called their capital; in the version of the origin of the dynasty given in the *Kathāsaritsāgara* the founder of the dynasty is said to have been born at Paiṭhan. . . . Majority of the inscriptions of the Sātavāhanas are to be found at Nasik; their earliest inscription is at Nānāghāt, in western India; their earliest coins are also found in western India. . . . It will thus appear that all the circumstances point to western India as the original home of the Sātavāhanas. . . . The evidence of the Jaina legends about the caste of the Sātavāhana princes is conflicting and of very little credence. One traditional account says that the Sātavāhana was born from a virgin aged four years; another traces his descent to a Yaksha. The epigraphic evidence, however, points definitely to the Sātavāhana as Brāhman."[1]

The result of Khāravela's expedition to the west was that Sātakarṇi was not defeated, and that he had to be content with the Mūṣika capital, which was taken by him to help the Kāśyapa kṣatriyas.[2] The Mūṣikas were very probably the subordinate ally of Sātakarṇi, and it appears that the Mūṣika country must have been between Paiṭhān and Goṇḍwānā. As Kosal came next to Orissa (north-west), the Mūṣika land must have been contiguous to the west.

Nothing particular has the fifth line to tell us but the fact that in the third year Khāravela was well versed in the science of music, with shows of dancing, singing, and so on.[3]

Line six is rather important. It is here that we get some reference to the Nanda era. It first tells us that after the march against Sātakarṇi and Mūṣikas the next campaign of Khāravela was carried into western India. In the fourth year of his reign he humbled the Rāṣṭrikas of the Marāṭhā country and Bhojakas of Berār, both feudatories of the Āndhras.[4]

Thus on two occasions, according to the inscriptional record, did Khāravela invade the Āndhra dominions in the Deccan. In his second year he sent a large army of horses, elephants, footsoldiers and chariots to the

1. *J.B.B.R.A.S.* (New Series), III., pp. 49-52.
2. *J.B.O.R.S.*, IV., p. 398, and XIII., p. 226.
3. Cf. ibid..
4. Ibid., IV., p. 399.

west in defiance of Sātakarṇi; and in his fourth year he humbled the Rāṣṭrikas of the Marāṭhā country and Bhojakas of Berār, both under the domination of the Āndhra king of Pratiṣṭhāna.[1] Such expeditions were undoubtedly in the nature of a challenge to the predominant power of the Deccan, but they appear not to have been pursued beyond the limit of safety. In the words of Professor Rapson: "We may suppose that the armies of Khāravela passed the valley of Mahanadi, and over the watershed into the valleys of Godavari and its great tributaries, the Wainganga and the Wardha. They could thus invade territory which the Āndhra monarch regarded as lying within the realm, but it is not stated, and there are no grounds for surmising, that the forces of the Kaliṅgas and the Āndhras came into actual conflict on either of these occasions, or that any important political results followed."[2]

This is not to minimize the greatness of the extent of Khāravela's conquests. No doubt as a military leader he played a great part in the political affairs of his time, but nothing more. He could very well stand by the side of the great Puṣyamitra or the great Śālivāhana, but if, as the expeditions of his second and fourth years seem to indicate, his ambition led him to entertain the project of wresting the suzerainty from the Āndhra king of Pratiṣṭhāna, the attempt must be held to have failed. That was not possible for him, and that is not what is meant by the inscription.

In his fifth year Khāravela caused a canal that was excavated in the year 103 of King Nanda, and the roads of Tanasuliya or Toṣalī,[3] to enter the city of Kaliṅga.[4] This and many other accurate statements and year figures in the body of the inscription made scholars like Fleet, Smith and others infer that a careful chronicle was kept at Orissa, and that all these long periods could not be reckoned without an era.[5] That the era taken into consideration here is the Nanda era is clear from the text of the line itself. It is so natural

1. The modern Paiṭhān, on the north bank of the Godāvarī in the Auraṅgābād district of Hyderabad, is famous in literature as the capital of King Sātakarṇi (Sātavāhana or Śālivāhana) and his son Śaktikumāra.
2. Rapson, *C.H.I.*, I., p. 536.
3. We would be justified in accepting that the capital of Khāravela was Toṣalī, in whose neighbourhood the Hāthīgumphā cave and River Prācī are to be found. According to Mr Haraprasad Sastri, Toṣalī is etymologically identical with Dhauli, the name of the place where a sect of the Kaliṅga edicts exists — Smith, op. cit., p. 546.
4. Cf. *J.B.O.R.S.*, IV., p. 399.
5. See Fleet, *J.R.A.S.*, 1910, p. 828 ; Smith, op. cit., p. 545.

that nobody would care to recollect such long intervals since the reign of a particular king unless an era founded by him were in continuous use. This king, in the opinion of Jayaswal, cannot be any other than King Nanda-Vardhana, whose date, according to his calculations, comes to about 457 BC.[1] As seen before, there is no historical basis or any other clue in the body of the inscription on which we can rest such an identification. Jayaswal believes that his era exactly corresponds to the information received by Alberuni about the era of Śrī Harṣa, and hence whatever Alberuni has put down in the form of local traditions about Śrī Harṣa[2] has been wrongly identified by the former with that of Nandivardhana.[3] To us there seems no reason for such a far-fetched identification. There is nothing unnatural if the era began with Nanda I of the Jainas or Mahāpadma Nanda of the Purāṇas. After all that we have seen from the Purāṇic and the classical accounts about Nanda it is certain that he was great enough for commencing an era in his name. We can thus safely identify it with one started by him. Thus the date of the canal referred to in the sixth line would roughly correspond to 320-307 BC, taking the *nirvaṇa* date of Mahāvīra to be 480-467 BC.

From what is said in the seventh line we get that Khāravela's wife was of the Vajra family,[4] and Jayaswal says: "The name of the queen is either not given or is "Ghusīta(ā).""[5] This was the seventh year of his reign, and it seems he had a prince by this time.[6]

The eighth year of his regnal period opens with an invasion on Magadha. He stormed the Gorathagiri fortress of great enclosure by a great army.[7]

Line eight is that important one about which we have already talked at length, and which because of a reference to the great Indo-Greek king Demetrios greatly solves the most difficult and at the same time the most important problem of Kaliṅga chronology — namely, the date of Khāravela.

1. *J.B.O.R.S.*, XIII., p. 240.
2. Cf. Sachau, *Alberuni's India*, II., p. 5.
3. Cf. *J.B.O.R.S.*, XIII., p. 240.
4. वजिर-घर-वंति घुसितघरिनि. . . . — Ibid., p. 227. This Vajra family has been identified by Dr K. Aiyangar with an ancient dynasty of considerable importance and holding the important territory of Bengal on this side of the Ganges. — *Some Contributions of South India to Indian Culture*, p. 39.
5. *J.B.O.R.S.*, XIII., p. 227.
6. . . . कुमार . . . etc. — Ibid.
7. महता सेना मह [त-भित्ति]-गोरधगिरिं घातापयिता, etc. — Ibid., IV., p. 399, and XIII., p. 227.

A literal translation of the line, with a portion of the previous line, made in the light of the latest readings of Jayaswal, which we have adopted for our purpose here, is as follows: "In the eighth year he (Khāravela) having got stormed the Gorathagiri (fortress) of great enclosure (*lit* "wall," "barrier") by a great army causes pressure around Rājagraha (lays siege to Rājagṛha). On account of this report (uproar), occasioned by the acts of valour (that is, the capture of Gorathagiri fortress and the siege of Rājagrha), the great King Demet(rios) drawing in army and transport or covering himself with his army and vehicles retreated to abandon Mathura."[1]

Thus we see that in the eighth year of his reign Khāravela invaded Magadha. This shows that he had not only become independent but also aggressive. He reaches as far as the Barābar Hills (Gorathagiri), on the old route from Gayā to Pāṭalīputra. Hearing of this advance on the part of Khāravela, Demetrios, the king of Indians, beat a retreat, in the result giving up Mathurā, and whose invasion in the interior and retreat from India are mentioned by historians of the Bactrian history.[2]

Most probably Puṣyamitra was on the throne at that time. According to the Purāṇas, Puṣyamitra reigned for thirty-six years,[3] and according to Mr Vincent Smith, Puṣyamitra dethroned Bṛhadratha, the last Maurya king, in 185 BC.[4] According to Mr Jayaswal this event took place in 188 BC,[5] and hence Puṣyamitra must have ruled from 185 to 149 BC or 188 to 152 BC.

There is hardly anything of importance in line nine of the inscription. It talks of some gifts of land to brāhmaṇas, and thereby supports the system of collective grant of land to brāhmaṇas prevalent during the Hindu rule.[6] As we have already remarked about the Vedic coronation of Khāravela, here also the mere fact that he was a Jaina in no way interfered with the national constitutional rites of the orthodox type. Another inference that we might draw from this is that the original organization of the Āryans had some of its permanent effects on the social life of the people irrespective of the religion to which they belonged. Jainism and Buddhism of Mahāvīra's

1. *J.B.O.R.S.*, IV., pp. 378, 379, and XIII., pp. 228, 229.
2. Meyer (Eduard), op. cit., IX., p. 880.
3. Cf. Pargiter, op. cit., p. 70.
4. Smith, *Early History of India*, p. 204.
5. *J.B.O.R.S.*, XIII., p. 243.
6. Cf. ibid., IV., p. 400, and XIII., p. 229.

time might have been direct revolutions against the prevalent form of Brāhmanism, but that real or superstitious respect for brāhmaṇas and their social claims over other castes hardly suffered in any way from these revolutions.

No doubt in such a case as this, much depended upon the broad-minded outlook of the person concerned, and that, like Aśoka, Khāravela was also the emperor who was always above any kind of blind religious fervour about his own or about any particular faith, and, like his predecessor's edicts, he has this inscription to prove his aloofness from any sort of petty-minded bigotry. Tolerance was his chief characteristic, and he seems to have been a magnificent ruler, of liberal tendencies, and styles himself "a worshipper of men of all sects."[1]

Coming to the tenth line we find that Khāravela got built the royal residence *mahāvijava* (the palace of victory), at the cost of thirty-eight hundred thousand coins.[2] After this he, "with the policy of war, peace and conciliation," causes departure for northern India (Bhārata-varṣa) for further conquests, and obtains the precious things of those who have been invaded upon.[3] It should be noted here that the third division of Hindu foreign policy — namely, *bheda*— that is, "dissension"— is omitted here, probably as considered too low and not honourable for the policy of Khāravela.[4]

The next line is also not very important for our purpose here. It talks of some *maṇḍa* (throne) being ploughed down by Khāravela with a plough drawn by big asses.[5] The throne, it is said, was erected, by some bad (perverse) king — bad because the king's religious heresy must be connected with Jainism. The throne referred to here must be a decorated stand or a covered throne. For the identification of the "bad king" there is nothing in the inscription to help us. Furthermore, Khāravela breaks the lead-bodied figure (or figures) or the assemblage of leaden bodies made a century and thirteen years ago, or in the year 113.[6] With the reading 113 years before the eleventh year of Khāravela the date of these "lead figures" would be 285 BC; but if we take the other reading the year would be in the Nanda era, as in line six, and would be equal to 345 BC.

---

1. सव-पासंड-पूजको. . . . — *J.B.O.R.S.*, IV., p. 403.
2. Cf. ibid., IV., p. 400.
3. Cf. ibid., and XIII., p. 230.
4. Cf. ibid.
5. Ibid.
6. Ibid., p. 232.

The first incident is about the *apa-rāja* (bad king), and there seems some form of aggression on the part of the said king, but the latter incident is inexplicable. That the images were not other than Jaina images seems certain, because there is no such reference as that, and because that would contradict the generous policy of Khāravela. As we shall see in line seventeen, Khāravela was a respecter of all religions,[1] and therefore it seems possible that these must be images representing ugly caricatures of some Jaina *tīrthaṅkaras*.

Over and above these two incidents the line tells us that Khāravela causes consternation amongst the kings of Uttarāpatha (northern Punjab and the frontier countries).

Again, the twelfth line is also very important for our purpose. It is important not only from the standpoint of this chapter on Khāravela, but it is also a great support to some such problems as "the Nandas and their faith," "Jainism and the Nanda dynasty," "the Antiquity of Jainism," "the Image worship among the Jainas," and so on. To some of these problems we have already referred in our previous chapters. The remaining ones will be dealt with during the course of this and other chapters that are to follow, and hence to refrain from undue repetition we need not take up any discussions here. For the present we shall be satisfied with a literal translation of the line, with a portion of the previous line, which goes as follows :

"In the twelfth year (he) causes consternation amongst the kings of Uttarāpatha and causing great panic amongst the peoples of Magadha (he) makes his elephants enter the *Su-gāṅgeya*, and he makes the king of Magadha, Bahasati-mitra, bow at his feet. (He) brings home the image known as the Jina of Kaliṅga which had been carried away by King Nanda (and) the home *Ratnas* as recaptures as the riches of Aṅga and Magadha."[2]

Thus the countries of the north-western frontiers are subdued and the king of Magadha is made to pay homage at his feet. Furthermore it seems from this that King Nanda of Magadha had taken away some Jaina image to Pāṭalīputra which Khāravela had brought back to Orissa along with other trophies from Aṅga and Magadha after the defeat of Bahasati-mitra. At first sight it seems strange why this image is called "the Jina of Kaliṅga." It

1. सव-देवायतन-संकारकारको. . . . — *J.B.O.R.S.*, IV., p. 403.
2. सेहि वितासयतो उतरापथराजानो मगधानं च विपुलं भयं जनेतो . . . अंगमागध-वसुं च नेयाति. — Ibid., IV., p. 401, and XIII., p. 232.

does not refer to any *tīrthaṅkara* whose life-history was connected with Kaliṅga, but it seems, according to the interpretation of Muni Jinavijaya, that it is a practice still prevalent to designate the image of a particular *tīrthaṅkara* after the name of the locality of the establishment.[1] The first *tīrthaṅkara* (Ṛṣabhadeva) at Śatruñjaya for instance is called Śatruñjaya *jina*. Similarly the image at Abu is called "the Arbuda *jina*," and the one Dhulew (Mewar) is called "the Dhulew *jina*."[2] Thus it is not necessary that the image must be of a *jina* associated with Kaliṅga in his life-history. The expression "the *jina* of Kaliṅga" merely means that the Jaina image was worshipped at Kaliṅga or at the Kaliṅgan capital.

Before we pass on to the next line we shall deal firstly with the questions as to who this Bahasati-mitra was, and with whom he can be identified, and secondly, the antiquity of Jainism in Kaliṅga.

Looking to the contemporary history of the time it is certain that this Bahasati-mitra was the great Śuṅga king Puṣyamitra. He, a brāhmaṇa like the Sātavāhanas of the west, having brought about the orthodox revolution which pulled the Mauryas from the throne, founded his dynasty. What we mean by orthodox revolution is that Puṣyamitra was the outcome of the revival of the old Brāhmanism, in the beginning of the second entury BC. The evidence of Tāranātha (AD 1608, resting on old works), as correctly translated by Schiefner, agrees with that of the *Divyāvadāna*[3] in stating that Puṣyamitra was the ally of unbelievers, and himself burned monasteries and slew monks:

"There took place a war of the Brahman king Pushyamitra with the rest of the *Tīrthyas*. He burnt a number of monasteries from Madhyadeśa up to Jalandar."[4]

Again, coming to the orthodox revolution, the fact is that there may be some strong political reasons at its back, but nevertheless it must be said that Aśoka, the great Maurya emperor, little thought how his lack of political instinct, his religious policy, his theocracy, and his partition undermined the strength of the empire. Otherwise it is not possible that the military despotism so well established could disappear only forty or fifty years after the death of the greatest Indian monarch, whose memory is cherished with affection all over the Buddhist world, and who is regarded as a great and good ruler

1. Cf. *J.B.O.R.S.*, IV., p. 386.
2. Ibid.
3. Cf. Cowell and Neil, op. cit., p. 434.
4. Schiefner, *Tāranātha's History of Buddhism*, p. 81.

all over the world. His death was welcome news to the brāhmaṇas of north India, to the powerful Āndhras of the south, and to the enemies of India outside. The Mauryan control up to the Hindukush became weak soon after Aśoka's death. The north-western frontiers, ever exposed to foreign attacks, now became a tempting field to the Greek provinces of Bactria, Parthia and the warlike races of the borders.

Notwithstanding his toleration the brāhmaṇas, who feared that their religion was in danger, were embittered against Aśoka. Besides this they should also have lost many of their former privileges. This led to a great reaction against Mauryan ascendancy, which was promoted for some time in secret by the brāhmaṇas and culminated in open revolution in the time of the later Mauryas. The descendants of Aśoka retained only Magadha and the neighbouring home provinces. Bṛhadratha, the last king of the imperial Mauryan line, was finally treacherously murdered by his commander-in-chief, Puṣyamitra — "the Indian Macbeth."[1] Now, considering this from the chronological point of view, we find that the whole duration of the Maurya dynasty, according to Purāṇic authority, was one hundred and thirty-seven years; and if this period be accepted, and reckoned from the accession of Candragupta in 322 BC, the dynasty must have come to an end about 185 BC.[2] This date, as we have seen before, is certainly approximately correct. Thus the brāhmaṇa dynasty which uprooted the Buddhist Mauryas succeeded to the throne of India about 185 BC.

Thus at the instigation of the brāhmaṇas Puṣpa or Puṣyamitra faithlessly slew his master, imprisoned the ministers, usurped the throne, proclaimed himself king, founded the Śuṅga or Mitra dynasty, which lasted for about a decade and a century, and brought about an orthodox revolution in literature and Hindu society.[3] Bāṇabhaṭṭa, in his life of Harṣavardhana (seventh century AD), alludes thus to this military *coup d'état*: "And reviewing the whole army, under the pretext of showing him his forces, the base-born general, Pushyamitra, crushed his master Vṛhadratha, the Maurya, who was weak in keeping his coronation oath."[4]

Writing on this very point the learned author of *The Hindu History* opines

1. Mazumdar, op. cit., p. 626.
2. See Pargiter, op. cit., p. 27.
3. *J.B.O.R.S.*, X., p. 202.
4. The rendering combines the versions of Cowell and Thomas (*Harṣacarita*, p. 193), of Bühler (*I.A.*, II., p. 363) and of Jayaswal. Cf. Smith, op. cit., p. 268, n. 1.

that "Pushyamitra, when old, claimed the honour of lord paramount of north India. An imperial sacrifice and a horse sacrifice were magnificently performed by Pushyamitra under the guidance and presidentship of his *Guru* Patañjali, the noted commentator of Pāṇini's Grammar. Pushyamitra tried his best to revive the Brahmanic faith. His sacrifice was rather a Brahmanic victory over the Buddhists. Buddhist writers have branded Pushyamitra as a persecutor. It is alleged that he burned monasteries and slew monks from Magadha to Jālandhar in the Punjab. There may be some truth in it. The motive of Pushyamitra was that there was widespread Buddhist and Jain conspiracy against him."[1]

Taking into consideration all these points one thing is clear — that the reaction of the inquisitorial tyranny of Aśoka's system gave a death-blow first to the Buddhist faith, and secondly, for other political reasons, to the Mauryan predominance in north India. The extreme favour which Aśoka showed to the Buddhists, and to some extent also to the Jainas, resulted in a serious fall in the privileged position of the brāhmaṇas. They were also dissatisfied by the prohibition of bloody sacrifices and the irritating proceedings of the censors. Thus the moment the strong hand of the old emperor dropped the sceptre brāhmaṇa influence reasserted itself and produced a revolt which, as we have seen, resulted in the foundation of the new dynasty known as that of the Śuṅgas.[2] Coming to the territorial extent of the Śuṅgas we find that Pāṭalīputra, the modern Patna, the ancient Pālibhotra and then the capital of north India, continued to be the capital of the Śuṅgas, who perhaps owned authority over all the central or home provinces. The kingdom extended south of Narmadā. Besides it embraced Behar, Tirhoot, and the modern united provinces of Agra and Oudh. The Punjab, it seems, was probably long lost to the later Mauryas and the Śuṅgas.

Again, this identification of Bṛhaspati with Puṣyamitra on the basis of temporary history is further supported by the connection between Bṛhaspati and Puṣya asterisms. Writing on this Mr Smith says: "Bahapati is identical with Bahasati Mitra of certain coins and short inscriptions, both names being Prākṛt variations of the Sanskrit Brahaspati, who was believed to be the regent of the zodiacal asterism (*Nakshatra*) named Pushya or Tishya which

1. Mazumdar, op. cit., p. 636.
2. Cf. *J.P.A.S.B.*, 1910, pp. 259-62.

forms part of the constellation Cancer or the Crab. Bahapati certainly is an alternative name for Pushyamitra, the first Suṅga king according to the list in the *Purāṇas*."[1]

Emphasizing the similar standpoint Mr Haraprasad Sastri says to the following effect:

"Aśoka was, to all intents and purposes, a Buddhist monarch, and a bigoted one too. . . . He put a stop to all animal sacrifices throughout his vast empire. . . . This is an order which was certainly directed against the Brahmans, a privileged class wherever they settled. . . . This was followed by another edict in which Aśoka boasted that those who were regarded as gods on earth have been reduced by him in a short time into false gods. If it means anything it means that the Brahmanas, who were regarded as *Bhūdevas* or gods on earth, had been shown up by him. . . . The appointments created by Aśoka of *Dharma Mahāmātas* — that is, of superintendents of morals — was a direct invasion of the right and privileges of the Brahmanas. They were not the persons to brook the injury done to them quietly. And to crown all, Aśoka, in one of his edicts, insisted upon all his officers strictly observing the principle of *Daṇḍa-samatā* and *Vyavahāra-samatā* — that is, the equality of punishment and the equality in lawsuits, irrespective of caste, colour and creed. . . . Under such circumstances the prospects of being huddled together in prison with the unspeakable non-Āryans, whipped, impaled alive and hanged, were very offensive to the highly educated, respectable and privileged community. They tolerated these indignities heaped on them as long as the strong hand of Aśoka was guiding the empire. . . . They began to cast their eyes for a military man to fight for them, and they found such a man in Pushyamitra, the commander-in-chief of the Maurya Empire. . . . He was a Brahmanist to the core and hated the Buddhists."[2]

In short, there is no difficulty about the identification of Bahapatimitra with Puṣyamitra Śuṅga, and moreover no historical fallacy is committed by such an identification.[3] Everything fully agrees with the contemporary historical personages and well suits the events of the time.

---

1. *J.R.A.S.*, 1918, p. 545.
2. Sastri (Haraprasad), *J.P.A.S.B.*, 1910, pp. 259-60.
3. It may be noted here that such alternative names are common in Indian history — i.e. Bimbisāra — Śreṇika, Ajātaśatru — Kūṇiya, Aśoka — Piyadasi, Candragupta — Narendra, Balamitra — Agnimitra, Bhānumitra — Vasumitra, etc.

That Puṣyamitra was a brāhmaṇa and Khāravela a Jaina is a point which adds to the importance of the latter's reign from the viewpoint of Jaina history. If Khāravela had not been there to safeguard the Jaina faith against the Brāhmanical crusades of Puṣyamitra the revolution of Mahāvīra would have suffered the same fate as that of Buddha at the hands of one who was known to fame as the "annihilator of Buddha's doctrines."[1]

According to what we have said before, Khāravela attacked Magadha twice during his rule. In his first attack he advanced within a few miles of Pāṭalīputra. Puṣyamitra made a strategic withdrawal to Mathurā, and Khāravela apparently considered it wise at the moment not to proceed farther than the Barābar Hill (Gorathagiri).

In his second attack Khāravela was more successful. Entering northern India and marching at the foot of the Himālayas he suddenly appeared before the capital of Magadha, on the north side of the Ganges, which he crossed with the help of the famous elephants of Kaliṅga.[2] Puṣyamitra was forced to submit, and the treasures of his capital were seized by the victor. Among them was an image of the *jina* of Kaliṅga which at one time had been carried away by King Nanda of Magadha. His temporary success affected only the eastern frontier of the Śuṅga kingdom. He may have conquered Bengal and eastern Behar, where numerous instances of Jaina influence still survive.[3]

Mr Jayaswal, in connection with this victory of Khāravela, says: "Pushyamitra seems to have avoided staking his throne on the issue of a battle by returning those objects which epitomised the Magadha-Kaliṅga history of the past three centuries. Most likely it was the power of the Magadha sovereign which rendered the object of the campaign little more than a diplomatic victory, for otherwise it was too tempting for any human being to let go the imperial throne of India without ascending it."[4]

That Khāravela could not actually usurp the throne of Puṣyamitra is clear from the text of the inscription. It is no use stretching the imagination so far as that. What really took place is that, as with Sātakarṇi, here also Khāravela seems to have been forced to remain satisfied with what little moral supremacy he could establish over his neighbours, because after the

---

1. *Divyāvadāna*, pp. 433-34.
2. Smith, op. cit., p. 209.
3. Mazumdar, op. cit., p. 633.
4. *J.B.O.R.S.*, III., p. 447.

murder of Bṛhadratha, the last Maurya, the political atmosphere of the time was surging with conflicts between powers eager to share in the spoils of the Mauryan Empire. It was a struggle for supremacy among those powers which arose on the ruins of the great empire. In this struggle for supremacy it may safely be said that Khāravela played a prominent part and fully acquitted himself wherever he laid his hands.

Coming to the second point, about the antiquity of Jainism in Kaliṅga, we find that the only clue we get from this inscription is about the image of the *jina* of Kaliṅga. As we have said before, it is clear from the phraseology used here that this must be an image worshipped at Kaliṅga, or at the Kaliṅgan capital. Now, as the inscription tells us, this image was carried away by King Nanda, which might have been from Kaliṅga to Magadha. We have seen that this King Nanda is Nanda I of the Jainas and not Nandivardhana, as Smith has taken it, in accordance with Jayaswal and others.[1] If all these factors are taken as historically sound, there is no exaggeration in stating that, long before Buddhism managed to secure a foothold in Kaliṅga, Jainism had its sway and was popular with the people of the place.

In short, at the time of the conquest of Kaliṅga by Nanda I, Jainism appears to have been the prevailing religion. Substantiating this statement Mr Jayaswal says: "Jainism had already entered Orissa as early as the time of King Nanda, who, as I have shown, was Nanda Vardhana of the Śaisunāga dynasty. . . . Before the time of Khāravela there were temples of the Arhats on the Udayagiri Hills, as they are mentioned in the inscription as institutions which had been in existence before Khāravela's time. It seems that Jainism had been the national religion of Orissa for some centuries."[2]

This is also corroborated by a Jaina tradition which regards Orissa as a kṣatriya centre as early as the sixth century BC. It tells us that in Orissa a kṣatriya friend of the father of Mahāvīra was ruling and that Mahāvīra went there.[3]

---

1. "The Nanda Rāja referred to appears to be Nandivardhana, the ninth Śaisunāga king of the Purāṇas. It seems to be necessary to treat him and his successor, Mahanandin, No. 10, as Nandas, distinct from the nine Nandas who come between No. 10 and Candragupta. In the third edition of my *Early History of India* (1914) I placed the accession of Nandivardhana about 418 BC. He must now go back to *c.* 470 BC or possibly to an earlier date." — Smith, *J.R.A.S.*, 1918, p. 547.
2. *J.B.O.R.S.*, III., p. 448.
3. ततो भगवं मोसलिं गओ, . . . तत्थ सुमागहो नाम रट्ठिओ पियमित्तो भगवओ सो मोएइ, ततो सामी तोसलिं गओ. . . . — *Āvaśyaka-Sūtra*, pp. 219-20.

The learned author of *Orissa and her Remains* says about it that "Jainism was so deeply rooted in that we find traces of it as late as the 16th century AD Pratāp Rudra Deva,[1] the king of Orissa of the *Sūryavaṁśa* dynasty, had a great leaning towards Jainism."[2]

Before we pass on to the next line we may merely note that there are good grounds to infer from the inscription that image worship was prevalent among the Jainas so early as the beginning of the fifth century BC. The question of image worship we shall deal with in detail in the latter part of this thesis.

In taking note of this incident in the inscription Mr Jayaswal makes three important inferences, which are as follows: "(1) that Nanda was a Jaina, and (2) that Jainism was introduced in Orissa very early, probably just after Mahāvīra or in his time (the Jaina tradition mentions his visit to Orissa and line 14th of the inscription implies that Kumārī Hill (Udayagiri) was the place where religion had been preached and promulgated). It also proves (3) that to have Jaina images about or rather before 450 BC means that the date of Mahāvīra-Nirvāṇa must be what we get from the various Jaina chronological data read with the Purāṇic and Pāli materials which all harmonise in fixing it to be 545 BC (*J.B.O.R.S.*, I., 99-105)."[3] All the three inferences have been mostly dealt with by us.

We now take the following line. This has also a political event to note — namely, the year of his great victory was marked with the pouring in of riches from the extreme south. In the beginning it tells us that Khāravela built excellent towers with carved interiors, and that "he the capable one" caused to be brought into Kaliṅga wonderful and marvellous elephant-ships[4] with choice horses, rubies and numerous jewel pearls from the king of the Pāṇḍya country (in the extreme south opposite Ceylon).[5]

There is no mention here of an invasion over the Pāṇḍya country by the Kaliṅga Emperor. Perhaps looking to the greatness of Khāravela and

---

1. "Pratāp Rudra Deva, one of the Gajapati kings who ruled from AD 1503, renounced the Jaina doctrines. . . ." — Long, *J.A.S.B.*, XXVIII., nos. I to IV and V, 1859, p. 189.
2. Ganguly, op. cit., p. 19.
3. *J.B.O.R.S.*, XIII., pp. 245, 246.
4. The Ceylonese constructed ships expressly for the export of their elephants. It seems these were of the class of the "elephant-ship" of the inscription.
5. तु जठर-लिखिल-वरानिसिहिरानि नीवेसयति . . . पंडराजा चेदानि अनेकानि मुतमणिरतनानि — *J.B.O.R.S.*, IV., p. 401, and XIII., p. 233.

his supremacy over the Āndhras and the Śuṅgas all these trophies may be in the form of a tribute from the Pāṇḍyas. As we shall see just now, besides this account of Khāravela's military prowess the inscription records the pious deeds of the king. It affords good grounds for the belief that the king and his family had a leaning towards Jainism, and his successors also were apparently adherents of that religion.[1]

From line fourteen to the end of the inscription we find that King Khāravela was not a Jaina only in name, but one who had given it a proper place in the daily routine of his life. It is apparent from what is mentioned there that during the thirteenth year of his reign, having satisfied himself with the extension of his empire, he devotes his energies to religious acts. He spends large sums of money on the pious sites of the Kumārī Hill,[2] and incises the inscription full of glory. The State maintenances to be given on completion of the vow were ordered by him to be given to the *yāpa* professors who had ended their course of births[3] by austerities at the depository of the remains of the body on the sacred Kumārī Hill, where "the wheel of the Conqueror"[4] was fully established. It says further that Khāravela having finished the layman's vows realized or experienced the beauty of (i.e. the distinction between) "soul" (*jīva*) and "matter" (*deha*).[5]

What better proof than this is required of Khāravela's firm and rigid devotion to his faith? His gifts to *yāpa* professors and others who observed certain vows, and his love for the study of the technical importance of *jīva* and *deha* in the Jaina philosophy, show very clearly that he was not a blind Jaina. He first tried to understand in detail the chief characteristics of his faith, and thus having realized the greatness of the religion of his birth he was always ready to help and encourage those who had become *sādhus*, or who were out to live or die for the divine message of Lord Mahāvīra.

There are some references in the line which throw great light on certain practices of the Jainas of bygone days, and about a class which no more

1. *B.D.G.P.*, p. 24.
2. It was sacred as the place where Jainism was preached (line 14).
3. The perfect ideal Jaina ascetics, who are believed to have freed themselves by means of austerities. This is much idealized in Jaina philosophy.
4. This suggests that amongst the Jainas also *cakra* symbolized the spread of conquest of religion. This is confirmed by the representation of the wheel found at the Jaina *stūpa* of Mathurā.
5. तेरसमे च वसे सुपवत-विजय-चक कुमारीपवते अरहिते यप-रवीण-संसितेहि काय . . . जीव-देह-सिरिका परिखिता. — *J.B.O.R.S.*, IV., pp. 401, 402, and XIII., p. 233.

exists. The class of the *yāpa* professors mentioned seems to be one of the Jaina priesthood of those days. As laid down by Indrabhūti in his *Nītisāra* it formed one of those heterodox *saṁgha*s into which the Digambaras of the south were divided:

गोपुच्छकः श्वेतवासा द्राविडो यापनीयकः।
निःपिच्छिकश्चेति पञ्चैते जैनाभासाः प्रकीर्तिताः ॥[1]

It is strange to find the *yāpanīya*s included in this list, because in the inscription of the Cāḷukya king, Ammarāja II, they are described as part of the "pure and worthy *Nandi-gaccha*," and their *saṁgha* is addressed as "the holy *yāpanīya-saṁgha*."[2] Furthermore, according to one of the inscriptions at Śravaṇabeḷgoḷa this *Nandi-saṁgha* was considered as orthodox by Arhadbali. In his opinion it was an "eye to the world."[3] He did not mind any difference being made "in the case of all heterodox *saṁgha*s such as the Sitāmbara and others, which are of a form contrary to rule"; but anyone who thought such a thing "in the case of the *sena, nandi, deva* and *siṁha saṁgha*s" was branded by him as "a heretic."[4]

Speaking on this Mr Jayaswal states: "The *Bhadrabāhucarita* in giving the history of Jainism immediately after the teacher Bhadrabāhu, a contemporary of Candragupta, says that amongst the disciples of Bhadrabāhu who worshipped the bones of their master a school called *Yāpana-saṁgha* arose, and that they finally decided to remain without clothes. The *Yāpana-saṁgha* flourished in the south, as they prominently appear in Carnatic inscriptions. They are extinct now. Muni Jinavijaya is of opinion that some tenets of theirs bore affinity to the Digambara school and some to the Śvetāmbara. In view of this opinion the *Yāpana* school marked the stage before the great schism. Our inscription shows that *yāpa*, which gave the name to the school, consisted of certain pious practices. If we take it in the sense in which it is used in *Caraka* — "mitigating pain" — or as in the *Mahābhārata* — "supporting life" — the *yāpa* teachers emphasised the duty of alleviating the physical misery of others."[5]

Moreover, the inscription tells us that these *yāpa* professors were at the

---

1. Premi, *Vidvadratnamālā*, I., p. 132.
2. Hultzsch, *E.I.*, IX., p. 55, V. 18, L. 50.
3. *E.C.*, II., *S.B.*, 254.
4. Ibid.
5. *J.B.O.R.S.*, IV., p. 389.

Kāyya niṣīdi or the Kumārī Hill. That this *niṣīdi* was a *niṣīdi* of the *arhat* is proved by the next line. *Niṣīdi* or *niṣīdhi* seems to have been employed in Jaina literature as figuratively denoting ornamental tombs of their saints, but meaning thereby resting places.[1]

Writing on this Dr Fleet says: "As regards the word *niśīdhi* — which also occurs as *niśīdhi, nishidhi* and *nihidige* — Mr K.B. Pathak tells me that it is still used by the older members of the Jaina community, and that it means "a tomb erected over the remains of a Jaina ascetic." And he has given me the following passage from the *Upasargakevaḷigaḷa Kathe* in which it occurs:

"*Ṛshi-Samudāyaṁ=ellaṁ dakshiṇāpathadiṁ baṁdu bhaṭṭārara nishidiyan=eydid—āgaḷ,* etc.:

The whole assemblage of the saints having come by the region of the south, and having arrived at the *nishidhi* of the venerable one, etc."[2]

The *niṣīdhi* at the Kumārī Hill, where the inscription is engraved, seems to be not an ornamental tomb but a real *stūpa*, for it is qualified by *kāyya*, "corporeal" (i.e. "having remains of the body"). Taking the inscription into consideration Mr Jayaswal observes: "Thus it seems that the Jainas called their *Stūpas* or *Caityas*, *Nishīdis*. The Jaina *Stūpa* discovered at Mathura and the datum of *Bhadrabāhu-carita* saying that the disciples of Bhadrabāhu worshipped the bones of their master establish the fact that the Jainas (at any rate the Digambaras) observed the practices of erecting monuments on the remains of their teachers."[3] By the by, it may be mentioned here that this was a custom confined not only to the Jainas or the Bauddhas, but to erect monuments — *caityas* — in memory of teachers had been a national custom.

As laid down before, line fifteen also places before us Khāravela in the robes of a devout Jaina. It talks of some act being done by Khāravela for ascetics and recluse philosophers, but as some words are missing in the beginning of the line it is not possible to know actually what that act must have been. Anyhow it is clearly put down that the act was meant for "accomplished *Śramaṇas*, for those of good deeds, for the wise ones from a hundred directions, and for the leaders of *Saṁghas*."[4]

---

1. *E.I.*, II., p. 274.
2. *I.A.*, XII., p. 99.
3. *J.B.O.R.S.*, IV., p. 389.
4. सुकति समण-सुविहितानं च सत-दिसानं . . . तपसि. — Ibid., IV., p. 402, and XIII., p. 234.

It further tells us that near the Depository of the Relics of the *arhat*, on the slope of the mountain, King Khāravela establishes the "*siṁ-hapura* (=*prastha*)"[1] palace for his Queen Sindhuḍā, with stones from excellent mines brought over from many miles, and with pillars with bells attached, like the beautiful mediaeval pillars of this description standing in Nepal, and inlaid with beryls at the cost of seventy-five hundred thousand *paṇa*s (the then rupees).[2]

Mr Jayaswal identified this place with the grand rock-cut buildings known as the *rānī-naur* or "queen's palace."[3] It is close to the Hāthīgumphā, on the slope of the hill, and it may be noted that it has got "lions" (*siṁha*) in the round, prominently placed. Thus the reliquary — monument — the *arhat*'s *niṣīdi* — must have been, according to the inscription, near the queen's shelters.

As seen before, the latter part of the sixteenth line is the most important portion of the inscription from the point of view of the controversy that has been going on for the last few decades. From the point of information about Khāravela and his relation with the Jaina history it has hardly anything particular to say. With the previous line it fully confirms the fact that Khāravela was a great Jaina. It clearly states the profound interest he had in Jaina scriptures and their well-being, for we find in the line that:

"The fourfold *Aṅga-Saptika* of 64 sections, lost in the time of the Maurya king, he restores."[4]

As we have seen before, the interpretation of Dr Fleet is now more or less the same, and it is as follows: "The whole passage does not present any date, but tells us that Khāravela restored some text and the 64th chapter or other division of the collection of the seven *Aṅgas* which had been neglected since(?) the time of the Maurya kings or king."[5]

Here we are reminded of the great famine in Magadha, which lasted for twelve years, and which has been referred to in the previous chapter. As we have seen, this resulted in the abduction and flight of Candragupta with his *guru* Bhadrabāhu and other emigrants to the south, and finally was followed by the council of Pāṭalīputra[6] under the great pontiff Sthūlabhadra, who was

1. Cf. Aiyangar (K.), op. cit., pp. 75, 76.
2. Cf. *J.B.O.R.S.*, IV., p. 402, and XIII., pp. 234, 235.
3. Ibid., XIII., p. 235.
4. Ibid., p. 236.
5. *J.R.A.S.*, 1910, pp. 826-27.
6. The modern Patna, a place historic in the annals of their order, and at that time the capital of the Mauryan Empire.

one of those who had preferred to cling at any risk to the hallowed scenes at home. Our text thus serves as a good confirmation of the tradition about the controversy or the loss of certain Jaina texts in the time of Candragupta; and Kaliṅga, being more or less under the influence of Bhadrabāhu and his colleagues in the south, evidently did not accept the restoration of the council which met in Magadha.[1]

The last line of the inscription — namely, the seventeenth — is also to be read with a portion of the previous line, and it characterizes in short the chief attributes of Khāravela, and puts down in a few words the extent of his power. There may be certain exaggerations, especially in this part of the inscription, and it is natural, but since there is nothing else before us to make a comparative study of Khāravela we shall remain satisfied with a literal translation of the line, which runs as follows:

"He is the King of Prosperity (*Kshema*), the King of Extension (of the Empire) (or, a "King to the old people"), a King to the *Bhikshus* (or, though king yet a *Bhikshu*), the King of *Dharma* who has been seeing to, listening to and experiencing welfare (*Kalyāṇas*). . . .

"King Khāravela-Śrī, the great conqueror, descended from a family of the dynasty of royal sages, one whose empire has been extended, with an empire which is kept protected by the leader of the empire (or army), one whose chariots and army have not been obstructed, one who is the restorer of every temple, one who respects every sect, one who is an expert by virtue of special qualities. . . ."[2]

Here ends the autobiography of *bhikṣurāja* Khāravela, the great Emperor of Kaliṅga and one of the greatest royal patrons of the Jaina faith. The invocation of the *arhat*s and *siddha*s in the first line, the building of temples and caves for the Jaina *śramaṇa*s, the gifts of lands and other accessories to the *yāpa* professors, and last but not least the restoration of the image of the *jina* of Kaliṅga carried away by King Nanda prove beyond doubt that Khāravela was a Jaina. He came to the throne about 183 BC, at the age of twenty-four. At the time of his first invasion of Magadha he was only thirty-

1. This council fixed the canon of the Jaina sacred literature, consisting of eleven *aṅga*s and fourteen *pūrva*s.
2. खेमराजा स वढराजा . . . अनुभवंतो कलाणानि . . . सव-पासंड-पूजको . . . खारवेलसिरि. — *J.B.O.R.S.*, IV., p. 403, and XIII., p. 236.

two, and at the time of the second he was thirty-six. According to Mr Jayaswal he was probably dead before 152 BC.[1]

He is that imperial king about whose dynasty we know hardly anything, and about whose career there is absolutely no historical source but this long inscription, which also, as usual, could not escape the ravages of time. With all this it may be justly stated that it will not be surprising if on some happy day a scholar were to come across a better and more comprehensive document about this *dharmarāja*, "the illustrious descendant of the dynasty of royal sages." It is really strange, nay unbelievable, that the Jainas have got nothing to say about one whose contribution to Jaina history is second to none.

About the extent of Khāravela's rule and of the fresh conquests then made by him after his succession we have not a single contemporary record, historical or otherwise, on which we can lay our hands. It is just like a voice from the other world telling us that in days gone by there was some great Kaliṅga Emperor Khāravela, and that you must take him as such and place him as one of the contemporary historical luminaries on the sole basis of these seventeen lines commemorating his memory on the Hāthīgumphā inscription.

The inscription tells us that our hero subdued the great Śuṅga king, Puṣyamitra, in the north; that the great Indo-Greek king, Demetrios, retreated and left Mathurā just on hearing of his victories against the Śuṅgas; that he subdued the great Sātakarṇi and his feudatories in the south, and that with all these military triumphs his fame spread so far that even the Pāṇḍya king in the remote south sent him complimentary gifts.

With no other document at our disposal the questions as to how much to believe and with what limitations to interpret the facts laid down by the inscription present a great difficulty. This becomes extremely intricate when such military expeditions, as is abundantly proved by inscriptions, form part of the ordinary routine in a state of society in which war had become a profession and the soldier was an hereditary member of a professional caste, and in which desire to extend one's rule was, according to the law books, one of the chief qualifications of kingship.[2] This characteristic feature

1. *J.B.O.R.S.*, XIII., p. 243.
2. Manu, IX., 251 ; X., 119, etc.

of the life of ancient and mediaeval India is well marked in the eulogies of kings, which fill so large a proportion of the inscriptions that have come down to our time, and with whatsoever broadmindedness we may look at them we have to confess that these works are only the output of grateful beneficiaries or court poets, whose object was rather to glorify their royal patron than to hand down to posterity an accurate account of his reign. It is clear that successes are evidently exaggerated, while reverses are passed over in complete silence. The statements of the inscriptions are very frequently those of prejudiced witnesses, and they must be weighed as such if we are to estimate rightly the value of these few scattered fragments of historical evidence which time has preserved. The achievements of Khāravela loom large in the Hāthīgumphā inscription, and in the words of Sir Ashutosh Mookerji: "Stone has again yielded a complete record, full of faithful details, of the Emperor Khāravela of Orissa, whose name had disappeared from the annals of our country and passed into complete oblivion, though there was hardly a great town in India in the second century before the Christian era which did not tremble at the sight, if not at the very name, of his mighty legions."[1]

Anyhow there is no doubt that Khāravela was a prominent figure in his day, and that morally he had reached a height where he was secure, and where he was standing on no slippery ground. In short, he was a great man in his time, who gave ample proofs of his greatness when he was called upon by Providence to guide the destinies of a great people at a critical and unsettled period in Indian history.

---

1. *J.B.O.R.S.*, X., p. 8.

CHAPTER V

Mathurā Inscriptions

THE Jaina inscriptions in Mathurā form the beginning of the next landmark in the history of Jainism in north India, the Hāthīgumphā inscription of Khāravela terminating the former period. The recorded period between the two — i.e., *c.* 150 BC to C. 16 BC — need not be taken as blank, because after the great Jaina king of Kaliṅga we have Vikramāditya of Ujjain, a greater ruler perhaps than the *Kaliṅgādhipati,* who is claimed by the Jainas as a royal patron of their own church. We shall, after a brief survey of the epigraphic evidence found there, see that, simultaneously with Kaliṅga and Mālwā, Mathurā had become the home of the Jaina community in the north.

We have referred to this Vikrama and his era — which begins in or about 57 or 56 BC — in connection with the *nirvāṇa* date of Mahāvīra. The Jainistic recension of the *Vikramacarita* tells us that "Vikrama in his pious exaltation, after listening to the instruction of the Jaina teacher Siddhasena Divākara, freed the whole earth from debt, and (in so doing) effected a change (literally, a turning-point) in the era of Vardhamāna."[1] It is he who handed down to later India its first persistent era, which is still the common era of north India. To quote Edgerton : "Such has been the belief of the Hindus, not only Jainas but others, for many centuries."[2] This great Avantī lord, whose glorious days and superhuman virtues are so extensively praised in both Jainistic and Brāhmaṇistic literature, used to call himself Vikramāditya, etymologically meaning "like the sun in his prowess." This title seems to have appealed powerfully to the fancy of many a king who succeeded, since many indeed are the kings who have assumed it of their own accord, with no connection of lineage whatever. This shows that the first Vikramāditya must have been a very great king, because, otherwise the title would not have been so very enviable.

---

1. Edgerton, *Vikrama's Adventures,* pt. I., Int., p. lviii. Cf. Tawney, *Prabandhacintāmaṇi,* p. 11 ff. ; *Śatruñjaya Māhātmya, Sarga* XIV, v. 103, p. 808.
2. Edgerton, op. cit., Int., p. lix.

It is this Vikramāditya who is considered to be a Jaina by the traditional literature of the Jainas. Referring to his predecessor, Gardabhilla, they tell us that their great Jaina saint, Kālikācārya, being insulted by him by the abduction of his sister, who had joined the order with him, approached one of the Scythian kings and with his help successfully wreaked his vengeance.[1] To quote Dr Charpentier: "This legend is perhaps not totally devoid of all historical interest. For it records how the Jaina Kālaka, having been insulted by King Gardabhilla of Ujjain, who, according to various traditions, was the father of the famous Vikramāditya, went in his desire for revenge to the land of the Śakas, whose king was styled 'King of Kings' (*Sāhāṇusāhi*).[2] This title, in its Greek and Indian forms, was certainly borne by the Śaka kings of the Punjab, Maues and his successors, who belong to this period; and as it actually appears in the form *Shaonano Shao* on the coins of their successors, the Kuṣāṇa monarchs, we are perhaps justified in concluding that the legend is to some extent historical in character. However this may be, the story goes on to tell us that Kālaka persuaded a number of Śaka Satraps to invade Ujjain and overthrow the dynasty of Gardabhilla; but that some years afterwards his son, the glorious Vikramāditya, repelled the invaders and re-established the throne of his ancestors.[3] What the historical foundation of this legend may be is wholly uncertain; perhaps it contains faint recollections of the Scythian dominion in Western India during the first century BC. In any case, it seems undoubtedly to give further proof of the connection of the Jains with Ujjain — a fact indicated also by their use of the Vikrama era, which was established in the country of Mālwā, of which Ujjain was the capital."[4]

In connection with Saint Kālaka of the Jainas it may be mentioned here that he went to King Sātayāna of Pratiṣṭhānapura in the Deccan. During the *paryuṣaṇa* — the sacred festival at the close of the Jaina year — the king, being engaged in the observance of the festival of Indra, found it difficult

1. *Kalikācārya-kathā*, vv. 9-40, pp. 1-4. Cf. Konow, *E.I.*, XIV., p. 293. "Kālakasūri, the uprooter of Gardabhilla, lived 453 v." — Klatt, *I.A.*, XI., p. 251. Cf. ibid., p. 247 ; Charpentier, *C.H.I.*, I., p. 168 ; Stevenson (Mrs), op. cit., p. 75 ; *M.A.R.*, 1923, p. 11.
2. वशीकृतः मूरिवैरः स साहिः — *Kālakācārya-kathā*, v. 26, p. 2 ; साहानसाहिः स च भण्यतेऽत्र. — Ibid., V. 27, p. 3. Cf. ". . . the Jaina work, *Kālakācārya-kathānaka*, states that their kings were called *Sāhi*." — Raychaudhuri, op. cit., p. 274 ; Jacobi, Z.D.M.G., XXXIV., p. 262. Cf. Konow, op. cit., p. 293.
3. "He (Vikramāditya) saved the nation and Hinduism by signally defeating the Scythians, whose political importance and outlandish manners had appalled the Indians." — Mazumdar, op. cit., p. 63. Cf. ibid., p. 638. "Vikramāditya ousted the Śakas and became king, whereafter he established his own era." — Konow, op. and loc. cit.
4. Charpentier, op. and loc. cit.

to come on the fifth of Bhādrapada, and accordingly the great *guru* is said to have changed his appointment to a day earlier — viz. the fourth of Bhādrapada. Since then the whole Jaina community have begun that fast on the fourth, though very late in history with the rise of certain *gaccha*s the fourth was replaced by the fifth of the same month.[1] This event, if it is true, is significant from two points of view — the first, that it refers to the Śvetāmbara contact with the south, and secondly, because it alludes to a Jaina prince in the Deccan who was important enough to be so much respected by a great saint like Kālakācarya, and who had a share in fixing the date of an important festival of the Jainas like *pajjuṣaṇa*.[2]

Coming to Vikramāditya, the successor of Gardabhilla, Jaina sources tell us that Siddhasena Divākara, one of the most prominent stars of the history of Jaina literature, lived about this time at the king's court, and they also credit him with the conversion of the great Vikrama,[3] and, according to Mrs Stevenson, of Devapāla, "king of Kumārapura" as well.[4] Two other events are likewise supposed to have happened about this time — the defeat of the Buddhists in a great argument by a famous Jaina controversialist, an ascetic called Ārya Khapuṭa, who lived in Broach;[5] and the foundation of Pālitāṇā where Śatruñjaya, the holiest of the Jaina *tīrtha*s, is situated.[6]

The *Kharataragaccha Paṭṭāvali* tells us that Vajrasvāmī (496-584 v.), the sixteenth on the list, extended the Jaina religion southward in the kingdom of the Bauddhas.[7] The second event, about the founding of Pālitāṇā, seems

1. ततश्चतुर्थ्यां क्रियतां नृपेण, विज्ञप्तमेवं गुरुणाऽनुमेने. — *Kālakācārya-kathā*, v. 54, p. 5. Cf. Stevenson (Mrs), op. cit., p. 76. This, as Klatt tells us, is supported by the *Paṭṭāvali* of the *Tapagaccha* (*I.A.*, XI., p. 251); on the other hand, the *Kharataragaccha Paṭṭāvali* informs us that the Kālaka, who transferred the *paryuṣaṇāparvan*, lived in 993 v., and that there were two more of the same name prior to him, one of whom lived in 453 v. and was connected with Gardabhilla. — *I.A.*, XI., p. 247.
2. That the King Sātayāna was a devout Jaina is clear from the *Kālakācārya-kathā* (vv. 50-54, pp. 4-5), but it is not known who he was. Pratiṣṭhānapura is known to us as the western capital of the Sātavāhanas. Jaina tradition claims Hala of this dynasty as belonging to its own religion. Cf. Glasenapp, *Der Jainismus*, p. 53 ; Jhaveri, *Nirvāṇa-Kalika*, Int., p. xi.
3. "He (Siddhasena Divākara) converted Vikramāditya 470 years after Mahāvīra's *Nirvāṇa*." — Klatt, op. cit., p. 247. Cf. ibid., p. 251 ; Edgerton, op. cit., p. 251 ff. ; Stevenson (Mrs), op. cit., p. 77 ; Tawney, op. cit., pp. 116 ff. ; *M.A.R.*, 1923, p. 10.
4. Cf. Stevenson (Mrs), op. and loc. cit.
5. विद्यासिद्धा आर्यखपुटा आचार्याः, . . . भृगुकच्छे . . . बुद्धो निर्गतः, पादयोः पतितः — *Āvaśyaka-Sūtra*, pp. 411-12. Cf. Jhaveri, op. and loc. cit.
6. Cf. ibid., Int., p. xix ; Stevenson (Mrs), op. cit., pp. 77-78.
7. Cf. Klatt, op. cit., p. 247 ; Hemacandra, *Pariśiṣṭaparvan*, Canto XII, vv. 311, 388 ; *Āvaśyaka-Sūtra*, p. 295.

to refer to Pādaliptācārya, who is reported to have been a contemporary of the great Vikrama.[1] According to the Jainas he was gifted with a power of flying through the air.[2] In a note to this Mrs Stevenson observes: "Śatruñjaya, the Jainas say, was built by a monk who had the power of rising through the air, and by a disciple of his who had the power of creating gold. This fortunate conjunction of talents has resulted in one of the loveliest temple cities in the world."[3] In connection with this *tīrtha* the *Kharatara Paṭṭāvali* tells us that it was demolished in 570 v., and restored by Jāvaḍa, whose father, Bhāvaḍa, was a contemporary of Vikrama.[4] According to the Jaina tradition both the king and Jāvaḍa are said to have gone on pilgrimage to Pālitāṇā, and both of them spent a lot for the upkeep of the *tīrtha* during their stay there.[5]

In connection with Pādalipta also it may be mentioned here that he too, like Kālaka, is connected with the Śvetāmbara contact with the south. It appears from the *Saṁyaktva-Saptati* of Haribhadrasūri that the great *ācārya* went to Mānyakheta,[6] and that in all these places there existed Jaina *saṁgha*s "noted for their good qualities."[7] Thus from the traditions connected with Kālaka and Pādalipta it seems certain that about the first century BC Śvetāmbara Jainas must have predominated in the Deccan. King Śālivāhana of Pratiṣṭhānapura, in the *Saṁyaktva-Saptati*, describes Pādalipta as having put an end "to all bad religious systems." From this it becomes clear that Śālivāhana too must have been of the same religion as Pādalipta — i.e. Śvetāmbara.[8]

---

1. Klatt, op. cit., pp. 247, 251. "Palitta-Sūri (Pādalipta) is definitely connected with the foundation of the Pālitāṇā City." — Jhaveri, op. and loc. cit.
2. "Pādalipta had acquired the flying-lore by applying medical ingredients to feet, and daily performed pilgrimage of the five sacred places including Śatruñjaya (Pālitāṇā) and Girnār or Revantagiri." — Ibid., Int., p. xi. Cf. Tawney, op. cit., p. 195.
3. Stevenson (Mrs), op. cit., p. 78, n. 1. "Nāgārjuna . . . the pupil of Pādaliptasūri . . . was trying to acquire '*Suvarṇa Siddhi*' (power to make gold) . . ." etc. — Jhaveri, op. cit., Int., p. xii.
4. "Jāvaḍa, a merchant of Saurāshṭra (Kathiawar), sent a fleet to China and the Eastern Archipelago, which returned after twelve years with a burthen of gold. The father of Jāvaḍa lived in the time of Vikrama. . . ." — Mazumdar, op. cit., p. 65. Cf. *Śatruñjaya Māhātmya, Sarga* XIV, vv. 104, 192 ff., pp. 808, 816 ff. ; Jhaveri, op. cit., Int., p. xix.
5. Cf. *Śatruñjaya Māhātmya, Sarga* XIV, V. 280, p. 824.
6. Mānyakheta or Mānyakṣetra is to be identified with Mālkheḍ, in the Nizam's territory. — Dey, *Geographical Dictionary*, p. 126. This Mālkheḍ or Mānyakheta, which Pādalipta visited, became famous in the succeeding centuries as the capital of the Rāṣṭrakūṭas who counted among them not a few patrons and followers of the Jaina religion.
7. *Saṁyaktva-Saptati*, vv. 96, 97. See *M.A.R.*, 1923, pp. 10-11. "For the greater part of his life Pādalipta resided at Manakhetapura." — Jhaveri, op. cit., Int., p. x.
8. *Saṁyaktva-Saptati*, V. 158. Cf. *M.A.R.*, 1923, p. 11 ; Jhaveri, op. cit., Int., p. xi.

Taking stock of all these facts connected with Vikrama and his period it must be said that they are based mostly on the long list of teachers, "often more or less apocryphal, which have been preserved by the modern subdivisions of the Jaina community,"[1] and on the literature of the period in no way connected with the one under our consideration. What is to be discovered is whether these circumstances can warrant the conclusion that Jaina traditions are without any foundation, and that Vikrama, the most noted of the quasi-historical heroes of mediaeval India, is a purely legendary monarch.

A thorough examination, as far as possible, of the various theories propounded in regard to this by different scholars has been made by Edgerton in his Introduction to his *Vikrama's Adventures*.[2] Without repeating the arguments put forth by the learned scholar in their refutations, suffice it to say that, leaving aside Vikramāditya, nothing can be stated with absolute certainty about many other personages in ancient India whose historicity is unquestioned either on epigraphic or numismatic evidence. There is no reason why the reality of this "Hindu King Arthur"— a model for real kings to follow — should be doubted when it is based on "both Jainistic and Brahmanistic literature." To quote Edgerton: "It seems that the *Paṭṭāvalis*, or lists of Jaina pontiffs, have the look of being in the main as reliable, certainly, as any other native literary source of Indian history (which, to be sure, may not be saying very much). . . . I am not aware that there is any definite and positive reason for rejecting the Jainistic chronicles completely, and for saying categorically that there was no such king as Vikrama living in 57 BC. Do we know enough about the history of that century to be able to deny that a local king of Malava, bearing one of the names by which Vikrama goes, may have won for himself a somewhat extensive dominion in Central India (for we do not of course need to swallow whole the characteristic Hindu exaggerations which could make him a universal Emperor)?"[3]

Besides Edgerton there are other scholars, like Bühler and Tawney, who also defend the historicity of the Jainistic chronicles. "In particular," observes Dr Bühler, "must it be admitted that the persons introduced in the older, as well in the more recent, narratives are really historical characters. Although it is frequently the case that an individual is introduced at a period earlier or

1. Charpentier, op. cit., p. 167.
2. Edgerton, op. cit., Int., p. lviii ff.
3. Ibid., p. lxiv.

later than that to which he really belonged or that the most absurd stories are told with regard to him, yet there is no case forthcoming in which we could affirm with certainty that a man named by these chroniclers is a pure figment of the imagination. On the contrary, every freshly discovered inscription, every collection of old manuscripts, and every really historic work that is brought to light, furnishes confirmation of the actual existence of one or other of the characters described by them. In the same way all exact dates given by them deserve the most careful attention. When they are found to agree in two works of this class that are independent of one another they may, without hesitation, be accepted as historically correct."[1]

Dr Sten Konow goes a little further, and clearly indicates that scholars are becoming less disdainful of the Indian traditions about Vikrama. He rightly welcomes the story of the great saint *Kālakācārya-kathānaka,* and how he was insulted and so on. To quote the eminent scholar: "I know that most European scholars, though many of them speak with respect about Indian tradition, do not usually take any notice of it, but I am unable to see why. And with regard to the narrative *Kālakācārya-kathānaka* I see no reason whatever why we should disbelieve it. I have shown elsewhere that there are good reasons for assuming the existence of the Malava King Vikramāditya at an early date," etc.[2]

Thus on the authority of scholars like Charpentier, Edgerton, Bühler, Tawney and Sten Konow we come to this conclusion — that the traditional literature of the Jainas can rightly claim to be considered historical, and that the reality of Vikrama and his era need not be denied. Such seems to have been the latest opinion of Vincent Smith also, for he observes: "it is possible that such a *Rājā* may have existed."[3] Moreover, as seen before, the kingdom of Avantī or Malava was a centre of Jainism even in the days of Mahāvīra. During the times of the Mauryas it came more and more to the forefront, and finally at the end of their rule the Jainas, gradually losing their position in the kingdom of Magadha, had begun their migration towards the western part of India, where they settled, and where they have retained their settlement

1. Bühler, *Ueber das Leben des Jaina-Mōnches Hemacandra*, p. 6. Cf. Tawney, op. cit., Int., pp. vi-vii ; ibid., pp. V. ff.
2. Konow, op. cit., p. 294.
3. Smith, *Oxford History of India*, p. 151.

even to the present day.[1] No doubt Kaliṅga has its own contribution to make to the history of north Indian Jainism, but the general tendency was towards the west. Another locality in which the Jainas appear to have been firmly established, from the middle of the second century BC onwards, was Mathurā. Since the days of Candragupta, and after him Samprati and Khāravela, the Jaina spread seems to have been uncommonly vigorous. Leaving aside the sentiments and the religious outlook of these great kings, an uncommonly vigorous spread of the Jainas is evident from the great number of *kula*s and *śākhā*s which we find in the Jaina *saṁgha* from the Mathurā inscriptions dating more or less from the second century BC.

The Mathurā inscriptions bring us to the Indo-Scythian rule in northern India. We have seen that Candragupta placed himself at the head of the Indians, who chafed under the Macedonian yoke, and after Alexander's departure defeated his generals and "shook the yoke of servitude from the neck" of India. What happened in India immediately after the departure of Alexander is not clear. "The mists of obscurity cling heavily round the course that events took in India during the years that immediately followed the death of Alexander the Great."[2] However, this much is certain, that for about a century after his death, the strong arms of the Mauryan emperors held India for the Indians against all comers, and treated their Hellenistic neighbours on equal terms.[3]

After the Mauryas we have seen how the Magadhan monarchy under the Brāhmanical Śuṅgas and the Greek power in the north-west were falling before the onslaughts of the Cedis under Khāravela. We have already referred to the feuds of Demetrios and Eucratides, which greatly weakened the power of the Greeks. As regards other Indian enemies of the Bactrian Greeks and onslaughts of the Sātavāhanas on the Śuṅgas we do not propose to say anything. For the purposes of a connected history we need say only this much: "that in the second and first centuries BC Greek rule in parts of Kafiristan and Gāndhāra was supplanted by that of the Śakas."[4] To quote Rapson: "The political isolation of India was completed by the Scythian conquest of Bactria

1. Cf. Charpentier, op. and loc. cit.
2. Macdonald, *C.H.I.*, I., p. 427.
3. Cf. Smith, *Early History of India*, p. 253.
4. Raychaudhuri, op. cit., p. 273.

c. 135 BC and by the long struggle between Rome and Parthia which began in 53 BC."[1] It was also with one of these Śaka rulers, known to us by the name Muraṇḍa, that the great Pādalipta was closely connected. Muraṇḍa is known to us from the traditional literature of the Jainas as the ruler of Pāṭalīputra, and Pādalipta seems to have gained complete influence at his court.[2] The great *ācārya* is said to have cured the king of the terrible headache he was suffering from. This incident is related by the *Prabhāvaka-Carita* in the following words:

"So quickly as Pādalipta turns his first finger round the knee-joint does the headache of King Muraṇḍa come to an end."[3]

However the Scythian (Śaka) invaders of Bactria were succeeded by the Yuch-chi; and when, in the first century AD, the predominant tribe of the Yuch-chi, the Kuṣāṇas, extended their dominion in Turkestan and Bactria to north-west India, the Kuṣāṇa Empire formed a connecting link between China and India, and provided the means of an intercourse which was fruitful in results. As the explorations of recent years have shown, an Indian culture, Indian languages and the Indian alphabets were established in Chinese Turkestan. Particularly, to repeat it once more, according to Mr N.C. Mehta even Jaina subjects came to be painted in the cave-temples of Chinese Turkestan.

With this shadowy background of Indian history in general we shall now refer to the Mathurā inscriptions, and examine their importance in connection with the Jaina church. The historical importance of these inscriptions cannot be better summed up than in the following words of Cunningham: "The information derived from these inscriptions is of the greatest value for the ancient history of India. The general purport of all of them is the same — to record the gifts of certain individuals, for the honour of their religion, and for the benefit of themselves and their parents. When the inscriptions are confined to this simple announcement they are of little importance, but as the donors in most of these Mathurā records have added the name of the reigning kings, and the *saṁvat* date at the time of the gift,

1. Rapson, *C.H.I.*, I., p. 60.
2. पाटलीपुरे . . . राजास्ति मुरण्डो नाम . . . स . . . हृतान्तःकरणो नृपः सूरेर्बालस्य पादानां प्रणामेच्छू रवेरिव. — *Prabhāvaka-Carita, Pādalipta-Prabandha*, vv. 44, 61. Cf. *Saṁyaktva-Saptati*, v. 48 ; *M.A.R.*, 1923, p. 11 ; Jhaveri, op. cit., Int., p. x.
3. *Prabhāvaka-Carita*, v. 59. Cf. *Saṁyaktva-Saptati*, v. 62 ; *M.A.R.*, 1923, op. and loc. cit.

they form in fact so many skeleton pages of the lost history.[1] The direct amount of information which they give belongs to an early and very interesting period — just before and after the Christian era — when, as we learn from the Chinese authorities, the Indo-Scythians had conquered the whole of northern India, although the actual extent of their conquest was quite unknown. Hence the great value of the present inscriptions, from which we learn that the permanent occupation of Mathurā had been effected some time before the *Saṁvat* year 9, when the Indo-Scythian prince Kanishka filled the throne of north-west India and the Punjab."[2]

Most of the Jaina inscriptions from Mathurā are from the mound known as Kaṅkālī Ṭīlā, about half-a-mile due south from the Kaṭrā, which is situated just one mile to the westward of the old fort of Mathurā. The Kaṅkālī mound seems to have been a very extensive one; the number of statues of all sizes, from the colossal downwards, which it has yielded has scarcely been surpassed by the prolific returns of Buddhist sculpture from the Jail mound.[3] There seems to have been two magnificent temples where the mound rises at present. Most of the inscriptions are incised on pedestals or bases of naked *jina*s either seated or standing, and some of which form a quadruple or a four-faced image called *caturmukha*. Chronologically the earliest inscription, according to Dr Bühler, is the following one :

समनस माहरखितास अंतेवासिस वछीपुत्रस सावकास (स्रावकास) उतरदासक[ा]स पासादोतोरनं ॥

"An ornamental arch for the temple (the gift) of the lay-hearer Utaradāsaka (Uttaradāsaka), son of Vachî (Vātsī mother and) disciple of the ascetic Māharkhita (Māgharakshita)."[4]

Because of exceedingly archaic characters and other linguistic peculiarities the learned scholar feels that it may be assigned to the middle of the second century BC.[5] Next in age come the two inscriptions that are connected with the Satraps of Mathurā. Of these the first one is complete, while the other

1. The Buddhistical inscriptions at Mathurā also are similar to the Jaina inscriptions in their style and contents. Cf. Dawson, *J.R.A.S.* (New Series), v., p. 182.
2. Cunningham, *A.S.I.*, III., pp. 38-39.
3. Cf. ibid., p. 46. "The Kankālī Tīla has been . . . prolific . . . both in sculptures and inscriptions, all of which . . . are pure Jaina monuments. On the upper level stands a large Jaina temple dedicated to Jambū Svāmī . . . an annual fair is held at this place. . . ." — Ibid., p. 19. This temple is near the Caurāsī mounds, which is the seat of another Jaina establishment. Cf. ibid., XVII., p. 112.
4. Bühler, *E.I.*, II., Ins. No. I, pp. 198-99.
5. Ibid., p. 195.

merely mentions some *kṣatrapa mahārāja* whose name begins with "*Ma*."[1] The former is dated in the year 42 of the Lord, the Mahākṣatrapa Śoḍāsa, in the second month of winter, and refers to a votive tablet that was set up by some female Āmohinī.[2] It is not clear what era is made use of in this inscription.

However, the existence of this Mahākṣatrapa Śoḍāsa was first made known by Cunningham, who found another inscription in that king's name in the Kaṅkālī Ṭīlā.[3] On the evidence of his coins, which resemble those of Azes, the learned archaeologist placed Śoḍāsa about 80-57 BC, and conjectured that he was a son of Rājubula or Rañjubula, another Satrap of Mathurā.[4] This conjecture is also confirmed by the Mathurā Lion capital, which mentions Śoḍāsa as a Chatrava (Satrap) and as the son of Mahāchatrava Rājūla (Rañjubula).[5] To quote Professor Rapson : "The Great Satrap Rājūla, whose name appears as Rājuvula in other inscriptions, is unquestionably the Rañubula who, both as Satrap and as great Satrap, struck coins in imitation of those of Strato I and Strato II, the last of the Yavana kings to reign in the E. Punjab . . . ; and he was the father of Śoḍāsa, in whose reign as Satrap the monument was erected. Subsequently Śoḍāsa himself appears as great Satrap in the Āmohinī votive tablet at Mathurā, which is dated in the second month of winter of the year 42."[6]

As to the era of the inscription, opinion is divided;[7] but, looking to the way in which the date is recorded, it seems highly probable that an Indian era must have been used.[8] If this is granted, as seems likely, it is the era of Vikrama (57 BC.), and the inscription is dated in 16-15 BC. Dr Konow also adduces good grounds for believing that Śoḍāsa dated his inscription in the Vikrama era.[9] "So far as I can see," observes the learned scholar, "we have a

1. Cf. Bühler, *E.I.*, II., Ins. No. III, p. 199.
2. Cf. ibid., Ins. II, p. 199.
3. Cf. Cunningham, op. cit., p. 30, Ins. No. I.
4. Cf. ibid., pp. 40-41. "Rañjubula, Rājuvula or Rājūla is known from inscriptions as well as coins. An inscription of Brāhmī characters at Mora near Mathura calls him Mahākshatrapa. But the Greek legend on some of his coins describes him as "King of Kings, the Saviour," showing that he probably declared his independence." — Raychaudhuri, op. cit., p. 283.
5. Ibid.
6. Rapson, *C.H.I.*, I., p. 575.
7. Cf. Raychaudhuri, op. cit., p. 283 ff. ; Smith, op. cit., p. 241, n. 1.
8. Cf. Rapson, op. cit., pp. 575-76.
9. Cf. Konow, *E.I.*, XIV., pp. 139-41.

distinct indication that the dating according to three seasons, each comprising four months, was later on considered as a characteristic feature of the Vikrama era. It is well known that in the oldest inscriptions which give name to this era it is designated as a Malava reckoning. In two of the most ancient instances of its use — in the Mandasor inscription of the time of Naravarman and in the Mandasor inscription of the time of Kumāragupta I — the season is expressly mentioned. I think we are forced to the conclusion that Śoḍāsa dated his inscription in the Vikrama era, and that the method of dating used in that reckoning was adopted by Kanishka and his successors in such records as were destined for India proper, because it was the national north Indian way of dating."[1]

After these two Satrapa inscriptions follow a few more which have been grouped under the name "Archaic," and which in the opinion of Bühler belong to the period before Kaniṣka.[2] Of these the following one needs particular mention:

"Adoration to the Arhat Vardhamāna! A tablet of homage was set up by Śivamitrā (of) the Kauśika (family), (wife) of Gotiputra (Guptiputra), a black serpent for the Pothayas and Śakas."[3]

According to Dr Bühler both Gotiputra and Kośika Śivamitrā were of noble or royal descent, and the expression "Gotiputra, a black serpent for the Pothayas and Śakas," points also to his belonging to the warrior tribe. "The wars to which it alludes," observes the learned scholar, "may have occurred either before the Scythians conquered Mathura — i.e. before the time of Kanishka — or when their domination had passed away. The letters of the inscriptions, which are particularly old-fashioned and may belong to the first century BC, speak in favour of the first alternative. If the inscription was incised before the Scythian conquest, it also furnishes valuable testimony for the antiquity of the Jaina temple in which it was found."[4]

The next in age to these follows a group consisting of dated inscriptions which explicitly mention Kaniṣka, Huviṣka, and Vasudeva. There are other dated ones that are taken to belong to their period, although they do not name any of these Kuṣāṇa monarchs. "The next group, Nos. XI-XXIV," observes Dr Bühler, "consists of the dated inscriptions which in my opinion

1. Cf. Konow, *E.I.*, XIV., pp. 139, 141.
2. Bühler, *E.I.*, II., Ins. Nos. IV-X, p. 196.
3. Ibid., Ins. No. XXIII, p. 396.
4. Ibid., p. 394.

belong to the time of Kanishka, Huvishka and Vāsudeva. Not one shows the name of a king. Nevertheless, I believe that nobody, who carefully compares them with the dated documents, mentioning the three kings, will come to a different conclusion."[1]

These dated Kuṣāṇa inscriptions range within the well-known limits from *saṁvat* 4 to *saṁvat* 98.[2] It is not possible to exactly lay down whether the mode of reckoning made use of in these inscriptions is the *saṁvat* era of the Great Vikrama or some other era. "The chronology of this period has been one of the most perplexing problems in the whole of Indian history; and the problem can scarcely be said to be solved positively even now — that is to say, it has not yet been placed beyond all possibility of doubt."[3] There is a lot of difference of opinion about the crucial point of the Kuṣāṇa chronology.[4] All the same, along with several scholars of eminence and repute, we feel that the era made use of in these inscriptions is the one known as the Śaka era, commencing AD 78.[5]

One of the inscriptions on a Jaina pedestal at Kaṅkālī mound runs as follows: "*siddham mahārājasya kanishkasya saṁvatsara navame . . . māse prath . . . divase 5,*" etc.[6]

No doubt as in the Śoḍāsa and other Kuṣāṇa inscriptions and "as characteristic of the old Vikrama-Malava era,"[7] we find here also the ancient Indian way of dating, with mention of the season, the number of the month within the season, and the day of the month; but this does not mean that the mode of reckoning adopted by the Kuṣāṇas under no circumstances can be connected with the Śaka era. On the other hand there is nothing impossible if what is characteristic of the old Vikrama-Malava era were

---

1. Bühler, *E.I.*, II., p. 196.
2. Cf. ibid. ; Cunningham, op. cit., p. 14.
3. Rapson, op. cit., p. 583.
4. For the various theories of Kaniṣka's date see Raychaudhuri, op. cit., p. 295 ff.
5. "According to Fergusson, Oldenberg, Thomas, Banerji, Rapson and many other scholars, Kanishka was the founder of the reckoning commencing AD 78, which came to be known as the Śaka era." — Ibid., p. 297. Cf. Hoernle, *Uvāsaga-Dasāo*, Int., p. xi. There is great difference of opinion as to who was the real founder of the Śaka era, though this much is certain — that it must have been some foreign ruler who founded it. As Pandit Ojha remarks, it is not possible to lay down anything for certain regarding the person behind this era. Cf. Ojha, *Palaeography of India*, pp. 172-73 (2nd edn.).
6. Cunningham, op. cit., Ins. No. IV, Plate XIII, p. 31.
7. Konow, op. cit., p. 141.

adopted by Kaniṣka and his successors in their Brāhmī records, and this conjecture gains ground when we know that one of the Kuṣāṇas is named Vāsudeva, which is a purely Indian name.[1]

Moreover, the adoption of the Vikrama era in connection with the Kuṣaṇas also makes it difficult to adjust their position as the successors of the Mathurā Satraps. This becomes more so when we know that under Kaniṣka's dynasty Mathurā formed part of one and the same empire.[2] Finally, "the evidence obtained by Sir John Marshall from his excavations of the ancient sites of Takshaśilā proves conclusively that the period of Kaniṣka's reign must have been somewhere about the end of the first century AD; and a comparison of this evidence with the statements of Chinese historians and with the dates supplied by inscriptions makes it seem almost certain that Kanishka was the founder of the well-known era which began in 78 AD."[3] Thus the period concerning the Kuṣāṇa inscriptions, which range within the limit from *saṁvat* 4 to *saṁvat* 98, may be approximately laid down as AD 82-176.

Of the Kuṣāṇa inscriptions two are to be particularly noticed, and of the two the following one is of great importance with respect to the history of the Jaina sect:

"The year 79, the fourth (month of the) rainy-season, the twentieth day — on that (date, specified as) above, — the image, the gift of the female lay-disciple Dinā (Dattā), wife of . . . , was set up at the *Vodva Stūpa*, built by the Gods."[4]

From this inscription we learn that an ancient Jaina *stūpa* existed in Mathurā which, as Bühler rightly remarks, in AD 157 (Śaka 79) was considered to have been built by the gods — i.e. was so ancient that its real origin had been completely forgotten.[5] The importance of the other lies inasmuch as the history of the Kuṣāṇa kings is concerned. It gives us the name of the "Mahārāja Devaputra Huksha (Hushka or Huvishka),"[6] whence we have the,"certainty that the name Hushka, which the *Rājataraṅgiṇī* has preserved and which still survives in the name of the Kashmirian village Ushkar — Hushkapura — was actually used in ancient times for Huvishaka."[7]

---

1. Cf. Cunningham, op. cit., p. 41.
2. Cf. Raychaudhuri, op. cit., p. 284.
3. Rapson, op. cit., p. 583.
4. Bühler, op. cit., Ins. No. XX, p. 204.
5. Ibid., p. 198. Cf. Charpentier, op. cit., p. 167.
6. Bühler, op. cit., Ins. No. XXVI, p. 206.
7. Ibid., p. 198.

Next in age to the Kuṣāṇa inscriptions come some three others which, in the opinion of Dr Bühler, belong to the Gupta period,[1] and another inscription which clearly belongs to the eleventh century AD.[2] Mathurā would thus seem to have been popularly frequented as a religious site for a period extending continuously over more than a thousand years.[3] Opinions about the Gupta inscriptions we reserve meanwhile till the next chapter. For the present, having dwelt mainly on the political bearing of all these Jaina inscriptions, we shall see if they are equally great for the history of the Jaina church. Their importance in this respect lies in two ways: first, from the standpoint of particular aspects of Jainism or the history of the Jaina church, and secondly, from their general importance in connection with the history of the northern Jainas.

Taking the first we find that some such points as the dedication of certain inscriptions to *tīrthaṅkara*s other than the last one, and the reference to more than one *arhat* in the body of the inscriptions, have been already referred to by us in connection with the problem of the historicity of Pārśva and his predecessors. Furthermore, as seen before, some of the records end as follows: "May it be for the welfare and happiness of all creatures," and we have referred to this while considering the Jaina ideal of *ahiṁsā* or non-violence. Besides these few points that are already dealt with by us a point of very great importance in connection with the Mathurā inscriptions is their mentioning several female ascetics, and their showing that these persons developed a very considerable activity.[4] There can be no doubt that Aryya-Saṅgamikā and Aryya-Vasulā in the following inscription are nuns: . . . अर्य्यसङ्गमिकये शिशीनिनं अर्य्यवसुलये निर्वर्तनं . . ., etc. ("At the request of the venerable Vasulā, the female pupil of the venerable Saṅgamikā . . ."), etc.[5] This follows from their title *aryya* ("The venerable"), their being called *śiśīni* or *śiśini* ("female disciples"), and from the statement that the gifts were made at, or by, their *nirvartana*, their request or advice. With so much certainty gained, it is not difficult to recognize that the Mathurā documents point to the existence of female ascetics among the Jainas of Mathurā. Thus the Śvetāmbara Caturvidha *saṁgha*, the community consisting of monks, nuns, lay-brothers and lay-sisters,

---

1. Bühler, op. cit., Ins. Nos. XXXVIII-XL, p. 198.
2. Ibid., Ins. No. XLI, p. 198.
3. Cf. Growse, *I.A.*, VI., p. 219.
4. Cf. Bühler, *E.I.*, I., Ins. Nos. II, V, VII, XII, XIV., etc., pp. 382, 384-86, 388-89.
5. Ibid., Ins. No. II, p. 382.

can be traced as far back as the beginning of the Christian era,[1] and this is further confirmed by a Jaina inscription found by Cunningham on a broken slab at Mathurā which reads *caturvarṇa saṁgha*.[2]

In connection with this fact of the existence of nuns it is worthy of note that only in one case we find a nun who appears as adviser of a layman. Here the venerable Kumāramitrā induces Kumārabhaṭi, her son during her worldly life, to dedicate an image of Vardhamāna.[3] In all the other inscriptions we find that the nuns exhorted female lay-members of the *saṁgha* to make their donations. Whether Kumāramitrā joined the order after the death of her husband or along with him we cannot positively say, because both the alternatives are equally possible. It may even be this — that she might have done so alone with the consent of her husband during his lifetime.[4] Bühler takes her to be a widow, and remarks : "It agrees with this that in modern times, too, the order of Jaina nuns mostly consists of widows, . . . who, according to the custom of most castes, cannot be married, and are got rid of in a convenient manner by being made to take the tonsure."[5]

As to the number of *kula*s and *śākhā*s appearing in the Mathurā inscriptions, suffice it to say that they furnish some well-preserved names which can be rightly identified with those appearing in the traditional literature of the Jainas.[6] Of these divisions of the Jaina community it seems that the adherents of the Koṭṭiya-Koṭika *Gaṇa* must have been more numerous in Mathurā than those of the other school. In the words of Dr Bühler: "It deserves to be noted that it is the only *Gaṇa* whose name survived in the fourteenth century AD. Its great age, as well as the great age of its ramifications, the *Brahmadāsika* family,

1. It is a characteristic Jaina doctrine that the *śrāvaka*s and *śrāvikā*s form part of the *saṁgha*. On this point the Jainas differ very markedly from the Buddhists.
2. Our transliteration of the said inscription is as follows : नमो अरहंतानं नमो सिद्धानं सं ६२ गृ ३ दि ५ . . . शिष्या चतुर्वर्णस्य संघस्य . . . वापिकाये देत्ति. The inscription is not clear. Some vowel-marks and letters cannot be accurately deciphered. However the date portion and the portion referring to the donation are more or less legible. It is dated in the year 62, and seems to talk of a well, possibly for the चतुर्वर्ण congregation. The donor looks like some female pupil (शिष्या). For the inscription see Cunningham, *A.S.I.*, XX., Ins. No. VI, Plate XIII. Cf. Bühler, op. cit., p. 380.
3. Cf. ibid., Ins. No. VII, pp. 385-86; ibid., p. 380.
4. Cf. Burgess, *I.A.*, XIII., p. 278.
5. Bühler, op. cit., p. 380.
6. Cf. ibid., pp. 378-79.

the *Uccenāgarī* [1] branch and the Śrīgṛha district community, is attested by our No. IV. The latest possible date of this inscription is *Saṁvat* 59, or AD 128-29. The preacher then living, the venerable Sīha, enumerates four spiritual ancestors, the first among whom must have flourished about the beginning of our era. The *Gaṇa* was, as we learn, much divided at that early period, and this fact speaks in favour of the statement of the tradition which places its origin about the year 250 BC."[2]

The language of the inscriptions is a mixed dialect, consisting partly of Prākṛt and partly of Sanskrit words and forms. However, some of the inscriptions are said to be recorded in pure Prākṛt of the Pāli type. As seen before, they show exceedingly archaic characters, and merely on this ground they are taken to be as old as the second and first century BC. Certain inscriptions of Sir A. Cunningham's collection shows the Jaina Prākṛt and Mahārāṣṭrī forms *Pūrvvāye* or *Pūrvvaye*.[3] It is not possible to say for certain what influenced the language of these documents unless we know exactly the character of the vernacular of Central India used in the first and second centuries AD. However it seems, as Dr Bühler observes, "to have been in some points more similar to the Jaina Prākṛt and the Mahārāshṭrī than to the Pāli and to the language of Aśoka's edicts and of the older Āndhra inscriptions."[4]

As regards the origin of this mixed dialect, with Dr Bhandarkar[5] and others the learned scholar remarks that "it is the result of half-educated people, trying to express themselves in Sanskrit, of which they possessed an insufficient knowledge and which they were not in the habit of using largely. All the Jaina inscriptions from Mathurā were no doubt composed by the monks, who acted as the spiritual directors of the laymen, or by their pupils. Though no inscription has been found in which the author is named, the above inference is warranted by the fact that numerous later documents of the same character contain the names of *yati*s who are said to have composed them or to have

1. This geographical name seems to be identical with the fort of Unchanagara, which belongs to the modern town of Bulandshahr, in the north-western provinces. Cf. Cunningham, *A.S.I.*, XIV., p. 147.
2. Bühler, op. cit., pp. 379-80. Cf. Klatt, op. cit., *I.A.*, XI., p. 246. The schools connected with the Koṭṭiya *gaṇa* offer no difficulty, as they agree with the corresponding names of the *Kalpa-Sūtra*. Cf. Jacobi, *Kalpa-Sūtra*, p. 82.
3. Cunningham, *A.S.I.*, III., Ins. Nos. II, III, VII and XI, pp. 30-33.
4. Bühler, op. cit., p. 376.
5. Cf. Bhandarkar, *I.A..*, XII., p. 141.

written them. The *yatis* in the first and second centuries no doubt, just as now, for their sermons and the exposition of their scriptures, used the vernacular of the day, and their scriptures were certainly written in Prākṛt. It was a matter of course that their attempts to write in Sanskrit were not very successful. This theory receives the strongest support from the fact that the character and the number of the corruptions vary almost in every document, and from various single sentences, such as *vācakasya aryya — baladinasya śishyo aryya — mātridinaḥ tasya nirvvarttanā*, which latter reads like a piece from a stupid school-boy's exercise."[1]

As to the general importance of the Mathurā inscriptions in connection with the history of Jainism in north India there can be no denying the fact that they afford most unequivocal evidence of the flourishing state of the Jaina religion during the period of Indo-Scythian rule, both before and after the Christian era. They tell us about a widespread and firmly established Jaina community, strongly supported by pious lay-devotees, and very zealous in the consecration and worship of images and shrines dedicated to Mahāvīra and his predecessors. After the Hāthīgumphā inscription of Khāravela the Kaṅkālī mound at Mathurā has now given us the most complete and satisfactory testimony that the Jaina religion, even before the beginning of the Christian era, must have been in a condition almost as rich and flourishing as that of Buddha.

1. Bühler, op. cit., p. 377.

CHAPTER VI

State of Jainism during the Gupta Period

THE Mathurā inscriptions bring us more or less to the end of the Kuṣāṇas. Tradition, monuments and inscriptions of this time prove that their sway extended all over north-western India, probably as far south as the Vindhyas, as well as all over the remote regions beyond the Pāmīr passes. There are grounds also for the belief that from the time of Kaniṣka to the reign of Vāsudeva the Kuṣāṇa rule extended over Bihar.[1] This paramount power in north India seems to have come to an end after the death of Vāsudeva, the last Kuṣāṇa king who continued to hold extensive territories in India.

"It is evident," observes Smith, "that the Kushān power must have been decadent during the latter part of the long reign of Vāsudeva, and apparently before its close, or immediately after that event, the vast empire of Kanishka obeyed the usual law governing Oriental monarchies and broke up into fragments, having enjoyed a brief period of splendid unity. Probably numerous *Rājas* asserted their independence and formed a number of short-lived states; but historical material for the third century is so completely lacking that it is impossible to say what or how many those states were."[2]

Nothing definite is recorded concerning the dynasties of northern India, excluding the Punjab, during the third century and the early part of the fourth. The period between the extinction of the Kuṣāṇas and the rise of the Imperial Gupta dynasty, nearly a century later, is one of the darkest in the whole of Indian history.[3] However, with the rise of the Guptas the veil of oblivion is lifted and the history of India regains unity and interest.

---

1. Cf. Smith, op. cit., pp. 274, 276 ; Jayaswal *J.B.O.R.S.*, VI., p. 22.
2. Smith, op. cit., pp. 288, 290.
3. "The period evidently was one of extreme confusion, associated with foreign invasions from the north-west, which is reflected in the muddled statements of the Purāṇas concerning the Ābhīras, Gardabbilas, Śakas, Yavanas, Bāhīlkas and other outstanding dynasties named as the successors of the Āndhras." — Ibid., p. 290.

With the advent of the Guptas Magadha again came to the forefront. "Twice in history did it establish a great empire — the Maurya Empire in the fourth and third centuries BC, and the Gupta Empire in the fourth and fifth centuries AD."[1] The extent of the Gupta Empire was by far the greatest that had been seen in India since the days of Aśoka, six centuries before. It comprised all the most populous and fertile countries of north India. It extended from the Brahmaputra on the east to the Jamunā and Cambal on the west; and from the foot of the Himālayas on the north to the Narmadā on the south. Beyond these wide limits the frontier kingdoms of Assam and the Gangetic delta, as well as those on the southern slopes of the Himālayas, and the free tribes of Rājpūtānā and Mālwā, were attached to the empire by bond of subordinate alliance; whilst almost all the kingdoms of the south had been overrun by the emperor's armies and compelled to acknowledge his irresistible might.[2]

As to the state of religion during the Gupta period this much is certain, that officially the kings of this dynasty were Brāhmanical Hindus, with special devotion to Viṣṇu, but followed the usual practice of ancient India in looking with a favourable eye on all varieties of Indian religion. Buddhism and Jainism, though by no means favoured religions, were allowed to continue. The inference seems to be one of non-interference, a universal toleration, with special preference for Vaiṣṇavism.[3] For instance Candragupta Vikramāditya or Candragupta II, the fifth in the Gupta list, "although tolerant of Buddhism and Jainism, was himself an orthodox Hindu, specially devoted to the cult of Vishṇu."[4]

Besides this eclectic spirit of the Guptas, as seen before, we have from the Mathurā inscriptions the epigraphic evidence of their sympathy towards the Jainas. Of these Jaina records three in the opinion of Dr. Bühler belong to the Gupta period.[5] This is of course indisputable with the following one, which is incised on the base of a large sitting *jina*, and which is dated in the reign of Kumāragupta :

"Success! In the year 113, in the victorious reign of the supreme lord and

1. Rapson, op. cit., p. 310.
2. Cf. Smith, op. cit., p. 303.
3. "The *Mānasāra* seems, therefore, to point to the Gupta period . . . ; the existence of an empire comprising the whole of India ; . . . the popularity of the Brāhmanical religion with predilection for the Vishṇu cult and non-interference and toleration of Buddhism and Jainism. . . ." — Acharya, *Indian Architecture according to Mānasāra Śilapaśāstra*, p. 194.
4. Smith, op. cit., p. 309.
5. Cf. Bühler, *E.I.*, II., Ins. Nos. XXXVIII-XL, p. 198.

supreme king of great kings, the illustrious Kumāragupta, on the twentieth day (of the winter-month Kārttika) — on that (date, specified as) above an image was set-up by Śāmāḍhyā (Śyāmāḍhyā), daughter of Bhaṭṭibhava (and) housewife of the ferry-man (?) Grahamittrapālita, who had received the command (to make the dedication) from Datilācāyya (Dattilācārya) out of the Koṭṭiya Gaṇa (and) the Vidyādharī-Śākhā."[1]

With regard to the other two inscriptions, one of them is not in good condition, and so no continuous translation is possible. It apparently records the building or restoration of a temple.[2] The other one, however, on palaeographical grounds has been considered by Bühler to belong to the Gupta period. The said inscription, which is incised on the base of a small statue, runs as follows :

"In the fifty-seventh, 57, year, in the third month of winter, on the thirteenth day, on the (date specified) as above. . . ."[3]

To quote the learned scholar : "The shape of the letters, and especially the peculiar method of marking the long and short — i.e. by turning the former to the right of the consonant and the latter to the left — makes it, I think, impossible to assign No. XXXVIII to an earlier period."[4]

As to the exact period of the above two inscriptions, dated in the years 113 and 57 of the Gupta period, we shall have to refer to the era founded by the Guptas. From the words "*Guptakāla,*" "*Guptavarṣa,*" etc., which were found in the Gupta epigraphical and other records, it appears that this era must have been started by some king of the Gupta dynasty. No recorded evidence has been available up till now for this, but from Samudragupta's inscription at Allahabad we find that Candragupta I, who was his predecessor, is the first Gupta king who calls himself *mahārājādhirāja*. His predecessors, both Gupta and Ghaṭotkaca, are entitled simply as *mahārāja*.[5] This, combined with the inscriptional records of the period of

1. Bühler, *E.I.*, II., Ins. No. XXXIX, pp. 210-11.
2. Ibid., Ins. No. XL, p. 211.
3. Ibid., Ins. No. XXXVIII, p. 210.
4. Ibid., p. 198. This is Mr Growse's No. V (*I.A.*, VI., p. 219). Speaking about it the learned scholar observes : "If the date is really the year 57 of the same era as that employed in the inscriptions of Kanishka and Huvishka, it is the earliest unmistakably Jaina figure yet found in this neighbourhood. I cannot, however, believe but that it is comparatively modern. . . ." — Growse, op. cit., p. 218.
5. "Who (Samudragupta) was a mortal only in celebrating the rites of the observances of mankind, (but was otherwise) a god, dwelling on the earth — who was son of the son's son of the *Mahārāja*, the illustrious Gupta; who was the son's son of the *Mahārāja*, the illustrious Ghaṭotkaca ; who was the son of the *Mahārājādhirāja*, the glorious Candragupta I," etc. — Fleet, *C.I.I.*, III., Ins. No. I, pp. 15-16. Cf. Ojha, op. cit., p. 174.

Candragupta II, the successor of Samudragupta, of the Gupta era 82 to 93,[1] made it possible for the scholar-world to put down the starting-point of the Gupta era from Candragupta I.

"His political importance," observes Smith, "was sufficient to warrant him in establishing, after the Oriental manner, a new era dating from his formal consecration or coronation, when he was proclaimed as heir to the Imperial power associated by venerable tradition with the possession of Pāṭalīputra. The first year of the Gupta era, which continued in use for several centuries, and in countries widely separated, ran from February 26, AD 320, to March 13, 321; of which dates the former may be taken as that of the coronation of Candragupta I."[2]

This year, AD 319-20, as the date of the beginning of the Gupta period has been based on Alberuni's statement that the Gupta era was posterior to the Śaka era by 241 years, or, in other words, the Gupta era begins with AD 319-20.[3] This statement of the Arabic traveller has been found correct,[4] and, according to Fleet, the Mandasor inscription confirms this conclusion.[5]

Thus, taking AD 319 as the beginning of the Gupta era, we find that the two Mathurā inscriptions of the year 57 and 113 of the Gupta period will fall in AD 386 and 432 respectively. According to the accepted chronology of the Gupta dynasty the first would fall in the reign of Candragupta II, and the other, in confirmation of what is laid down in the inscription itself, in the reign of Kumāragupta I.[6] As seen before, the earliest inscriptional records

---

1. Cf. Smith, *I.A.*, XXXI., p. 265 ; Ojha, op. and loc. cit.
2. Smith, *Early History of India*, p. 296, Cf. Ojha, op. cit., p. 175 ; Barnett, *Antiquities of India*, p. 46.
3. "As regards the *Guptakāla*, people say that the Guptas were wicked, powerful people, and that when they ceased to exist this date was used as the epoch of an era. It seems that Valabha was the last of them, because the epoch of the era of the Guptas falls, like that of the Valabha era, 241 years later than the *Śakakāla*." — Sachau, *Alberuni's India*, II., p. 7.
4. "I have shown, so far, that the early Gupta dates and, with them, any others that can be proved to the same uniform series, are to be preferred to the epoch of AD 319-320, or thereabouts, brought to notice by Alberuni and substantiated by the Verāwal inscription of Vallabhī-saṁvat 945." — Fleet, op. cit., Int., p. 69. Cf. Dutt, *Ancient India*, p. 50 ; Bhandarkar, *A Peep into the Early History of India*, p. 48. For a detailed discussion about the Gupta era see Fleet, op. cit., Int., pp. 16 ff.
5. Cf. ibid., Int., p. 23.
6. Cf. Smith, *I.A.*, XXXI., pp. 265-66. Candragupta's rule extended from *c.* AD 380 to *c.* 412, and that of Kumāragupta from *c.* AD 413 to *c.* 455. Cf. ibid.; Smith, *Early History of India*, pp. 345-46 ; Bhandarkar, op. cit., pp. 48-49 ; Barnett, op. cit., pp. 47-48.

of the Guptas begin from the year 82; and hence Dr. Bühler has rightly remarked, about the one which we have put down in the reign of Candragupta II, that if his conjecture about it were accepted, "its date, the year 57, is the earliest Gupta date yet found."[1]

Besides these two Mathurā inscriptions there are two more Jaina records connected with the Guptas. The first in chronological order is the Udayagiri cave inscription, which refers to the period of the early Gupta kings, and not to the reign of any particular sovereign. The recorded date, however, shows that it also belongs to the time of Kumāragupta I. It is dated, in words, in the year one hundred and six (AD 425-26), on the fifth solar day of the dark fortnight of the month of Kārttika.[2] That it is a Jaina inscription is clear from the following translation of a part of the inscription : "He (i.e. Śaṁkara, whose name occurs in the 6th line) who has conquered the enemies (of religion), (and) is possessed of tranquillity and self-command, caused (and set up) in the mouth of (this) cave, this image of a Jina, richly endowed with (the embellishments of) the expanded hoods of a snake and an attendant female divinity, (and) having the name of Pārśva, the best of Jinas. He is, indeed, the disciple of the Saint, the *Ācārya* Gośarman . . ."etc.[3]

Thus the object of the Udayagiri cave inscription is to record the installation of an image of the *tīrthaṅkara* Pārśva or Pārśvanātha at the mouth of the cave. The other inscription, mentioned above, is the Kahāum[4] Stone Pillar Inscription of Skandagupta I, the successor of Kumarāgupta I.[5] The grey-sandstone column on which the inscription is, stands at a short distance to the north of Kahāum village. The inscription itself refers to the reign of the early Gupta king, Skandagupta. It is dated, in words, in the year one hundred and forty-one (AD 460-61), and in the month of Jyeṣṭha.[6] The object of the inscription is clear from the following passage of the record itself :

---

1. Bühler, op. and loc. cit.
2. Cf. Fleet, op. cit., Ins. No. LXI, p. 258.
3. Ibid., p. 259. Cf. Hultzsch, *I.A.*, XI., p. 310.
4. "Kahāum or Kahāwam, the ancient Kakubha or Kakubhagrāma of this inscription, is a village about five miles to the west by south of Salampur-Majhaulī, the chief town of the Salampur Mahaulī Pargaṇā in Deoriyā Tahsīl or subdivision of the Gorakhpur district in the north-west provinces." — Fleet, op. cit., p. 66. Cf. Bhagwanlal Indraji, *I.A.*, X., p. 125.
5. Cf. Smith, op. cit., p. 346. He is said to have succeeded Kumārāgupta I in *c.* AD 455. Cf. ibid. ; Barnett, op. cit., p. 48.
6. Cf. Fleet, op. cit., Ins. No. XV, p. 66 ; Bhagwanlal Indraji, op. and loc. cit.

"He (i.e. Madra, whose name occurs in the 8th line of the inscription), being alarmed when he observed the whole of this world (to be ever) passing through a succession of changes, acquired for himself a large mass of religious merit (and by him), — having set up for the sake of final beatitude (and) for the welfare of (all) existing beings, five excellent (images[1]), made of stone, (of) those who led the way in the path of the Arhats who practise religious observances, — there was then planted in the ground this most beautiful pillar of stone, which resembles the tip of the summit of the best of mountains, (and) which confers fame (upon him)."[2]

Thus the Kahāum inscription records that a certain Madra set up five stone images of *ādikartri*s or *tīrthaṅkara*s, and this is testified by the sculptures of the column itself. Of these the most important are the five naked standing figures, which, according to Dr. Bhagwanlal Indraji, represent the five favourite *tīrthaṅkara*s of the Jainas — Ādinātha, Śāntinātha, Neminātha, Pārśva, and Mahāvīra.[3]

Besides these epigraphical evidences of the relations between the Guptas and the Jainas, thanks are due to Muni Jinavijaya[4] that his learned exposition of the *Kuvalayamālā*[5] throws a lot of light on the history of the Jainas during the Gupta period. Udyotanasūri, the learned author of this piece of the *Kathā Sāhitya* of the Jainas, introduces himself in the body of the book in a manner which is really characteristic of the times in which the great Sūri lived and had his being. We are told that this interesting Prākṛt *kathā* was finished in the year 700 of the Śaka era — i.e., in AD 779.[6] This is the age in which we find innumerable immortal works, where very often the writers have not even

1. Fleet, op. cit., p. 68 ; Bhagwanlal Indraji, op. cit., p. 126.
2. The exact wording of this part of the inscription is as follows : नियमवतामर्हतामादिकर्तॄन् पञ्चेन्द्रांस्थापयित्वा . . . etc. Dr Indraji has translated it as follows : "Having established . . . five chief *Ādikartris* (Tīrthaṅkaras) in the path of the ascetic Arhats." — *I.A.*, X., p. 126. To this the learned scholar makes a note as follows : "*Ādikartri* — 'Originators,' the first who lead in the path, but usually applied to the Tīrthaṅkaras. See *Kalpa-Sūtra, Śakrastava.* नमोत्थुणं समणस्स भगवओ महावीरस्स . . . चरमतित्थयरस्स. Sanskrit trans. : नमोस्तु श्रमणाय भगवते महावीरायादिकर्त्रे चरमतीर्थंकराय." — Ibid., p. 126, n. 16.
3. Ibid., p. 126. Cf. Fleet, op. cit., p. 66.
4. Jinavijaya, *J.S.S.*, III., pp. 169 ff.
5. This is a piece of the narrative literature of the Jainas of the eighth century AD. It was completed in Jābālipura, situated at present in Mārwār, though at one time it was considered to be a part of Gujarat.
6. सगकाले वोलीणे वरिसाण सएहि सत्तहि गएहिं।
एगदिणेणूणेहिं रइया अवरण्हवेलाए॥
— Ibid., V. 26, p. 180.

cared to give their names. However, the *Kuvalayamālā*, with the historical sense rightly ingrained in it, gives us more or less an exact picture of the period and the surroundings in which this work was composed, and the lineage of the great Sūri who brought it into existence. The following are the first few of the important introductory verses that have come down to us[1] :

(१) अत्थि पुहईपसिद्धा दोण्णि पहा दोण्णि चेय देस त्ति।
तत्थत्थि पहं णामेण उत्तरावहं बुहजणाइण्णं॥

(२) सुइदिअचारुसोहा विअसिअकमलाणणा विमलदेहा।
तत्थत्थि जलहिदइआ सरिआ अह चंदभाय त्ति॥

(३) तीरम्मि तीय पयडा पव्वइया णाम रयणसोहिल्ला।
जत्थत्थि ठिए भुत्ता पुहइं सिरितोररारएण॥

(४) तस्स गुरु हरिउत्तो आयरिओ आसि गुत्तवंसाओ।
तीय णयरीय दिण्णो जेण णिवेसो तहिं काले॥

(५) तस्स वि सिस्सो पयडो महाकई देवउत्तणामो त्ति।[2]

The substance of these verses is as follows : "In the world there are two paths and only two countries (*Dakshiṇāpatha* and *Uttarāpatha*), which are widely known. Of these *Uttarāpatha* is considered to be a country full of scholars. In that country flows the River Candrabhāgā, appearing as if she were the sweetheart of the ocean. On the bank of that river is situated the well-known prosperous town of Pavvaiyā. It is when he was here that Śrītorarāya enjoyed his authority over the earth. *Ācārya* Harigupta, who was born of the Gupta dynasty, was the *Guru* of this king, and at that time he was practically residing there. Devagupta, who was a great poet, became the pupil of this Ācārya."

These introductory verses of Udyotanasūri are of equal importance both

1. Jinavijaya informs us that only two manuscript copies of *Kuvalayamālā* are available at present — one in the Government collection at Poona and the other in the Jaina *bhaṇḍāra* at Jesalmer. Both copies differ from each other in minor points as well as in points of great historical importance. The learned scholar ascribes these differences to the author himself, and believes that in both the texts they come down from the original sources themselves. Cf. ibid., p. 175.

2. Cf. ibid., p. 177. In the Poona manuscript the first two verses are not to be found; it begins with the third verse, and the opening portion completely differs from that of the Jesalmer manuscript; it is as follows : अत्थि पयडा पुरीणं। For तोररायेण in the Poona manuscript we find तोरमाणेण. For the first half of the fifth verse we find the following whole verse in the Poona copy :

[तस्स] बहुकलाकुसलो सिद्धान्तवियाणओ कई दक्खो।
आयरिय देवगुत्तो ज[स्स]ज्जवि विज्जरए कित्ती॥

— Ibid.

from the standpoint of the Jaina community in the north and of Indian history in general. The King Toramāṇa, or Torarāya, referred to in the third strophe, is none else but the powerful leader of the Hūṇas,[1] who is known to have led the Hūṇa hordes which had burst through the north-western passes and spread in a destructive flood all over northern India. There is no historical fallacy committed in taking this Torarāya for the Hūṇa chieftain Toramāṇa, because there is only one पृथ्वीभोक्ता Toramāṇa — i.e., Toramāṇa enjoying the sovereignty of this earth — in all Indian history. He seems to be one of the very important figures of his time, because, as just remarked, it was he who was at the back of the Hūṇa invasion and the consequent break-up of the Gupta Empire. Leaving Central Asia he and his followers poured into India, and having conquered the Punjab and Delhi came down, as far inland as the country of Mālwā in Central India. To quote Vincent Smith : "The leader in this invasion of India, which, no doubt, continued for years, was a chieftain named Toramāṇa, who is known to have been established as ruler of Mālwā in Central India prior to AD 500. He assumed the style and titles of an Indian "sovereign of *Māhārājas*"; and Bhānugupta, as well as the king of Vallabhī and many other local princes must have been his tributaries."[2]

Naturally this *Hūṇādhipati*, the leader of the Āryans of Central Asia, must have brought about a great revolution in the political, religious and social conditions of India. No doubt the period of his domination was rather short, but when he died — in the first decade of the sixth century AD — the Indian kingdom which he had acquired was consolidated sufficiently to pass to his son and successor, Mahāvīra Mihirakula.[3] Anyhow it is not yet known for certain to antiquarians what was his capital. From various sources we know this much — that Sākala, the modern Siālkoṭ in the Punjab, was the metropolis of his successor, Mihirakula.[4] However, according to the

1. The Hūṇas were a tribe of Āryans in Central Asia. They shattered the Gupta Empire, and dominated a large part of it for a short period. The dominion of the Hūṇas did not long survive the defeat and death of Mihirakula, the son and successor of Toramāṇa, and this can be put down approximately in the middle of the sixth century AD. For further information about the Hūṇas see Ojha, *History of Rajputana*, I., pp. 53 ff., 126 ff.
2. Smith, op. cit., p. 335. Cf. Barnett, op. cit., p. 49.
3. Cf. Smith, op. and loc. cit. ; Ojha, op. cit., p. 128.
4. Cf. Smith, op. and loc. cit. ; Ojha, op. cit., p. 129 ; Barnett, op. cit., p. 50.

Kuvalayamālā tradition, Toramāṇa's headquarters was Pavvaiyā, situated on the bank of the River Candrabhāgā, now known to us as the Cenāb.

It is really difficult to identify this Pavvaiyā — having in Sanskrit some such form as Pārvatikā or Pārvatī — with any definite place in the map of northern India. Nevertheless, from *Yuan Chwang's Travels in India* we get to know that from Mou-lo-San-pu-lu — i.e. Multan — the pilgrim went north-east about 700 li to Po-fa-to country.[1] "The Po-fa-to of this passage," observes Watters, "is supposed to be for Po-la-fa-to — that is, Parvata."[2] Can we infer from this that Parvata of the Chinese traveller may be Pavvaiyā, the capital of Toramāṇa? However, there is no one opinion about this in the scholar-world.[3] Suffice it to say for our purpose that, according to the Jainas, the capital of Toramāṇa was Pavvaiyā, and that it remains to be seen as to where exactly this place can be located in the map of northern India.

What we are chiefly concerned with is the fact of some *ācārya* Harigupta being the *guru* of the great Toramāṇa. The significance of this note of the *Kuvalayamālā* is really great. Up till now, barring a few inscriptions, to which we have already referred above, there is practically nothing which could enlighten us about the state of the Jainas during the Gupta period. A foreign and triumphant ruler like Toramāṇa having a Jaina *ācārya* as his *guru* is a matter of no little importance for Jaina history. Howsoever insignificant it may seem, it is the basis on which we can infer that, as with the Śaiśunāga, Nanda and the Maurya periods, so also in the golden age of Indian history Jaina *sādhus*, enjoyed the privilege of becoming *rājagurus*.

Coming next to Harigupta, the great *ācārya*, it seems he must have been a man of great importance in his time. He is introduced to us as one belonging to the Gupta dynasty. It is very difficult to say whether he belonged to the royal dynasty of the Guptas or to any other ordinary dynasty of that name. There is hardly any evidence before us on which we can make such an

---

1. Cf. Watters, *Yuan Chwang's Travels in India*, II., p. 255 ; Beal, *Si-Yu-Ki*, II., p. 275.
2. Watters, op. and loc. cit. Cf. Beal, op. and loc. cit.
3. According to Vincent Smith Po-fa-to (Parvata) indicates the reign of Jamū (Jammoo), in the south of Kashmir state as at present constituted. Cf. Watters, op. cit., p. 342. Cunningham identifies Po-la-fa-to with Shorkot, though he believes that the position directed by the traveller agrees with the site of Jhang, on the Chenab. Cunningham, *Ancient Geography of India*, pp. 233-34. In the opinion of Dr Fleet, Po-fa-to cannot be anything else but the ancient place of Harppā. — Fleet, *J.R.A.S.*, 1907, p. 650.

assertion. However, according to Jinavijaya,[1] it is a common convention with the Jaina clergy that when a member of some particularly good family or dynasty joins the order, a note is carefully made to that effect for the glory of their religion. Generally the Jaina *sādhus* during their preachings before the laymen of the *saṁgha* mention such facts of their ecclesiastical history, and thus try to impress upon the mind of the audience the greatness of the religion and the following of Lord Mahāvīra. Thus if we were to infer from this that the *vaṁśa* of Harigupta, particularly noted by Udyotanasūri, who came about three centuries after the great Toramāṇa and his Jaina *guru*, must be some respectable and highly esteemed dynasty, such inference need not be considered as far-fetched or unworthy of historical notice. On the other hand the very fact that Harigupta was so closely connected with the Hūṇa *samrāṭ* greatly confirms the above hypothesis. No doubt the tradition of a member of the royal dynasty of the Guptas becoming a Jaina *sādhu* may seem a little strange and unbelievable, but there is no reason for any such attitude. Furthermore, the same introductory verses of Udyotanasūri tell us that Harigupta had a pupil named Devagupta, who was a great poet. This Devagupta is addressed later on in his preface by the *sūri* as *rājaṛṣi* (Royal Saint) of the Gupta dynasty.[2] It is clear from this that Devagupta must be somebody from the royal family of the Guptas. No doubt, before all these facts can be taken as historical truths, we stand in need of some more definite contemporary evidence which can lead us to this conclusion. However, there can be no denying the usefulness of these facts as the basis for any historical structure such as this.

With all this, when we have come so far we shall go a step further, and see if it is possible to identify either Harigupta or Devagupta with any member of the royal dynasty of the Guptas. Whatever historical records of the Guptas have been collected as yet, we nowhere find the name of Harigupta. However, in 1894, Cunningham found a copper coin in Ahicchatra on one side of which there is a flower vase (*kalaśa*) on a pedestal, and on the other side are the following words : *śrī mahārāja harigupta*."[3] From

1. Jinavijaya, op. cit., p. 183.
2. सो जयइ देवगुत्तो वंसे गुत्ताण रायरिसी — Chaturavijaya, *Kuvalayamālā-Kathā* (*Jaina Ātmānanda Sabhā*), Int., p. 6.
3. Cf. Allan, *Catalogue of Indian Coins, Gupta Dynasties*, p. 152 and Plate XXIV, 16 ; Cunningham, *Coins of Mediaeval India*, p. 19, Plate II, 6. It may be mentioned here that, as Jinavijaya has rightly remarked, *kalaśa* is one of the popular symbols of the Jainas. Cf. Jinavijaya, op. cit., p. 184.

the form and shape of the letters, and from the comparison of the name given on it, it is believed by those interested in numismatics that the coin must have been struck by some king of the Gupta dynasty.[1] However, it is not possible to trace the relations of this Harigupta with any of the Gupta kings. On epigraphic grounds it seems that he must have existed in the middle of the sixth century of the Vikrama era.[2] Thus from the standpoints of the date and the place where it was found the description of the coin meets with that of the Jaina Harigupta. The latter comes from the district of Punjab, and being the contemporary of Toramāṇa he also belongs to the middle of the sixth century of the Vikrama era. Thus, considering the similarity of the date, the place name and the dynasty, there is nothing wrong if the Harigupta of the coin and that of the Jaina tradition are one and the same person.

Coming to Devagupta we are faced with a similar difficulty. Nevertheless, from Bāṇa's *Harṣacarita*, which is considered to be "a very early attempt at an historical romance,"[3] we know that on the throne of Mālwā sat a king, a contemporary of the great king of Kanauj and Thāṇeśar, who was defeated by Harṣavardhana's elder brother, Rājyavardhana, because the Mālwā king was declared the enemy of Grahavarman, the king of Kānyakubja, who was married to the sister of Harṣavardhana.[4] This king of Mālwā has been identified by Dr. Bühler with the Devagupta of the Madhuban inscription.[5] Here arises the question whether it is possible to identify Devagupta of the Jaina tradition with the king of Mālwā spoken of in the *Harṣacarita*. The difficulty that comes

1. Cf. Cunningham, op. cit., pp. 18-19. "The form of the letter '*H*' is peculiar to the Guptas." — Ibid., p. 19.
2. "Coin of Harigupta seems to belong to the fifth century, from its epigraphy." — Allan, op. cit., p. cv.
3. Cowell and Thomas, *Harsacarita*, Int., p. viii.
4. Cf. Ibid., Int., pp. xi-xii. ". . . the illustrious Rājyavardhana, by whom, playing his whip in the battle, the Kings Devagupta and others — who resembled wicked horses — were all subdued with averted faces." — Bühler *E.I.*, I., p. 74. Cf. Barnett, op. cit., p. 52 ; Mookerji (Radhakumud), *Harṣa*, pp. 16-19, 53.
5. "Assuming the correctness of Bāṇa's account . . . it may be suggested that Devagupta was the name of the Mālava king. The latter certainly was the chief foe, and the conquest of his kingdom is attested by the further statement of Bāṇa that Bhaṇḍin, who had accompanied Rājyavardhana, brought the booty from Mālava to Harsha when the latter had reached the territory of Kumāra-Bhāskaravarman on his expedition of revenge against the King Gauḍa. I may add that the word Mālava need not refer here or in the other passages of the *Śrīharshacarita* to the Mālava in Central India. There was another Mālava in the Punjab, much nearer to Thāṇeśar, which may be meant." — Bühler, op. cit., p. 70. Cf. Mookerji (Radhakumud), op. cit., pp. 25, 50 ff.

XIII : Coins of "Śrī Mahārāja Harigupta."

in the way of such an identification is that of the chronological adjustment of both the Devaguptas.

Among the various dates of Toramāṇa the latest possible is that of about AD 516. Even if this is accepted there remains a difference of more than seventy-five years, which can be adjusted only on the following suppositions: that Toramāṇa may have died a few years later than *c.* AD 516; that Harigupta may have lived a long time after the death of his royal patron, and that Devagupta may have joined the order in the last days of his *guru*. Whatever it may be, we need not stress this point any further, because that would be going beyond the period which we have marked out for our examination, and moreover, about the tradition left to us by Udyotanasūri there is no choice for us but to await the further revelations of archaeology for a final answer. Thus the fact that also in the Gupta period Jainism was a living religion is evident from all that we have seen up till now. This is clear from "a multitude of inscriptions, which are almost all either Buddhist or Jaina," and from the Gupta princes being "perfectly tolerant of both Buddhism and Jainism."[1]

One thing still remains to be seen, and that is the rise of the dynasty of Vallabhī towards the close of the fifth century AD. This rise of the Vallabhīs more or less coincides with the end of the golden age of the Guptas, which at the most comprised a period of a century and a half. The death of Kumāragupta I, which can be definitely fixed as having occurred early in 455, marks the beginning of the decline and fall of the empire, while in the reign of Kumāragupta II began the actual break-up of the Gupta Empire.[2]

This new dynasty, which lasted until about AD 770, was established at Vallabhī in the east of the peninsula of Saurāṣṭra (Kāṭhiāwār), by a chief named Bhaṭārka, "who belonged to a clan called Maitraka, probably of foreign rule."[3] This Bhaṭārka of the Vallabhī dynasty had four sons, all of whom are included by Captain Wilberforce-Bell and others in their list of

1. Smith, op. cit., pp. 318, 320.

2. Ibid., p. 346. ". . . the power of the Guptas continued to wane, and deprived of possessions and powers, at the end of the sixth century AD, they died out." — Wilberforce-Bell, *The History of Kathiawad*, p. 37.

3. Smith, op. cit., p. 332. "Meanwhile, about the year AD 470, the history of Saurāshṭra again underwent a change. In this year Skanda Gupta died, and the bards relate that at the time, one Bhaṭṭārka, of the Maitraka clan, was Commander-in-Chief of the army. This man came to Saurāshṭra and, having declared his independence, established a dynasty which lasted for nearly 300 years." — Wilberforce-Bell, op. and loc. cit. Cf. Barnett, op. cit., p. 49.

Vallabhī kings. Of these Dhruvasena I, the fourth in the list, was naturally the third son of the founder of this dynasty.[1] We particularly refer to him because, along with Devardhigaṇi, the high-priest of the Jaina church of his time, he marks the end of the unrecorded period of Jainism in north India. Beyond this we are assured by Smith that "the earlier kings of Vallabhī do not appear to have been independent, and were doubtless obliged to pay tribute to the Huns."[2] Thus Dhruvasena must also be a dependent potentate under the Hūṇas, because the period of his rule has been put down by Charpentier and others as terminating about AD 526.[3] This date becomes more of a certainty on the authority of Smith and Wilberforce-Bell that Bhaṭārka founded the dynasty in *c.* 490 AD.[4] The two brothers that intervened between Bhaṭārka and Dhruvasena might have ruled for a short time, and thus Dhruvasena I might have succeeded to the throne in about AD 526. This is further strengthened when we know that Dharasena II, the seventh in the Vallabhī list, rules from AD 569.[5]

Of the great Jaina council under the protection of the *Vallabhīpati* Dhruvasena we shall speak in the next chapter. What need be said at present is that the canonical and other literature of the Jainas was put down in writing during this period, and thus the unrecorded period of Jaina history was brought to an end. It is significant to note that this important event of Jaina history is connected also with the Gupta period. That by this time the Jainas had more or less spread all over India is a fact which cannot be denied. The inscriptions referring to the Jaina communities become very numerous from the sixth century AD onwards.

1. Cf. Wilberforce-Bell, op. cit., pp. 38-39 ; Barnett, op. cit., pp. 49-50.
2. Smith, op. and loc. cit. "This dynasty was at first subordinate to the Guptas and then to the Hūṇas, and later became independent." — Barnett, op. cit., p. 49.
3. Dhruvasena I, Maitraka, king of Vallabhī, was reigning AD 526-40. — Barnett, op. cit., p. 50. "Now, as King Dhruvasena I of Vallabhī is supposed to have succeeded to the throne in AD 526. . . ."— Charpentier, *Uttarādhyayana-Sūtra*, Int., p. 16. This date of the learned scholar is based on the date of Mahāvīra's *Nirvāṇa* in 467 BC, and on 993 A.V., as the date of the redaction of the Jaina canon. The other date for the redaction of the canon is AD 980, and, counting upon this, the date of the council comes to *c.* AD 514. Cf. Jacobi, *Kalpa-Sūtra*, Int., p. 15 ; Farquhar, *Religious Literature of India*, p. 163. The difference between these two dates is based on this ground, that in 980 A.V. the Jaina canon was put in a definite form and in 993 A.V. *Kalpa-Sūtra* was read before the *Saṁgha*, under the patronage of Dhruvasena I in Ānandapura. नवशताशीतितमवर्षे कल्पस्य पुस्तके लिखनं, नवशतत्रिनवतितमवर्षे च कल्पस्य पर्षद्वाचनेति. — *Kalpa-Sūtra, Subōdhikā-Ṭīkā, sūt.* 148, p. 126. For the two dates of 980 A.V. and 993 A.V. see also Jacobi, S.B.E., XXII., p. 270.
4. Cf. Smith, op. and loc. cit. ; Wilberforce-Bell, op. cit., p. 38.
5. Cf. ibid., p. 39. "Dharasena II . . . was reigning 571-89." — Barnett, op. cit., p. 51.

Hiuen-Tsang, who travelled through India after the Gupta Empire had come to an end, found them spread through the whole of India, and even beyond its boundaries.[1] It would be very interesting indeed to follow this scattered information about Jainism, yet such lucubrations would be beyond our purpose. The documents quoted suffice, however, to confirm the assertion that during the first five centuries after Mahāvīra's *nirvāṇa* both the statements of Buddhist tradition and real historical sources give evidence to the existence of the Jainas as an important religious community independent of Buddhism, and that there are among the historical sources some which entirely clear away the suspicion that the tradition of the Jainas themselves is in any way falsified.

1. "Hiuen-Tsang's note on the appearance of the Nirgrantha or Digambar in Kiapishi . . . points to the fact that they had, in the north-west at least, spread their missionary activity beyond the borders of India." — Bühler, *Indian Sect of the Jainas*, pp. 3-4, n. 4 ; Beal, op. cit., I., p. 55.

CHAPTER VII

Jaina Literature of the North

THE Jainas have developed at all times a rich literary activity. "This literature is extremely extensive and full of interest. Indian and even European libraries contain a huge mass of Jaina manuscripts, which hitherto have not yet been utilised."[1] The Jaina authors belong mostly to the priest-class. They are monks who make use of the four months of the rainy-season, during which time they are forbidden to wander about, for literary purpose. To the prevalence of this clerical element among the writers there corresponds the one in the substance and contents of the Jaina literature. It has in the main points a religious character, in which it meets also with the Brāhmanical and Buddhist literature. Theological and philosophical treatises, legends of saints, religious tracts, and songs of praise in honour of the *tīrthaṅkaras* are the principal items in it. The religious atmosphere also predominates in the works of profane contents, as in scientific books, in poems and in works of the narrative literature, in dramas and in inscriptions.

The period of Jaina history under our consideration is solely concerned with the unrecorded state of its literature. Devardhigaṇi stands like a lighthouse and marks the end of this period, in which the canonical literature of the Jainas as the *Siddhānta* mostly predominates. However, by way of a few preliminary remarks regarding the whole literature of the Jainas, it may be mentioned here that the subjects treated in this huge literature are very multifarious. "First of all, there is the *Siddhānta* accompanied by a very extensive literature of commentaries. Moreover, there is a very rich scientific literature. The Jainas have created special systems of dogmatics, of logics, and of philosophy; on the other hand, they very successfully cultivated all the Brāhmanical sciences. They composed grammars and dictionaries of Sanskrit as well as of Prākṛt. There are even some grammars and vocabularies of the Gujarātī, and a vocabulary of the Persian language. Numerous are the Jaina treatises on poetics, on metrics, and on *nīti* in its two branches — the

1. Hertel, *On the Literature of the Śvetāmbaras of Gujarat*, p. 4.

rājanīti or statecraft, and the *sāmānyanīti*, which contains rules for the clever conduct of life. For the education of princes, Jaina authors wrote treatises on the sciences of elephants, of horses, of war-carriages and of bows, and on erotics; and for the use of the rest of the population they composed works on magic and on astrology, on *omina* and *portenta*, and on *oneirocritics*, which has played so important a role in Indian life. They even composed manuals of architecture and of music, and treatises on gold and on jewels. . . . They are the creators of a very extensive popular literature."[1]

With these introductory remarks we come to the *Siddhānta*, or the Holy Scriptures of the Jainas, which according to them come within the period under our consideration. As seen before, and as we shall see during the course of this chapter, we cannot disbelieve the traditions of the Jainas about their literary heritage. However for the present we give below the list of the scriptures of the Jaina canon which has been more or less accepted by scholars like Weber,[2] Winternitz,[3] Charpentier[4] and others:

I. Fourteen Puvvas or Pūrvas (not extant)

1. *Uppāya (Utpāda).*
2. *Aggeṇiya* or *Aggāṇiya* (?*Agrāyaṇīya*).[5]
3. *Vīriyappavāya* (*Vīryapravāda*).
4. *Atthinatthippavāya* (*Astināstipravāda*).
5. *Nāṇappavāya* (*Jñānapravāda*).
6. *Saccappavāya* (*Satyapravāda*).
7. *Āyappavāya* (*Ātmapravāda*).
8. *Kammappavāya* (*Karmapravāda*).
9. *Paccakkhāṇappavāya* (*Pratyākhyānapravāda*).
10. *Vijjāṇuppavāya* (*Vidyānupravāda*).
11. *Avaṁjha* (*Avandhya*).
12. *Pāṇāum* (*Prāṇāyuh*).
13. *Kiriyāvisāla* (*Kriyāviśāla*).
14. *Logavindusāra* (*Lokabindusāra*).

1. Hertel, op. cit., pp. 5-6.
2. Cf. Weber, *I.A.*, XVII., pp. 279 ff., 339 ff. ; XVIII., pp. 181 ff., 369 ff. ; XIX., p. 62 ff. ; XX., pp. 18 ff., 170 ff., 365 ff. ; and XXI., pp. 14 ff., 106 ff., 177 ff., 210 ff., 293 ff., 327 ff., 369 ff.
3. Cf. Winternitz, *Geschichte der Indischen Literatur*, II., p. 291 ff.
4. Cf. Charpentier, op. cit., Int., p. 9 ff. ; Belvalkar. *Brahma-Sūtras of Bādarāyaṇa*, p. 107 ff.
5. Cf. Charpentier, op. cit., Int., p. 12.

II. Twelve Aṅgas

1. *Āyāra* (*Ācāra*).
2. *Sūyagaḍa* (*Sūtrakṛta*).
3. *Thāṇa* (*Sthāna*).
4. *Samavāya*.
5. *Viyāhapaṇṇatti* (*Vyākhyāprajñapati*), mostly called *Bhagavatī*.
6. *Nāyādhammakahāo* (*Jñātādharmakathāḥ*).
7. *Uvāsagadasāo* (*Upāsakadaśāḥ*).
8. *Antagaḍadasāo* (*Antakṛddaśāḥ*).
9. *Aṇuttarovavāiyadasāo* (*Anuttaraupapātikadaśāḥ*).
10. *Paṇhāvāgaraṇāiṁ* (*Praśnavyākaraṇāni*).
11. *Vivāgasuyam* (*Vipākaśrutam*).
12. *Ditthivāya* (*Dṛṣṭivāda*), no longer extant.

III. Twelve Upāṅgas (corresponding to the twelve Aṅgas)

1. *Ovavāiya* (*Aupapātika*).
2. *Rāyapaseṇaijja* (*Rājapraśnīya*).
3. *Jīvābhigama*.
4. *Pannavaṇā* (*Prajñāpanā*).
5. *Sūriyapannatti* (*Sūryaprajñapti*).
6. *Jambuddīvapannatti* (*Jambudvīpaprajñapti*).
7. *Candapannatti* (*Candraprajñapti*).
8. *Niryāvalī*.
9 *Kappāvadaṁsiāo* (*Kalpāvataṁsikāḥ*).
10. *Pupphiāo* (*Puṣpikāḥ*).
11. *Pupphacūliāo* (*Puṣpacūlikāḥ*).
12. *Vaṇhidasāo* (*Vṛṣṇidasāḥ*).

IV. Ten Painnas or Prakīrṇāni

1. *Causaraṇa* (*Catuḥśaraṇa*).
2. *Āurapaccakkhrāṇa* (*Āturapratyākhyāna*).
3. *Bhattapariṇṇā* (*Bhaktaparijñā*).
4. *Samthāra* (*Samstāra*).
5. *Taṇḍulaveyāliya* (? *Taṇḍulavaitālika*).
6. *Candāvijjhaya* (*Candravedhyaka*).
7. *Devindatthava* (*Devendrastava*).
8. *Gaṇivijjā* (*Gaṇitavidyā*).
9. *Mahāpaccakkhāṇa* (*Mahāpratyākhyāna*).
10. *Vīratthava* (*Vīrāstava*)

V. Six Chedasūtras

1. *Nisīha* (*Niśītha*).
2. *Mahānisīha* (*Mahāniśītha*).
3. *Vavahāra* (*Vyavahāra*).
4. *Āyāradasāo* (*Ācāradaśāḥ*), or *Desāsuyaskhandha* (*Dasaśrutaskhandha*).
5. *Bṛhatkalpa*.
6. *Pañcakalpa*.

VI. Four Mūlasūtras

1. *Uttarajjhayaṇa* (*Uttarādhyayana*).
2. *Āvassaya* (*Āvaśyaka*).
3. *Dasaveyāliya* (*Daśavaikālika*).
4. *Piṇḍanijjutti* (*Piṇḍaniryukti*).

VII. Two Solitary Texts

1. *Nandīsutta* (*Nandīsūtra*) :
2. *Aṇyuogadārasutta* (*Anuyogadvārasūtra*).

All these scriptures form the canon of the Śvetāmbaras alone, because they are disowned by the Digambaras. This tradition of the latter is connected with the great famine which broke out in Magadha during the glorious days of Hindu rule under Candragupta Maurya. After the emigration of Bhadrabāhu and his followers to the south it so happened that the holy texts of the Jainas were threatened with the danger of falling into oblivion, and a council was called by Sthūlabhadra and his followers, who had preferred to remain at home, early in the third century BC, at Pāṭalīputra, a place historic in the annals of their order and at the same time the capital of the Mauryan Empire. This council of the Jainas, as Dr Charpentier tells us, "may have discharged pretty much the same functions as are recorded of the first Buddhist council."[1] A canon was fixed by the council including both the *Aṅga*s and the *Pūrva*s, and this is undoubtedly the first origin of the *Siddhānta*.[2] Now the monks who had returned home from the south were by no means satisfied with these

1. Charpentier, op. cit., Int., p. 14.
2. "Thus, according to Sthūlabhadra's tradition, a canon was established including the ten first *Pūrvas* and *Aṅgas*, as well as other scriptures which are recorded to have been composed by Bhadrabāhu — e.g. the *Kalpa-Sūtra*." — Ibid. "Therefore a council was called at Pāṭalīputra in which the 11 *Aṅgas* were put together and the rest of the 14 *Pūrvas* were incorporated into the 12th *Aṅga*, the *Diṭṭhivāya*." — Winternitz, op. cit., p. 293. Cf. Farquhar, *Religious Literature of India*, p. 75 ; Jacobi, *Kalpa-Sūtra*, Int., pp. 11, 15. For Hemacandra's version about the synod at Pāṭalīputra see *Pariśiṣṭaparvan*, Canto IX, vv. 55-76, 101-03.

arrangements. They refused to acknowledge the canon, and declared that the *Pūrvas* and the *Aṅgas* were lost to them.[1] Thus here lies the basis of the belief of the Digambaras — that what exists as the *Siddhānta* of the Jainas is not in its original form. We shall once again see presently that this tradition on their part carries very little weight considering the grounds in favour of the Śvetāmbara belief.

However, before we come to this we shall refer to the next Jaina council, that met at Vallabhī in Gujarat under Devardhigaṇin, the Buddhaghoṣa of Jaina literary history, in the beginning of the sixth century AD. What happened after the first great council in Magadha is that in course of time the canon of the Śvetāmbaras fell into disorder, and was even in danger of being lost. Therefore, as seen before, in the year 980 or 993, after the death of Mahāvīra, "a famous teacher, Devardhigaṇin, called the Kṣamāśramaṇa, who saw that the sacred lore was in danger of becoming obsolete — no doubt because of the scarcity of manuscripts — convoked a second great council at Vallabhī."[2] The twelfth *Aṅga*, which contained the *Pūrvas*, was already lost by that time, and whatever could be available was put down in a definite written form. Thus Devardhigaṇin's activity must have consisted only in bringing about a canon of holy scriptures partly with the help of old manuscripts and partly on the ground of oral tradition.[3] As most of the modern scholars believe, we need no more doubt that the whole of the external form of the *Siddhānta* dates from the days of Dhruvasena, under whose patronage the great council was called.

Now, coming to the Digambara tradition of the Jaina *Siddhānta* being completely lost or forgotten immediately after the great famine in Magadha, we find that there is no evidence available on which we can make such a sweeping statement. Before we proceed any further one thing must be noted down — that even the Digambaras agree to the fact that the first disciples of Mahāvīra knew the *Pūrvas* and the *Aṅgas*. "They hold the twelve *Aṅgas* —

1. For the famine in Magadha, etc., see Charpentier, op. cit., Int., pp. 13-15 ; Winternitz, op. and loc. cit.
2. Charpentier, op. cit., Int., p. 15. Cf. Winternitz, op. cit., pp. 293-94 ; Jacobi, S.B.E., XXII., Int., pp. xxxvii-xxxviii. According to another tradition the *Siddhānta* was issued "at the hands of a council in Mathura under Śrī Skandilācārya." — Weber, *I.A.*, XVII., p. 282.
3. "*Pūrvaṁ sarvasiddhāntānām pāṭhanaṁ ca mukhapāṭhenai 'vā 'sit'.* " — Jacobi *Kalpa-Sūtra,* p. 117. Cf. Winternitz, op. cit., p. 294. For the work done and the exact method adopted by the redactors of this council see Charpentier, op. cit., Int., p. 16 ff. "To provide every teacher, or at least *Upāśraya*, with copies of the sacred books, Devardhigaṇin must have issued a large edition of the *Siddhānta*." — Jacobi, S.B.E., XXII., Int., p. xxxviii.

the *Dvādaśāṅgī* — in as high esteem as the Śvetāmbaras."[1] Now what remains to be confirmed is that the original *Siddhānta* was not lost for ever. The epigraphic evidence that we can produce for this is that of the Mathurā inscriptions. As we have seen, the number of *kula*s and *śākhā*s appearing in these records can very well be identified with those appearing in the writings which are "proclaimed by the Digambaras to be late and worthless works, although they seem to make use of them to a certain extent."[2] Furthermore, the Mahāvīra legend is also reproduced in the Mathurā sculptures as it appears in our texts, and the Jaina monks are mentioned with the title *vācaka*[3] — i.e. lecturer or preacher. This latter fact, according to Dr Winternitz, gives epigraphical evidence that there must have existed the holy scriptures of the Jainas even in the beginning of the Christian era.[4] Moreover, as seen before, the fact that as an alternative the Jaina monks could go about naked is also found in the Śvetāmbara texts. This shows they did not dare to make arbitrary changes in the text, but handed them down as true as possible. Finally, it is a great proof for the authenticity of the Jaina tradition that in many remarkable details it exactly corresponds with the Buddhist tradition.

The total absence in the most important parts of the canon of any ideas belonging to Greek astronomy, according to some scholars supplies a decisive proof of the suggestion that the texts must have remained almost unaltered at least since the very first century of our era.[5] "Moreover, the metrical parts of the Jaina canon suggested to such an acute observer and such an expert on Hindu metrics as Jacobi a *terminus a quo*; for as a general rule all the metres used by the Jainas in their canonical scriptures, whether vaitāliya, triṣṭubh or āryā, show types that are clearly more developed than those of

1. Cf. Bühler, *I.A.*, VII., p. 29. "However, we are told by the Śvetāmbaras, as well as the Digambaras, that besides the *Aṅgas* there existed other and probably older works, called *Pūrvas*, of which there were originally fourteen." — Jacobi, op. cit., Int., p. xliv.
2. Charpentier, op. cit., Int., p. 11. Cf. Bühler, op. and loc. cit.
3. वाचकस्य अर्य्यबलदिनस्य. . . . — Bühler, *E.I.*, I., Ins. No. III, p. 382. Cf. ibid., Ins. Nos. IV, VII, etc., pp. 383-86.
4. Cf. Winternitz, op. and loc. cit.
5. Cf. Charpentier, op. cit., Int., p. 25. "But an argument of more weight is the fact that in the *Siddhānta* we find no traces of Greek astronomy. In fact the Jaina astronomy is a system of incredible absurdity, which would have been impossible if its author had the least knowledge of the Greek science. As the latter appears to have been introduced in India about the third or the fourth century AD, it follows that the sacred books of the Jainas were composed before that time." — Jacobi, op. cit., Int., p. xl.

the Pāli canon, and at the same time distinctly older than those of the *Lalita Vistāra* and other northern Buddhist texts. Supported by this very powerful evidence, Jacobi concluded that the most important and oldest portions of the *Siddhānta* must have been fixed during a period lying between the *Tripiṭaka* and the first centuries of our era, say, roughly, between 300 BC and AD 200; and I, for my part, consider this conclusion quite justified."[1]

Besides all this there are certainly many other passages scattered through the whole of the canon which might lead us to draw further conclusions about the period of the *Siddhānta* of the Jainas. An enumeration of all such passages is out of the question, but we shall mention one instance that has a certain interest for the question of the date. To put it in the words of Dr Charpentier: "In the second *Upāṅga,* the *Rāyapaseṇaijja,* the interesting relations of which to the *Pāyāsisutta* of the *Dīgha Nikāya* were detected and dealt with by Professor Leumann, it is stated in a certain passage that any brāhmaṇas who have committed certain crimes should be stigmatised — i.e. the image of a dog (*sunakha*) or a *kuṇḍiya* should be branded upon their foreheads. This coincides with Kāuṭilya, p. 220, who prescribes that four marks should be used: for theft a dog (*śvan*), for incest (*gurutalpa*) a pudendum muliebre (*bhaga*), for manslaughter a headless trunk (*kabandha*), and for consuming intoxicating liquor a *madyadhvaja*. But this rule does not occur in Manu and the later law books, where corporal punishments on brāhmaṇas are not permissible. This usage had consequently become obsolete after the times of Kāuṭilya, and the conclusion is that the Jaina text where it occurs must be nearer to the time of Kāuṭilya than to that of the later Dharmaśāstras."[2]

Thus from all that has been seen one thing is certain — that the present *Siddhānta* of the Śvetāmbaras is no creation of later times, and that with all the additions and subtractions at various places it is based on the original texts. The question as to how far these texts can be chronologically traced is rather dubious, though of great interest. However there would be nothing wrong if in their definite forms they are traced back to the council of Pāṭalīputra, and in certain individual cases to a still earlier date.[3] We shall

---

1. Charpentier, op. cit., Int., pp. 25-26 ; Jacobi, op. cit., Int., p. xli ff.
2. Charpentier, op. cit., Int., p. 31.
3. ". . . I do not consider that the principal sacred scriptures represent even in their present shape the actual canon fixed at the council of Pāṭalīputra." — Ibid. Cf. Jacobi, op. cit., Int., pp. ix, xliii.

now consider in brief the separate works of the canon and, though rather superficially, shall mark their contents side by side with some points of importance individually attached to them.

First in order comes the group of the fourteen *Pūrva*s. They form the oldest portion of the canon, and even the Śvetāmbaras themselves tell us that they have been irrevocably lost along with *Dṛṣṭivāda*, the twelfth *Aṅga*, in which these oldest works were incorporated at the time when they ceased to exist independently of the *Aṅga* literature. As seen before, the *Pūrva*s were suggested by Mahāvīra himself, while his disciples, the *gaṇadhara*s or apostles, composed the *Aṅga*s. "This tradition," observes Dr Charpentier, "rejects the authorship of the mythic saint Ṛṣabha, and is certainly right in ascribing the original tenets of the canon to Mahāvīra himself. As a general account of the facts, the statement that the main part of the canon originated with Mahāvīra and his immediate successors may probably be trusted."[1]

After the *Pūrva*s come the *Aṅga*s, the single members of which are marked by certain formal peculiarities, which prove a connection closer in the case of some than in that of others. Taking the first of the twelve *Aṅga*s — namely, the *Āyārāṅga* or the *Ācārāṅga Sūtra* — we find that it is the oldest extant canon[2] in prose and in verse, and treats of the mode of life (*ācāra*) of the Jaina clergy. It contains two books, or *Śrutaskandha*s, very different from each other in style and in the manner in which the subject is treated. It is the first of these two *Śrutaskandha*s that gives the impression of its being one of the oldest, if not the very oldest, of the existing scriptures. Like the *Sūtrakṛtāṅga* and a few other texts of the *Siddhānta*, in *Ācārāṅga* also we find that the larger divisions close with the words *ti bemi* (*iti bravīmi*) ("Thus I say"); and according to the *scholia*, Sudharman, Mahāvīra's pupil, is regarded as the one who gives utterance to this formula. The prose portions begin with the formula: *suyaṁ me āusaṁ! teṇaṁ bhagavayā evam akkhāyam* ("I have heard, O Long-lived one ! Thus has that saint spoken."[3]) In this fashion, which characterizes the contents as the oral translation of the utterances of Mahāvīra, Jambū, a scholar of Sudharma, is addressed.

1. Charpentier, op. cit., Int., pp. 11-12.
2. Cf. Winternitz, op. cit., p. 296 ; Belvalkar, op. cit., p. 108 ; Weber, op. cit., p. 342. "I am of the opinion that the first book of the *Ācārāṅga-Sūtra* and *Sūtrakṛtāṅga-Sūtra* may be reckoned among the most ancient parts of the *Siddhānta*." — Jacobi, op. cit., Int., p. xli.
3. Cf. Weber, op. cit., p. 340 ; Jacobi, op. cit., pp. 1, 3 ; Vaidya (P.L.), *Suyagaḍam*, pp. 65, 80.

As seen before, the *Ācārāṇga-Sūtra* treats mainly of one of the four heads, or *anuyogas*, into which the sacred lore is divided — namely, *dharmakathā*, *gaṇita* (*kāla*), *dravya* and *caraṇakaraṇa*.[1] The sermons therein combine the voice of an indifferent and impartial adviser and the solemn warning of a *guru*, spiritual or otherwise. To quote a part of the *sūtra* itself:

"The Arhats and Bhagavatas of the past, present, and future, all say thus, speak thus, declare thus, explain thus; all breathing, existing, living, sentient creatures should not be slain, nor treated with violence, nor abused, nor tormented, nor driven away.

"This is the pure, unchallengeable, eternal law, which the clever ones, who understand the world, have declared. Having adopted (the law), one should not hide it, nor forsake it. Correctly understanding the law, one should arrive at indifference, for the impressions of the senses, and "not act on the motives of the world. . . ." These who acquiesce and indulge (in worldly pleasures), are born again and again. "Day and night exerting thyself; steadfast," always having ready wisdom, perceive that the careless (stand) outside (of salvation); if careful, thou wilt always conquer. Thus I say."[2]

The second *Aṅga* — the *Suyagaḍāṅga* or the *Sūtrakṛtāṅga* — comprises poetic exhortations and philosophic disquisitions, followed by a polemic against *kriyāvāda*, *akriyāvāda*, *vaināyika* and *ajñānavāda*.[3] The object of this *sūtra* is to protect young monks from heretic doctrines, to warn them of the perils and temptations involved in them, to confirm them in their creed and to lead them to the highest destination. Like the first *Aṅga* this is divided into two books, and according to Jacobi and others it is the first that may be reckoned among the most ancient parts of the *Siddhānta*.[4] As in the Buddhist literature, we meet here again a mixture of prose and verse, with some interesting parables scattered here and there. For instance we read: "As (birds of prey) — e.g. dhaṅkas — carry off a fluttering bird whose wings are not yet grown, . . . so many unprincipled men will seduce a novice who has not yet mastered the Law."[5]

---

1. अनुयोगः चाचारि द्वाराणि — चरणधर्मकालद्रव्यारथानि . . . रक्खिअज्जेहिं। जुगमासज्ज विभत्तो अणुयोगो तो कओ चउहा ॥ — *Āvaśyaka-Sūtra*, p. 296.
2. Jacobi, op. cit., pp. 36-37.
3. Cf. Vaidya (P.L.), op. cit., pp. 3-11.
4. Cf. Jacobi, op. cit., Int., p. xli ; Winternitz, op. cit., p. 297.
5. Cf. Jacobi, S.B.E., XLV., p. 324.

The *Sūtrakṛtāṅga* starts refuting the doctrines of Buddha and of other heretical teachers who are confronted with the main doctrines of Mahāvīra. With all this, as Winternitz has remarked, what we get from this *sūtra* about *karman* and *saṁsāra* does not differ much from that of "heretic" doctrines. Philosophical ideals such as the following can be found also in the Buddhist text:

"It is not myself alone who suffers, all creatures in the world suffer; this a wise man should consider, and he should patiently bear (such calamities) as befall him, without giving way to his passions."[1]

The difficulties and temptations that lie in the way of a monk are very minutely considered, and everywhere the young monk is advised to meet them all heroically. He is specially urged to beware of the temptations of women. Very often we find that such warnings are accompanied by a touch of genuine humour which makes the whole atmosphere more homely and realistic. For instance we read: "When they (women) have captured him, they send him on all sorts of errands: Look (for the bodkin to) carve the bottle-gourd, fetch some nice fruit. Bring wood to cook the vegetables. . . ; paint my feet, come and meanwhile rub my back. . . ! Give me the collyrium-box, my ornaments, the lute, . . . Fetch me the pincers, the comb, the ribbon to bind up the hair; reach me the looking-glass, put the tooth-brush near me !"[2]

The next two *Aṅga*s — namely, the *Sthānāṅga* and the *Samavāyāṅga* — we shall take together. Like the Buddhist *Aṅguttaranikāya*, both these texts of the *Āgamika* literature of the Jainas treat of several topics of religious importance in a numerical order, rising in the *Thānāṅga* from 1 to 10 and in the *Samavāya* from 1 to 100, and even up to 1,000,000.[3] As to the contents of the two, the former provides us with a Table of Contents of the lost *Diṭṭhivāya*, the twelfth *Aṅga* of the Jainas, and with an enumeration of the names of the seven schisms, together with those of their founders and of their localities.[4] The latter, or the *Samavāya*, contains some exact statements about the contents of all the twelve *Aṅga*s, and also consists of many statements and references about the doctrines, and the legendary hagiology and history of the Jainas.[5]

1. Cf. Jacobi, S.B.E., XLV., p. 251.
2. Ibid., pp. 276-77.
3. Winternitz, op. cit., p. 300 ; Belvalkar, op. and loc. cit.
4. Cf. Winternitz, op. and loc. cit. ; Weber, *I.A.*, XVIII., p. 370.
5. Cf. Winternitz, op. and loc. cit. ; Weber, op. cit., p. 377. "To the detailed consideration of the 12 *Aṅga*s there is appended here, as in the *Nandī*, a passage on the entire →

Thus both the *Aṅga*s combined together constitute a perfect treasure-house for the correct understanding of innumerable groups of conceptions and of the *Siddhānta*.

Coming to the *Bhagavatī*, the fifth *Aṅga* of the Jainas, we find that it is one of the most important and most sacred texts of the Jaina *Siddhānta*. Its importance, from the standpoint of Jaina history, is second to none. In our previous chapters about the period of Pārśva and Mahāvīra, and about their contemporaries, we have referred to it more than once. Besides this the work contains a circumstantial and complicated exposition of the Jaina dogma, partly in the form of catechism and partly in the form of legendary dialogues (*itihāsasaṁvāda*). Of the legends, especially important are those which treat of the predecessors and contemporaries of Mahāvīra, of the disciples of Pārśva, and of the founders of sects — Jamāli and Gośāla Makkhaliputta — to whom is dedicated the fifteenth book of the *Bhagavatī*.[1] "All these legends," observes Weber, "give us the impression of containing traditions which have been handed down in good faith. They offer, therefore, in all probability (especially as they frequently agree with the Buddhist legends) most important evidence for the period of the life of Mahāvīra himself."[2]

The *Nāyādhammakahāo*, or the sixth *Aṅga* of the *Siddhānta*, brings us to the narrative literature of the Jainas. It is a collection of tales or parables designed to serve as moral examples, and, as with almost all the narrative literature of India, the *Kathā* literature of the Jainas also serves didactic purposes. At the beginning of his homily a Jaina preacher usually gives, in a few prose words or verses, the topic of his sermon (*dharmadeśanā*), and then goes on to tell an interesting tale of considerable extent, as the most effective means of spreading the doctrines of Mahāvīra among his followers.

→ *Duvalasaṅgaṁ Gaṇipiḍagam*. This deals partly with the attacks which it was subjected to in the past, which it now experiences in the present and will experience in the future, partly with the devoted acquiescence which is its lot to meet with in these three periods, and concludes with the declaration of its certain existence for ever: *na kayāi na āsi, na kayāi na 'tthi, na kayāi na bhavissati*." — Ibid. To this Weber makes the following note : "According to Abhayadevasūri attacks at the hands of Jamāli, Goshṭhāmāhila, etc. — i.e. the representatives of the seven schisms." — Ibid., n. 65.

1. Cf. Winternitz, op. cit., pp. 300-01. "Of the legends which are adduced here, those claim a special interest which deal with predecessors or contemporaries of Mahāvīra, with the opinion of his heterodox opponents . . . and with their conversion." — Weber, *I.A.*, XIX., p. 64.

2. Ibid., p. 65.

According to Hertel the literary form of these Jaina sermons not only resembles that of the Buddhist *Jātaka*, but is also highly superior to it.[1] "Characteristic of Indian art," observes the great Orientalist, "are the narratives of the Jainas. The Jainas' way of telling their tales differs from that of the Bauddhas in some very essential points. Their main story is not that of the past but that of the present; they do not teach their doctrines directly, but indirectly; and there is no future Jina to be provided with a *rôle* in their stories."[2]

Most of these narratives of the Jainas are in the form of parables. Generally more stress is put on the parables than on the narration itself. In the first book of the *Aṅga* under our discussion there is one of this kind, which runs as follows. A merchant has four daughters-in-law. To test them he gives each one five grains of rice, with the instruction that they should keep them carefully until he would ask them back. In the meantime it so happens that one throws the grains away, thinking: "In the godown there are plenty of grains; I shall give him some others." The second one thinks the same and eats them up. The third one keeps them carefully in her jewel-box; but the fourth one sows them, and reaps a harvest again and again until she has a great stock of rice after five years. When the merchant inquires for the five grains of rice he condemns the first two daughters-in-law by entrusting them to do only the lowest kind of work in the house, while the third is asked to look after the whole property, and the fourth one is made the head- mistress of the house. Based on this simple story the moral to be taught is that with these four women may be compared monks, of whom some are not at all anxious to keep the five great vows; a few others who neglect them; the better ones, who keep the vows scrupulously; and the best ones, who are not only content to keep them, but also look for followers.[3]

Mostly of narrative contents are also the seventh, eighth and ninth *Aṅga*s. Of these the first — namely, the *Uvāsaga-Dasāo* — contains legends about ten pious *śrāvaka*s, many of whom are rich merchants, and who, by means of asceticism, in the end come so far that even as lay-followers they are rewarded with miraculous powers. Finally they die as real Jaina saints, by starving themselves voluntarily to death, and are then reborn as gods in the heaven of the pious.[4] The most interesting is the story of the rich potter, Saddalaputta,

1. Hertel, op. cit., p. 7.
2. Ibid., p. 8.
3. Cf. *Jñātā, sūt*. 63, pp. 115-20.
4. Cf. Hoernle, *Uvāsaga-Dasāo*, I., pp. 1-44, etc.

"the servant of the Ājīviya," who was finally convinced by Mahāvīra of the truth of his doctrine.[1] Likewise the eighth and ninth *Aṅga*s deal with legends concerning the pious, who, having put an end to their worldly life, attained the *mokṣa* and the highest heavenly world respectively.[2]

Taking the last two of the extant *Aṅga*s, known as the *Praśnavyākarṇāni* and the *Vipākaśrutam*, we find that the first is more of a dogmatic than of a legendary nature, while the other is the reverse of it. It treats of the ten moral duties — commandments and prohibitions — viz. first of the five *adharma*s, which must be avoided — injury to life, lying, robbery, unchastity, (love of) possession — and then of the five *dharma*s, the opposites of each of the above sins.[3] The *Vipāka-Sūtra*, on the other hand, contains legends on the reward of good and evil deeds, which are rightly, in the opinion of Dr Winternitz, similar to the Buddhist *karman* stories in the *Avadānaśataka* and the *Karmaśataka*.[4]

As to the twelfth *Aṅga* of the Jainas, it is no longer extant. It is irrevocably lost, along with the fourteen *Pūrva*s — the oldest portion of the canon — which were incorporated in it when they ceased to exist independently of the *Aṅga* literature.[5] However there is one question of capital interest connected with the loss of the *Dṛṣṭivāda*. Eminent Jaina scholars in Europe feel that the Jainas themselves give no convincing reason for the loss of what may be regarded as the oldest and the most venerable part of their sacred lore, and hence various explanations of what according to them seems to have been a startling fact have been attempted by them. To mention a few of these scholars: Weber thinks that the *Dṛṣṭivāda*, not being in complete agreement with the tenets of the orthodox doctrine, was wilfully rejected by the Jainas themselves.[6] According to Jacobi, *Dṛṣṭivāda* became obsolete because it consisted merely of discussions (*pravāda*) between Mahāvīra and his opponents, and that these would have gradually lost their interest and at last become wholly unintelligible to the Jainas themselves.[7] Last on the list, Dr Leumann propounds a totally different view as regards the loss of the *Dṛṣṭivāda*. According to him

1. Cf. Hoernle, *Uvāsaga-Dasāo*, I., pp. 105-40.
2. Cf. Barnett, *The Antagaḍa-Dasāo and Aṇuttarovavāiya-Dasāo*, pp. 15-16, 110, etc.
3. Cf. Weber, *I.A.*, XX., p. 23.
4. Cf. Winternitz, op. cit., p. 306.
5. The fourteen *Pūrvas* were included as the third great subdivision of the twelfth *Aṅga*. Cf. Weber, op. cit., p. 174.
6. Cf. Weber, *I.A.*, XVII., p. 286.
7. Cf. Jacobi, S.B.E., XXII., Int., pp. xlv ff.

this *Aṅga* of the Jainas must have contained a great number of texts concerning tāntric rites, sorcery, astrology, etc., and this would be the real reason for its becoming obsolete.[1]

All these explanations for the loss of the twelfth *Aṅga* of the Jainas seem to have one drawback in common — viz. that of suggesting that the *Dṛṣṭivāda* ("or the *Pūrvas*, which is much the same thing"[2]) was simply abandoned by the Jainas. This sounds rather strange, and especially so in the face of the traditions of the Jainas themselves; for they clearly tell us that the *Pūrva*s became obsolete only gradually, so that the loss was not complete until a thousand years after the death of Mahāvīra — i.e. just at the time of the final redaction of the canon. With whatsoever limitations we may take into consideration this tradition of the Jainas, along with Dr Charpentier, in our opinion also "the statement as a whole ought not to be totally disregarded."[3]

Coming to the second part of the *Siddhānta*, corresponding to the number of the *Aṅga*s, we get the twelve *Upāṅga*s. According to Weber and others "there are no instances of real inner connection between the *Aṅga*s and *Upāṅga*s having the same position in the series."[4] Taking *Aupapātika*, the first *Upāṅga*, as mentioned before, its historical importance rests in connection with the detailed treatment of the appearance and sermon of Mahāvīra in Campā under King Kūṇiya or Ajātaśatru, and of the pilgrimage of the king to Mahāvīra.

As to the second *Upāṅga*, the *Rājapraśnīya*, the largest portion of the text deals with the pilgrimage of the god Suriabha, with a numerous retinue, to Amalakappa, the city of King Śveta, in order to offer his reverence to Mahāvīra, especially by means of music, singing and dancing.[5] However, the quintessence of the work is in the inserted dialogue between King Paesi and the monk Keśi, which starts with the question in reference to the relation of the *jīva* (soul) to the *deha* (body), and which ends with the conversion of the open-minded king.[6]

---

1. ". . . des Diṭṭhivāya eine ganz analoge tantra-artige Texpartie gestanden hat, sondern lässt damit zugleich auch errathen, warum der Diṭṭhivāya veloran gegangen ist." — Leumann, "Beziehungen der Jaina-Literatur zu Andern Literaturkreisen Indiens," *Actes du Congress à Leide*, 1883, p. 559.
2. Charpentier, op. cit., Int., pp. 22-23. "Tradition indeed appears to regard the *Pūrvas* as identical with the *Diṭṭhivāya*." — Weber, *I.A.*, XX., p. 170.
3. Cf. Charpentier, op. cit., Int., p. 23.
4. Weber, op. cit., p. 366. Cf. Winternitz, op. and loc. cit.
5. Cf. *Rājapraśnīya-Sūtra* (Āgamodaya Samiti), *sūt*. 1 ff.
6. Cf. ibid., *sūt*. 65-79.

Of the remaining *Upāṅgas* the third and fourth may be taken together, being more or less similar in contents and form. The first of these treats in a dialogue form of the different forms and groups of animated nature, while the second treats of the different forms, conditions of life, etc. of the *jīva*.[1] However, *Prajñāpanā*, the fourth *Upāṅga* differs from nearly all the other canonical texts in this, that it is attributed to an author called Ayya Sāma (Ārya Śyāma, also Śyāmārya), who is placed by both the Kharatara and Tapa Gaccha *Paṭṭāvalis* in the fourth century after Vīra.[2]

The next group combines in it the fifth, sixth and seventh *Upāṅgas* of the Jainas. The *Sūryaprajñapti*, the *Jambudvīpaprajñapti* and the *Candraprajñapti* are the scientific works of the Jainas, and they treat of astronomy, legendary geography of Bhāratavarṣa, and of cosmography of the heavens and system of time-reckoning, respectively. Of these, *Sūryaprajñapti*, the fifth *Upāṅga*, needs special mention on our part. "In it," observes Dr Weber, "we find the most remarkable statements concerning the astronomy of the Jainas arranged in a systematic form of presentation. It is an open question whether Greek influence made itself felt in this rectification; at any rate we have to deal here with an indigenous style of Indian astronomy antecedent to the authoritative and prepondering influence of the Hellenes."[3] This fact of the *Sūryaprajñapti* being a unique specimen of "an indigenous style of Indian astronomy," even prior to the days of Greek influence in the East, is believed in by other scholars also,[4] and its importance in the light of Jaina history is self-evident.

With regard to the last five *Upāṅgas* they are also compiled as five sections of a single text, entitled the *Niryāvalisuttam*. According to Weber, "their enumeration as five separate texts was caused by the desire to have the number of *Upāṅgas* correspond to that of the *Aṅgas*."[5] The historical importance of the eighth *Upāṅga* lies in this, that it treats of how the ten half-brothers of

1. Cf. Weber, op. cit., pp. 371, 373.
2. Cf. Klatt, *I.A.*, XI., pp. 247, 251. According to Dr Charpentier, "*Upāṅga* 4 is expressly stated to be the work of Ārya Śyāma, a patriarch who is certainly identical with that Kālakācārya whom the tradition places in the time of Gardabhila, the father of Vikramāditya." — Charpentier, op. cit., Int., p. 27. Cf. Jacobi, Z.D.M.G., XXXIV., p. 251 ff.
3. Weber, *I.A.*, XXI., pp. 14-15.
4. Cf. Jacobi, S.B.E., XXII., Int., p. xl ; Leumann, op. cit., pp. 552-53. Thibaut, *J.A.S.B.*, XLIX., 1880, p. 108. For some facts of special interest in connection with the *Sūryaprajñapti* see ibid., pp. 107-21, 181-206.
5. Weber, op. cit., p. 23.

Kūṇika were killed in the campaign against Ceḍaga, the great Licchavi king, and how as a result they were reborn in different hells.[1]

This much about the *Upāṅga*s which form the second group of the *Siddhānta*. With regard to the third group of the texts of the *Siddhānta* it is formed by ten *Painna*s or *Prakīrṇa*s. These texts, "in the pregnant sense of the word, bear a name which, denoting "scattered," "hastily sketched" pieces, well suits their real nature as a group of texts corresponding to the Vedic *Pariśishṭas*. Like the *Pariśishṭa*s they are, with a few exceptions, composed in metre; and in fact in *āryā*, the metre which is usual in the *Kārikā* insertions in the *Aṅgas*," etc.[2] These *Painnas* treat of manifold subjects. Among them may be mentioned the prayers by means of which one is put under the fourfold protection of the *arhats*, *siddhas*, *sādhus* and the Religion; the genuine euthanasy; the life in embryo; the qualities of teachers and pupils; the enumeration of gods, etc.[3]

Next we shall take the *Chedasūtra*s, the fourth part of the *Siddhānta*. They discuss in general what constitutes prohibited conduct for monks and nuns, prescribing punishments or expiations for the same, though there is a large admixture of subsidiary matter of a legendary character. They correspond, consequently, to the *Vinaya* of the Buddhists, with which, despite all differences, they are closely connected in contents and in style of treatment.[4] As to the antiquity of the existing *Chedasūtra*s, in the opinion of both Winternitz and Weber a large portion of them is of considerable antiquity. This is because the quintessence of this group, the *Chedasūtra*s 3-5, belong to the oldest part of the canon.[5]

These three texts — namely, the third, fourth and fifth *Chedasūtra*s — come under one group, known as *Dasa-Kappa-Vavahāra*.[6] Of these the composition of the two texts, the *Kalpa* and the *Vyavahāra*, is frequently referred back to Bhadrabāhu, who is said to have extracted them out of the ninth *Pūrva*.[7] The authorship of Bhadrabāhu is also asserted by tradition of the

1. Cf. *Niryāvalika-Sūtra*, pp. 3-19.
2. Weber, op. cit., p. 106. Cf. Winternitz, op. cit., p. 308.
3. Cf. Weber, op. cit., pp. 109-12 ; Winternitz, op. and loc. cit.
4. Cf. Weber, op. cit., p. 179 ; Winternitz, op. cit., p. 309.
5. Cf. ibid., p. 308 ; Weber, op. cit., pp. 179-80.
6. Cf. Winternitz, op. cit., p. 309 ; Weber, op. cit., pp. 179, 210.
7. दसकप्पव्ववहारा, निज्झूढा जेण नवमपुव्वाओ। वंदामि भद्दबाहुं, . . . — *Ṛṣimaṇḍalastotra*, v. 166.

third member of this group of texts, the *Āyāradasāo*. The eighth section of this last-mentioned text is long known as the *Kalpa-Sūtra* of Bhadrabāhu. It is formed of the entire work called *Kalpa-Sūtra* — i.e. of the entire work of this name in its three parts; however Jacobi and others rightly hold that in reality only the last (the third) section, which is called "*Sāmācāri*" — i.e. rules for *yatis* — "comprised by the name *paryuṣaṇa kalpa*," belongs to this place, and that it alone could claim, together with the remaining *Āyāradasāo* to be ascribed to Bhadrabāhu.[1]

As to the contents of the *Kalpa-Sūtra* of Bhadrabāhu we need not enter into any more details here. We have referred to it more than once in connection with the life history of Mahāvīra, with that of his twenty-three predecessors, with the successors of Mahāvīra, pontiffs of the Jaina church, and in connection with the rules and prescriptions to be observed by *yatis*. With these few remarks about the *Chedasūtras* we shall next deal briefly with the *Mūlasūtras* and the two solitary texts which form the last two groups of the Jaina canon.

Taking first the *Mūlasūtras*, we find that the significance of this title of a group of the Jaina canon is rather doubtful. In ordinary parlance, however, it would mean original text, but it is likely, according to Dr Charpentier, that, like the Budhists, the Jainas also may have used *mūla* in the sense of "original text," and that too merely to denote the actual words of Mahāvīra himself.[2] As to the contents of these *sūtras* the first three also, from a literary standpoint, are of great importance. Of these the *Uttarādhyayana*, the first in the list, with its specimens of old ascetic poetry, belongs to the most precious part of the canon. It consists of direct ordinances in reference to a correct course of life, especially of the clergy, and of recitals and parables illustrating this life. According to the opinion of the old authorities summarized by Jacobi the aim of the text is "to instruct a young monk in his principal duties, to commend an ascetic life by precepts and examples, to warn him against the dangers in his spiritual career, and to give some theoretical information."[3]

Much of the contents, according to modern authorities on Jaina

1. Jacobi, *Kalpa-Sūtra*, pp. 22-23 ; Winternitz, op. and loc. cit. ; Weber, op. cit., p. 211.
2. Charpentier, op. cit., Int., p. 32.
3. Jacobi, S.B.E., XLV., Int., p. xxxix.

literature, makes upon us the impression of great antiquity, and recalls similar Buddhist texts, and especially *Aṅga* 2 — that is to say, the very oldest parts of the canon.[1] As just remarked, it resembles the *Sūtrakṛtāṅga* with regard to its object and parts of the subjects treated; however in the *Uttarādhyayana* "the heretical doctrines are only occasionally alluded to, not fully discussed. Apparently the dangers expected from that quarter grew less in the same measure as time advanced and the institutions of the sect were more firmly established. Of more interest to a young monk seems to have been an accurate knowledge of animate and inanimate things, as a rather long treatise on this subject has been added at the end of the book."[2]

As to the contents of the second *Mūlasūtra*, the *Āvaśyaka-Sūtra*, it deals with all the six *Āvaśyaka*s, or observances which are obligatory upon the Jaina, be he a layman or one of the clergy.[3] With these observances are connected narrations of historical or quasi-historical importance which are handed down to us in the commentaries. To quote Professor Weber: "It treats not merely of the doctrine of Mahāvīra on this point, but also of the history of the doctrine itself — i.e. of the predecessors of Mahāvīra, of himself, of his eleven *Gaṇadhara*s and of his opponents: the different schisms (*niṇhaga*s, *ninhava*s) which gradually gained a foothold in his teachings. The latter are chronologically fixed. Haribhadra quotes very detailed legends (*Kathānakas*) in Prākṛt prose (sometimes in metre) in this connection, and also in connection with *Diṭṭhaṁta* and *Udāharaṇa*, which are frequently mentioned in the text."[4]

Taking next the last two *Mūlasūtra*s we find that the contents of the first one — namely, the *Dasaveyāliya* — refer to the *Vinaya*, or rules of conduct of the Jaina clergy, and this according to Dr Winternitz reminds us of the *Dhammapada* of the Buddhists.[5] The authorship of this complete conspectus of the leading Jaina tenets is ascribed to Sayyambhava or Sajjambhava, the

---

1. Cf. Charpentier, op. cit., Int., p. 34 ; Winternitz, op. cit., p. 312 ; Weber, op. cit., p. 310.
2. Jacobi, op. and loc. cit.
3. समणेण सावएण य अवस्सकायव्वयं हवइ जम्हा। अंतोअहोणिसस्स य तम्हा आवस्सयं नाम. — *Āvaśyaka-Sūtra*, p. 53; the six *Āvaśyaka*s in order are as follows : — The *Sāmāiam*, or avoidance of evil deeds; the *Cauvisattho*, or praise of twenty-four *jina*s; the *Vaṁdanayam*, or veneration of the teachers; the *Paḍīkamaṇam*, or confession; the *Kāusagga*, or atonement of sins committed by penance and meditation; and the *Paccakkhāṇam*, or abstention from food, etc. Cf. ibid.
4. Weber, op. cit., p. 330.
5. Cf. Winternitz, op. cit., p. 315.

fourth patriarch after Mahāvīra. Mrs Stevenson looks upon this *Sūtra* "as a monument of a father's love persisting even in the ascetic life,"[1] because it was composed by the author for the benefit of his son named Manaka.[2] As to the last *Mūlasūtra*, it is a mere supplement to the previous one.

Finally, what remains to be seen of the *Siddhānta* of the Jainas are the two solitary texts known as *Nandīsūtra* and the *Anuyogadvārasūtra*. Both of them are somewhat related in contents, but they differ in style. They are more or less encyclopaedic, but systematic, reviews of everything that appeared necessary as a means of information with reference to the sources and forms of a correct knowledge and understanding of the sacred texts.[3] In this way, according to Weber, their author could present his readers with a hermeneutical introduction. To quote the learned scholar, "these two works are admirably adapted to the use of one who, having completed a collection or redaction of them, then seeks for knowledge concerning the nature of sacred knowledge itself."[4] Though according to the literary traditions of the Jainas Devardhigaṇi seems to be the author of these two solitary texts, to both Weber and Charpentier there seems, however, no external support for this conclusion, which is not borne out by any information to be derived from the contents.[5] "After all," observes the latter, "I think that the authorship of Devarddhi is not very strongly established, and we may regard him as a redactor rather than the author of the canonical works."[6]

This much about the canonical literature of the Śvetāmbara Jainas.[7] As to the language of the canon, from the unsettled state of the Jaina literature down to Devardhigaṇi's times it may be concluded that the language also in which it was handed down underwent a gradual alteration. However this much seems highly probable, that the religious reformers of the sixth century before Christ, who taught in opposition to the priestly wisdom of the brāhmaṇa

---

1. Stevenson (Mrs), op. cit., p. 70.
2. Cf. Jacobi, *Kalpa-Sūtra*, p. 118 ; Klatt, op. cit., pp. 246, 251. For the tradition about the composition of the *Daśavaikālika* see Hemacandra, *Pariśiṣṭaparvan*, Canto V.
3. Cf. Weber, op. cit., pp. 293-94 ; Winternitz, op. and loc. cit.
4. Weber, op. cit., p. 294.
5. Cf. ibid. ; Charpentier, op. cit., Int., p. 18.
6. Ibid.
7. About the *Siddhānta* of the Digambaras see Winternitz, op. cit., p. 316 ; Jacobi, op. cit., Int., p. 30.

scholars a way to salvation accessible to the bulk of the people, used for their sermons the language of the ordinary people and not the learned language of Sanskrit. This language of the people seems to have been the vernacular dialect of Magadha, the home of Mahāvīra. With all this the Māgadhī used by the Jainas "has very little of affinity with the Māgadhī either of Aśoka's inscriptions or of the Prākṛt grammarians."[1] This is why the actual language used by the Jainas is known as Ardha-Māgadhī, a mixed language, "which consists to a great extent of Māgadhī, but took up also elements of foreign dialects; Mahāvīra is said to have spoken this mixed language to be understood by all with whom he came in touch, therefore also by the people living on the boundaries of his mother-country."[2]

According to the tradition of the Jainas "the old *Sūtra* was exclusively composed in the language called Ardha Māgadhī,"[3] but the Jaina Prākṛt of "the old *Sūtra*" differs considerably from the language of the commentaries and poets. The Jainas call it *Ārṣam*, the language of the *Ṛṣis*, while the dialect in which the canon is written is nearer to Māhārāṣṭrī, and is known as the Jaina Māhārāṣṭrī. We shall not enter into any further details about the peculiarities of the language used and developed by the Jainas before the final rearrangement of the Jaina books. Suffice it to say that "the Jaina Māhārāshṭrī, being once fixed as a sacred language, continued to be the literary language of the Jainas until it was replaced by Sanskrit."[4]

Of the non-canonical literature of the Jainas we have, on the one hand, any amount of commentatorial works represented by the class of scriptures called the *Nijjutti*s or *Niryukti*s, and on the other, independent works consisting partly of learned works about dogmatics, ethics, and monks' discipline, and partly poetical products, of which some are hymns to glorify the Jainas while the rest belong to the highly increased narrative literature of the Jainas. It seems certain that long before the final compilation of the canon under Devardhi the Jaina monks must have begun composing explanations to the holy texts, for the oldest commentaries, the *Nijjutti*s or *Niryukti*s, are in some cases very closely connected with the *sūtra*s, or have even displaced them.

---

1. Jacobi, op. cit., Int., p. 17.
2. Glasenapp, *Der Jainismus*, p. 84.
3. पोराणमद्धमागहभासानिययं हवइ सुत्तं. — Hemacandra, *Prākṛt Grammar*, IV. 287.
4. Jacobi, op. cit., Int., p. 20. For further details about the language of the sacred writings of the Jainas see ibid., p. 17 ff. Glasenapp, op. cit., p. 81 ff.

Piṇḍa and *Oghanijjutti* appear in the canon itself, and *Oghanijjutti* is said to have been taken from some of the *Pūrvas*.[1]

According to Dr Charpentier, old as the *Niryukti*s are they certainly do not represent the very first set of Jaina commentatorial literature. They are not the oldest but the oldest existing set of commentaries on the canonical scriptures of the Jainas. This is because "the *Niryukti* is in its main parts only a sort of index, a collection of *versus memoriales* meant to give an abbreviation of an extensive commentary, where all these tales and legends were really told at length."[2] The oldest commentator seems to be Bhadrabāhu, who, as seen before, died one hundred and seventy years after the *nirvāṇa* of Vardhamāna. He is said to have composed ten *Niryukti*s on different works belonging to the canon — viz. the *Ācārāṅga*, the *Sūtrakṛtāṅga*, the *Sūryaprajñapti*, the *Daśaśrutaskandha*, *Kalpa* and *Vyavahāra*, the *Āvaśyaka*, the *Daśavaikālika*, the *Uttarādhyayana* and the *Ṛṣibhāṣita*.[3] According to Banarsi Das Jain, Bhadrabāhu's *Niryukti* on the *Āvaśyaka* is the earliest authority on the *Pūrvabhāva*s — i.e. former births of Ṛṣabha. This is because "the *Aṅgas* do not make any special mention of the *Pūrvabhavas* of the Tīrthaṅkaras, though they contain numerous references to the past and future lives of several of Mahāvīra's contemporaries."[4]

What makes all these commentaries so precious is the circumstance that they have preserved for us, on the one hand, very many old historic or quasi-historic traditions, and on the other, a vast amount of material for popular narrations. Like the Buddhist monks the Jaina monks also have at all times preferred to animate their sermons by narrating stories and legends of saints with a view to gaining and preserving as many followers as possible, by taking advantage of the Indian lust of hearing religious stories. Thus "there gradually accumulated a considerable stock of legends and tales, partly borrowed from collections among the people since time immemorial, partly belonging to the "legend aurea" of the Jainas themselves, and partly perhaps invented quite recently, which then formed a sort of permanent commentary on the holy texts."[5]

---

1. Cf. Winternitz, op. cit., p. 317.
2. Charpentier, op. cit., Int., pp. 50-51.
3. Cf. *Āvaśyaka-Sūtra*, vv. 84-86, p. 61 ; Jacobi, op. cit., Int., p. 12.
4. Jain, *Jaina Jātakas*, Int., p. iii.
5. Charpentier, op. cit., Int., p. 51.

To this famous Bhadrabāhu is also attributed the *Saṁhitā* known as the *Bhādrabāhavī-Saṁhitā* — an astronomical work — and the *Uvasaggaharastotra*, an ode to Pārśva. However it is doubtful whether the Bhadrabāhu of the *Saṁhitā* and of the *Niryukti*s mentioned above are one and the same person. Besides its being of the same character as the other *Saṁhitā*s, this *Bhādrabāhavī-Saṁhitā* is not cited by Varāhamihira, who names amongst his numerous authorities another Jaina astronomer, Siddhasena,[1] and consequently it is more modern than Varāhamihira. To quote Jacobi, "At any rate, its author cannot be the same Bhadrabāhu who composed the *Kalpa-Sūtra*, because its last redaction, the date of which (980 A.V. = AD 454 or AD 514) is mentioned in it, was already earlier than, at least contemporaneous with, Varāhamihira — not to speak of its composition."[2]

As for the *Uvasaggaharastotra* the tradition about its composition by Bhadrabāhu is based on the following verse:

उवसग्गहरं थुत्तं काऊणं जेण संघकल्लाणं।
करुणापरेण विहिअं स भद्दबाहू गुरु जयउ ॥[3]

"Victory to Guru Bhadrabāhu, who by composing the *Uvasaggaharastotra* bestowed, out of pity, happiness on the *Saṁgha*."

With regard to the contents of the *Stotra* it is a hymn in veneration of Lord Pārśva. This is clear from the last verse of the *Stotra*, which runs as follows: "Thus praised Glorious one! with a heart full of mighty devotion, Pārśva! mayest thou, O God! therefore, give perfect wisdom in every birth, Moon of the Jinas."[4] As to its composition by Bhadrabāhu, Jacobi believes that if that is granted, it is the oldest specimen of the now extensive literature of Jaina hymns.[5]

Besides Bhadrabāhu's there are many other independent works, but we shall limit ourselves to a few of the most important of them. Of these the first to draw our attention is the *Upadeśamālā* of Dharmadāsagaṇi, who is claimed by the Jainas to be a contemporary of Mahāvīra.[6] The text contains

1. Kern, *Bṛhat Saṁhitā*, Pre., p. 29.
2. Jacobi, op. cit., Int., p. 14. For the tradition of the Digambaras about Bhadrabāhu II and the legendary story of the Śvetāmbaras about Bhadrabāhu and Varāhamihira see ibid., pp. 13, 30. Vidyabhusana, *Mediaeval School of Indian Logic*, pp. 5-6.
3. *Kalpa-Sūtra, Subōdhikā-Ṭīkā*, p. 162.
4. Cf. Jacobi, op. cit., Int., p. 13.
5. Cf. ibid., p. 12.
6. Cf. Dharmadāsagaṇi, *Upadeśamālā* (Jaina Dharma Prasāraka Sabhā), p. 2.

moral instructions for laymen as well as for monks, and its popularity is witnessed by many commentaries, two of which go as far back as the ninth century AD.[1] After Dharmadāsa we may mention Umāsvāti, who is claimed by both the Śvetāmbaras and the Digambaras. According to Winternitz, because he represents views which do not correspond with those of the Digambaras, they are scarcely entitled to claim him as one of them. With what limitations this fact about Umāsvāti can be or should be understood we cannot say. However, the learned scholar is right in inferring, with others of his opinion, that probably the great *Ācārya* belongs to an earlier period, when both the sects were not so sharply divided.[2] This is further supported by the *Tapagaccha Paṭṭāvali* of the Jainas, according to which Śyāmārya, of the fourth century after Vīra and, as mentioned before, the author of the *Prajñāpanā*, was the pupil of Umāsvāti.[3] Nevertheless, according to Hiralal, "the solution may, however, lie in the fact that Umāsvāti does not touch the principles under controversy between the two sections."[4]

This Umāsvāti is better known as Vācaka-Śramaṇa. According to the Śvetāmbara recension of his *Tattvārthādhigama-Sūtra* it seems he was known also as Nagaravācaka. We are told by him that he was born in Nyagrodhika, but he resided in Kusumapura or Pāṭalīputra.[5] The Hindu philosopher, Madhavācārya, calls him Umāsvātivācakācārya.[6] As to the writings of this great *ācārya*, we find that no less than five hundred works are said to have been composed by him, of which, however, only five have survived. The colophon to all of these —viz. (i) *Tattvārthādhigama-Sūtra*; (ii) *Bhāṣya* on the above; (iii) *Pūjāprakaraṇa*; (iv) *Jambūdvīpasamāsa*; and (v) *Praśamarti*, as published by the Asiatic Society of Bengal — reads: "कृतिः सिताम्बराचार्यस्य महाकवेरूमास्वातिवाचकस्य इति।"[7]

1. Cf. Winternitz, op. cit., p. 343 ; Macdonell, *India's Past*, p. 74 ; Stevenson (Mrs), op. cit., p. 82.
2. Cf. Winternitz, op. cit., p. 351 ; Hiralal (Rai Bahadur), *Catalogue of MSS. in C.P. and Berar*, Int., pp. vii-ix ; Vidyabhusana, op. cit., p. 9.
3. Cf. Klatt, op. cit., p. 251. This account of the Śvetāmbara *Paṭṭāvali* assigns him to centuries before Christ. Ārya Mahāgiri the tenth pontiff after Mahāvīra, dies two hundred and forty-nine years after the latter. He had two pupils, Bahula and Balissaha. The pupil of the latter was Umāsvāti. Cf. ibid., pp. 246, 251. In the Digambara account Umāsvāti is mentioned as the sixth in succession from Bhadrabāhu, and as succeeding Kundakundācārya. His date of death is given V.S. 142 or AD 85. Cf. Hoernle, *I.A.*, XX., p. 341. For further information about Umāsvāti see Hiralal (Rai Bahadur), op. cit., Int., pp. vii-ix ; Peterson, *Report on San. MSS.*, IV., Int., p. XVI ; Jaini, S.B.J., II., Int., pp. vii-ix.
4. Hiralal (Rai Bahadur), op. cit., Int., p. ix.
5. *Tattvārthādhigama-Sūtra* (ed. Motilal Ladhaji), *Adhyayana* X, p. 203.
6. Cf. Cowell and Gough, *Sarva-Darśana-Saṁgraha*, p. 55.
7. Hiralal, op. cit., Int., p. viii.

Among the works mentioned above, *Tattvārthādhigama-Sūtra* is the one on which mostly rests his fame. Of the few priceless jewels that have been rescued from loss and oblivion this is about the most valuable. Umāsvāti is the first to put in the popular style of the philosophical Sanskrit *sūtra*s all the Jainistic principles that constitute the backbone of the Āgamic literature of the Jainas. This is why it is virtually known as the Jaina Bible and is revered by all sections of the Jaina community. How great and authoritative it is recognized to be will be further evident from the fact that it has perhaps received the greatest attention from most Jaina commentators. No less than thirty-one commentaries are known to be extant now. There is no Jaina doctrine or dogma which is not expressed or implied in these aphorisms. Verily *Tattvārtha-Sūtra* is a sacred epitome of Jainism.[1]

With these few introductory notes on the great Umāsvātivācaka we shall pass on to the period of Vikramāditya, with Siddhasena Divākara and Pādaliptācārya as the outstanding luminaries of the Jaina literary history.[2] With regard to the authenticity of the ancient and persistent Jaina tradition about the period of Siddhasena and his conversion of Vikrama we have already dealt, and hence we need not here enter into any further details about this moot question of the period of Divākara. However two facts may be adduced here in favour of this traditional date of Siddhasena. In the first place, like Vācaka-Śramaṇa, he also is claimed by both the Digambaras and the Śvetāmbaras, and secondly, references to him in the literature of both the sects are ancient.[3]

As to the literature left to us by the great Siddhasena, he is said to have written thirty-two independent works dealing with Jaina logic and philosophy. Leaving aside the minor question of the number of works composed by him he is precisely the first Śvetāmbara author of *Prakaraṇa*s in the technical meaning of the word. "A *Prakaraṇa* is a systematic treatise in which the subject is exposed in a scientific form, unlike the unsystematic, either diffuse or episodical, treatment of subjects in canonical books; it may be in Prākṛt, but as a rule it is in Sanskrit."[4] Such endeavours on the part of great teachers like Siddhasena and others during the first few centuries before and after the

1. Jaini, op. cit., Int., p. viii.
2. Rice (E.P.), *Kanarese Literature*, p. 41.
3. Hiralal (Rai Bahadur), op. cit., Int., p. xiii.
4. Jacobi, *Samarāicca Kahā*, Int., p. xii.

Christian era to raise the Śvetāmbaras to the high level of Indian mental culture were brought to their conclusion by Hemacandra, who provided them with admirable textbooks of the principal Indian sciences, besides such standard works as more directly concerned their own creed.

Siddhasena is known to us particularly as the famous author of *Nyāyāvatāra* and *Sammatitarka*. The first is a metrical work on logic, giving an exposition of the doctrine of *Pramāṇa* (sources of valid knowledge) and *Naya* (the method of comprehending things from particular standpoints), while the second is the only work in Prākṛt on general philosophy containing an elaborate discussion on the principles of logic. Before the inauguration of these two learned works it seems there had not perhaps existed any distinct treatise on Jaina logic, its principles having been included in the works of metaphysics and religion. To quote Dr Vidyabhusana: "Logic was mixed up with metaphysics and religion in the ancient writing of the Jainas as in those of other sects in India. The first Jaina writer on pure logic appears to have been Siddhasena Divākara. It was he who, for the first time among the Jainas, distinguished logic from the cognate branches of learning by composing a metrical work called *Nyāyāvatāra* on Logic in thirty-two stanzas."[1]

As with Bhadrabāhu so also with Divākara is connected one of the hymns of the Jainas which is also an ode to Pārśva. This is the *Kalyāṇamandirastotra*, the tradition about whose composition runs as follows:

"Once he (Siddhasena) presumptuously declared in the presence of his *Guru* that he would turn the whole sacred lore from Prākṛt into Sanskrit. For the expiation of the sin committed by this sacrilegious utterance he was administered by his *guru* the *Pārāṇhika Prāyaścitta*, which required him to remain dumb for twelve years and visit sacred places. In the observance of this vow he once went to Ujjain and lodged in the temple of Mahākāla. Here he incurred the displeasure of the priests for not making obeisance to the god Śiva. They called the King Vikramāditya, who compelled Siddhasena to bow before the god. Siddhasena did this, reciting the *Kalyāṇamandira* ode, which had the effect of splitting the image of Śiva in twain and manifesting

1. Vidyabhusana, *Nyāyāvatāra*, Int., p. 1.

out of it an image of a Jaina *tīrthaṅkara*. Being impressed with his power King Vikramāditya and many others became converted to Jainism."[1]

With regard to Pādalipta we have already referred to him as one who had converted his majesty King Maruṇḍa, "the emperor of the thirty-six hundred thousand people of Kanyākubja."[2] He is known to us as the author of the *Taraṅgavatī*, the most ancient and famous of Jaina romances. The original text has been lost, but a later recasting of it, *Taraṅgalolā*, has been preserved. Nemicandra, the author of the summary, abridged *Taraṅgavatī* by the omission of complex verses and "*lokapadas*" (popular sayings). The reason given by Nemicandra for abridging the original is that it was very extensive, complex, and full of pairs, sixes; and *Kulaka*s (collections) of verses, and that consequently it had become a work only for the learned, the ordinary people having lost interest in it.[3]

However, in spite of its being an abridged edition of *Taraṅgavatī*, *Taraṅgalolā* is also of great literary interest as a specimen, and reflex, as it were, of the more popular literature of fiction current in those days, which must have been a very extensive one, both in Sanskrit and Prākṛt, though very few works belonging to it have come down to us. As usual with other specimens of such literature, in our romance also the picture of the heroine ends in her renouncement of the world and entering the order. *Karma* remembrance of a previous birth, and its consequences, etc., serve to motivate the story, and the narrative is interspersed with a great deal of religious instruction, which, however, rarely degenerates into sermons.

Besides *Taraṅgavatī*, among other works of Pādalipta we mention the *Praśna-Prakāśa*, a work on astrology, and the *Nirvāṇa-Kalikā*, the oldest extant work dealing with ceremonials relating to the "Installation of Idols," and is known also as the "*Pratiṣṭhā-Paddhati*" — i.e. "Treatise on Installation."[4] The last-mentioned work is of great interest to the antiquarian, as it supplies "a link between the period of the composition of the Jaina holy scriptures and the date when they were systematically committed to writing. The work is written in Sanskrit, in departure from the usual practice to write in the Ardha-Māgadhī language of Jaina religious works of the time. . . . The

1. Hiralal (Rai Bahadur), op. cit., Int., p. xiii. Cf. this story with the one given in the Jainistic recension of *Vikramacarita*. — Edgerton, op. cit., p. 253.
2. Ibid., p. 251.
3. Cf. Jhaveri, *Nirvāṇa-Kalikā*, Int., pp. 12-13.
4. Ibid., Int., p. 1.

pomp attached to Ācāryship is great. Royal insignias, such as elephant, horse, palanquin, chowries, umbrella, as well as *yogapaṭṭaka* (diagram for worship) and *khaṭika* (pen), books, crystal-bead-rosary, and sandals are presented to Acarya on conferment of the dignity. . . . The reference in the *Nitya-Karma-Vidhi* to *Aṣṭa Mūrti* (eightfold form, Śiva) is important, and shows that Jaina worship was influenced by *Tāntrika Āgamas*, where the chief deity is Śiva."[1]

Thus from all that we have seen above this much is certain — that even the unrecorded period of Jaina history can safely claim to have had a copious and in part ancient literature. Though ours is in no sense an exhaustive survey of the traditional literature of the Jainas belonging to this period, there would be no exaggeration if we conclude that the Jaina literature of the period under discussion does not yield to any other Indian literature either in quality or in variety. All the species are represented in it, not only those which have an immediate bearing on the canonical writings — that is to say, the dogmatic, the moral, the polemic and the apologetic — but also history and legend, epic and romance, and lastly the sciences, such as astronomy and, above all, sciences like astrology and divination.

1. Jhaveri, op. cit., Int., p. 5.

CHAPTER VIII

Jaina Art in the North

We propose to deal in this chapter with the sculptural, architectural and pictorial contributions of the Jainas to the history of north Indian art in general. In the words of Dr. Guérinot, "the Hindu art owes to them a great number of its most remarkable monuments. In the domain of architecture in particular they have reached a degree of perfection which leaves them almost without a rival."[1] It is doubtless true that Jainism finds its best expression in architecture. It is consequent on the Jaina belief, which is greater than that of the other Indian sects, in the efficacy of temple-building as a means of salvation that their architectural performances bear so much larger a proportion to their members than is the case with other sects.

In the first place they possess picturesqueness in a great degree. They love to construct their sanctuaries on the slopes of woody or naked hills, in wild places with boundless scope for decoration. The mountain masses of Girnār and Śatruñjaya, which rise abruptly to a height of three or four thousand feet above the plains, have veritable cities of temples on their tops. The grouping together of their temples into what may be called "cities of temples" is a peculiarity which the Jainas have practised to a greater extent than the followers of any other religion in India.[2] "Specially on the summit of Śatruñjaya on every side sculptured chapels gorgeous in gold and colour stand silent and open; within are saints sitting grave and passionless behind the lights that burn on their altars. The multitude of calm stone faces, the strange silence and emptiness, unaccompanied by any sign of neglect or decay, the bewildering repetition of shrines and deities in this aerial castle, suggest nothing built with human purpose but some petrified spirit world."[3]

---

1. Guérinot, *La Religion Djaina*, p. 279.
2. Fergusson, *History of Indian and Eastern Architecture*, II., p. 24. Cf. Smith, *A History of Fine Art in India and Ceylon*, p. 11.
3. Elliot, *Hinduism and Buddhism*, I., p. 121.

ecclesiastical head of the neighbouring place on *saṁvatsarīka* — the last and the holiest of their eight-day festival of fasts; but all these distinctive traditions of Jaina aesthetics belong to the period of Jaina or Mediaeval Gujarat painting which begins from the twelfth century AD.[1]

Coming to the architectural and sculptural remains of the Jainas belonging to our period we find that our main sources lie in the Jaina caves on the Udayagiri and Khaṇḍagiri Hills in Orissa, on Mount Girnār in Junāgaḍh, and in the sculptural remains at the Kaṅkālī-Ṭīlā and other mounds in Mathurā. However, before we proceed any further we shall make a few preliminary remarks bearing on certain characteristics of Indian art in general.

The first thing that should be borne in mind is that a sectarian classification of Indian art in general, as Fergusson has assumed, is rather defective. Really speaking, there are no Buddhist, Jaina or Brāhmanical styles of architecture or sculpture, but only Buddhist, Jaina and Brāhmanical remains in the Indian style of their period.[2] It is the provincial variations in its formal development, existing side by side with the secular variations in pure style, that tempt us to a sectarian classification of Indian art, but it is not correct.[3] No doubt, as we shall see later on, the varying practical require-ments of the cult of each religion, of course, have an effect on the nature of the structure required for particular purposes, but otherwise "works of art, including architecture, should be classified with regard to their age and geographical position, not according to the creed for the service of which they were designed."[4]

Thus there is no such thing, for example, as a Jaina style of architecture or sculpture. This becomes quite evident from the fact that the principal sculptures of both the Bauddhas and the Jainas are so nearly identical that it is not

1. Cf. Mehta, *Studies in Indian Painting*, pp. 1-2 ; Percy Brown, *Indian Painting*, pp. 38, 51.
2. "Bühler has emphasised the lesson taught by the Mathura discoveries that Indian art was not sectarian. All religions — Buddhist, Jaina and Brāhmanical — used the art of their age and country, and all alike drew on a common storehouse of symbolic and conventional devices. *Stūpas*, sacred trees, railings, wheels and so forth were available equally to the Jaina, Buddhist, or orthodox Hindu as religious or decorative elements." — Smith, *The Jaina Stūpa and other Antiquities of Mathura*, Int., p. 6. Cf. Bühler, *E.I.*, II., p. 322.
3. Cf. Coomaraswamy, *History of Indian and Indonesian Art*, p. 106. "But, although nearly all Indian art is religious, it is a mistake to suppose that style was dependent on creed. Fergusson's classical *History of Indian Architecture* is grievously marred by the erroneous assumption that distinct Buddhist, Jaina and Hindu styles existed." — Smith, *A History of Fine Art in India and Ceylon*, p. 9.
4. Ibid.

always easy for the casual observer to distinguish what belongs to the one and what to the other, and it requires some experience to do this readily.[1]

The other point of importance for a student of Indian art is that although almost all Hindu art is religious,[2] to the Hindus religious, aesthetic and scientific standpoints are not necessarily conflicting, and in all their finest work, whether musical, literary or plastic, these points of view, nowadays so sharply distinguished, are inseparably united. No doubt it remains to be seen whether this limitation or discipline serves as a source of power or makes it the slave of a didactic purpose, but nevertheless, though religious story, symbolism or history may serve to move the artist to action, they cannot alone suffice to guide his hand. The moment he has commenced to work art will step in and take the reins of genius from all three. This is why the "fiery religious zeal of Renaissant Italy with all her pictorial symbols does not seem to have deterred her artists from becoming better painters than preachers, true to their kind as decorators rather than as missionaries; so that Signorelli could not help himself from utilising his sacred themes as vehicles chiefly for his discoveries in the art of drawing from the life; and the admirers of Fra Bartolommeo sadly removed from the church wall his masterly but too alluring St. Sebastian!"[3]

With these few introductory remarks about Indian art in general we now come to the particular remains of the Jainas. Of these the first to strike our notice are the caves of Orissa, which are amongst the most interesting, though at the same time the most anomalous, of the caves in India. That most of them are Jaina caves goes without saying. In our chapter entitled "Jainism in Kaliṅga Deśa" we have referred to the images of *tīrthaṅkaras* found in these caves and to the prominence given to Pārśva, whether among these images or by the use of his symbol, the serpent-hood. On examining the caves, however, no remains are found which could be clearly attributable to Buddhism: no

---

1. "The *Stūpas* of the Jainas were indistinguishable in form from those of the Buddhists, and a Jaina curvilinear steeple is identical in outline with that of a Brāhmanical temple." — Ibid. ". . . even highly educated people are not able to distinguish the one class of images from the other." — Rao, *Elements of Hindu Iconography*, I., pt. I., p. 220.
2. Cf. Coomaraswamy, *The Arts and Crafts of India and Ceylon*, p. 16. "(an Image made) according to rule (*śāstra*) is beautiful, no other forsmooth is beautiful ; some (deem) that beautiful which follows after (their own) fancy, but that not according to rule (appears) unlovely to the discerning." — Ibid. "The Hindus always present an aesthetic principle in the guise of a religious precept." — Smith, op. cit., p. 8.
3. Solomon, *The Charm of Indian Art*, pp. 86-87.

dāgoba, no Buddha or *bodhisattva*, no scene distinctly traceable to Buddhist legends. *Triśūla*s open or pointed, *stūpa, svastika*s, barred railings, railed trees, wheels, the goddess Śrī are found, but they are as common to Jainism as to other religions.[1] Furthermore this is a fact generally accepted by competent scholars, antiquarians and archaeologists like O'Malley,[2] Mon Mohan Chakravarti,[3] Bloch,[4] Fergusson,[5] Smith,[6] Coomaraswamy[7] and others.

Thus the oldest extant Jaina sculptures show that, like the other sects, Jainas also excavated cave-dwellings or *bhikṣugṛha*s for their recluses, but the practical requirements of their cult had an effect on the nature of the structure adopted by them. As a general convention Jaina monks did not live in large communities, and this combined with the nature of their religion did not necessitate them to have large assembly halls like the *caitya*s of the Buddhists. As seen before, the oldest and the most numerous of these earliest caves of the Jaina sects are in the hill on the east called Udayagiri; the modern in the western portion designated Khaṇḍgagiri. "The picturesqueness of their forms, the character of their sculptures and architectural details, combined with their great antiquity, render them one of the most deserving of a careful survey."[8]

If not from the architectural at least from the archaeological point of view the first to arrest our notice among the Udayagiri caves is the Hāthīgumphā cave, a great natural cavern, the brow of which must have been smoothed to admit of the inscription. As to the inscription, it has been already dealt with at length by us. Though as it stands now there is very little of architectural importance left in it, this much is certain — that in spite of its being a natural cavern, looking to the importance of the record the Hāthīgumphā must have been an excavation of no mean consideration. This is because the predilection for cutting temples or caves in the rock is

1. Cf. Chakravarti (Mon Mohan), op. cit., p. 5 ; Fergusson, op. cit., p. 11.
2. O'Malley, *B.D.G.P.*, p. 266.
3. "After having examined the caves carefully during my visits I have come to the conclusion that all the caves, so far as the present data are available, should be ascribed to the Jainas and not to the Buddhists." — Chakravarti (Mon Mohan), op. and loc. cit.
4. "That the caves contain nothing Buddhist, but apparently all belong to the Jainas, is a fact which is now, I think, generally . . . accepted by all competent scholars." — Cf. ibid., p. 20.
5. "Till comparatively recently, however, they were mistaken for Buddhist, but this they clearly never were." — Fergusson, op. cit., I., p. 177.
6. Cf. Smith, op. cit., p. 84.
7. Cf. Coomaraswamy, *History of Indian and Indonesian Art*, p. 37.
8. Fergusson, op. cit., II., p. 9.

to be found in the great desire for lasting merit; which the solid rock offers over a structural edifice; the merit gained by the work would last as long as the work. Moreover, the fact that the Hāthīgumphā cave was enlarged and improved by art gains further strength from the fact that as a general rule cave-cutters selected cliffs where the rock was solid and free from cracks and fissures, and not natural caverns, to facilitate their work. This is because a natural cavern means rotten rock, where fragments may drop at any time, and so make living within them dangerous.

As mentioned before, from the artistic point of view the greatest interest lies in the Rānī and the Gaṇeśa caves on the Udayagiri Hill. Both of them are two-storeyed caves with friezes, interrupted by the cell doorways, in both the upper and lower galleries. Of the two the Rānī is the largest and best decorated of all the caves,[1] and in it elaborately carved friezes represent various scenes of human activities. As to the scenes portrayed in these sculptures and those, more or less, repeated in the Gaṇeśa cave, the *District Gazetteer* and reputed scholars like Chakravarti and others are of opinion that they relate to various incidents, legendary or otherwise, of Pārśva's life. We have referred to this fact before, and have also touched a little in detail upon the subject-matter of these friezes.

As to the sculpture of these early Jaina remains we find that, like the Mathurā specimens which are to follow, there is here also a strange mixture of Greek and Indian elements in the dress of male and female figures, as well as in the draperies. This becomes confirmed in itself since the Yavanas were very much advanced during the centuries before the Christian era, and that Khāravela of the Hāthīgumphā inscription had his share in forcing the great Indo-Greek king, Demetrios, to retreat from India. Moreover the figures in these scenes are cut in bold relief, as at Mathurā, and the women here too wear very thick ring anklets. This characteristic of the Orissa and other Jaina remains rightly emphasizes the truth of the statement that "the interchange of ornamental motifs between the peoples of the earth must have been in progress since man first consciously produced decorative forms, and it is a psychological truth that such borrowed motifs invariably became modified in the process of application by the borrower. The extension of such borrowing and modification is endless, and motifs

1. Cf. Coomaraswamy, op. cit., p. 38.

XVI : Part of a frieze from the Gaṇeśagumphā, Udayagiri.
(from Mitra, *The Antiquities of Orissa*)

XVII : Portion of a frieze in the upper verandah of the Rānigumphā, Udayagiri. (from Mitra, *The Antiquities of Orissa*)

XVIII : Ancient Jaina brick *Stūpa* excavated, Mathurā.
(Copyright: Archaeological Survey of India)

frequently return to their earlier traces extraordinarily transformed — sometimes almost beyond recognition."[1]

Besides this fact of the introduction of foreign elements in the realm of Jaina or Indian art of the pre-Gāndhāra period we are of opinion that in this early Jaina sculpture there is a singular charm. Over and above its wealth of ornaments and skill in technique it is instinct with a remarkable freshness of feeling and wholesome joy of life, which ultimately breaks out into scenes of broad humour. These bas-reliefs, among other scenes of human activities, represent those of hunting, fighting, dancing, drinking and love-making, and, according to Fergusson, "anything, in fact, but religion or praying in any shape or form."[2] This warmth of healthy humanity is characteristic of all the best Buddhist and Jaina art, and was only partly repressed by the classic reserve of the Gāndhāra school, which next appears on the scene.

Space forbids any further discussion about the Jaina remains at Orissa. However two particular aspects of the Jaina contribution to art may be mentioned here before we pass on to the Mathurā remains. The first is the institution of relic worship in the form of *stūpa*s, and the second that of idolatry among the Jainas. As mentioned before, from the fourteenth line of the Hāthīgumphā inscription we learn that even prior to the age of the Mathurā sculptures — as with the Buddhists so also with the Jainas — was prevalent the practice of erecting monuments or *stūpa*s on the remains of their teachers. "Doubtless the oldest *stūpa*s were not symbols of a religious cult, but memorials of the dead associated with the practice of burial instead of cremation."[3] It may be that this line of worship was not so common with the Jainas as with the Buddhas, and it is certain that it was out of date after a short span of its popularity; but from the Vodva *stūpa* from Mathurā, which, as seen before, was built by the gods, we can affirm this much — that *stūpa*-worship with the Jainas also had reached a definite stage.

The chief ground for such an assertion is that "*Stūpa*s were, originally, great mounds of earth raised over the ashes of a chief or religious leader, and surrounded by wooden rails to protect them. Later they were built in brick or stone with an earthen core, a stone railing taking the place of a wooden one."[4] That the Vodva and other *stūpas* at Mathurā do not resemble

1. Andrews, *Influences of Indian Art*, Int., p. 11.
2. Fergusson, op. cit., p. 15.
3. Havell, *Ancient and Mediaeval Architecture of India*, p. 46.
4. Cousens, *Architectural Antiquities of Western India*, p. 8.

stūpa architecture in its primitive form is clear on the very face of it. We find in them a stone railing taking the place of a wooden one, and besides this a lavish decoration applied to the exterior.

The second point that we are to consider now is the iconography of the Jainas. From the Hāthīgumphā inscription we have seen that the Jainas used to have images of their Jinas as far back as the days of the Nandas. This is partially confirmed by the Mathurā remains that the Jainas of the Indo-Scythic period used for their sculptures materials from an old temple. In accordance with Smith this state of facts shows indeed at least this much, that there was a Jaina temple in Mathurā before 150 BC.[1] Moreover from the traditional literature of the Jainas we have seen that, even in the days of Mahāvīra, Pārśva was the *tīrthaṅkara* worshipped by his father and the Jaina *saṁgha* of those days. However, we need not concern ourselves with the question as to when exactly idol-worship was taken up by the Jainas, though this much seems certain, that in one form or the other it has been prevalent from the days of Mahāvīra.

What we are immediately concerned with is the iconography of the Jainas. The proper objects of worship are the twenty-four *jina*s or *tīrthaṅkaras*, but, like the Mahāyāna Buddhists, they also allow the existence of Hindu gods, and have admitted into their sculptures at least such of them as are connected with the tales of their saints — among which are Indra or Śakra, Garuḍa, Sarasvatī, Lakṣmī, Gandharvas, Apsaras, etc., forming a pantheon of their own, divided into four classes — *Bhavanādhipati*s, *Vyantaras*, *Jyotiṣka*s and *Vaimānikas*.[2] The *tīrthaṅkara*s, as already mentioned, are recognizable by a cognizance, or *cihna*, usually placed below the image. We have seen that more than one cave in Orissa is noted for the figures of Jaina *tīrthaṅkaras*, with their characteristic symbols or *lāñchana*s, and for those of seated *jina*s carved in moderate relief. Similar statues of the Jaina *tīrthaṅkara*s are found among the Mathurā remains also, and as a class they represent the Digambara mode of representation of the Jaina *tīrthaṅkaras*.[3] Thus even historically the series of twenty-four pontiffs (*tīrthaṅkara*s), each with his

---

1. Smith, *The Jaina Stūpa and other Antiquities of Mathura*, Int., p. 3.
2. Cf. Bühler, *Indian Sect of the Jainas*, p. 66 ff.
3. Cf. Vogel, *Catalogue of the Archaeological Museum at Mathura*, p. 41. For further details about the *tīrthaṅkara* images at Mathura Museum see ibid., pp. 41-43, 66-82.

distinctive emblem, was evidently firmly believed in at the beginning of the Christian era, and even earlier.

The *tīrthaṅkaras* are generally represented seated in the same cross-legged attitude as Buddha, with the same stolid, contemplative expression of countenance. If the dancing figures in both the Orissa and Mathurā sculptures stand for evolution, the everlasting becoming, the *yogī* type of seated *jina* is an equally dramatic image of withdrawal, of complete independence of evolution. It is well to remember that this does not represent any sort of mortification of the flesh; it is simply the position which has been adopted by Indian thinkers from time immemorial as most convenient for meditation. It need not also be considered as expressionless because it does not reflect the individual peculiarities which make up expression as we commonly conceive it. On the other hand, in the opinion of Rothenstein the plastic interpretation of *samādhi*, or religious absorption, forms one of the supreme conceptions in the history of art which the world owes to the genius of India. "This concrete crystallisation of a spiritual mood," observes the learned scholar, "was developed into a form so perfect and inevitable that it remains, after more than 2000 years, one of the most inspiring and satisfying symbols erected by man."[1]

Coming to the Jaina remains in Mathurā, a city of immemorial antiquity, it may be said that they were excavated from or near the Kaṅkālī or Jainī mound (Ṭīlā), about half-a-mile south of the Kaṭrā. The importance of this school in the history of Indian art lies as a link between old Indian and mediaeval sculpture and its close affinity with the Gāndhāra school, so-called because its centre was in the region of Gāndhāra, the north-western frontier, and most of its finest creations have been found there. "Geographically," observes Smith, "Mathura occupies a central position intermediate between Gandhāra to the north-west, Amarāvatī to the south-east, and Sārnāth to the east. It is therefore not surprising that the local school of art should display intermediate characters, linking it on the one hand with the Hellenistic art of Gandhāra, and on the other with the purely Indian schools of the interior."[2] This Gāndhāra-Mathurā school seems to have sprung up in the

---

1. Rothenstein, *Examples of Indian Sculpture*, Int., p. 8.
2. Smith, *History of Fine Art in India and Ceylon*, p. 133. Cf. Vogel, op. cit., p. 19.

first century BC, and flourished in full maturity between AD 50 and 200.[1] It arose from the adoption of the Hellenistic models to the older art of India, which gradually assimilated to its own spirit.

"The phrase "Gāndhāra school,"" observes Dr. Barnett, "is a collective term denoting the labours of many artists working in various materials through several generations with a considerable variety of technique. Sometimes they blindly copied Hellenistic models, with the dubious success due to clever imitation. Usually, however, they did more: together with the figures, draperies, and motives which they borrowed from Hellenism they imported a spirit of Greek refinement and dignity, of beauty and harmony, which raised the forms of the older art to a nobler level, without weakening its sincerity and humanity."[2]

This introduction of foreign elements into the art of India and the extension of Indian taste abroad are a natural outcome of the political and commercial intercourse which India had with the world outside. This is why the geographical India of today includes the homes of numerous races whose ideals of art, as of religion, are far from being identical, and who, being in many cases immigrant even down to late historical times, have introduced foreign elements of decorative art, which, like the immigrants themselves, have become naturalized and have also acquired a local patina. However, according to Andrews, on climatic and other grounds hardly any interesting facts concerning art matters can be gleaned from the lands most affected by contact with India, and hence "most of our knowledge of the Arts has to be compiled from the internal evidence of such objects as have survived the destructive forces of climate and fanaticism."[3]

With these few preliminary remarks about the Mathurā school in general we shall now study some specimens of Jaina sculpture found at the Kaṅkālī mound, and shall see how far Jaina artists were governed by the immutable law of the undisputed obedience which Art exacts from her votaries, and how far they succeeded in bringing about a healthy assimilation of Hellenistic elements.

Of the few specimens of Mathurā sculptures which we are to describe here we shall take first the very interesting and beautiful works technically known as *āyāgapaṭṭas*. "An *Āyāgapaṭṭa*," observes Dr. Bühler, "is an ornamental

1. "This culmination of the art of the school may be dated from about AD 50 to 150 or 200." — Smith, op. cit., p. 99.
2. Barnett, *Antiquities of India*, p. 253.
3. Andrews, op. cit., Int., p. 12.

slab, bearing the representation of a *jina* or some other object of worship, and the term may be appropriately rendered by "tablet of homage or of worship," since such slabs were put up in temples, as the numerous inscriptions on them say, "for the worship of the Arhats.". . . Among the Jainas they probably went out of fashion at an early period, as the inscriptions on them invariably show archaic characters, and are in no case known to be dated."[1]

The *āyāgapaṭṭa*s seem to be not the exclusive but a prominent feature of the ancient Jaina art. As usual, the aim that the Jaina sculpture had in view in these highly decorated tablets "was not the independent creation of beauty. Their art was the dependent art of the decorator of architectural monuments."[2] Nevertheless there is nothing strange if the central disc of the *yogī* type of seated *jina*, the highly ornamental *triśūla*s, accompanied by a great variety of sacred symbols, the exquisite curvilinear ornaments, and the massive pillars in the Persian-Achaemenian style were to prejudice the art-loving visitor so as not to easily believe that symbolism was a prime motive of Mathurā's sculptures in their handling of their chisels upon these "tablets of Worship." On the other hand, at least with regard to these *āyāgapaṭṭa*s, one may go even a step further and assert they showed their supremacy in the vitality and independence of their creations, and thus being enthusiastic artists themselves they must have often utilized religious themes as an excuse for, rather than as, the end and aim of their productions.

Of these, two *āyāgapaṭṭa*s may be mentioned here — the one set up by Śivayaśā, the wife of the dancer Phaguyaśa,[3] and the other by Āmohinī, as mentioned before, of the year 42 of the Lord, the Mahākṣatrapa Śoḍāsa. The first composition, in the words of Smith, "gives an interesting view of a Jaina *Stūpa*, which was surrounded by a perambulation path guarded by a railing. The path is approached through a highly decorated *Toraṇa* gateway, to which four steps ascend. A heavy wreath hangs from the lowest beam of the gateway. A dancing girl completely nude except for a sash of the usual jewellery round the hips stands in an immodest attitude on the railing on each side of the gate. Two massive pillars with peculiar bases are shown, and a small portion of the railing surrounding an upper perambulation path is visible."[4]

1. Bühler, *E.I.*, II., p. 314.
2. Chanda, *A.S.I.*, 1922-23, p. 166.
3. Cf. Bühler, op. cit., No. V., p. 200.
4. Smith, *The Jaina Stūpa and other Antiquities of Mathura*, p. 19, Plate XII.

On this beautifully carved *toraṇa* there is a brief dedication, and according to Smith the characters of this inscription are "little more archaic than those of Dhanabhūti's inscriptions on the gateway of the Bharhut *Stūpa*, dated in the reign of the Suṅgas, or about 150 BC."[1] Dr. Bühler also has grouped it under the name of "archaic," but he limits himself to the remark that it belongs to the period before Kaṇiṣka.[2] As to the artistic merits of this *āyāgapaṭṭa* one need not be guided by mere sentiment. There are tests more universal than those of particular canons or personal likes and dislikes. To Vincent Smith the attitude of the two female figures represented here seems immodest. Likewise the female statues appearing on some railings elsewhere are also considered by him indecently naked.[3] It seems, in cases such as these, it is the immediate or apparent subject-matter — the representative element — which gives vent to personal likes and dislikes, and the meaning of art no more remains for us far deeper than that of its immediate subject.

As it is, the female figures both in the *āyāgapaṭṭa* of Śivayaśā and on some railing pillars, either standing on crouching grotesque dwarfs or in some other pose, are not to incite good or bad actions, since nearly all art which has any conscious purpose is sentimental. The true ethical value of art appears in its quality of detachment and vision. The light in which the ancient Indian artists envisaged woman was serene, frank and generous. The thick ring anklets, the light wisp of drapery, the heavy ear ornaments, armlets, necklace and girdle enrich but do not conceal the all-conquering and triumphant nudity. There exists not a trace either of immodesty or the diffidence of false shame in this arborean beauty. Within no mean or narrow compass but in the palace of their souls did the artists at Mathurā, as at Sāñcī and elsewhere, enshrine woman, and so they enskied her image — the immortal symbol of all beauty — stamped, as was fitting, in everlasting stone, and outlined against the blue-black ground of heaven.

Coming to the tablet of homage set up by Āmohinī, Smith observes : "This fine votive tablet, which is essentially an *Āyāgapata*, though not so

1. Smith, *The Jaina Stūpa and other Antiquities of Mathura*, Int., p. 3.
2. Bühler, op. cit., p. 196.
3. According to Coomaraswamy these female figures are not dancing girls, as Smith has observed. In his opinion "they are *Yakṣīs*, *Devatās* or *Vṛkṣakas*, nymphs and dryads, and to be regarded as auspicious emblems of vegetative fertility, derived from popular beliefs." — Coomaraswamy, op. cit., p. 64. Cf. Vogel, *A.S.I.*, 1909-10, p. 77.

called, represents a royal lady attended by three women and a child. The attendant women, in accordance with the ancient Hindu fashion, which survived to modern times in southern India, are naked to the waist. One holds an umbrella over her mistress, whom another fans. The third holds a wreath (*hār*) ready for presentation. The execution is bold, and not altogether wanting in artistic merit."[1]

Next to these *āyāgapaṭṭas* we may mention the sculpture connected with the Vodva *stūpa* built by the gods. The sacred symbol in the centre of the composition consists of a *dharmacakra* supported by a *triśūla*, which itself rests on a lotus. The *dharmacakra*, or the Wheel of the Law, as the emblem of their respective creeds, is common to all three sects — the Jainas, the brāhmaṇas and the Bauddhas.[2] The particular *cakra* that appears here "differs from those on the Buddhist and other Jaina sculptures by the two earlike projections at the top, as well as by the addition of two śaṅkhas, which lean against the basis."[3] The group of worshippers on the right of the picture is formed of four female figures holding garlands in their hands, wherewith they evidently intend to worship the *arhat* mentioned in the inscription. Each of the first three figures holds up in her right hand a long-stalked lotus flower, while the fourth one, which looks smaller and apparently much younger, clasps her hands in an attitude of adoration, and is partly hidden behind the stiff Assyrian-looking lion which crouches at the end of the slab. According to Dr. Bühler the faces of these females look like portraits,[4] and their dress, which is a bit peculiar, consists of a single long robe covering the whole body to the feet and confined at the waist.

There is some difficulty about the mutilated portion of the slab. The male figure on the right of the *dharmacakra* is considered by Dr. Bühler to be that of a "naked ascetic, who, as usual, has a piece of cloth hanging over his right arm. This is probably the Arhat mentioned in the inscription."[5] It is

---

1. Smith, op. cit., p. 21, Plate XIV.
2. ". . . it would be surprising if the worship of *Stūpas*, of sacred trees, of the Wheel of the Law, and so forth, more or less distinct traces of which are found with all sects, as well as their representations in sculptures, were due to one sect alone instead of being heirlooms handed down from remote times before the beginning of the historical period of India." — Bühler, op. cit., p. 323.
2. Ibid., p. 321. For a specimen of Buddhist sculpture see Fergusson, *Tree and Serpent Worship*, Plate XXIX, Fig. 2.
3. Bühler, op. and loc. cit.
5. Ibid.

difficult to say if this is a naked figure of an ascetic. According to Smith it is one of the four male worshippers who have formed the other side of the slab.[1] In our opinion, too, Smith's view seems to be more acceptable, because then the whole sculpture would be representing a group of male and female lay-worshippers preparing for the homage of the *arhat* mentioned in the record.

The importance of this specimen of Mathurā sculpture lies in this, that it is connected with the Vodva *stūpa* built by the gods. We have already referred to the significance of the words "built by the gods." It must have been built several centuries before the beginning of the Christian era, for the name of its builder would assuredly have been known if it had been erected during the period when the Jainas of Mathurā carefully kept record of their donations. The Jaina tradition about it, as reproduced by Smith, runs as follows : "The *Stūpa* was originally of gold, adorned with precious stones, and was erected in honour of the seventh Jina, Supārśvanātha, by the goddess Kuberā, at the desire of two ascetics named Dharmaruci and Dharmaghosha. In the time of the twenty-third Jina, Pārśvanātha, the golden *Stūpa* was encased in bricks, and a stone temple was built outside."[2]

Besides these few specimens of Mathurā sculpture we may mention the *toraṇa*, showing the veneration of holy objects and places by human and mythological beings. The artist in these *toraṇa*s does not want to illustrate any particular text or legend, but merely wishes to show how eager gods and men are to pay homage to the *tīrthaṅkaras*, to their *stūpa*s and temples. This is why the scenes refer to the worship of one or several Jaina sanctuaries and to processions of pilgrimages undertaken for this purpose.

Amongst these sculptures is one which apparently possesses very considerable archaeological interest. It is a *toraṇa* bearing a relief which represents the worship of a *stūpa* by two *suparṇa*s — half birds and half men — and by five centaurs or *kinnara*s. All the five figures wear turbans, such as many males of rank represented on Buddhist sculptures wear. "A somewhat similar scene," observes Bühler, "where *Suparṇas* worship a *Stūpa* occurs on a rilievo at Sānchi.[3] But it must be noted that the Sānchi figures are much more

1. Smith, op. cit., p. 12.
2. Ibid., p. 15.
3. Cf. Fergusson, op. cit., Plate XXVII, Fig. 1.

XIX : Ayāgapata, or "Tablet of Homage", Mathura.

XXI : *Āyāgapaṭṭa* with Jina, Mathurā: first Century AD.
(Copyright: Archaeological Survey of India)

XXII : Votive Tablet set-up by Āmohini.
(Copyright: Archaeological Survey of India)

XXIII : Railing pillars with human figures (Mathurā).
(Copyright: Archaeological Survey of India)

XXIV : Sculpture connected with the Vodva *Stūpa*, "Built by the Gods"
(Copyright: Archaeological Survey of India)

XXV : Obverse and reverse of a *Toraṇa*, representing Gods and men paying homage to *Tīrthaṅkaras*.

(Copyright: Archaeological Survey of India)

XXVI : Obverse and reverse of a *Toraṇa*, Mathurā.
(Copyright: Archaeological Survey of India)

XXVII : Ornamental slab representing female dancers and musician rejoicing at Nemeṣa's feat.

XXVIII : Four mutilated statues representing the transfer of Mahāvīra's embryo

like Greek harpies, while those on our slab are done in a more conventional manner, like the winged figures on the Assyrian and Persian sculptures. Among Brāhmanical representations those of *Garuḍa*, the king of *Suparṇas*, on the Gupta seals[1] are worthy of comparison. Centaurs have been discovered on the Buddhist monuments in Gayā and elsewhere, and in all probability they go back to Greek models. What is particularly remarkable in those on our slab is the branch which hides the place where the human body is united with the rump of the horse.[2] As far as I have been able to ascertain from my colleagues versed in classical archaeology there are no Greek sculptures showing this particular."[3]

As to the figures on its reverse, the *toraṇa* beam retains a fragment of a procession, apparently about to visit some sacred place. The cart closely resembles a modern *Shighrām*, and the driver, who lifts his goad, is seated, as is still the custom, on the pole. The trappings of the several animals are exactly like those represented on the Sāñcī sculptures. But similar carts are not traceable on the latter, where very Greek-looking chariots[4] drawn by horses appear instead.[5]

Taking last the ornamental slab, the obverse of which represents Nemeṣa's feat of transferring the embryo of Mahāvīra, and the reverse showing female dancers and musicians rejoicing at the great feat, once again we realize that the religious stories and moral lessons which the Indian artist was employed to advertise did not interfere with his freedom to perfection. The Mathurā carver seems to have succeeded in creating the most satisfying aesthetic forms precisely at the periods when their services were in the greatest request for purposes of propaganda among the priestly and royal patrons. Especially when he was employed to illustrate some well-known story or legend he could, to an unusual degree, use traditional canons of proportion and gesture, and reconcile these with a daemonic energy.

Besides this slab representing the popular tradition of the transfer of Mahāvīra's embryo there are four mutilated statues lithographed by Cunningham. Two of these figures represent seated females. Each of them

1. Cf. Fleet, *C.I.I.*, III., Plate XXXVII ; Smith, *J.A.S.B.*, LVIII., p. 85 ff., Plate VI.
2. "No other example is known of a leaf being used to mask the junction between the human and equine bodies in the centaurs." — Smith, *History of Fine Art in India and Ceylon*, p. 82.
3. Bühler, op. cit., p. 319.
4. Fergusson, op. cit., Plate XXXIII ; ibid., Plate XXXIV, Fig. 1.
5. Bühler, op. and loc. cit.

has a small child lying in a dish on her lap. The left hand supports the dish, but the right is raised up to the shoulder. Both females appear to be naked. The other to figures are those of Naigameṣa, and rightly are they "goat-headed," according to Dr. Bühler, as also the figure in the other sculpture. Comparing this slab[1] with that of the four figures of Cunningham[2] the eminent Orientalist observes : "The very close resemblance of the position of the infant, and the attitude of the female holding it, is at once apparent. And this point, taken together with the unmistakable figure of Naigamesha-Nemeso, irresistibly leads to the conclusion that the legend referred to must be the same in both cases."[3]

In fact, the cave temples and dwellings excavated in Orissa and at Junāgaḍh or Girnār in Gujarat, with their elaborately carved friezes and finished to the minutest detail and ornament, and the richly decorated *āyāgapaṭṭa*s and *toraṇa*s of the Mathurā find, stand before us not as remains but as living oracles of art. They combine in them the Triune Entity of Indian art — a sublime union of the purely Decorative, the Realistic and the purely Spiritual. This is felt rather than seen; for the differences between the one and the other are to be found, not in the fields of artistic knowledge, however wide, but in the *terra incognita* of taste.

1. Bühler, op. cit., Plate II, a.
2. Cunningham, *A.S.I.*, XX., Plate IV.
3. Bühler, op. cit., p. 318.

Conclusion

IF nothing succeeds like success, the great triumph of Jainism in holding its own against its numerous rivals in the north discredits the view that Jainism, like Buddhism, did not strike deep roots in north India, and that there was nothing like a Jaina period in the history of India.[1] With all deference to the scholars who maintain such views, we venture to believe that the study of Jainism in north India attempted in the foregoing pages, inadequate as it is in many ways, is sufficient evidence to the contrary. Whatever may be the antiquity of Jainism in north India, no one can deny that there is enough conclusive evidence to the effect that, at least from the days of Pārśva or from 800 BC down to the conversion of the great Vikrama by Siddhasena Divākara in the beginning of the Christian era, and to some extent even throughout the Kuṣāṇa and the Gupta periods, Jainism was the most powerful religion in the north. During this glorious period of more than a thousand years there was not a single dynasty in the north, whether great or small, that did not come under its influence at one time or another.

Leaving aside a few points of historical importance here and there, almost every chapter in the present work deals with matters about which long researches have been made, and various opinions have been recorded. Thus, more or less, ours has been a humble attempt to string together, in methodical order, the results of the labours of able scholars, in order to produce a readable work on the unrecorded period of Jaina history — and not to compose an elaborate work of discussions on Jaina antiquities. In fulfilment of this any betrayal into conjectures and suppositions should be accepted as such, and not as historical discoveries. As far as possible details have been suppressed; nevertheless repetition has not been avoided where such repetition seemed necessary to bring out cardinal facts and salient features of this period of north Indian Jainism, which happily coincides with the hey-day of its powers.

However, until the numerous Jaina inscriptions and manuscripts which exist everywhere in the north are collected and translated, and until plans

1. Cf. Smith, *Oxford History of India*, p. 55.

are made of the architectural remains and statistics gathered, it is idle to speculate either about the extent and strength of Jainism in the north or about its vicissitudes during its existence there. It is a task worthy of being attempted, for, if successfully carried out, it would add to our scanty stores of knowledge one of the most interesting chapters still available for the religious and artistic history of the people of India.

General Bibliography

Sources

I. *Archaeological and Epigraphical*

Allan, John, *Catalogue of the Coins of the Gupta Dynasties and of Śaśāṅka, King of Gauḍa*, London, 1914.

Annual Report of the Mysore Archaeological Department for the Year 1923, p. 10 ff, Bangalore, 1924.

Banerji, R.D., Inscriptions in the Udayagiri and Khaṇḍagiri Caves, *E.I.*, XIII., 1915-1916, p. 159ff.

Banerji, R.D., Note on the Hāthīgumphā Inscription of Khāravela, *J.B.O.R.S.*, III., 1917, p. 486 ff.

Beglar, J.D., Tours in the South-Eastern Provinces, *A.S.I.*, XIII., 1882.

Bhagwanlal Indraji, Pandit, The Hāthīgumphā and three other Inscriptions in the Udayagiri Caves near Cuttack, *Actes du Sixième Congrès International des Orientalistes*, Troisième Partie, Section 2, Aryenne, Liede, 1885, p. 133 ff.

Bhagwanlal Indraji, Pandit, The Kahāuṅ Inscription of Skandagupta, *I.A.*, X., 1881, p. 125 ff.

Bhandarkar, R.G., On Dr Hoernle's Version of a Nasik Inscription and the *Gāthā* Dialect, *I.A.*, XII., 1883, p. 139 ff.

Bloch, T., Conservation in Bengal, *A.S.I.*, 1902-1903, 1904, p. 37 ff.

Bühler, G., New Jaina Inscriptions from Mathura, *E.I.*, I., 1892, p. 371 ff.

Bühler, G., Further Jaina Inscriptions from Mathura, *E.I.*, I., 1892, p. 393 ff.

Bühler, G., Further Jaina Inscriptions from Mathura, *E.I.*, II., 1894, p. 195 ff.

Bühler, G., The Nānāghāṭ Inscriptions, *A.S.W.I.*, V., 1883, p. 59 ff.

Bühler, G., Aśoka's Rock Edicts according to the Girnār, Shāhbāzgarhī, Kālsī and Mansehra Versions, *E.I.*, II., 1894, p. 447 ff.

Bühler, G., The Pillar Edicts of Aśoka, *E.I.*, II., 1894, p. 245 ff.

Bühler, G., The Three New Edicts of Aśoka, *I.A.*, VII., 1878, p. 141 ff.

Bühler, G., Indische Palaeographie, *Encyclopaedia of Indo-Aryan Research*, p. 1 ff.

Bühler, G., Specimens of Jaina Sculptures from Mathura, *E.I.*, II., 1894, p. 311 ff.

Bühler, G., The Barābar and Nāgārjunī Hill Cave Inscriptions of Aśoka and Daśaratha, *I.A.*, XX., 1891, p. 361 ff.

Bühler, G., The Madhuban Copper-Plate of Harsha, dated Saṁvat 25, *E.I.*, I., 1892, p. 67 ff.

Bühler, G., The Jaina Inscriptions from Śatruñjaya, *E.I.*, II., 1894, p. 34 ff.

Burgess, James, Caves in Junāgaḍh, and elsewhere in Kāṭhiāwāḍ, *A.S.W.I.*, Kāṭhiāwāḍ and Kachh, 1874-1875, 1876, p. 139 ff.

Chakravarti, Mon Mohan, *Notes on the Remains in Dhauli and in the Caves of Udayagiri and Khaṇḍagiri*, Calcutta, 1902.

Chanda, Ramaprasad, Dates of the Votive Inscriptions on the Stūpas of Sānchi, *Memoirs of the Archaeological Survey of India*, No. 1, 1919, p. 1 ff.

Chanda, Ramaprasad, Khāravela, *J.R.A.S.*, 1919, p. 395 ff.

Chanda, Ramaprasad, The Mathura School of Sculpture, *A.S.I.*, 1922-1923, p. 164 ff.

Colebrooke, H.T., On Inscriptions at Temple of the Jaina Sect in South Bihar, *Miscellaneous Essays*, II., Madras, 1872, p. 315 ff.

Cunningham, Alexander, Inscriptions of Aśoka, *C.I.I.*, I.,1879.

Cunningham, Alexander, *A.S.I.*, 1871-1872, III., 1873.

Cunningham, Alexander, *A.S.I.*, 1878-1879, XIV., 1882.

Cunningham, Alexander, *Coins of Mediaeval India*, London, 1884.

Cunningham, Alexander, *A.S.I.*, 1881-1882, XVII., 1884.

Cunningham, Alexander, *A.S.I.*, 1882-1883, XX., 1885.

Dowson, J., Ancient Inscriptions from Mathura, *J.R.A.S.*, V., (New Series), p. 182 ff.

Fleet, J.F., Records of the Somawaṁsi Kings of Katak, *E.I.*, III., 1894-1895, p. 323 ff.

Fleet, J.F., The Hāthīgumphā Inscription, *J.R.A.S.*, 1910, p. 824 ff.

Fleet, J.F., The Rumindei Inscription and the Conversion of Aśoka to Buddhism, *J.R.A.S.*, 1908, p. 471 ff.

Fleet, J.F., Sanskrit and Old Canarese Inscriptions, *I.A.*, VII., 1878, pp. 15 ff., 33 ff., 101 ff.

Fleet, J.F., Inscriptions of the Early Gupta Kings and their Successors, *C.I.I.*, III., 1888.

Gardner, Percy, *Catalogue of Indian Coins, Greek and Scythic*, London, 1886.

Growse, F.S., Mathura Inscriptions, *I.A.*, V., 1877, p. 216 ff.

Hultzsch, E., Maliyapundi Grant of Ammarāja II, *E.I.*, IX., 1907-1908, p. 47 ff.

Hultzsch, E., Inscriptions of Aśoka, *C.I.I.*, I., (new edn.), 1925.

Hultzsch, E., Inscriptions on the Three Jaina Colossi of Southern India, *E.I.*, VII., 1902-1903, p. 108 ff.

Hultzsch, E., Two Inscriptions from General Cunningham's Archaeological Reports. *I.A.*, XI., 1882, p. 309 ff.

Jayaswal, K.P., Hāthīgumphā Inscription of the Emperor Khāravela (173-160 BC), *J.B.O.R.S.*, III., 1917, p. 425 ff.

Jayaswal, K.P., A Further Note on the Hāthīgumphā Inscription, *J.B.O.R.S.*, III., 1917, p. 473 ff.

Jayaswal, K.P., Hāthīgumphā Inscription Revised from the Rock, *J.B.O.R.S.*, IV., 1918, p. 364 ff.

Jayaswal, K.P., Hāthīgumphā Inscription of the Emperor Khāravela, *J.B.O.R.S.*, XIII., 1927, p. 221 ff.

Jayaswal, K.P., Hāthīgumphā Notes, *J.B.O.R.S.*, XIV., 1928, p. 150 ff.

Jayaswal,. K.P., An Inscription of the Suṅga Dynasty, *J.B.O.R.S.*, X., 1924, p. 202 ff.

Jayaswal, K.P., The Statue of Wema Kadaphises and Kushan Chronology, *J.B.O.R.S.* VI., 1920, p. 12 ff.

Jinavijaya, Muni, *Prācīna Jaina Lekha Saṁgraha*, I., Bhavanagar, 1917.

Konow, Sten, Epigraphy, *A.S.I.*, 1903-1906, 1909, p. 165 ff.

Konow, Sten, Taxila Inscription of the Year 136, *E.I.*, XIV., 1917-1918, p. 284 ff.

Konow, Sten, The Ara Inscription of Kanishka II: the Year 41, *E.I.*, XIV., 1917-1918, p. 130 ff.

Lüders, H., A List of Brāhmī Inscriptions from the Earliest Times to about CE 400. *E.I.*, X., 1912, Appendix 1.

Mazumdar. R.C., Hāthīgumphā Inscription, *I.A.*, XLVII., 1918, p. 223 ff.

Mazumdar R.C., Second Note on the Hāthīgumphā Inscription of Khāravela, *I.A.*, XLVIII., 1919, p. 187 ff.

Narasimachar, R., Inscriptions at Śravaṇa Beḷgoḷa, *E.C.*, II., 1923.

Prinsep, James, Note on Inscriptions at Udayagiri and Khaṇḍagiri in Cuttack, in the Lāṭ Character, *J.A.S.B.*, VI., 1837, p. 1072, ff.

Prinsep, James, Translation of Inscription in the Society's Museum — Brahmeswara Inscription, from Cuttack, *J.A.S.B.*, VII., 1838, p. 557 ff.

Prinsep, James, Facsimiles of Ancient Inscriptions, *J.A.S.B.*, VII., 1838, p. 33 ff.

Sastri, Banerji A., The Lomaśa *Ṛṣi* Cave Façade, *J.B.O.R.S.*, XII., 1926, p. 309 ff.

Senart, E., The Inscriptions of Piyadasi, *I.A.*, XX., 1891, p. 229 ff.

Smith, Vincent A., *The Jaina Stūpa and other Antiquities of Mathura*, Allahabad, 1901.

Smith, Vincent A., Inscribed Seal of Kumāra Gupta, *J.A.S.B.*, LVIII., 1889, p. 84 ff.

Vogel, J. Ph., Mathura School of Sculpture, *A.S.I.*, 1909-1910, 1914, p. 63 ff.

Vogel, J. Ph., *Catalogue of the Archaeological Museum at Mathura*, Allahabad, 1910.

Wilson, H.H., On the Rock Inscriptions of Kapur di Giri, Dhauli and Girnār, *J.R.A.S.*, XII., p. 153 ff.

II. *Literary*

The Mahābhārata, Vana Parva (Ganapat Krishnaji), Bombay, *Saka*, 1798.

Kālikācārya-Kathā (Devchand Lalbhai), Bombay, 1914.

Brahma Purāṇa (Anandasrama Series), 1895.

Abhayadevasūri, *Bhagavatī-Sūtra of Sudharma, I-III* (Āgamodaya Samiti), Bombay, 1918-1921.

Abhayadevasūri, *Aupapātika-Sūtra*, with Commentary (Āgamodaya Samiti), Bombay, 1916.

Abhayadevasūri, *Jñātā Dharma Kathāṅga of Sudharma* (Āgamodaya Samiti), Bombay, 1919.

Abhayadevasūri, *Sthānāṅga of Sudharma, II* (Āgamodaya Samiti), Bombay, 1920.

Barnett, L.D., *The Antagaḍa-Dasāo* and *Aṇuttarovavāiya-Dasāo*, London, 1907.

Bechardas, Pandit, *Bhagavatī-Sūtra of Sudharma, I, II* (Jināgama Prakāśakasabhā.) Bombay, 1918.

Belvalkar, S.K., *The Brahma-Sūtras of Bādarāyana*, Poona, 1923.

Bhandarkar, R.G., *Report on the Search for Sanskrit Manuscripts in the Bombay Presidency during the Year 1883-1884*, Bombay, 1887.

Bühler, G., The Laws of Manu, S.B.E., XXV., 1886.

Bühler, G., Vasishṭha and Baudhāyana, S.B.E., XIV., 1882.

Candraprabhasūri, *Prabhāvaka-Charita*, I., Bombay, 1909.

Candrasūri, *Saṁgrahaṇī-Sūtra*, Bombay, 1881.

Candrasūri, *Niryāvalika-Sūtra*, with Commentary (Āgamodaya Samiti), Bombay, 1922.

Chakravarti, A., *Pañcāstikāyasāra* by Kundakundācārya, S.B.J., III.,1920.

Charpentier, Jarl, *The Uttarādhyayana-Sūtra*, I., II. Upsala, 1922.

Chaturavijaya, Muni., *Kuvalayamālā-Kathā of Ratnaprabhasūri* (Jaina Ātmānanda Sabhā), Bhavanagar, 1916.

Cowell, E.B., and Gough, A.E., *Sarva-Darśana-Saṁgraha* of Mādhavācārya, (Popular edn.) London, 1914.

Cowell, E.B., and Neil, R.A., The *Divyāvadāna*, Cambridge, 1886.

Dhaneśvarasūri, *Śatruñjaya-Māhātmya*, Jamanagar, 1908.

Dharmadāsagaṇi, *Upadeśamālā*, Jaina Dharma Prasāraka Sabhā.

Dhruva, K.H. *Sāchuṅsvapna* (1st edn.), Ahmedabad, 1916.

Dvivedi, Mahamahopadhyaya Sudhakara, *The Bṛhat-Saṁhitā* of Varāhamihira, I., II. Benares, 1895.

Edgerton, Franklin, Vikrama's Adventures, I., *H.O.S.*, XXVI., Cambridge, 1926.

Fausbüll, V., *The Jātaka*, III., IV, London, 1883, 1887.

Feer, M. Léon, *Saṁyutta-Nikāya*, II, London, 1888.

Geiger, Wilhelm, The *Mahāvaṁsa*, London, 1908.

Ghosal, Sarat Chandra, *Dravyasaṁgraha of Namicandra*, S.B.J., I.,1917.

Griffith, Ralph T.H., *Hymns of the Rigveda*, II. (2nd edn.), Benares, 1897.

Guérinot, A., *Essai de Bibliographie Jaina*, Paris, 1906.

Haribhadrasūri, *Āvaśyaka-Sūtra of Sudharma* (Āgamodaya Samiti), Bombay, 1916-1917.

Haribhadrasūri, *Ṣaḍdarśanasamuccaya*, Benares, 1905.

Hemacandra, *Abhidhānacintāmaṇi*.

Hemacandra, *Triṣaṣṭi-Śalākā-Puruṣa-Caritra*, *Parvas*, IX., X. (Jaina Dharma Prasāraka Sabhā), Bhavanagar, 1908, 1909.

Hemacandra, *Yogaśāstra*, MS. No. 1315 of 1886-1892. *B.O.R.I.L.*, Poona.

Hemacandra, *Yogaśāstra*, with Commentary, Bhavanagar, 1926.

Hemacandra, *Prākṛt Vyākaraṇam* (Ed. Kripachandraji), Surat, 1919.

Hemavijayagani, *Pārśvanāthacaritram*, Benares, 1916.

Hiralal, Rai Bahadur, *Catalogue of Sanskrit and Prakrit MSS. in the Central Provinces and Berar*, Nagpur, 1926.

Hoernle, Rudolf A.F., *Uvāsaga-Dasāo*, I., II, Calcutta, 1888, 1890.

Hoernle, Rudolf A.F., Three Further *Paṭṭāvalis* of the Digambaras, *I.A.*, XXI., 1892, p. 57 ff.

Hoernle, Rudolf A.F., Two *Paṭṭāvalis* of the *Sarasvati-Gaccha* of the Digambara Jainas, *I.A.*, XX., 1891, p. 341 ff.

Jacobi, Hermann, *Sthavirāvali Carita or Pariśiṣṭaparvan of Hemacandra*, Calcutta, 1891.

Jacobi, Hermann, *Samarāicca Kahā of Haribhadra*, Calcutta, 1926.

Jacobi, Hermann, *Kalpa-Sūtra of Bhadrabāhu*, Leipzig, 1879.

Jacobi, Hermann, *The Ācārāṅga-Sūtra and the Kalpa-Sūtra*, S.B.E., XXII., 1884.

Jacobi, Hermann, *The Uttarādhyayana-Sūtra and the Sūtrakṛtāṅga Sūtra*, S.B.E., XLV., 1895.

Jacobi, Hermann, *Das Kālkācārya-Kathānakam*, Z.D.M.G., XXXIV., 1880, p. 247 ff.

Jain, Banarsi Das, *Jaina Jātakas*, Lahore, 1925.

Jaini, J.L., *Tattvārthādhigama-Sūtra* of Umāswāmi, S.B.J., II., 1920.

Jarrett, H.S., *The Āīn-i-Akbarī of Abul Fazl*, Calcutta, 1891.

Jayasiṁhasūri, *Kumārapāla-Bhūpāla-Caritra-Mahākāvya*, Bombay, 1926.

Jhaveri, Mohanlal B., *Nirvāṇa-Kalikā of Pādaliptācārya*, Bombay, 1926.

Jinabhadragaṇi, *Viśeṣāvaśyakabhāshya*, Benares, 1918.

Jolly, J., *Arthaśāstra of Kauṭilya*, Lahore, 1923.

Kern, H., *Bṛahat-Saṁhitā of Varāhamihira*, Calcutta, 1865.

Kern, H., *The Bṛahat-Saṁhitā*, or Complete System of Natural Astrology of Varāhamihira, *J.R.A.S.*, VI. (New Series), pp. 36 ff., 279 ff.

Laxmi-Vallabha, *Uttarādhyayana-Dīpikā* (Ed. Rai Dhanapatsimha), Calcutta, 1880.

Malayagiri, Ācārya, *Rājapraśnīya Upāṅga* (Āgamodaya Samiti), Bombay, 1925.

Merutuṅga, *Vicāraśreṇi*, MS. No. 378 of 1871-1872. *B.O.R.I.L.*, Poona.

Merutuṅga, *Vicāraśreṇi*, *J.S.S.*, II., 1903-1925, Appendix.

Meyer, John Jacob, *Hindu Tales*, London, 1909.

Motilal Ladhaji, *Syādvādamañjarī of Hemacandra*, Poona, 1926.

Motilal Ladhaji, *Tattvārthādhigama-Sūtra of Umāsvātivācaka* (*Sabhāṣya*), Poona, 1927.

Munibhadrasūrī, *Śāntinātha Mahākāvyam*, Benares, 1911.

Pansikar, Sastrī, *Brahmasūtra-Bhāṣya* (2nd edn.), Bombay, 1927.

Penzer, N.M., Tawney's *Somadeva's Kathā-Sarit-Sāgara*, I, London, 1924.

Peterson, P., *Report of Operations in search of Sanskrit MSS. in the Bombay Circle*, IV. (1886-1892), London, 1894.

Premi, Nathuram, *Darśanasāra of Devasena*, Bombay, 1918.

Premi, Nathuram, *Vidvadratnamālā*, I, Bombay, 1912.

Rhys Davids, T.W., Buddhist Suttas, S.B.E., XI., 1881.

Rhys Davids, T.W., Dialogues of the Buddha, I., *S.B.B.*, II., 1899, and II., *S.B.B.*, III., 1910.

Rhys Davids, T.W., and Rhys Davids, C.A.F., Dialogues of the Buddha, III., *S.B.B.*, IV., 1921.

Rhys Davids, T.W., and Oldenberg, Hermann, Vinaya Texts, I., S.B.E., XIII., 1881, and III., S.B.E., XX., 1885.

Rhys Davids, Mrs. *The Book of Kindred Sayings*, I, London, 1917.

Śākṭāyanacārya, *Strīmukti-Kevalibhukti, J.S.S.*, II., 1923-1925, Appendix II.

Śāntyācārya, *Uttarādhyayana-Śishyahitā*, Bombay, 1916.

Śilāṅkācārya, *Ācārāṅga-Sūtra of Sudharma* (Āgamodaya Samiti), Bombay, 1916.

Śilāṅkācārya, *Sūtrakṛtāṅga of Sudharma* (Āgamodaya Samiti), Bombay, 1917.

Soni, Pannalal, *Bhāvasaṁgrahadih* (Manikchandra Digambara Jaina Grantha Mālā), Bombay, *Saṁvat*.

Stevenson, The Reverend J., *The Kalpa-Sūtra and Nava Tattva*, London, 1848.

Sukhlal, Sanghvi, and Bechardas Doshi, *Sammatitarka of Siddhasena*, III, Ahmedabad, 1928.

Tawney, C.H., *Merutuṅga's Prabandhacintāmaṇi*, Calcutta, 1901.

Tawney, C.H., *The Kathākośa*, London, 1895.

Telang, Kashinath Trimbak, The *Bhagavadgītā* with the *Sanatsujatiya* and the *Anugītā*, S.B.E., VIII., 1882.

Vaidya, P.L., *Suyagaḍam*, Poona, 1928.

Vidyabhusana, Satis Chandra, *Nyāyāvatāra of Siddhasena Divākara*, Arrah, 1915.

Vinayacandrasūri, *Mallinātha Caritram*, Benares, 1912.

Vinayavijayagaṇi, *Kalpa-Sūtra, Subodhikā-Ṭīkā* (Devchand Lalbhai), Bombay, 1923.

Warren, Henry Clarke, Buddhism in Translations, *H.O.S.*, III., Cambridge, 1909.

Weber, A., Fraugment der *Bhagavatī*, Berlin, 1866.

Wilson, H.H., *Viṣṇu Purāṇa*. London, 1840.

III. *Travels, etc.*

Beal, Samuel, *Si-Yu-Ki*, I., II., London, 1906.

Beal, Samuel, *The Life of Hiuen-Tsang* (Popular edn.), London, 1914.

McCrindle, J.W., *Ancient India as described by Megasthenes and Arrian*, London, 1877.

McCrindle, J.W., *Invasion of India by Alexander the Great*, Westminster, 1893.

Sachau, Edward G., *Alberuni's India*, I., II., London, 1910.

Watters, Thomas, *On Yuan Chwang's Travels in India*, II., London, 1905.

Literature

I. *Works*

Acharya, Prasanna Kumar, *Indian Architecture according to Mānasāra-Śilpaśāstra*, Oxford, 1927.

Aiyangar, Krishnaswami, *Some Contributions of South India to Indian Culture*, Calcutta, 1923.

Aiyangar, Ramaswami, and Rao, Seshagiri, *Studies in South Indian Jainism*, Madras, 1922.

Barnett, Lionel D., *Antiquities of India*, London, 1913.

Barodia, U.D., *History and Literature of Jainism*, Bombay, 1909.

Barth, A., *The Religions of India*, London, 1882.

Belvalkar, S.K., and Ranade, R.D., *History of Indian Philosophy*, II., Poona, 1927.

Beni Prasad, *The State in Ancient India*, Allahabad, 1928.

Bhandarkar, R.G., *A Peep into the Early History of India*, Bombay, 1920.

Bird, James, *Historical Researches*, Bombay, 1847.

Brown, Percy, *Indian Painting* (Heritage of India Series), Calcutta.

Bühler, G., *On the Origin of the Indian Brahma Alphabet*, Strassburg, 1898.

Bühler, G., *The Indian Sect of the Jainas*, London, 1903.

Bühler, G., *Uber das Leben des Jaina-Mönches Hemacandra*, Wien, 1889.

Bühler, G., *Indian Studies*, No. III., Wien, 1895.

Coomaraswamy, Ananda K., *The Arts and Crafts of India and Ceylon*, London, 1913.

Coomaraswamy, Ananda K., *History of India and Indonesian Art*, London, 1927.

Cousens, Henry, *The Architectural Antiquities of Western India*, London, 1926.

Cunningham, *Ancient Geography of India* (Ed. Mazumdar), Calcutta, 1924.

Dasgupta, Surendranath, *A History of Indian Philosophy*, I., Cambridge, 1922.

Dey, Nando Lal, *The Geographical Dictionary of Ancient and Mediaeval India*, London, 1927.

Dubreuil, G. Jouveau, *Ancient History of the Deccan*, Pondicherry, 1920.

Dutt, R.C., *Ancient India*, Calcutta, 1890.

Elliot, Charles, *Hinduism and Buddhism*, I, London, 1921.

Farquhar, J.N. *An Outline of the Religious Literature of India*, Oxford, 1920.

Fergusson, James, *History of Indian and Eastern Architecture*, I, II, London, 1910.

Fergusson, James, *Tree and Serpent Worship*, London, 1868.

Fergusson, James, and Burgess, James, *The Cave Temples of India*, London, 1880.

Frazer, R.W., *A Literary History of India*, London, 1920.

Ganguly, Mano Mohan, *Orissa and her Remains — Ancient and Mediaeval*, Calcutta, 1912.

Glasenapp, Helmuth V., *Der Jainismus*, Berlin, 1925.

Guérinot, A., *La Religion Djaina*, Paris, 1926.

Havell, E.B., *The Ancient and Maediaeval Architecture of India*, London, 1915.

Hertel, J., *On the Literature of the Śvetāmbaras of Gujarat*, Leipzig, 1922.

Hiralal, H., *Ancient History of the Jaina Religion*, II, Jamanagar, 1902.

Hopkins, E.W., *The Religions of India*, London, 1910.

Jaini, Jagmandarlal, *Outlines of Jainism*, Cambridge, 1916.

Kannoomal, Lala, *The Saptabhaṅgī Naya*, Agra, 1917.

Kern, H. *Manual of Indian Buddhism*, Encyclopaedia of Indo-Aryan Research, p. 1 ff.

Kunte, N.M., *The Vicissitude of Aryan Civilization in India*, Bombay, 1880.

Latthe, A.B., *Introduction to Jainism*, Bombay, 1905.

Law, Bimala Charan, *Some Ksatriya Tribes of Ancieht India*, Calcutta, 1924.

Law, Bimala Charan, *The Life and Work of Buddhaghosha*, Calcutta and Simla, 1923.

Law, Narendra Nath, *Aspects of Ancient Indian Polity*, Oxford, 1921.

Lilly, W.S., *India and its Problems*, London, 1902.

Macauliffe, Max Arthur, *The Sikh Religion*, V, Oxford, 1909.

Macdonell, A.A., *India's Past*, Oxford, 1927.

Macphail, James M., *Aśoka* (The Heritage of India Series), Calcutta.

Mazumdar, Akshoy Kumar, *The Hindu History*, Calcutta, 1920.

Mehta, N.C., *Studies in Indian Painting*, Bombay, 1926.

Mitra, Rajendralal, *The Antiquities of Orissa*, I., II. Calcutta, 1880.

Mitra, Rajendralal, *The Sanskrit Buddhist Literature of Nepal*, Calcutta, 1882.

Monahan, F.J., *The Early History of Bengal*, Oxford, 1925.

Mookerji, Radhakumud, *Aśoka* (Gaekwad Lectures), London, 1928.

Mookerji, Radhakumud, *Harsha*, Oxford, 1926.

Nariman, G.K., *Literary History of Sanskrit Buddhism* (2nd edn.), Bombay, 1923.

Ojha, Pandit G.H., *The History of Rajputana*, I, Ajmer, 1916.

Ojha, Pandit G.H., *The Palaeography of India*, Ajmer, 1918.

O'Malley, L.S.S., *Bengal District Gazetteers, Puri*, Calcutta, 1908.

O'Malley, L.S.S., *Bihar and Orissa District Gazetteers, Patna*, Patna, 1924.

Pargiter F.E., *The Purāṇa Text of the Dynasties of the Kali Age*, Oxford, 1913.

Pargiter F.E., *Ancient Indian Historical Tradition*, London, 1922.

Poussin, L. De. La Vallée, *The Way to Nirvāṇa*, Cambridge, 1917.

Pradhan, Sita Nath, *Chronology of Ancient India*, Calcutta, 1927.

Radhakrishnan, S., *Indian Philosophy*, I., London, 1923.

Ralston, W.R.S., *Schiefner's Tibetan Tales*, London, 1882.

Rao, Gopinatha T.A., *Elements of Hindu Iconography*, I., pt. 1., Madras, 1914.

Rawlinson, George, *Parthia* (*The Story of the Nations*), London, 1893.

Raychaudhuri, Hemachandra, *Political History of Ancient India* (2nd edn.), Calcutta, 1927.

Rhys Davids, T.W., *Buddhist India* (5th edn.), London, 1917.

Rice, E.P., *Kanarese Literature* (The Heritage of India Series, (2nd edn.), Calcutta, 1921.

Rice, Lewis B., *Mysore and Coorg from the Inscriptions*, London, 1909.

Rockhill, W., Woodville, *The Life of the Buddha*, London, 1884.

Samaddar, J.N., *The Glories of Magadha*, Patna, 1927.

Schiefner, Anton, *Tāranātha's Geschichte-Buddhismus*, St. Petersburg, 1869.

Smith, Vincent A., *The Oxford History of India*, Oxford, 1925.

Smith, Vincent A., *The Early History of India*, Oxford, (1st edn.), 1904; (3rd edn.), 1914; (4th edn.), 1924.

Smith, Vincent A., *Aśoka*, Oxford (1st edn.), 1901; (3rd edn.), 1919.

Smith, Vincent A., *A History of Fine Art in India and Ceylon*, Oxford, 1911.

Solomon, Gladstone W.E., *The Charm of Indian Art*, London, 1926.

Srinivasachari C.S., and Aiyangar, N.S. Ramaswamy, *A History of India*, I, Madras, 1927.

Stevenson, Mrs Sinclair, *The Heart of Jainism*, Oxford, 1915.

Thomas, Edward, *Jainism, or the Early Faith of Aśoka*, London, 1877.

Tiele, C.P., *Outlines of the History of Religion* (3rd edn.), London, 1884.

Tod, Colonel James, *Travels in Western India*, London, 1839.

Vaidya, C.V., *History of Mediaeval Hindu India*, III, Poona, 1926.

Vidyabhusana, Satis Chandra, *History of Indian Logic*, Calcutta, 1921.

Vidyabhusana, Satis Chandra, *History of Mediaeval School of Indian Logic*, Calcutta, 1909.

Vijaya, Rājendra Sūri, *Abhidhānarājendra*, II., Rutlam, 1910.

Warren, Herbert, *Jainism* (2nd edn.), Arrah, 1916.

Wilberforce-Bell, Captain H., *The History of Kathiawad*, London, 1926.

Wilson, H.H., *His Works*, I., London, 1862.

Winternitz, M., *Geschichte der Indischen Litteratur*, II., Leipzig, 1920.

II. *Articles*

Andrews, F.N., Introduction, *The Influences of Indian Art*, The India Society, London, 1925.

Bakhle, V.S., Sātavāhanas and the Contemporary Ksatrapas, *J.B.B.R.A.S.* (New Series), III., 1928, p. 44 ff.

Barnett, L.D., The Early History of Southern India, ch. XXIV., *C.H.I.*, I., 1922, p. 593 ff.

Barua, Benimadhav, The Ājīvikas, *J.D.L.*, II., 1920, p. I ff.

Bhagwanlal Indraji, Pandit, Some Considerations of the History of Bengal, *I.A.*, XIII., 1884, p. 411 ff.

Bühler, G., Pushpamitra or Pushyamitra?, *I.A.*, II., 1874, p. 363 ff.

Bühler, G., The Digambara Jainas, *I.A.*, VII., 1878, p. 28 ff.

Burgess, J., Papers on Śatruñjaya and the Jainas, *I.A.*, II., 1874, pp. 14 ff., 134 ff.; XIII., 1884, pp. 191 ff., 276 ff.

Charpentier, Jarl, The History of the Jainas, ch. VI. *C.H.I.*, I., 1922, p. 150 ff.

Charpentier, Jarl, The Date of Mahāvīra, *I.A.*, XLIII., 1914, pp. 118 ff., 125 ff., 167 ff.

Colebrooke, H.T., Observations on the Sect of Jainas, *Miscellaneous Essays*, II., Madras, 1872, p. 191 ff.

Colebrooke, H.T., On the Philosophy of the Hindus, *Miscellaneous Essays*, I., Madras, 1872, p. 227 ff.

Crooke, W., Bengal, *E.R.E.*, II:, 1909, p. 479 ff.

Dey, Nando Lal, Notes on Ancient Aṅga or the District of Bhagalpur, *J.A.S.B.* (New Series), X., 1914, 1918, p. 317 ff.

Fleet, J.F., Nisīdhi and Guḍḍa, *I.A.*, XII., 1883, p. 99 ff.

Fleet, J.F., Bhadrabāhu, Candragupta, and Śravaṇa-Beḷgoḷa, *I.A.*, XXI, 1892, p. 156 ff.

Fleet, J.F., Dimensions of Indian Cities and Countries, *J.R.A.S.*, 1907, p. 641 ff.

Fleet, J.F., Notices of Books: Archaeological Survey of India — Annual Report for 1905-1906, *J.R.A.S.*, 1910, p. 240 ff.

Heras, Rev. H., Aśoka's Dharma and Religion, *Q.J.M.S.*, XVII., 1926-1927, p. 255 ff.

Hermann Oldenberg, Jacobi's *Kalpa-Sūtra* of Bhadrabāhu, Z.D.M.G., XXXIV., 1880, p. 748 ff.

Hoernle, Rudolf A.F., Ājīvikas, *E.R.E.*, I., 1908, p. 259 ff.

Jacobi, Hermann, On Mahāvīra and his Predecessors, *I.A.*, IX., 1880, p. 158 ff.

Jacobi, Hermann, The Dates of the Philosophical Sūtras of the Brahmans, *J.A.O.S.*, XXXI., 1909-1910, p. 1 ff.

Jacobi, Hermann, Automic Theory (Indian), *E.R.E.*, II., 1909, p. 199 ff.

Jacobi, Hermann, Ueber die Entstehung der Śvetāmbara und Digambara Sekten. Z.D.M.G., XXXVIII., 1884, p. 1 ff.

Jayaswal, K.P., The Saisunāka and Maury Chronology and the Date of the Buddha's Nirvāṇa, *J.B.O.R.S.*, I., 1915, p. 67 ff.

Jayaswal, K.P., The Empire of Bindusāra, *J.B.O.R.S.*, II., 1916, p. 79 ff.

Jayaswal, K.P., Demetrios, Khāravela and the *Garga-Saṁhitā*, *J.B.O.R.S.*, XIV., 1928, p. 127 ff.

Jinavijaya, Muni, *Kuvalayamālā*, *J.S.S.*, III., p. 169 ff.

Kamta Prasad Jain, The Jaina References in the Buddhist Literature, *I.H.Q.*, 1926, p. 698 ff.

Ketkar, S.V. Jainism, *M.E.*, XIV., Poons, 1925, p. 319 ff.

Klatt, Johannes, Extracts from the Historical Records of the Jainas, *I.A.*, 1882, p. 245 ff.

Lassen, Papers on Śatruñjaya and the Jainas, *I.A.*, II., 1874. pp. 193ff., 258 ff.

Leumann, E Beziehungen der Jaina — Literatur Zu Andern Literaturkreisen Indiens, *Actes de Sixième Congrès*, Troisième Partie, Section 2, Aryenne, Leide, 1885, p. 467 ff.

Long, Rev. J., Notes and Queries suggested by a Visit to Orissa in January 1859., *JA.S.B.*, XXVIII., 1859, p. 185 ff.

Macdonald, George, The Hellenic Kingdoms of Syria, Bactria, and Parthia, ch. XVII, *C.H.I.*, I., 1922, p. 427 ff.

Marshall, J.H., The Monuments of Ancient India, ch. XXVI. *C.H.I.*, I., 1922, p. 612 ff.

Meyer, Eduard, Demetrius, *E.B.*, VII (11th edn.), 1910, p. 982 ff.

Meyer, Eduard, Eucratides, *E.B.*, IX (11th edn.), 1910, p. 880 ff.

Mookerji, Ashutosh, Historical Research in Bihar and Orissa, *J.B.O.R.S.*, X., 1924, p. I ff.

Pargiter, F.E., Ancient Indian Genealogies and Chronology, *J.R.A.S.*, 1910, p. I ff.

Pathak, K.B., The Date of Mahāvīra's Nirvāṇa as determined in Śaka 1175, *I.A.*, XII., 1883, p. 21 ff.

Rapson, E.J. The Scythian and Parthian Invaders, ch. XXIII. *C.H.I.*, I., 1922, p. 563 ff.

Rapson, E.J., Indian Native States after the Period of the Maurya Empire, ch. XXI, *C.H.I.*, I., 1922, p. 514 ff.

Rapson, E.J., The Purāṇas, ch. XIII, *C.H.I.*, I., 1922, p. 296 ff.

Rapson, E.J., A. Peoples and Languages; B. Sources of History, ch. II, *C.H.I.*, I., 1922, p. 37 ff.

Rhys Davids, T.W., The Early History of the Buddhists, ch. VII, *C.H.I.*, I., 1922, p. 171 ff.

Rice, Jewis, Bhadrabāhu and Śravaṇa Beḷgoḷa, *I.A.*, III., 1874, p. 153 ff.

Rothenstein, William, Introduction. Examples of Indian Sculpture in the British Museum, p. 7 ff. The India Society, London, 1923.

Sastri, Banerji A., The Ājīvikas, *J.B.O.R.S.*, XII., 1926, p. 53 ff.

Sastri, Haraprasad, Causes of the Dismemberment of the Maurya Empire, *J.A.S.B.*, VI., 1910, p. 259 ff.

Shah, C.J., The A B C of Jainism, *J.G.*, XXIII., 1927, pp. 103 ff., 133 ff., 185 ff., 212 ff.

Smith, Vincent A., New Light on Ancient India, *J.R.A.S.*, 1918, p. 543 ff.

Smith, Vincent A., Revised Chronology of the Early or Imperial Gupta Dynasty, *I.A.*, XXXI., 1902, p. 257 ff.

Sterling, A., An Account, Geographical, Statistical and Historical, of Orissa proper, or Cuttack, *A.R.*, XVII., 1825, p. 163 ff.

Subrahmanian, K.R., The Early Religious History of Kaliṅga, *A.H.R.S.*, I., 1926, p. 49 ff.

Thibaut, G., On the *Sūryaprajñapti*, *J.A.S.B.*, XLIX., pt. 1, 1880, p. 107 ff.

Thomas, Edward, Jainism, *I.A.*, VIII., 1879, p. 30 ff.

Thomas, F.W. Political and Social Organisation of the Maurya Empire, ch. XIX, *C.H.I.*, I., 1922, p. 474 ff.

Thomas, F.W., Candragupta, the Founder of the Maurya Empire, ch. XVIII, *C.H.I.*, I., 1922, p. 467 ff.

Turnour, George, An Examination of the Pāli Buddhistical Annals, No.5, *J.A.S.B.*, VII., 1838, p. 991 ff.

Vijayadharmasūri, *Jainatattvajñāna*, *Bhandarkar Commemoration Volume*, Poona, 1917, p. 139 ff.

Weber, The Sacred Literature of the Jainas, *I.A.*, XVII., 1888, pp. 279 ff., 339 ff.; XVIII., 1889, pp. 181 ff., 369 ff.; XIX., 1890, pp. 62 ff.; XX., 1891, pp. 18 ff., 170 ff., 365 ff.; XXI., 1892, pp. 14 ff., 106 ff., 177 ff., 210 ff., 293 ff., 327 ff., 369 ff.

Wilford, Captain, Of the Kings of Magadha: their Chronology, *A.R.*, IX., 1819, p. 82 ff.

Wilson, H.H., An Essay on the Hindu History of Cashmir, *A.R.*. XV, 1825, p. 1 ff.

Index